DEVELOPMENTAL PSYCHOLOGY
The school-aged child

The Dorsey Series in Psychology
Advisory Editors
Wendell E. Jeffrey
University of California, Los Angeles

Salvatore R. Maddi
The University of Chicago

Bruce Ekstrand
University of Colorado

Ellen A. Strommen
John Paul McKinney
Hiram E. Fitzgerald

all of the
Department of Psychology
Michigan State University

DEVELOPMENTAL PSYCHOLOGY

The school-aged child

1983   Revised edition

THE DORSEY PRESS   Homewood, Illinois   60430

© THE DORSEY PRESS, 1977 and 1983

ISBN 0-256-02409-X
Library of Congress Catalog Card No. 83–70059
Printed in the United States of America

1 2 3 4 5 6 7 8 9 0 ML 0 9 8 7 6 5 4 3

To the half-remembered school child
who shaped each of us

PREFACE

Developmental periods are divided from one another in different ways. Adolescence, for example, is usually thought to begin at about the time of onset of puberty, an event with roots in biology and physiology. The school years, however, are defined primarily on the basis of a sociocultural event—at least in industrialized settings, they begin when children first start spending a good deal of their time away from family, under the supervision of an adult who is not a parent, and in the company of a more-or-less stable group of same-aged peers. This change is no less real for being socially rather than biologically defined. Through it, children's social experience is substantially restructured. Peers assume a new role in their lives, a role which continues to grow throughout these years and adolescence. Through exposure to adults other than parents, children encounter new modes of socialization and also begin to learn about the range of social roles which adults may hold. And school itself is the source of new knowledge, of new ways of applying and using intellectual skills.

All of these changes are facilitated by the fact that children starting school are adapting to the new sets of situations and expectations they encounter there. But it is apparently not solely because children start school that changes begin to take place at this time. Over a diversity of cultures, some of which provide formal schooling and some of which do not, the modal age at which children are first assumed to be teachable and responsible on a variety of dimensions is between the ages of about five and seven (Rogoff, Sellers, Pirotta, Fox, & White, 1975). Evidently there is something about children who are arriving at this age which leads to widespread agreement that they are now becoming capable in ways that they were not before, and that they are now ready to begin a new developmental period in their lives. The sociocultural definition of these years as the time when most children start school appears to be rooted in relevant changes in the children themselves.

In the course of these new experiences children grow and develop in a variety of ways. Their development during the school years is heavily influenced by the events of the early years of their lives, but a great deal is added during the school years, and the outcomes of this period will serve in turn as the foundation for development in adolescence and in the subsequent periods of adult life. If there is a theme for the changes taking place during this period, it is the marked changes in competence that one can see in the children—competence in motor skills and coordination; in learning, thinking, and remembering; in social skills and in interactions with others; in knowledge about self, others, and relationships. Preliminary formulations of attitudes and values are established; first steps toward independence from family are taken; personality patterns begin to stabilize; and for the first time friendships based on interpersonal trust and intimacy become evident. By the end of elementary school one can get some idea of what the child will be like as a young adult; and the changes that take place during adolescence depend to a great extent on the person that the schoolchild has become. We hope that readers will come away from this volume with not only increased knowledge of the changes that take place in school children and the social and psychobiological influences that influence them, but also of the roles these changes may play in the overall scheme of growing up.

Acknowledgment and thanks are due to Nancy Heath, Carolyn Osborne, Mary Ann Reinhart, Karen Tyree, and Mary Lee Nitschke for their assistance at different points throughout the preparation of this revision.

Ellen A. Strommen

CONTENTS

Hemispheric lateralization of the brain and reading. Comprehension. Meta-cognition and cognitive monitoring.

Occupations and work: *Premature occupational foreclosure.* Social group membership and prejudice: *Attitudes toward one's own social group. Attitudes toward other social groups.*

DEVELOPMENTAL PSYCHOLOGY
The school-aged child

BOX 1–1
Study questions

What do the major theories of personality say about personality development during the school years?

What are some of the disagreements between continuity and discontinuity theorists of development?

What are the major stages of intellectual development according to Piaget, and by what processes do children move through the stages?

Describe the life-span theoretical orientation and the psychobiological theoretical orientation.

How do the bodies of school-aged children typically change during the school years?

What difference do children's physical attributes make for the reactions they elicit from adults?

CHAPTER 1

SCHOOL-AGED CHILDREN: WHO ARE THEY?

School-aged children—children between about 4 or 5 to about 12 years of age—are all around us. In fact, we probably see more children of that age than any other because they are old enough to be out and about on their own but not yet old enough to have to forego hours of play for other obligations and responsibilities. Yet we have tended, parent and professional alike, to pay less attention to these children as a group than we have to children in other periods of development. This relative neglect may reflect the lingering effects of early but influential theories of personality development according to which relatively little of importance took place during these years; or it may be because school-agers are not so cute as younger children nor so troublesome as adolescents; or because the changes that do take place are neither so obvious nor so dramatic as those in younger or older children.

But changes need not be obvious or striking to be important. Any close examination makes it abundantly clear that important changes are taking place during these years. In this chapter we shall begin our study of school-aged children, first by looking at theoretical perspectives on children's development during these years and then by examining the physical changes which children typically undergo while they are in elementary school.

THEORETICAL PERSPECTIVES

What have psychologists had to say about school-aged children? Ideas are often dismissed as "just theory," as though theories had no connection with the real world. It is true that theories are interpretations which can—and should—

be challenged. But these attempts to make sense of the world are based upon real events. Perhaps more important for our purposes, theories are often sources of orienting attitudes and implicit assumptions about what is true. Certainly our ideas about development during the school years reflect theoretical interpretations in important ways.

Personality development

The legacy of Freud   Sigmund Freud's (1856–1939) theory of psychosexual development, though much criticized, is nonetheless the origin of many widely held ideas concerning personality development. It is also the source of many issues with which psychologists are still concerned.

FIGURE 1–1   Sigmund Freud

National Library of Medicine

Freud was the first theorist to recognize and emphasize the importance of the early years of life for personality development, a point of view which we now take for granted. Freud believed that *libido,* an innate drive or motivating force which is sexual in nature, is present from birth. With development there are successive shifts in the locus, or part of the body, which is the primary site for the satisfaction of libidinal drives. Each such shift corresponds to a stage of personality development (see Table 1–1). The term *psychosexual stages* reflects Freud's emphasis on the sexual basis of personality development. The term *psychodynamic theory* refers to theories like Freud's, which emphasize motivational dynamics of personality.

TABLE 1–1
Freud's psychosexual stages, Erikson's psychosocial stages, and the periods of development during which they occur

Period of development	Freud: Psychosexual stages	Erikson: Psychosocial stages
Infancy....................	Oral stage	Basic trust versus mistrust
Toddler years..............	Anal stage	Autonomy versus shame and doubt
Early childhood............	Phallic stage	Initiative versus guilt
SCHOOL YEARS...........	LATENCY PERIOD	INDUSTRY VERSUS INFERIORITY
Adolescence...............	Genital stage	Identity versus role diffusion
Young adulthood...........		Intimacy versus isolation
Adulthood.................		Generativity versus stagnation
Late adulthood.............		Ego integrity versus despair

School-aged children are in a period which intervenes between the third and fourth stages of psychosexual development. The third stage of psychosexual development, the *phallic or early genital stage,* occurs approximately between the ages of three and five. Its consequences persist until the fourth stage begins at puberty, so to understand Freud's view of the school years we must look at the phallic stage more closely.

In this stage, the genital area is the focus of libidinal pleasure, although not yet in the ways that will characterize adult sexuality. The major event of this stage is the *Oedipus conflict.* For boys, the attachment to mother which began in infancy intensifies, and strong feelings of rivalry and jealousy develop toward father. But these feelings are of course unacceptable, and since fathers are powerful compared to their small sons, the son experiences *castration anxiety*— fear that his father will punish or injure him for his unacceptable feelings. This is an unresolvable conflict for the child. To cope with it, he resorts to *repression,* which means that the anxiety, and the feelings of attachment for mother and rivalry with father which produce it, are pushed from conscious awareness. Simultaneously he *identifies* with his father, meaning that he incorporates attributes of his father into his own personality. It is as though by being like his father he might vicariously share both his father's strength and his special privileges.

Girls are assumed to undergo a similar conflict, sometimes called the *Electra conflict.* However, Freud never developed his theory as fully for women as he did for men, and some of his assumptions about women have been sharply criticized. Because the female genitals do not include a penis, Freud thought that girls experience *penis envy* and that as a result they devalue femininity. This in turn causes them to turn away from their earlier attachment to mother and toward father. The consequence is an unresolvable conflict analogous to that experienced by boys: There is strong attachment to father and rivalry with and devaluation of mother. Girls, like boys, deal with this unresolvable conflict through repression and through identification with the same-sex parent. For both boys and girls, the identification established at this point is assumed to be a major source of sex role development and of conscience.

The repression of feelings growing out of the Oedipus and Electra conflicts has taken place by the time children are about five years old and persists until they approach puberty and adolescence. During the years in between, the dynamic influences on personality development are repressed and *latent,* or inactive; hence the name *latency period.* Children enter this period with the beginnings of sex role identity and of conscience. During the period they learn many new facts, skills, and roles; conscience and sex role identity became more stable and better organized. But from the dynamic perspective of Freudian theory, these are simply refinements on already established aspects of personality. It is as though personality development is "on hold" until the increasing intensity of maturing sexual feelings accompanying the approach of puberty becomes strong enough to cause the repression to break down. This marks the beginning of the *genital stage.* At this point the conflicts repressed during the phallic stage re-emerge, but now the individual can transfer to a peer the feelings originally directed toward the opposite-sex parent, thus resolving the earlier conflict. Notice that though the resolution is new, the conflict is not. The formative conflict itself took place during the phallic stage. This is why Freud believed that personality was basically determined by the time children reached the age of five. And this position of Freud's is very likely one reason why the school years receive less attention than earlier periods of development.

Two neo-Freudians: Erikson and White Neo-Freudians are theorists who accept many but not all of Freud's ideas, often adding important contributions of their own. Of these theorists, Erik Erikson has had perhaps the greatest influence on contemporary thinking about children's personality development.

Erikson (1950) accepts Freud's stages of psychosexual development but believes that there are also stages of *psychosocial development*—predominant patterns of social interaction characteristic of different periods of life—and that these psychosocial stages are at least equally important for understanding per-

FIGURE 1–2 Erik Erikson

Courtesy Harvard University News office

sonality development. Erikson suggests that there are eight stages of psycho-social development (see Table 1–1). The first five correspond roughly in time to the stages of psychosexual development, but the eight stages cover the entire life span—quite a different view from the notion that personality is basically deter-mined by about five years of age! At each stage, social interactions are pervaded by a predominant theme which has both positive and negative extremes. Of course, everyone has both positive and negative interactions with others, and at some time or other every child experiences the range of outcomes characterized by the dimensions of each stage. But if the balance of interactions within each stage is positive, the positive side of the dimension will prevail, whereas if the balance is negative, the negative side of the dimension will prevail.

The school years correspond most closely to Erikson's fourth stage, during which the predominant dimension is a *sense of industry versus feelings of inferi-ority*. The sense of industry grows out of the rapidly expanding skills and com-petencies which are so characteristic of this period of life. Of course, com-petence has roots in earlier years (see Fitzgerald, Strommen, & McKinney, 1982), but it is during the school years that it becomes central to personality devel-opment. The sense of competence is a sense of oneself as capable, as being able to do meaningful tasks in the real world and not just "baby stuff." It also includes taking on tasks and projects for their inherent interest, and working to complete them for the satisfaction of seeing the outcome. The sense of industry is a major component of work habits and skills that will be important in later periods of life. If children's use of their expanding skills and competence meets mostly with success, finding support and approval from family, friends, and teachers, then the children develop a sense of industry. But if the predominant experience is of failure and disapproval, then the sense of themselves as inferior will predom-inate. In either case, the outcome will color children's feelings about themselves, and their consequent development in later periods of life.

Robert White (1959, 1960) takes a very similar view of the school years, though he arrives at it in a different way. Like Erikson, White accepts Freud's stages of psychosexual development. However, he argues that although psycho-sexual development is crucial for the development of love and sexuality, it is not very helpful in accounting for work and for pride in performance, which make up a second major component of adult identity. White suggests that the libidinal drives of the psychosexual model need to be supplemented with *effectance motivation*, the satisfaction intrinsic to gaining mastery over one's world. Effec-tance motivation results in the development of *competence*, "fitness or ability to carry on those transactions with the environment which result in its [the individ-ual's] maintaining itself, growing, and flourishing" (White, 1960, p. 100). Effec-tance motivation is relevant at all stages of development—the infant, for in-stance, must give up the breast or bottle (Freud's oral stage), but at the same time gains the satisfaction of being able to feed itself.

But the concept of competence is especially relevant for school-aged chil-dren. On all fronts—social, intellectual, emotional, motoric—school-aged chil-dren begin as awkward, inexpert novices and move toward sophisticated, com-petent performance. The competence developed during the school years, and the children's sense of themselves as competent or incompetent, may have profound influences on their personality development, in some cases altering or redirecting patterns established within the family during the earlier years of life.

Social learning theory and developmental tasks *Social learning theory* came into being when U.S. psychologists who were interested in Freud's ideas, but concerned because those ideas did not readily lend themselves to experimental testing, began to translate Freudian concepts into the terms of learning theory. Freud's influence is evident not only in the origins of social learning theory but in the continuing interest of social learning theorists in issues originally deriving from his theory, such as imitation (related to identification, see Chapter 6) and resistance to temptation and deferment of gratification (related to moral development, see Chapter 7).

Beyond this, contemporary social learning theory is very different from the psychodynamic theories of Freud, Erikson, and White. Social learning theorists do not accept the libidinal model of development, stressing instead what children do and how their behavior is influenced by environmental events and circumstances.

As for the processes through which developmental change takes place, the emphasis of the social learning theorists is on learning processes, which are assumed to operate in much the same way at any period of life. Personality styles and modes of interacting with others are learned in much the same way that intellectual or other skills are learned. Nor do social learning theorists believe that development proceeds through stages, if by "stage" anything more is meant than a description of developmental differences at different periods. Stage theorists believe that behavior changes *qualitatively,* meaning that genuinely new and different forms of behavior become possible with successive stages; thus there are discontinuities between one stage and the next. Furthermore, they believe that the achievements of one stage are necessary foundations for the newly emerging processes of the next stage, so that the sequence of stages is necessarily invariant (that is, occurs in the same order). In contrast, social learning theorists believe that behavior development is continuous; children learn to do more as they develop, and to put things together in more complex forms, but this is a matter of *quantitative change*—being able to do more of the same things, and in better ways. Thus the same principles and processes that account for behavior development in school-aged children should apply to infants, adolescents, and adults as well. This disagreement over whether development is continuous or discontinuous, whether or not there are stages in development, is one of the recurring and continuing disagreements among different groups of developmental psychologists. Both groups can point to evidence in which they find convincing support for their position. We will have occasion to revisit this debate in later chapters.

Social learning theorists may not believe in stages, but they do recognize that there are differences between children in different age periods. To account for such differences they are likely to borrow from sociology the notion of *developmental tasks* (Havighurst, 1972)—societally defined tasks that everyone is expected to master during given periods of life. The developmental tasks faced by school-aged children include at least the following: making the transition from home to school; learning to get along with peers; learning to interact with teachers, and adults in many other roles, outside of the family; becoming literate and mastering basic school-related information; developing independence of family and self-regulation of their own behavior; learning about sex-roles and other socially defined expectations for their behavior. Obviously if children are growing up in a cultural setting where there is no formal schooling, the developmental tasks for this same age span would be quite different.

Intellectual development: Piaget

Jean Piaget (1896–1980) has had at least as great an influence on our ideas about intellectual development as Freud had on our ideas about personality. Early in his career Piaget worked with Binet and Simon—developers of the first IQ tests—on the standardization of test materials. He did not find this work particularly stimulating, but he became intrigued with children's reasoning, especially when they gave incorrect responses, and this work set him off on the studies of intellectual development to which he devoted the remainder of his life.

What Piaget had to say about the thinking of school-aged children must be put in context as part of a complex and comprehensive theory which covers development from birth through adolescence and adulthood. Piaget thought of intelligence as a characteristic of all living organisms, in much the same way that digestion or metabolism characterizes all living organisms. His main concern was with intelligence as a universal attribute which characterizes all human beings, *not* with individual differences in intelligence or with conceptions which lead to the classification of people by their level of intelligence. Since intelligence as Piaget views it is a biological characteristic of human beings, he also contends that two basic and universal attributes which hold for all biological characteristics apply to intelligence as well. One of these universals is *or-*

FIGURE 1–3 Jean Piaget

Courtesy World Health Organization

ganization, or structure. In the case of intelligence, structure is manifested in recurring and identifiable sequences of behavior. In infants, for example, such behavior sequences as sucking, looking, grasping, and mouthing are instances of the identifiable structures which Piaget calls schemes. In school-aged children, addition and multiplication are examples of the identifiable structures which he calls *operations.* These structures or behavior sequences are not identical from occurrence to occurrence, but they do have common properties which make them identifiable as instances of the particular organization.

The second universal attribute of intelligence is *adaptation.* It is through adaptation to new and different circumstances that the changes in intellectual structures take place. Adaptation consists of two simultaneous processes, accommodation and assimilation. *Accommodation* refers to the reshaping of intellectual structures so that they can now handle new information or a new event, whereas *assimilation* refers to the incorporation of the event or information into the intellectual structure. As a rather imperfect analogy, think of putting on a long-sleeved sweater. As you pull the sleeve on, the sleeve *accommodates* itself to the shape of the arm, and simultaneously the arm is *assimilated* or enters into the sleeve. In much the same way, children encountering unfamiliar information simultaneously change their intellectual structures to fit the new information and incorporate the new information into their intellectual structures.

Accommodation and assimilation occur simultaneously, but one or the other may predominate in. any given adaptation. Piaget is careful to distinguish between the two because he believes that their roles in intellectual development differ. The comparison of play and imitation illustrates the ways in which accommodation or assimilation may predominate in a given adaptation (Piaget, 1962). When a child imitates someone, accommodation predominates. Imitation requires changing one's own behavioral sequence to match that of a model as closely as possible, with little regard for incorporating new knowledge. But when children play, assimilation predominates. Any number of objects or ideas may be incorporated into the ongoing play, with minimum reshaping of intellectual structures. If a "fort" or a "house" is needed, children will make do with items as diverse as packing crates, tables, low-hanging tree branches, or even sticks or stones lined up to represent walls. The concept "fort" or "house" is relatively unchanged (there is little accommodation of structure), but a wide variety of possible objects may be assimilated to the concept for the purpose of play.

Two additional themes must be mentioned. The first of these is the *active nature of intelligence.* Children *use* their intellectual structures. They apply them spontaneously and repeatedly to the environment around them, and in the course of this intellectual activity new information is encountered. The second theme involves the concept of *equilibration.* When the available intellectual structures can cope successfully with external circumstances, they are said to be in equilibrium; when they cannot cope successfully, so that the child encounters contradiction or discrepancy with present knowledge, they are in disequilibrium. Whenever there is disequilibrium, the intellectual structures begin to adapt, moving toward a higher and more complex state of equilibrium in which the contradiction or discrepancy is resolved.

The motivation for cognitive development resides in these processes, according to Piaget. Intellectual structures are used for their own sake, and when disequilibrium occurs in the course of their use, growth through equilibration inevitably and spontaneously follows. Intelligence develops, not as a result of what someone else does to the child, but through the child's own intellectual activity. From this perspective, it is quite incorrect to think in terms of "motivating" children to learn, which implies that they are passive and must be gotten to learn by forces external to themselves. Adults may find it necessary to maneuver (that is, motivate) children into doing what *adults* think they should do when *adults* think they should do it, or to get children to exercise their intellectual structures on materials that *adults* consider important for them, but this is a quite different issue. What the children will get out of time spent on such materials depends completely on the children and on the intellectual activity they direct toward those materials.

The stages Piaget believed that there are four major periods or stages of intellectual development, each distinguished from the preceding stages by evidence that children are beginning to use a new type of intellectual structure. During each period, use of the new structure is gradually applied to more and more areas of the children's thinking. Because each stage grows out of and builds on the intellectual activities of the earlier stages, the order or sequence in which children go through the stages is always the same. They do not go through the stages at the same rate however, and there may be large individual differences in the ages at which different children enter the different stages.

In the first, *sensorimotor period,* intellectual growth is evident in children's sensory and motor actions (see Fitzgerald, Strommen & McKinney, Volume 1 of this series). The main achievement of this period is the development of *object constancy.* As soon as children show evidence that they are beginning to use mental representations or symbols (such as delayed imitation, which requires some remembered representation of the original event), they have entered the second major period, the *preoperational period.* This usually happens sometime around 18 months or 2 years of age. Throughout this period, children extend their newly acquired symbolic skills to increasingly wide ranges of their experiences. The rapid expansion of mental representations and symbolic skills during this period is evidenced in the rapid growth of language, the appearance and elaboration of imaginative play, and the first evidence of dreams.

By the end of the preoperational period, children have sizable arrays of representations and symbols at their command, but they use them in ways that indicate they do not yet grasp relationships among them—relationships of the sort embodied in such previously mentioned operations as equivalence, addition, and implication. Use of operations first begins to appear sometime around the ages of five to seven for most children, and once this occurs, they have entered the *period of concrete operations.* This period continues until children are 11 to 15 years of age, so by far the majority of school-aged children are in this period of intellectual development. With the development of concrete operations, children first become capable of types of reasoning that adults would recognize as logical. At the outset of the period, children show such reasoning only occasionally, and only on some types of problems. As the period progresses, they gradually extend their newly developed use of operations to more and different problems, much as preoperational children expand their use of mental representation and symbols.

However, the typical thinking children do during this period is still limited. They can reason quite logically when they are working with concrete, immediately present materials (hence the name concrete operations). But they still have a great deal of difficulty if asked to apply similar skills to hypothetical situations or to problems with elements not concretely present. Sometime around early adolescence these limitations begin to be overcome, and children enter the *period of formal operations,* so named because the children can now deal with problems presented formally and are no longer dependent upon concrete instances. (See McKinney, Strommen, & Fitzgerald, volume 3 of this series.)

Notice that each stage builds on what has gone before. The emergence of mental operations embodying relationships among symbols presupposes the availability of symbols to be related; the emergence of mental representations and symbols presupposes sensorimotor experience through which rudimentary "concepts" are established which can then be represented or symbolized. Transitions from one stage to the next are not abrupt leaps, but rather the gradual emergence of new skills growing out of accumulated experience with the limitations of the previous, less flexible modes of thinking. Note, too, that although the stages occur in an invariant sequence, this does not mean that the sequence is innate or that intellectual development is a simple matter of physical and physiological maturation, occurring regardless of children's experience. Piaget regards maturation as basic in the sense that intellectual development could not occur without it. But how intellectual growth proceeds once the physical and physiological structures are present depends on children's experience in the form of their intellectual interactions with the world.

Finally, the newly emerging skills of each stage never replace or completely supplant the prior modes of thinking. Rather, older structures are partially integrated into and reorganized by newer structures. Children do not stop using symbols when they begin using concrete operations. Rather, they begin to coordinate symbols into new structural relationships. But even adults, presumably capable of formal operational thinking, often still use concrete operational, preoperational, or even sensorimotor intelligence.

Are the stages universal? If Piaget's theory does describe processes of knowing which apply for all human beings, one should find children going through similar stages of development regardless of the cultural context in which they grow up. This is partly true. The evidence indicates that the younger the children, the more likely they are to show similar reasoning cross-culturally; and development through concrete operations has been documented across diverse cultural groups which include not only Western industrialized countries of the Americas and Europe, but also tribes in the African bush, Australian aborigines,

Eskimos, and other diverse groups (e.g., Dasen, 1972, 1977; Laboratory for Comparative Human Cognition, 1979). Formal operations, however, have proved to be culture dependent, appearing primarily in industrialized settings in which prolonged formal schooling is required of children. Even in such settings—including the United States—not all adolescents or adults use formal operations, and those that do may use them only in some problem situations but not in others.

However, if intellectual development depends upon children's active processing of their experience, there should also be cultural variations in the particulars of intellectual development that reflect the varying experience of children from different cultural settings—and there are (Dasen, 1972, 1977; Carmi, 1981; Laboratory for Comparative Human Cognition, 1979; Piaget, 1966b). Though concrete operations are found in all cultural settings, the typical ages at which they are achieved vary considerably from one group to another, and in some settings not all adults may use them (as not all adults in industrialized settings use formal operations). Similarly, rates of acquisition of particular skills may reflect particular cultural experiences. Children from pottery-making families are more likely to be able to conserve quantity (and perhaps other properties) than are children from nonpottery-making families, probably because of their greater experience and skill in manipulating quantities of clay (Price-Williams, Gordon, & Ramirez, 1969; Adjei, 1977, though Steinberg & Dunn, 1976, did not replicate their finding). Conservation means recognizing that changes in shape, arrangement, appearance, and so on, do not alter such properties as quantity, number, area; see Chapter 2 for more detailed discussion. And Wolof children in Africa appear to learn how to apply concrete operations through different means than do children in the United States (Greenfield, 1966).

Patterns of good and poor performance on different types of tasks evidently vary from culture to culture, even though all cultures achieve concrete operations. Such variations in performance reflect, not differences in competence or in the capacity to develop intellectually, but rather differences in the types of skills important to the cultural group. To understand the performance of individuals in any group, one must understand the cultural setting or context within which that performance takes place (Cole & Bruner, 1971; Cole & Scribner, 1974; Piaget, 1966b; Goodnow, 1969; Laboratory for Comparative Human Cognition, 1979).

General theoretical orientations

Theoretical orientations differ from theories in that they represent general points of view that influence the way we think about an area of interest, rather than more-or-less articulated sets of principles such as those summarized in the preceding section. Two theoretical orientations in particular have been important for the development of these volumes.

The *life-span development orientation* emphasizes that psychological development is a lifelong process, not just a process characteristic of those who have not yet reached adulthood. It also emphasizes that processes of development are multiple, that they are frequently (but not necessarily) age-related, and that they interact with the context in which one grows up (e.g., Baltes, Reese, & Lipsitt, 1980).

One important determinant of context is historical time—when, in time, did you grow up? A *cohort,* or generation, is a group who were born and grew up in the same historical period. So children born in 1965 (that is, members of the 1965 cohort) would have been fourth graders in about 1975—the *only* cohort for which this can ever be true. For this group, and others born in the 1960s, far more would experience family breakups and single-parent families than was true for 1950s cohorts; television is virtually universal, which wasn't true in the 1930s; not only is universal elementary education taken for granted (a product of the 19th century which, together with child labor laws, significantly affected the life experience of very large numbers of school-aged children) but that education will include high school and post-high school education for a majority, rather than terminating at the end of elementary school as was the case for many in the 1890s and early 1900s. These factors and many others affect not only the experience of middle childhood itself, but the way in which this period relates to later periods of life.

Another feature of the life-span orientation is an interest in the ways in which the events and processes from earlier periods together with events and processes particular to the life period under study work together to help understand that period. For school-aged children, their experiences as infants and toddlers affect (but do not entirely explain) their experiences and attributes as school children, and these, in turn, affect (but do not entirely explain) what they will be like as adolescents and as adults. We will examine these linkages from time to time as we proceed.

The *psychobiological orientation* emphasizes that human beings are biological beings; their behavior and experience cannot exist independent of their biological attributes. Through the middle decades of the 20th century, U.S. psychologists tended to emphasize environmental influences on behavior and learning to the exclusion of other factors, in part in reaction against still earlier thinkers who emphasized biological determinism to the exclusion of environment (there are cohort effects in science too!). Especially since the 1970s, contemporary researchers are more likely to speak of the interaction of inherent biological attributes and environmental influences, emphasizing that behavior depends integrally on both. Attempting to specify more precise linkages between biology and behavior is difficult. Among fields of study where such linkages are of special interest are behavior genetics and ethology, especially (for our purposes) human ethology. Behavior geneticists attempt to clarify the relationship between genetics and hereditary processes on the one hand and behavior on the other; we will encounter some of their ideas when discussing intelligence (Chapter 3) and when discussing personality (Chapter 6). Ethologists approach the study of behavior with the assumption that many patterns of behavior are innate, or at least that innate behavioral predispositions contribute importantly to behavior development. If so, we need to know what those behavioral predispositions are and how they operate in different settings if we are to understand behavior development. Human ethologists bring this orientation to the study of human behavior. Many have been especially interested in development issues (e.g., see Hess, 1970).

PHYSICAL CHARACTERISTICS OF SCHOOL-AGED CHILDREN

Given that there are important links between biological characteristics and behavior, it is important to know something about the physical and physiological attributes of school-aged children, even though we may not yet be able to specify all the ways in which their physical attributes are related to their behavior.

Physical growth

The most visible signs of growth—in fact, what many people think of when growth is mentioned—are changes in height and weight. At age six, the average child is a little over 3½ feet tall and weighs about 37 pounds. By age 12, the average child is about 5 feet tall and weighs about 66 pounds. Body proportions change somewhat during this period, though not nearly so markedly as they did during the first five years of life as the body lost its "babyish" contours, nor as rapidly as they will during adolescence, when the relatively similar bodies of boys and girls take on the stature and secondary sex characteristics of young men and women.

Figure 1–4 shows the *typical* growth curves from birth to age 20 for four different types of body tissue, expressed as a percentage of adult size. The unshaded part of the figure shows growth during the school years. Height and weight both follow the general curve of development. They increase steadily during middle childhood, but at slower rates each year. Compared to the rates of change during early childhood and adolescence (the shaded portions of the figure), changes in height and weight are much slower in middle childhood.

However, other types of tissue follow different patterns of growth. Reproductive tissue grows very little either before or during middle childhood. In contrast, lymphoid tissue grows very rapidly during both early childhood and middle childhood, actually exceeding adult levels during middle childhood and declining during adolescence. Finally, brain and head tissues are approaching their adult levels during middle childhood, following their very rapid growth in the first few years of life. By five years of age, the brain has reached about 90 percent of its adult weight; most of its remaining growth takes place during middle childhood.

Physical growth follows these general patterns for all children, unless it is hampered by such factors as severe malnutrition, endocrine dysfunction, and severe chronic illness. In fact, if malnutrition or chronic illness is terminated during the years of growth, a period of very rapid growth typically follows during which the child regains much of the lost ground. This is called the *"catch-up" phenomenon.*

FIGURE 1–4 Comparison of growth rates of four major types of body tissue during middle childhood (unshaded center portion) with their growth rates before and after middle childhood (shaded portions). Growth is expressed as a percentage of adult size. Different types of tissue grow at different rates.

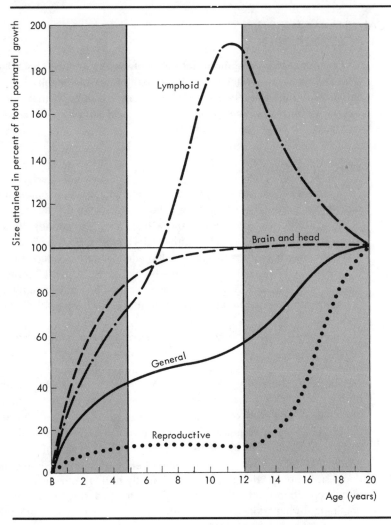

Source: J. M. Tanner, *Growth at Adolescence*, 2d ed. (Oxford: Blackwell Scientific Publications, 1962), p. 9.

Though all children follow these general patterns, the growth rates of individual children vary considerably. In a large group of Scottish boys, excluding the 3 percent who were tallest and the 3 percent who were shortest for their age, the average height at age eight was nearly 51 inches, or 4 feet 3 inches (Tanner, 1962). But even excluding the tallest and shortest children, there were boys who were only about 45 inches tall (3 feet 9 inches) and boys who were about 54 inches tall (4 feet 6 inches). Such differences partly reflect differences in body build—after all, full-grown adults differ in height too—but they also reflect the fact that some children grow rapidly and others grow slowly.

Any individual child's rate of growth is quite stable. Children ahead of the average for their age on one indicator are likely to be ahead on other indicators. Children who are behind their age-mates will be consistently behind. This will usually be true throughout the years of growth. One effect of these differential rates of growth for individual children is that any group of children of about the same chronological age will contain children who vary considerably in physical maturity and capacities. This is already evident when children start school, but it becomes especially apparent in the later school years, when children who are early maturers enter puberty while still in elementary school (see Figure 1–5). The average age at the onset of puberty is about 12 for girls and about 14 for boys in the United States, but normal girls may begin puberty by the age of 9 or 10, normal boys by 11 or 12. This great range of development levels poses a considerable challenge for teachers and others working with young people during these years. It also poses a challenge of a different sort for those attempting to define developmental periods—here are children who by the criterion of physical development are adolescents, although by other criteria they are still in middle childhood.

What determines physical growth, the rate at which it occurs, and the final level that will characterize the child as an adult? The major determinant is undoubtedly heredity. Tall parents are likely to have tall children; short parents are likely to have short children. Growth rates are more similar for identical twins than for siblings, and for siblings than for unrelated children. But other factors also influence growth, in complex interactions. These factors include nutrition, amount of rest, the quality of the home and the adequacy of child care, climate, the presence or absence of disease, even the time of year—children grow more in summer than in winter. Severe psychological disturbance can also interfere with normal growth. So the relationship between physical development and psychological development works both ways: psychological attributes can affect physical development as well as the other way around.

Physiological changes

Figure 1–4 showed growth in the amount of brain tissue with age. But such gross changes as brain weight *per se* do not in themselves tell us much about important qualitative changes that may be taking place in the child's brain and nervous system. For instance, developmental changes in brain weight do not mean that older children have more neurons (the basic cells of the nervous system) than do younger children. All, or effectively all, neurons are already present before birth. Instead, the weight changes in brain tissue represent such changes as the development of *dendrites* (the interconnecting fibers between neurons), *neuroglia* (the cells which form the supporting tissue of the brain), and *myelin sheaths* (a fatty covering of nerve cells which is not present at birth). Until changes of this kind are sufficiently advanced, many skills and behaviors are beyond the competence of the child. Interconnections between relevant nerve cells must be present before many behaviors can develop; and although the role of myelination is not fully understood, many experts maintain that fully effective functioning of nerve cells is not possible until these cells have been myelinated. Although behaviors cannot appear until the neurophysiological structure has developed, structural maturation does not guarantee that the behaviors it makes possible will appear. Such factors as experience, motivation, and practice determine whether and how a child will use available structures behaviorally. However, the maturation of neurophysiological structures does make it possible for the behavioral functions to develop.

Though there is as yet little specific information on the relationships between physiological structure and behavioral function in middle childhood, there are some significant hints. For instance, Tanner (1970) points out that the interconnections within the brain which are necessary for fine control of voluntary movement are not fully myelinated until about the age of four. If nerve cells are not fully functional until they have their myelin sheaths, fine motor coordination must be difficult or impossible for most children before they are four years of age or older, regardless of experience or practice. But once fine motor coordination is physically possible, it may be exercised and developed in many forms. The very rapid development of skills and abilities which is a hallmark of the school years may very well depend on this neurophysiological structural development. As another instance, the reticular formation is a brain structure that plays an important role in the maintenance of attention and consciousness. Myelinization within the reticular formation continues at least until puberty, and maybe longer. This progressing myelinization of structures important for attention may play a role in the increased capacity for concentration and directed attention which appears so much more characteristic in middle childhood than in earlier years.

The implications of such changes may be far-reaching indeed. Tanner (1970) points out that even though brain weight is nearing adult levels in the school years (Figure 1–4) there could still be considerable development of interconnections among dendrites, since they weigh very little and take up little space. Such an increase in interconnections within the brain could, he argues, be a necessary foundation for progress through intellectual stages of development like those described by Piaget (see Chapter 2).

Adult reactions to changes in apparent age

Before reading this section, look at Figure 1–5.

Children's physical attributes influence behavior both directly and indirectly. In the preceding section we argued that many skills may be impossible before certain levels of physical and neurological maturation are reached. Here, children's behavioral development is directly dependent upon their physical development. On the other hand, if a child's physical attributes elicit particular reactions from others, such as teasing or ridicule, such reactions will inevitably affect at least self-image and interactions with others. In cases like this, the child's physical characteristics influence psychological development indirectly, being mediated by other persons' evaluations of and expectations for an individual having such physical characteristics. Since children's bodies are constantly

FIGURE 1–5   First-grade and sixth-grade class photographs show some of the variations in the size of children who are about the same age.

Cary Wolinsky—Stock Boston

Jean-Claude Lejeune

changing as they grow, it seems likely that there may be systematic changes in the responses of others to these regularly changing physical characteristics.

Adults' reactions to children's apparent age provide a clear illustration of one such indirect effect. There are many ways in which children's behavior is expected to change as they grow up. Think of crying. The reactions to a child's crying are likely to be quite different for a 6-year-old and for a 12-year-old, even though they are doing the same thing (crying). However, not all changes in expectations for growing children involve such specific and easily recognized behaviors. In fact, it is likely that many changing expectations are implicit rather than explicit, and may be neither recognized nor understood. Fry and Willis (1971) report a very suggestive study which may demonstrate a change in one such implicit category of behaviors. They observed adult reactions to unfamiliar children of 5, 8, and 10 years of age who invaded the adults' "personal space."

Personal space refers to zones of distance which people maintain from one another. The zone immediately surrounding one's own body (up to about 18 inches in our culture) is usually maintained as a zone of privacy. Only intimates are allowed to enter this zone. If someone else comes this close, the individual will move away or show signs of discomfort. Most people are not aware that they pattern the space around their bodies in this way.

Fry and Willis' subjects were 60 men and 60 women standing in the ticket lines of movie theaters in urban shopping centers. The child confederates were told to stand as close to the adults as possible without actually touching them, a degree of proximity that would not be tolerated between adults. To be sure that it was the child's apparent age to which the adults responded rather than some other attribute of a particular child, the child confederates included two boys and two girls at each age level. They had been chosen to be representative of height and weight norms for their age. In addition, a large class of college undergraduates had been able to judge their ages from photographs with reasonable accuracy.

There was a clear difference in the adults' reactions to the children, depending upon the child's apparent age. Closeness was accepted from 5-year-olds, but not from 10-year-olds. Eight-year-olds were in between; they were tolerated or ignored (5-year-olds and 10-year-olds were never ignored). Adults of both sexes were likely to turn toward, smile at, or speak to five-year-olds. With 10-year-olds, however, they showed the same reactions that they would show to another adult standing too close: They moved away, leaned away, fidgeted (showed excessive motor behavior). The message to 10-year-olds was very different from the message to 5-year-olds.

This study provides a clear illustration of a subtle change in adult responses to children which shifts markedly during the school years, depending upon the child's apparent age. There are undoubtedly many other patterns of behavior which are as subtle and as little recognized as personal space. These behavior patterns certainly are not taught to children explicitly, since adults themselves are not very well aware of them. Rather, the change in adult "messages" to younger and older children represents a real change in the children's social environment, one to which the children must adapt by changing their own behavior patterns in relation to adults. Such adaptation is undoubtedly one process through which childish behavior patterns are replaced by more "grown-up" patterns.

Because it is apparent age or maturity to which adults respond, the great variation in the growth of children of the same chronological age means that changes in the responses of others will have quite different effects on children of different apparent maturity. Children who look young for their age may "get away with" babyish behavior for a much longer time than the average child. Children who look mature for their age will not only encounter the effects of these changes at an earlier age than average, but will run an additional risk. If at six they look eight, they may be advanced for their age in many respects, but not yet have the skills or actual maturity of the eight-year-old. People who forget that the children are only six are likely to think of them as immature, incompetent, maybe even a bit stupid because they do not act as old as they look. Evidently the appearance of maturity has a strong effect; even parents and teachers sometimes talk about slipping into a pattern of making unrealistic demands of mature-looking children.

Fry and Willis' study illustrates one other general point, namely, that much of what goes on in interactions between adults and children depends as much on the child as on the adult. Traditionally, interactions between children and adults have been conceptualized as a one-way process, with emphasis on the effects of adult behavior, attitudes, or personality on the child. Here we have a first illustration of ways in which the attributes of the child are important too. In this study, children's apparent maturity influenced the behavior of adults. Later chapters will discuss the effects of some other attributes of children on the interactions between children and adults.

SUMMARY

The psychodynamic theories of Freud, Erikson, and White all conceptualize personality as developing through stages fundamentally characterized by changes in the psychosexual orientation of the child. Freud thought that school-aged children were in a latency period, between times of dynamic growth. Erikson and White, however, stress the competencies that develop so rapidly during these years. Social learning theorists, in contrast, think of development as a continuous process in which individuals must master the culturally influenced developmental tasks appropriate for their age.

Piaget's theory deals with developmental stages in how children know or understand their world. The organization or structure of intelligence is assumed to change as children, through active use of their intelligence, encounter new information which results in disequilibrium. When this occurs, intellectual structures adapt to incorporate the new information. School-aged children are typically mastering the use of concrete operations.

The life-span orientation reminds us that childhood is linked in important ways with other periods of life and that the historical time in which one is growing up makes a difference for the kinds of experiences which children have.

The psychobiological orientation reminds us that people are physical beings and that their physical attributes necessarily shape their experiences in important ways.

Height, weight, and body proportions change during the school years, though less dramatically than in early childhood or adolescence. Children grow at different rates. As a consequence, any group of children of the same chronological age will include children who are very different in their physical attributes. For individual children, though, rates of growth are very stable and consistent.

All aspects of a child's development, including physical growth, are interrelated. Many behaviors cannot appear until the physical and physiological structures necessary for them have developed. The dramatic development of skills and abilities in middle childhood may depend on the maturation of physical and physiological structures necessary for fine motor coordination. However, psychological development may influence physical development as well as be influenced by it, as demonstrated by the interfering effect of severe emotional disturbance on physical growth.

Adult reactions to, and expectations for, children change with a child's apparent maturity. As a consequence, fast-growing and slow-growing children—children who look old or young for their age—may encounter quite different expectations and behaviors from adults, which may very well influence the children's development differently. Children's adaptations to these adult reactions to their changing bodies are one factor contributing to the progressive change in behavior with age as children come to act more "grown-up."

TERMS AND CONCEPTS

libido
psychosexual stages
psychodynamic theory
phallic stage
Oedipus conflict
castration anxiety
repression
identification
Electra conflict
penis envy
latency period
psychosocial development
industry vs. inferiority
effectance motivation
competence
social learning theory
qualitative vs. quantative view of development

continuous vs. discontinuous views of development
developmental tasks vs. stages
organization or structure of intelligence
operations
adaptation as a property of intelligence
accommodation
assimilation
active nature of intelligence
equilibrium
sensorimotor period
preoperational period
period of concrete operations
period of formal operations
life-span development orientation
cohort

psychobiological orientation

human ethology

growth curve

catch-up phenomenon

dendrites

neuroglia

myelin sheaths

structure vs. function in

    physiological development

personal space

SUGGESTED ADDITIONAL READING

Tanner, J. M. Physical growth. In P. Mussen (Ed.), *Carmichael's manual of child psychology* (3rd ed.) (Vol. 1). New York: John Wiley & Sons, 1970.

Lerner, Richard M. *Concepts and theories of human development.* Reading, Mass.: Addison-Wesley, 1976.

CHAPTER 2

INTELLIGENCE AS PROCESS: PIAGET'S THEORY

Let us now return to Piaget's theory of intellectual development, which we considered in overview in Chapter 1. First we wish to discuss in more detail what Piaget had to say about the intellectual performance of school-aged children. Second, we shall take up some of the questions and criticisms of his theory which researchers are raising with increasing frequency. Finally, we shall spend some time discussing *social cognition,* one's knowledge and understanding of social interactions and social relationships.

THE THINKING OF SCHOOL-AGED CHILDREN: CONCRETE OPERATIONS

The years during which most children are in the period of concrete operations correspond quite closely to the elementary school years. There are individual differences, of course. Some children have concrete operations before they begin school, whereas others may not begin using them until they have been in school for some time. Some children use formal operations before they finish elementary school, though many do not. Nonetheless, by far the majority of school-aged children are in the period of concrete operations. What does this mean for understanding their characteristic modes of thinking?

The achievements

Conservation   One particularly dramatic achievement is the appearance of conservation of the properties of objects, such as quantity, length, number,

25

weight, density, area, and volume. To adults it is obvious that if you pour liquid from one container to another, differently shaped container, there is still the same amount of liquid in the second container; that if 10 objects in a row are spread out, rearranged into a circle, or piled up, there are still 10 objects. These adults are demonstrating conservation of the properties liquid quantity and number, respectively. They recognize that these properties of objects remain the same, or are conserved, in the face of changes irrelevant to the properties in question, or of transformations that make the objects look different but do not actually affect the properties themselves. But what is so obvious to older children and adults is not at all obvious to preoperational children. Piaget was the first person to discover this, although it has certainly been true of children all along.

The procedure for determining whether or not a child has achieved conservation of some property begins by showing the child two identical displays. Some examples are shown in Figure 2–1. The child must first be satisfied that both displays are the same for the property in question. Then, *while the child watches,* the examiner transforms one of the two objects in some way that does not affect the property. The child is then asked whether there is more in the unchanged object, more in the changed object, or whether both have the same amount (or number, or length). The child is also asked why he or she gave the judgment. Piaget believes that children's reasons for their judgments are more important in indicating whether or not they are conserving the property than are the judgments themselves, since children can give a "right" answer for the "wrong" reasons. (And it does make a difference whether one uses responses, judgments, or both in classifying children as conservers; see Brainerd, 1973.)

Both preoperational and concrete-operational children see the same "evidence" in tasks like these, but they come to quite different conclusions. Preoperational children say that there is now more in one display or the other. Children may fail to conserve number even though they can count, because children can learn to count by rote memorization of number names without fully understanding the properties of numbers, just as they can memorize "addition facts" (2 + 2 = 4), "subtraction facts" (4 − 2 = 2), or any other computational "facts" without grasping the processes that they represent.

To justify their answers, preoperational children usually point out some single attribute that looks different after the transformation. The flattened ball of clay isn't as high, so there is less clay in it; one stick extends beyond the other, so it is longer; one row of objects is longer than the other, so it has more. They fail to recognize that in each case other attributes which also look different compensate for the first attribute. For instance, the flattened ball of clay isn't as high, but it is wider. This tendency to focus on a single perceptual feature of a problem, without being able to conceptualize changes in that feature in relation to other features of the problem, is a general characteristic of preoperational thinking called *centration.* But children with concrete operations are no longer limited in this way; their thinking is decentered. They can conceptualize the apparent changes in relation to each other, and can recognize that the changes cancel each other out, so that although the transformed display looks different, the relevant attribute is still conserved.

FIGURE 2–1 Examples of some conservation tasks. Children are shown the original displays and agree that both objects are equivalent. Then they watch the examiner transform the displays. Conservers agree that the displays are still equivalent; non-conservers do not.

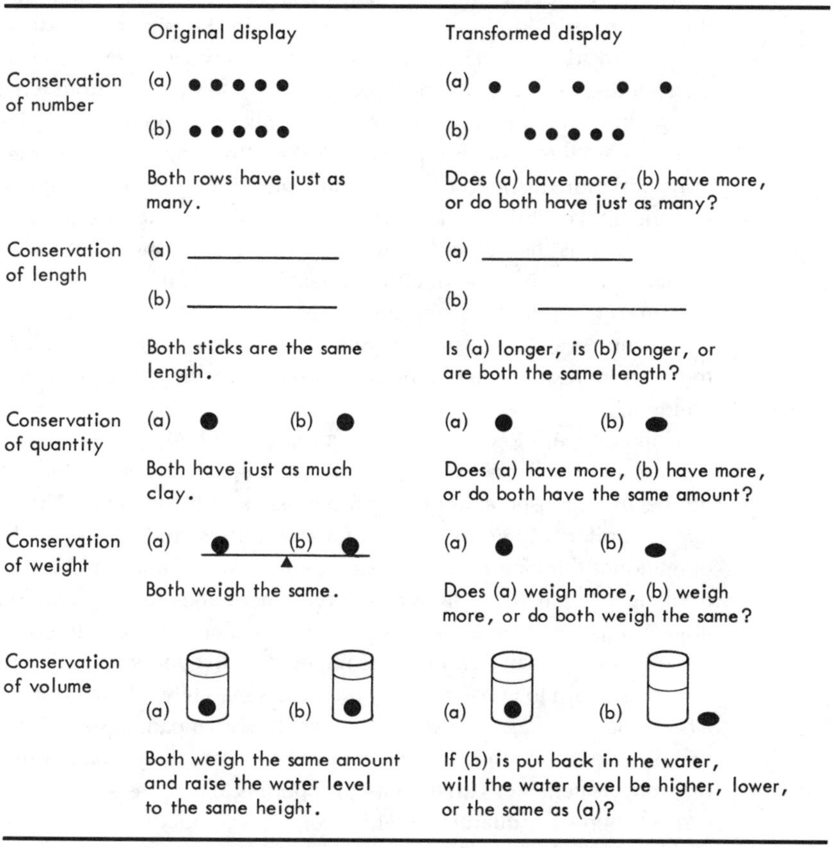

A second very important change which accompanies the acquisition of concrete operations and is related to decentering is *reversibility*. Children become able to perform operations or transformations mentally; they can mentally retrace the steps of a problem. There are several forms of reversibility. Children who say that the property remains the same because there are two simultaneous changes that cancel each other out are using reciprocity or compensation. Children may also argue that the changed display is still the same because nothing was added and nothing was taken away, or they may argue that if things were put back the way they were before, they would be the same, so they must still be the same now. These last two forms of reversibility are called *identity* and *negation*, respectively. In each case, the children can mentally "undo" the change made by the examiner, whereas preoperational children seem to simply go from one state (the original display) to another (the transformed display), reacting to each as a separate event. In much the same way, an adult seeing a pitcher of milk on one trip into the kitchen, then later seeing four glasses of milk, would be hard put to say whether the amount in the four glasses was the same as the amount in the pitcher. In this case, it is because the adult does not know the relationship, if any, between the milk in the pitcher and the milk in the glasses. An adult might make educated guesses based on estimates of the dimensions of the various containers, but this is quite different from what happened when older children or adults watch the milk being poured. They know that the amounts are the same. But preoperational children, even when they watch the transformation, respond in terms of individual states. They may be able to show empirical *reversibility;* asked what would happen if the examiner were to put things back as they were before, they may well answer that the two displays would be the same—but their argument would be that the two would *become* the same *again,* not that they are, therefore, *still* the same now. Through decentering and reversibility, the thinking of concrete operational children becomes much more flexible and mobile compared to the static thinking of preoperational children.

Children learn to conserve many properties of objects. Among these properties are quantity, number, length, area, weight, density, and volume. Children do not begin to conserve all of the properties at once, however. There is indeed a *formal* similarity to conservation of all properties, and adults capable of formal operational thinking may be misled by their recognition of that similarity into thinking that, having mastered conservation for one property, children should be able to apply conservation to all properties, since conservation is always "the same." But the formal similarity is not evident to concrete operational children; they must learn to conserve each property separately. There is what Piaget calls a *horizontal décalage* (*décalage* is a French word meaning something like gap or lag) as, over time, children apply their newly acquired operations to new and different content areas (in this case, properties to be conserved). Conservation of such properties as quantity and number are at about the same level of difficulty; children in the United States usually show conservation of these properties early. But children may conserve quantity and not number, or vice versa. There is, in addition, a well-documented sequence of acquisition of conservation of some properties. Quantity is conserved first, followed a year or more later by conservation of weight; and not until children begin to achieve formal operations do they demonstrate conservation of volume, which requires that they simultaneously coordinate three dimensions (height, width, and depth) rather than the two that sufficed for the other conservations discussed.

In addition to horizontal décalages, where children apply the same intellectual structures to different content areas, there are also *vertical décalages,* where a problem mastered with one set of intellectual structures must be remastered at a different level when new structures develop. As early in life as the sensorimotor period, children show evidence of what might be called operations-in-action. An 18-month-old child whose ball rolls under a sofa may immediately detour around and behind the sofa to retrieve the ball. But children cannot solve such problems *mentally* until the period of concrete operations. As for conservation, in a very real sense any child's first conservation is conservation of the object itself, in the form of the object permanence which develops in the course of the sensorimotor period. There are some very clever studies with preoperational children as young as three years of age in which the number of objects in a display containing a small number of objects changed "magically" in ways that violated conservation of number (Gelman, 1972). When this happened, the children were surprised. Their surprise indicated that they expected number to be conserved and that they could recognize and react to a situation in which number was not conserved. Yet it would probably be some time before these same children would conserve number in the traditional conservation task. On occasion, researchers get into heated interchanges with one another over when some intellectual capacity "really" develops. In fact, any intellectual skill is "really" developing all along through a succession of increasingly complex manifestations. It is less a case of *when* an intellectual skill develops than of what the successive manifestations of the skill might be and how these successive manifestions are related to one another.

Classification   Another important series of changes takes place in children's *classification* of objects. Fully developed classification skills require that one know the defining attributes of different classes of objects, as well as recognize the system of relationships between subordinate and superordinate classes. For instance, dachshunds and collies are distinguishable subordinate classes of the superordinate class dogs; dogs, cats, horses, and birds are distinguishable subordinate classes of the superordinate class animals. Each subordinate class has defining attributes by which all of its members can be identified and distinguished from members of other subordinate classes; and there is a hierarchical organization of subordinate and superordinate classes.

If young preoperational children are given a set of objects—blocks of different form and colors, say, or toys representing people, animals, and buildings—and asked to put together the ones that go together, they group them in idiosyncratic and inconsistent ways. They do not yet use the defining attributes of the objects themselves to form classes. With blocks of different shapes and colors, they may make up patterns of pictures—"graphic collections," as Inhelder and Piaget (1964) call them (see Figure 2–2). Toys may be grouped by stories or themes relating the objects to one another. Such collections are based on whatever notions the child happens to come up with at the time; they differ from occasion to occasion and from child to child.

Later, children begin to group objects according to attributes of the objects themselves. All blocks of the same color or the same form are put together; animals, people, and buildings are put into separate groups; and every object goes into an appropriate group. But such groupings may still be "nongraphic collections" rather than classes, depending upon whether or not the child organized the groupings into a classification *system*. Children who have classification systems understand the relationships among different parts of a system and can move easily from one part of the system to another. They recognize that objects may be simultaneously members of different subclasses (a block is simultaneously blue and square) and that they are simultaneously members of both

FIGURE 2–2 Examples of a type of graphic collection called "collective objects."

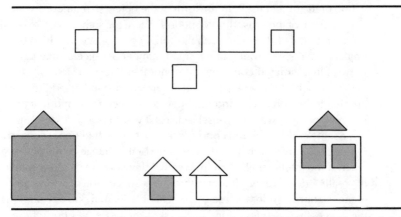

Source: B. Inhelder and J. Piaget, *The Early Growth of Logic in the Child.* Trans. from the French by E. A. Lunzer and D. Papert. English Translation Copyright © 1964 by Routledge & Kegan Paul Ltd. By permission of Harper & Row, Publishers, Inc.

subordinate and superordinate classes (the blue, square block is a wooden block, as is the red, triangular block; a dog is an animal). At this level, children who have sorted according to their colors blocks that differ in form and color can, if asked to do it a different way, readily re-sort the blocks according to form because they recognize the multiple-class membership of the blocks. But children who do not have a classification system cannot do this. Having once sorted by a given attribute, they can see no other way to do it. They "know" perfectly well that the blocks have different colors, and that they also have different shapes, but they cannot coordinate this information so as to simultaneously recognize both types of attributes. Here again, the attributes of decentration and reversibility are evident once concrete operations are being used. The children can then mentally "undo" the groupings they have just made and find an alternative way of doing it. Then performance is no longer centered on just one of the available attributes of the objects which they are sorting.

Many of children's apparent "misunderstandings" seem to stem from the lack of fully organized classification systems. Their use of concepts that refer to members of a class is unstable until they can use defining attributes consistently in identifying members of the class. Such errors are more frequent and more noticeable to adults in young preoperational children than in school-aged children who have begun to use concrete operations, since the latter use defining attributes more consistently. But errors stemming from failure to coordinate parts with wholes, subordinate with superordinate classes, show up in many ways well into the school years. Children may, for instance, have great difficulty in grasping the idea that someone can be both Protestant and Republican, that is, have simultaneous membership in two classes. (One boy asked about this is said to have answered, "Yes, but only if he moves.") Likewise, they may have difficulty in understanding their own multiple citizenship in their local community, their state, and their country, which requires understanding their simultaneous membership in a system with superordinate (national) and subordinate (state, local) classes. Again, this is true even though if asked about any one level—for instance, "Do you live in the United States?"—they answer promptly and correctly.

Relational thinking   Children's understanding of *relational concepts*— concepts such as brother and sister, right and left, which express relationships between objects and events—also changes with the acquisition of concrete operations.

A preoperational boy may insist that he has a brother but that his brother doesn't have any brothers. He fails to understand the reciprocal nature of the brother relationship, that he cannot have a brother without himself being a brother. Children also have difficulty with concepts such as right and left, which are sometimes used in an absolute sense (your right hand is always your right hand) but which are more often used in a relational sense: the table or door is to your right or left, depending on, or relative to, the position of your body.

Initially, children use such concepts only in an absolute sense. One of Piaget's tasks consists of showing children a board on which three objects are lined up left to right. When asked if the middle object is on the right side of one end object, or to the left side of the other end object, they could answer correctly. But when asked how the middle object could be to the right and to the left at the same time, they were baffled and confused. This confusion concerning the relative usage of *right* and *left* persists until second grade or later for many children. Similar inability to understand relational concepts is apparent in quite different contexts. For instance, foreigner is a relative concept that depends on where persons hold citizenship as well as where they are now. A citizen of the United States is a foreigner in France or India, but not in the United States. But until well into the school years, children may define foreigners absolutely. A foreigner is a foreigner no matter where he is, and they themselves would never be foreigners no matter where they were. Other relationships, such as friend and enemy, are given similar absolute interpretations (Piaget, 1966a). However, re- lational thinking does not appear all at once for all relational problems. Kinder- garten and second-grade children were given both the right-middle-left task described above and another exactly analogous task in which the objects were lined up front-middle-back (Harris, 1972). Relational questions concerning right and left flummoxed all of the kindergartners and about half of the second graders, but these *same* children gave, and insisted on, relational answers con- cerning front and back.

Changes in egocentrism   *Egocentrism,* as Piaget uses the term, is a failure to differentiate subject from object, self from experience, that stems directly from one's level of intellectual functioning. Children begin life as completely ego- centric beings, because at the outset they do not differentiate any external events from their experience of those events. By the end of the sensorimotor period, their egocentrism as regards objects has been overcome; the appearance of object permanence is evidence that they do indeed differentiate objects from themselves and from their sensory and motor contact with objects. But this is just the first round. Each time a new type of intellectual structure emerges, ego- centrism reappears in a new form; and so one finds characteristic forms of egocentrism associated with each period of intellectual development. Egocentrism in this sense is something that children cannot avoid. It is a direct and inevitable consequence of their intellectual development. This is a very different conception from the interpretation of egocentric as selfish or egotistical, which implies differentiation of one's own self and concerns from those of others, and voluntarily or deliberately placing one's own concerns before those of others. Further, this second sense of egocentrism is essentially social, describing an orientation of one individual in relation to other individuals. But egocentrism, as Piaget uses the term, is not basically social. Instead, it is a general phenomenon which permeates everything children do, including their social interactions.

With the acquisition of concrete operations, children begin to overcome the forms of egocentrism characteristic of preoperational thinking. (Remember that the period of concrete operations begins when children first begin to use operations; most of their thinking is still preoperational.) The most frequent characterization of the egocentrism of preoperational children is that they are trapped within their own point of view, unable to take a perspective different from their own. This form of egocentrism stems from a failure to differentiate between symbols and their referents, between a child's thinking about an object or an event and the object or the event itself. Children seem to take their own thoughts as part of the situation in much the same sense that the event itself is part of the situation. As a result, they appear to be unaware that they could have any other thoughts, or that others might have thoughts, information, or points of view different from their own. Others do have different points of view, of course, and encounters with other points of view which children must reconcile with their own are one important factor in the development of an awareness that other points of view exist.

By the beginning of the school years, children do realize that other points of view exist, but they are not yet very skilled at recognizing what those other points of view might be or at coordinating them with their own. Children's performance on a task requiring them to coordinate spatial perspectives, which literally requires them to take the spatial perspective of another, is one good illustration of preoperational egocentrism and its decline with the acquisition of concrete operations. The task originally designed by Piaget and Inhelder (1948) consists of showing children an array of three model mountains which differ in size, shape, color, and landmarks (see Figure 2–3). Children first view the array from all sides. Then they are seated on one side, and asked what would be seen by someone seated in a different location—opposite them, or to their right or left relative to the model mountains. Young children who are just approaching or entering the period of concrete operations are likely to pick the picture or reconstruct the same scene that they themselves see, regardless of the location of the other figure. Their responses are egocentric.

Later, children recognize that the scene should be different from what they themselves see, but they are not yet able to keep the spatial relationships among the objects straight "in their heads." They no longer pick the scene that they themselves see, but not until about fourth grade or later can they consistently

FIGURE 2–3 Top and side views of model mountains used to study coordination of spatial perspectives. While seated at position A, the child must indicate how the mountains might look to someone at positions B, C, or D.

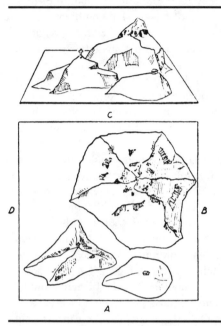

Source: J. Piaget and B. Inhelder, *The Child's Conception of Space* (New York: W. W. Norton, 1967).

pick the picture showing what someone would see from a location other than their own.

But again, there is evidence of prior development. If familiar objects having clearly identifiable backs and fronts (cars, houses) are used instead of model mountains, even second graders can often make nonegocentric responses (Strommen, 1976). And if children look through a peephole at a scene consisting of three familiar objects, such as a doll in a toy chair watching a toy TV, then look at the same objects through a peephole on the other side, even four-year-olds show surprise if the scene has been surreptitiously rotated so that the objects are still in the same spatial orientation relative to themselves (Shantz & Watson, 1970, 1971). These children already expect the spatial relationships among objects to change as their own position relative to the objects changes, and they recognize violations of this expectation.

The limitations

Problem solving Concrete-operational children are able to think logically about problems, but there are still limitations on their thinking. They cannot yet formulate hypotheses, coordinate operations to solve multidimensional problems, or conceptualize possible alternatives which may not exist in reality. Contrasting the performance of concrete-operational and formal-operational children on different tasks may help to clarify the nature of these limitations.

One task requires children to discover what combination of four colorless liquids will yield a yellow color when combined with a fifth liquid, g (see Figure 2–4). They must discover that it is a combination of the first and third liquids, so that pairing g with just one liquid will not produce the color; and haphazardly trying different pairs or triads of liquids without some system to keep track of what combinations have been tried is more likely to result in confusion than to produce the color. Yet this is what concrete-operational children are likely to do. It may not even occur to them to try pairs of liquids unless the examiner suggests it.

However, formal-operational children behave as though they have an overall coordinating system which they follow systematically. They also usually begin by combining g with each liquid individually, but when this does not work, they change hypotheses—if it's not an individual liquid, it must be a combination—and begin systematically combining pairs of liquids with g: $1 + 2 + g$, $1 + 3 + g$. Here the color appears. A concrete-operational child would probably stop here. But formal-operational children are as likely as not to continue trying out the remaining combinations: $1 + 4 + g$, $2 + 4 + g$, and so on. One 13-year-old, discovering in this way that liquid 4 bleached out the color, concluded that 4 could not be water because "if this liquid 4 is water, when you put it with $1 + 3$, it wouldn't completely prevent the yellow from forming" (Inhelder

FIGURE 2–4 Materials for studying combinations of colored and colorless liquids. Four large flasks and a fifth, smaller flask (g) contain odorless, colorless liquids. A combination of liquids from flasks 1, 3, and g will produce a yellow color. The child is also presented with two glasses, one containing $1 + 3$, the other water. The experimenter demonstrates that a drop from g produces a yellow color in the glass containing $1 + 3$, but not in the glass containing water. The child is then asked to reproduce the yellow color by combining liquids from any or all of the flasks.

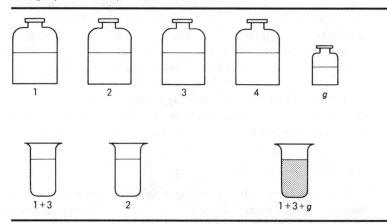

Source: Figure 6 from *The Growth of Logical Thinking: From Childhood to Adolescence* by Barbel Inhelder and Jean Piaget, translated by Anne Parsons and Stanley Milgram, © 1958 by Basic Books, Inc., Publishers, New York.

& Piaget, 1958, p. 117). This last argument postulates a circumstance that is possible (4 contains water) but is contrary to fact (4 actually contains something else). It is a type of argument that concrete-operational children almost never use.

Children using concrete-operational reasoning also have difficulty recognizing the implications of contradictory evidence. In one study, children were shown pictures in which pairs of objects differed in an obvious way (tools versus means of transportation) and in a less obvious way (wheels versus no wheels) (Elkind, 1966). The obvious contrast was irrelevant; children had to select pictures according to whether or not there were wheels. Children were presented pairs of pictures which differed on both dimensions. A horse (no wheels) might be paired with a lawn mower (wheels), and an automobile (wheels) with a saw (no wheels). Both adolescents 13–14 years old and school-aged children 9–10 years old initially focused on the obvious (and irrelevant) tools-transportation contrast, but their strategies were very different. The adolescents responded to signals that a response was incorrect as disconfirming the hypothesis on which the response was made and shifted to something else. So they quickly ruled out both tools and transportation, looked for another contrast, and solved the problem. But only about half of the school-aged children solved the problem, and those who did required many trials to do so. Their difficulty was that, having come up with a hypothesis, they tended to stick with it regardless of disconfirming evidence, which they tended to discount as mistaken interpretations of the object chosen. One child hypothesized that the correct pictures were "things that move;" when told that a picture of a horse was incorrect, he said, "I guess horses move in a different way." Here the inability of the younger children to think of alternative hypotheses clearly interfered with their learning. It is very likely that such interference occurs in classroom situations as well.

Egocentrism   Even as children are overcoming preoperational egocentrism, a new form of egocentrism associated with the concrete operations themselves is becoming increasingly evident. Concrete-operational egocentrism consists of failure to distinguish between facts and hypotheses. Assumptions and hypotheses are treated as though their truth were firmly established. As a consquence, disconfirming evidence may fail to change children's minds, and verification of their assumptions or their interpretations of events is not sought—exactly the quality of thinking that characterized the performance of concrete-operational children described in the preceding section. This type of egocentrism sometimes shows up in humorous incidents, as when an eight-year-old girl visiting one of the authors refused to touch some tiny half-inch-long toads on the grounds that touching them would make her fingers dissolve. Her friend had told her so. Despite the direct disconfirming evidence that no one else's fingers dissolved (several people were handling the little toads), as well as a good bit of reasoning and some teasing, her conviction remained unshaken.

Elkind (1981) refers to such assumptions-taken-as-facts as *assumptive realities,* "assumptions about reality that children make on the basis of limited information and which they will not alter in the face of new and contradictory evidence" (p. 79). Some assumptive realities, such as the idea that adults aren't very smart, may be widely held over much of the school years (see Chapter 8). Other assumptive realities may be situational and short-term. For example, assumptive realities regarding school course work may contribute to some learning difficulties and, if exaggerated in form and complicated by emotional involvement, may become serious "learning blocks." This could occur if children accept some principle as fact and persist in applying it indiscriminately despite being shown more appropriate solutions (disconfirming evidence). In such instances, the assumptive reality would interfere with continued learning.

The egocentrism of concrete operations may be most characteristic among school-aged children, but it does not entirely disappear as children become adults. Remember that adults, though many are *capable* of formal operations, may actually use concrete-operational thinking much of the time. As one such assumptive reality, Elkind mentions "the romantic image of love and marriage held by so many young women in our society, despite all of the everyday evidence which gainsays this image" (1981, p. 89). Other examples are not difficult to find. Arguments over politics, religion, drugs, and many other topics often have attributes that suggest assumptive realities are at work, as when the participants take their own positions as truth and have great difficulty in seeing that other positions may be valid alternative interpretations rather than perverse stupidity. Many such arguments seem to be characterized by a grand imperviousness to evidence of any sort, and rarely seem to end with any perceptible expansion of the participants' thinking.

Training studies

Whether children can be trained to use intellectual structures before the structures would develop "naturally" has been a topic of great interest to investigators in the United States. Such studies are useful for looking more closely at how intellectual growth takes place, since successful training is evidence that the procedures used were relevant. Far more training studies have dealt with the transition from preoperational to concrete-operational performance than with other transitions. Piaget believed, and the early studies as reviewed by Flavell (1963) concurred, that standard learning procedures such as reinforcing correct response should not be effective as training procedures; only those procedures through which children could discover the relevant principle for themselves should be successful and then only when children were about to achieve the new skill on their own anyway.

However, since then a variety of training procedures have been found to be effective, maybe even more effective than the discovery process considered necessary by the Piagetians (Brainerd, 1978). Some studies suggest that the transition may be fostered by influences other than (though not necessarily incompatible with) those suggested by Piaget, such as learning to attend to the relevant cues (Gelman, 1969) or learning through observation (Charbonneau, Robert, Bourassa, & Gladu-Bissonnette, 1976); or that the process described by Piaget may not work in just the way that he thought (for example, Brainerd, 1976). And whether training appears effective often depends upon method—

how the task is presented to children, what part of their answer is used to judge successful performance, and so forth (e.g., Brainerd, 1973; Brainerd & Hooper, 1975). Such training studies, producing results not predicted from a strict interpretation of Piaget, have been one important source of criticism of his theory.

As for the children, however, it is hard to see what they gain (or lose) by acquiring some skill a little before they might gain it on their own. Some argue that "all things come in due time," that there is a developmental timetable for each child with which we tamper at the child's cost. We don't, for example, give children shots of growth hormone in order to get them to develop faster physically; if we were to do so we might very well upset the whole hormonal system regulating the child's growth. Is there some parallel argument relevant for cognitive development as well? We don't know, although when one looks at the range of environmental settings within which children develop cognitively, one is tempted to believe that considerable flexibility must characterize intellectual development. Certainly there is no strong evidence that would suggest that children might be harmed by achieving mastery of some cognitive tasks through training. On the other hand, there is also no strong evidence that would suggest that they have much to gain from such accelerated development. On present evidence there is no more reason for assuming that if concrete operations are good, mastering them sooner must be better, than there is for assuming that training children in concrete observations is likely to upset some developmental timetable.

Criticisms of Piaget's theory

As the preceding section suggests, research investigations of issues relating to Piaget's theory have raised, and continue to raise, questions and criticism about the theory. In general, these criticisms do not apply to the actual descriptions of children's performance; as an observer Piaget was unexcelled, and the phenomena he described can often be replicated even by novices. (You might find it interesting to try some conservation tasks yourself, choosing materials similar to those described in Figure 2–1). However, there is increasing disagreement about how the changes take place and what they mean (e.g., Siegel & Brainerd, 1978; Flavell, 1977). Many such questions relate to the issue of the relationship between competence and performance: Given what you see a child do (performance), what does that tell you about the child's cognitive skills (competence)? A six-year-old who doesn't conserve may lack concrete operations (a Piagetian interpretation) but it may also be the case that the particular task was too difficult for that child, or there might have been other factors involved in the child's performance (e.g., Siegel & Brainerd, 1978). Or we ourselves might not yet understand how to adequately conceptualize, assess, and measure the cognitive skill of interest, which upon close examination proves to be a much more complex endeavor than it appears at first glance (Flavell, 1977, Chapter 7).

Several researchers have roundly criticized Piaget for describing the thinking skills of preoperational children in negative terms, that is, in terms of the operations that they lack, rather than in terms of what they can do cognitively. As a consequence, our knowledge of the thinking of preoperational children has been severely limited (e.g., Gelman, 1979; Borke, 1978). We referred before to Gelman's demonstration that with an innovative technique, and with small numbers, even three-year-olds behave as though they expect number to be conserved. Gelman and her co-workers have studied a variety of early number-related skills in preschool children, skills upon which they build their later mastery of the usual conservation tasks as well as their mastery of more complex arithmetic and mathematical skills (Gelman & Gallistel, 1978). Similarly, a simplistic interpretation of the nature of preoperational egocentrism as "inability to take the point of view of another" can lead the unwary to assume that preoperation children show no sensitivity to others (an assumption any obser-vant nursery school teacher could challenge). Yet children as young as three can not only differentiate basic emotions, such as happiness, anger, and sadness, but can appropriately relate such feelings to simple stories—not a very demanding version of such tasks, perhaps, but important in its own right, and clear evidence that they are capable of some awareness of others (e.g. Borke, 1978). We need to know much more about what young children can do cognitively if we are to fully appreciate their characteristics and competencies when they begin school.

A related concern questions whether it is reasonable to think of general stages of intellectual development as Piaget does (e.g., Flavell, 1977). From such a conception it follows that there should be links or connections between the levels of any given child's performance across a wide domain of intellectual tasks. But the evidence for such generality has not been very strong, and such evidence as does exist is open to other interpretations. Based on years of re-search and reading in the area, Flavell (1977) suggests that we would do better to think in terms of domain-specific sequences rather than in terms of general stages. For any category of tasks, no one can do the hard ones without first understanding the easy tasks; thus, for any domain, such as number or classi-fication, there will necessarily be sequences of tasks through which children will progress. But there is no strong reason in the evidence available to assume any necessary connection between children's performance levels in different domains.

Where does this leave us? First, we know substantially more about children's intellectual development than we would have had Piaget not made his con-tribution. The fact that we are now raising questions which we would not have a few years back is as it should be; these are now different questions, raised for different reasons, growing out of our increased understanding and sophistication regarding how children think. Second, even though we are less sure than we were about Piaget's interpretations of them, we still have the rich legacy of his descriptions of the changes which children's performance undergoes from pre-school on into the school years.

SOCIAL COGNITION

Social cognition is one of the research areas that has expanded dramatically since we first wrote about it several years back. Then, we defined social cognition as ". . . the ability to understand other people: To conceptualize their attributes, to recognize what they feel, think, or intend; to be able to take their point of view while maintaining one's own" (Strommen et al., 1977, pp. 204–205). Now we would define social cognition more generally as one's understanding and knowledge of persons, social relationships, and social institutions. This more inclusive definition allows us to take into consideration the expansion of social cognition to include not only knowledge of other persons but also of the self (e.g., Bandura, 1981; Mischel, 1981); not only understanding of persons but of relationships such as friendship (e.g., Berndt, 1981; Hartup, 1978; Youniss & Volpe, 1978) or marriage and divorce (Lowry, 1979); and social institutions such as money, commerce, and community (Furth, 1978). Furthermore, understanding persons implies understanding their intellectual characteristics as well as their personal and social characteristics (Flavell & Wellman, 1977) so one can ask what children know about their own and others' memories (Flavell & Wellman, 1977), comprehension skills (Markman, 1981), communication skills (Dickson, 1981), and so forth. These latter skills are also called *metacognition*—knowing about what and how one knows.

What can one say about such a diverse array of competencies? We can make some very general statements, such as that older children show better understanding than younger children, and that the school years appear to be a period of especially rapid development in most areas of social cognition. Also, many social cognitions or metacognitions may play an important role in regulating behavior through a process of checking how things are going against what is known about such situations; this process is called *cognitive monitoring* and it also appears to show considerable gains during the school years (for further discussion, see Flavell, 1979, 1981, 1981a).

Beyond this, however, we run into difficulties. The expanded field of social cognition draws upon not only a very wide range of content domains, both social and personal, but upon a range of theoretical perspectives as well. Piaget's ideas were an important source of much of the early interest in social cognition, and we shall come back to some of the work influenced by his ideas shortly. But in addition, there is increasing convergence between developmental and social psychology, which has its own tradition of studying social cognition; in particular, ideas from *attribution theory*—which studies our inferences about the causes of behavior and the consequences of such inferences—are becoming increasingly prevalent in studies with children. In the cognitive areas, much of the research draws on information processing theory. We have no reason to assume that there are general or unifying principles of social cognition which apply across all of these diverse content domains and theoretical orientations. So, rather than deal with all of social cognition here, we shall come back to particular areas in the context of discussion of the more general behavioral topics to which they are most closely related.

Piaget's influence   As for Piaget's influence on studies of social cognition, researchers were interested in how well his conceptions, developed in the context of thinking about the physical world, would apply to the social world. (Despite his research emphasis on the physical world, Piaget himself argued that development is affected by both social and physical environments, and further that feelings and thinking are inextricably mixed—you can't have a thought without some kind of feeling, or a feeling without some kind of knowledge of it.) Researchers were also interested in Piaget's contention that preoperational children are egocentric in that they could not differentiate their own point of view from another person's point of view. When Shantz reviewed social cognition research in 1975, much of the work she reviewed reflected these interests. She suggested that most of the then-current work related to one or another of five questions.

1.   The first question Shantz identified was, what does the other *perceive?* Studies relevant to this question are those dealing with recognizing another's spatial perspective, discussed in an earlier section of this chapter (pp. 32–33).

2.   What does the other person *intend?* Piaget (1965) argued that preoperational children judge actions as good or bad according to their consequences, but that by eight or nine they have shifted to judging acts according to the actor's intentions. (Of course it isn't that simple. Even preschoolers can use intentions in some circumstances.) We will deal with these ideas, and Kohlberg's extensions of them, in greater detail in Chapter 7.

3.   What does the other *feel?* At issue here is children's capacity for empathy, the ability to experience the feelings of another person. We mentioned previously that, contrary to what simplistic interpretations of egocentrism might imply, one can find evidence of awareness and sensitivity to others' feelings even in very young children (see p. 38 above; Borke, 1978). The major change during the school years appears to be in children's ability to recognize the feelings of persons unlike themselves in unfamiliar situations (Rothenberg, 1970; Chandler & Greenspan, 1972). Even though young children can recognize emotions, children as old as 8½ may still have difficulty in recognizing the feelings, of say, adults in situations typical for adults, but not familiar for children. By 10½ this ability has improved significantly (Rothenberg, 1970). One can argue, as do Chandler and Greenspan (1972) that the younger children's recognition of familiar feelings in familiar situations is primarily identification or projection of their own feelings, rather than responsiveness to others' feelings. One can counter-argue, as does Borke (1978), that the experimental tasks used by Chandler and Greenspan and by other researchers are so complex that one is studying cognitive development—ability to understand the task—rather than empathy. (She also attributes this error to Piaget.) The problem with this interpretation is that it does not show us how we can study empathy once away from very simple situations. Surely identifying common emotions in simple situations is not all there is to empathy, with all subsequent elaboration a matter of cognitive gain. It seems more reasonable to us to agree with Borke that preoperational children do indeed have rudimentary empathic skills, but to also agree with Chandler and Greenspan and others that coping with understanding others' feelings in more complex situations requires both empathic and cognitive growth, and that such growth proceeds rapidly during the school years.

4.   What is the other person *like?* This is *person perception,* how children perceive and describe other people. (It is the one area discussed in this section

which did not originally draw heavily on Piaget's ideas.) When children start school, their descriptions of others are typically nonpsychological and often superficial. They focus on concrete, observable attributes and behaviors, such as what the other person wears, owns, does—especially as it affects the child making the description (Sally is nice because she lets me ride her bike). By the end of the school years, however, children's descriptions of other persons include not only more attributes, but substantial proportions of psychological attributes which require inferences from behavior (shy, dishonest, friendly, generous), and sometimes statements about why the other person has the attributes in question. The descriptions of movie scenes in Box 2–2 illustrate some of these changes. In a major study which asked children between age 7 and age 15 to describe people they knew, there was a steady and significant increase with age in the total number of statements that the children made about others and in the number and proportion of psychological statements (Livesley & Bromley, 1973). A particularly interesting finding was that the most marked change took place between 7½ and 8½ years of age. The authors note that in some instances the differences between 7- and 8-year-olds were greater than those between 8-

---

BOX 2–2
Changes in social cognition illustrated in children's descriptions of scenes from movies

The following interpretations of a movie scene, the first by a 6-year-old and the second by a 12-year-old, illustrate the changes in children's responsiveness to psychological attributes, feelings, and motives. Compare the 6-year-old's simple description of events with the 12-year-old's interpretations of feelings and motives.

At the beginning her daddy was sitting in the chair in the living room looking at the paper. And the little girl got out of her bed and said, "Pa, will you kiss me goodnight?" And the daddy said, "Go to bed," and the little girl went to bed crying. And he tore up the paper and he threw it down on the floor. Then he went into the kitchen and was getting ready to go out to the barn. And the lady said, "Where are you going?" And he said, "Out to the barn." And the lady said, "At this time of the night?" And the man said, "Yes."

The father was reading the newspaper, but he was thinking about something else. He couldn't really read it. And the little girl was looking down and asked her father if he didn't want to kiss her good night. The father wanted to say good night, but then he thought she did something bad, so he said, "No. Go back to bed." And the girl was crying and did go back to bed. And the father tried to read the newspaper again, but he couldn't read it, so he threw it away. He wanted to go up to her and say it wasn't so bad. But he decided he better not. So he went to the kitchen and said to his wife he was going out. And the mother said, "I think you just want to be by yourself." And he said, "Yes." And the mother said, "There is a circus coming to town tonight." I think he is going to the circus with the girl now.

Source: D. Flapan, *Children's Understanding of Social Interaction* (New York: Teacher's College Press, 1968), pp. 31, 32.

and 15-year-olds. Borke (1978) suggests that this increasing attention to psychological characteristics of others may be intertwined with children's increasing capacity for empathy.

Summarizing a review of person perception studies with children, Rogers (1978) suggests that the person perceptions of six- or seven-year-olds differ from those of older children and adults in three ways. First, they differ in *content*. The six- or seven-year old uses simple, unqualified descriptions, and in a given situation may infer different psychological states from those an older child would infer. Second, the *orientation* of the younger child is different, focused as it is on the immediate, the concrete, and the "what" of persons and events rather than the abstract, the long term, and the "why." And finally, the child's *information processing skills* are limited. The child may infer information appropriately, but lack the intellectual skills to proceed effectively with that piece of information. This is a more general point about which more will be said when we discuss learning and information processing in more detail (Chapter 4).

5. What does the other person *think?* At issue here is children's ability to recognize another person's intellectual perspective, that is, to differentiate between what they themselves know and think compared to what another person might know and think. Primary grade children may have considerable difficulty in overcoming an "egocentric" perspective to recognize that another person does not know or think what they do. Flavell, Botkin, Fry, Wright, and Jarvis (1968) showed children a set of seven pictures in which a boy walks down a street, is chased by a dog, climbs a tree to escape, and ends up sitting in the tree eating an apple. Three pictures showing the dog can be removed, leaving a different story: A boy walks down the street, climbs a tree, and sits there eating an apple. Children were first shown the entire seven pictures and asked to tell the story, which all the children could do easily. Then the pictures showing the dog were removed, a new person was brought into the room, and the children were asked to tell the story they thought the new person would tell about the pictures. Through third grade, most of the children still told the story appropriate for the complete set of pictures. They were unable to get outside their own perspective to realize that the new person could not know about the dog from the pictures now visible. By fourth grade, most children changed the story appropriately, though if asked why the boy climbed the tree, they were likely to say it was to get away from the dog.

Understanding what another person is thinking requires not only being able to distinguish between one's own perspective and someone else's, but being able to relate the two perspectives to each other. Selman and Byrne (1974) suggest that children go through a developmental sequence of levels in acquiring this ability. At *Level 0, Egocentric Role-Taking,* children do not yet distinguish between their own perspectives and those of others. *Level 1* is called *Subjective Role-Taking.* At this level, children realize that others feel or think differently because they are in different situations or have different information, but the children cannot put themselves in the position of the other person in judging what the other person does, nor can they take the other person's perspective in judging themselves. At *Level 2, Self-Reflective Role-Taking,* children have become aware that people think or feel differently, not just because they have different information, but because they have their own particular values and interests. They can also put themselves in the other person's shoes and recognize that the other person can do the same thing, so that they can begin to anticipate how others will react to their own actions or ideas. *Level 3, Mutual Role-Taking,* is reached when children not only differentiate their own perspective from another person's, but can look at both person's perspectives from the point of view of some third person, such as a typical member of some group (most people, the other kids, grown-ups, and so on). Now they can think about their own point of view and the other person's point of view simultaneously, and evaluate both points of view from the perspective of an outside observer.

Selman and Byrne (1974) presented children with social dilemmas similar to those used in studies of moral judgment (Chapter 7), then analyzed the children's responses in terms of the level of role-taking evident in them. Table 2-1 shows the proportions of 4-, 6-, 8-, and 10-year-olds at each level of role-taking.

In subsequent work, Selman and his co-workers have suggested that not only is there a stage hierarchy in social perspective taking (what we called role-taking above), but that there are parallel hierarchical developments in school-aged boys' conceptions of interpersonal relationships and other social concepts (e.g., Selman, 1976; Selman, 1977; Selman & Jaquette, 1978). When they compared the performance of clinic-referred boys who had emotional problems with the performance of nonclinic boys, they found (among other things) that the two groups were more different in social reasoning than in physical-logical reasoning, as assessed by typical Piaget tasks; that there was much more variation in the performance of the clinic boys than of the others, with some of the clinic children performing at very low levels of social reasoning while others were quite similar to nonclinic children; that children whose social reasoning was poor, compared to other children their own age, were also quite likely to be unpopular with their peers; and that the clinic children were more likely than nonclinic children to behave in very unsophisticated ways even when their levels of social reasoning were fairly good, especially if they were under social pressure.

TABLE 2-1
Percentage of 4-, 6-, 8-, and 10-year-old children reaching a given role-taking level
($N = 10$ per age group)

Stage	Age 4	Age 6	Age 8	Age 10
0	80	10	0	0
1	20	90	40	20
2	0	0	50	60
3	0	0	10	20

Source: R. L. Selman and D. F. Byrne, "A Structural Developmental Analysis of Levels of Role-taking in Middle Childhood," *Child Development* 45 (1974), pp. 803–6. Copyright 1974 by The Society for Research in Child Development, Inc.

In addition, there are the studies mentioned in the beginning of this section which examine children's reasoning about a variety of social topics. (For collections of studies many of which are in this category, see Damon, 1978; McGurk, 1978.) Typically, children's responses to relatively open-ended questions on topics of interest are examined. Some of these topics will be treated in more detail later. For now, some examples of typical results will suffice. For one, results in these studies often resemble those discussed for person perception above, showing that primary grade children are unlikely to show much awareness of psychological processes or relationships which require inference from observed behavior, whereas by the end of grade school children do typically use such concepts. For another, primary grade children are likely to view social roles and relationships as absolute, and to talk of them in terms of concrete, immediate, personal experience, whereas older children are becoming more able to take more abstract, impersonal, and flexible positions. For instance, concepts of government or of community require comprehension of an abstract, impersonal social entity which can serve the common good. Primary grade children are likely to answer questions about such constructs as though they referred to people who do things for others, especially for children (government is an old man who makes parks for children to play in). Not until the late elementary years or even adolescence do children begin to show a more general grasp of such topics (e.g., Furth, 1978; Adelson & O'Neil, 1966). And finally, concepts about psychological processes that require simultaneous coordination of several ideas for their comprehension are not understood until much later than concepts that require only comprehension of a single idea (e.g., Chandler, Paget, & Koch, 1978).

How might these social cognitive skills be related to one another or to cognitions about the physical world? Low to moderate relationships are found when such questions are examined (e.g., Shantz, 1975; Selman, 1976), but as we pointed out earlier, such correlations do not necessarily reflect some underlying stage structure, but could exist for a variety of reasons. If Flavell (1977) is right that cognitions about the physical world develop in sequences whose relationship to one another is yet to be spelled out, we would hardly expect to find any closer relationship among cognitions about the social world or between physical and social cognitions. Children appear to enter the school years with some basic social cognitive skills already established; in all the areas considered, the school years appear to be a period when there is a substantial increase in the level and sophistication of such skills. Certainly, it is possible that there is some underlying structural organization of children's cognitions. But it is equally likely that children's changed social and intellectual circumstances once they begin school, with its associated social and cognitive experiences, are responsible for the parallel changes described here.

One might ask also how these skills are related to children's behavior in real life situations; with few exceptions (e.g., Selman, 1976; Selman & Jaquette, 1978), we have little information. Addressing this question of the relationship between social cognition and social behavior is one direction in which research in this field is beginning to move.

SUMMARY

In Piaget's terms, most school-aged children have begun to use concrete operations, so that they have begun to think logically for the first time. Operations permit them to deal with relationships between objects and events, making possible the beginning of such major changes as conservation of properties of objects, the development of classification systems, improvements in relational thinking, and the overcoming of preoperational egocentrism. These achievements do not appear suddenly. They have antecedents in earlier periods of development; initially they appear only occasionally, later generalizing to become increasingly typical of the children's thinking.

There are still limits to what children using concrete operations can do, however. They do best with concrete immediate situations; they have difficulty conceptualizing alternatives or formulating hypotheses. And they demonstrate a new form of egocentrism characterized by failure to distinguish assumptions from facts.

Similarly, changes are evident in children's thinking about persons and social relationships. As with cognitions about the physical world, children's social cognitions have antecedents in earlier years of development. Children enter the school years with some basic social cognitive skills, though they have difficulty with tasks that require inferring psychological attributes or processes, or with going beyond absolute interpretations of immediate, concrete, personally experienced situations. By the end of the school years, they are much more competent with psychological constructs and much more capable of thinking in relative terms about abstract and impersonal social constructs. Their much expanded social experience throughout the school years undoubtedly contributes substantially to these changed social cognitions.

However, while most researchers agree that Piaget correctly observed the changes in the ways in which children think, they increasingly disagree with him about what these changes mean or how they take place. It is quite likely that intellectual development proceeds, not in general stages which are evident in all of a child's thinking, but rather in sequences within different content areas which may or may not be related to one another. The contrasts between stages have been overdrawn too; preschool children have far more cognitive skills than was evident when they were described only in terms of their inability to perform correctly on the difficult and demanding tasks used to assess concrete-operational thinking. One of the main tasks now facing researchers is to delineate in clearer detail the many small steps and alternate routes through which sequences of development proceed.

TERMS AND CONCEPTS

social cognition	**horizontal décalage**
conservation	**vertical décalage**
centration	**classification**
reversibility	**graphic collection**

classification system
relational concepts
egocentrism
spatial perspective
assumptive realities
competence vs. performance
sequences vs. stages
metacognition

cognitive monitoring
attribution theory
empathy
person perception
egocentric role-taking
subjective role-taking
self-reflective role-taking
mutual role-taking

SUGGESTED ADDITIONAL READING

Ginsburg, H., & Opper, S. *Piaget's theory of intellectual development: an introduction* (2nd ed.). Englewood Cliffs, N.J.: Prentice-Hall, 1979.

Siegel, S., & Brainerd, C. J. *Alternatives to Piaget: Critical essays on the theory.* New York: Academic Press, 1978.

Damon, W. *Social cognition. New directions for child development.* No. 1, 1978. San Francisco: Jossey-Bass, 1978.

BOX 3–1
Study questions

What is a psychological construct?

Define IQ. Why are average IQ scores always 100 for children of any age?

In what sense is the validity of IQ tests quite good? In what sense can one challenge this point?

If you know a child's IQ score at age 6, what can you say about that child's probable score at age 12?

What environmental and personal attributes are related to IQ scores?

What do average group scores tell you about the abilities of individual members of those same groups?

How is heredity related to IQ scores?

What are some of the problems for which IQ tests are criticized?

Compare and contrast process and product orientations toward intelligence.

CHAPTER 3

INTELLIGENCE: TESTS OF MENTAL ABILITIES

It is one of those fascinating bits of historical trivia that Piaget, with his orientation toward intelligence as an attribute shared by all human beings, made his initial observations in the laboratories of Alfred Binet, developer of the first intelligence test and thus founder of a movement which has focused almost exclusively upon individual differences in intellectual functioning. Both orientations toward understanding human intelligence have thrived, but their emphases have been so different that it often seems one is dealing with two separate topics.

Binet's test was introduced into this country in revised form as the Stanford-Binet intelligence test in 1916. It was received with enthusiasm and psychologists soon began to develop other scales not only of intelligence, but of personality, social interaction skills, and diverse other psychological attributes. At present there are hundreds of tests available for use in human assessment and in research, including the large body of tests of mental abilities which are one of the facts of life for the vast majority of school-aged children.

Yet mental ability testing became, and has continued to be, controversial despite the widespread use of tests in academic and vocational settings—and this was especially true during the 1970s. On the one hand, there is a substantial body of information available now regarding tests and the factors influencing children's performance on them. On the other hand, there is considerable concern, both public and professional, about issues such as the adequacy of the tests for the tasks for which they are often used in practice, the meaning of scores obtained from them, and their relation to the larger social and political contexts within which their use takes place. (See Glaser & Bond, 1981, for articles reviewing varied perspectives on these issues.)

We should point out at the outset that theorists have not yet come up with a definition of intelligence upon which they can all agree. Certainly they concur with the general position that intelligence involves mental competence in some way, but beyond that different definitions have emphasized a variety of attributes such as comprehension, invention, direction, and censorship; the ability to plan, to solve new problems, or to benefit from experience; and the ease with which new behaviors are learned.

The difficulty in defining intelligence (and many other psychological attributes as well) is that it cannot be seen or measured directly. Intelligence is a psychological *construct*—an abstract conceptualization based on, or inferred from, what people do. Most of us, when we judge someone as being intelligent or unintelligent, have in mind specific things that we have seen the person do, such as come up with interesting ideas, figure out how something works, cope with new situations, and so forth. From such observations we then judge or infer that the individual is smart or stupid—but we have not seen smartness or stupidity *per se,* just what the person has done.

Mental ability tests simply provide us with a more systematic and standardized basis for making such an inference or judgment. What we actually observe is the number of questions of different types which an individual answers correctly out of a standard set. Since we measure performance on the tests rather than intelligence, some researchers suggest that intelligence should be defined as what the tests measure. Though this definition may sound nonsensical, it is useful because it reminds us that we observe *test scores* rather than intelligence, and that our generalizations about intelligence are limited by the nature of the tests.

Though there is no generally accepted definition of intelligence, this does not mean that tests of mental abilities are an unrelated hodge-podge of items. Different parts of any given test are correlated with one another, and scores from different tests correlate highly too (see discussion of reliability and validity, below). Such correlations suggest that some common processes underly performance on the tests. Further, test scores show properties that fit with theoretical notions of what intelligence should be like. For these reasons, among others, it makes sense to accept the construct of intelligence as a useful one even though we may not be able to specify exactly what we think it is (Scarr-Salapatek, 1975).

Still, it is clearly important to pay close attention to the tests themselves. We will begin by doing so, moving on to discussion of the correlates of children's test performance, and finally coming back to some of the points of controversy about use of the tests in educational practice.

TESTS AND IQ SCORES

The tests

Most IQ tests consist of items chosen to require different types of intellectual skills—reasoning, comprehension, memory, numerical skills, and so forth. The items vary from easy to difficult. On the Stanford-Binet—several times revised since its introduction in 1916, but still one of the best tests available—items of different types are grouped together by age levels, all items at a given level being of about equal difficulty. Box 3–2 shows descriptions of the items that you would find at the 7-year and 12-year levels on this test. On the Wechsler Intelligence Scale for Children—another of the best tests for school-aged children—items are organized into subtests containing items of a given type arranged from easiest to most difficult. Some of the subtests require verbal skills such as information, vocabulary, numerical reasoning. Other subtests require performance skills such as arranging pictures to tell a story, copying block designs, and assembling puzzle-like pieces to form an object. On this test children are scored for verbal IQ, performance IQ, and full-scale (or overall) IQ.

Other tests are arranged in yet other ways, and—unlike the above two, both of which are individually administered—may be administered to groups of children in their classrooms or other settings. For example, Thurstone's tests of

---

BOX 3–2
Descriptions of test items at the 7- and 12-year levels of the Stanford-Binet, Form L-M

Year 7

1. *Picture absurdities.* The child is asked to pick out what is "funny or foolish" in each of a set of pictures containing a nonsensical element.

2. *Similarities.* The child is asked to tell in what way several pairs of objects are alike.

3. *Copying a diamond.* The child is shown a picture of a diamond shape and asked to copy it.

4. *Comprehension.* The child is asked questions requiring an understanding of structures or events, such as why sailboats move.

5. *Opposite analogies.* The child is asked to complete statements of the form "Coal is black; snow is _____."

6. *Repeating five digits.* The child must repeat five digits in the order in which they are spoken by the examiner.

Alternate: Repeating three digits reversed. The child must repeat three digits in the opposite order from that in which they are spoken.

Year 12

1. *Vocabulary.* The child must define words of increasing difficulty.

2. *Verbal absurdities 2.* The child is asked to state what is foolish about sentences containing contradictory or illogical information.

3. *Picture absurdities 2.* As at year 7, the child is asked to pick out the nonsensical element in each of a set of pictures, but identifying the element is more difficult.

4. *Repeat five digits reversed.* The child must repeat five digits in the opposite order from that in which they are spoken.

5. *Abstract words.* The child is asked to define such words as *pity, curiosity,* and *grief.*

6. *Minkus completion.* The child is shown printed sentences lacking connectives (*and, but, because*) and asked to complete them.

Alternate: Memory for designs. The child is shown a design for 10 seconds, then asked to draw it from memory.

Primary Mental Abilities provide separate scores for each of several different mental abilities—verbal, spatial, numerical, reasoning, and so forth. The Peabody Picture Vocabulary test and the Ammons Quick Test, both based entirely on vocabulary items to which the child responds by pointing to the item's referent in a picture, can be very useful in working with children who have language problems or physical handicaps.

IQ scores   IQ scores indicate whether children's test scores are high or low compared to the scores of other children of the same chronological age. IQ was originally defined as mental age divided by chronological age multiplied by 100: IQ = MA/CA × 100. Mental age was gotten by comparing the number of items answered correctly with age norms showing the number of items answered correctly on the average by children of different ages. If mental age is the same as chronological age, the child's IQ score will be 100, which is the average score at any age because of the way the score is defined; and IQ will be above or below average depending on whether mental age is higher (above average) or lower (below average) than chronological age.

Adequacy of the tests

The adequacy of a test (or, for that matter, of any experiment or measurement) depends on its reliability and validity. *Reliability* refers to the consistency of the test: Can it be counted on to give about the same information when given to the same individual at different times (test-retest reliability), or when scores from odd-numbered questions are compared with scores from even-numbered questions (odd-even reliability), or when the same individual is given two forms of the same test (alternate form reliability)? If individuals' pairs of scores are highly correlated when compared in these ways, the test is reliable. Tests of mental abilities are usually very reliable. Many of them are among the best available tests by this criterion.

Validity refers to whether a test measures what it claims to measure. A test must be reliable before its validity can be judged, but it may be highly reliable and still not be valid. To find out the time, you look at a clock, not a thermometer. The thermometer gives reliable information, but it is invalid for judging time of day.

To judge the validity of a test, one must compare performance on the test with some other, independent criterion of what the test claims to measure. For intelligence tests, the independent criterion could be any other behavior which is assumed to reflect intelligence. The most frequently used criteria are school grades and other, different intelligence tests. If one takes performance on some other test of mental abilities as a criterion, then most of the tests of mental abilities have good validity. Children who get high scores on a group test of intelligence administered in the classroom will usually get high scores on the Stanford-Binet as well.

Intelligence test scores also predict school grades in academic subjects quite well—that is, after all, what the tests were designed to do. The highest correlations are between IQ scores and grades in such subjects as reading compre-

hension and history. For such subjects as geometry, the correlations are somewhat lower. However, there is little relationship between intelligence test scores
and grades in such subjects as music, art, and shop. Of course, even the high
correlations are not perfect, and there is room for fluctuation. Otherwise, no
children could be classified as overachievers or underachievers, since the
school grades of overachievers and underachievers are by definition higher or
lower than would be expected from their intelligence test scores.

Children's performance on IQ tests

Stability of IQ scores It used to be thought—and some still mistakenly
think—that a person's IQ is like eye color, a characteristic which remains stable
over the course of the person's life. This is not true. IQs do remain fairly stable
for most people, at least from the school years on, but they can also change
dramatically. In one study of a large group of children from the time they were
6 until they were 18, more than half of the children's scores changed by 15
points or more, and some scores changed as much as 50 points (Honzik, Macfarlane & Allen, 1948).

Some typical patterns of stability are illustrated in Figure 3–1, which shows
the relative intelligence scores of five girls who were tested repeatedly as they
grew up. There is no consistent relationship between their scores in the first years
of life and their scores at later ages. But beginning at about school age, test

FIGURE 3–1 Relative intelligence test scores of five girls between birth and age 36. The
girls were chosen to represent high, low, and average performance. Boys' records show
similar patterns.

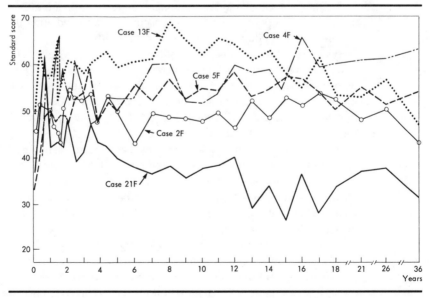

Source: N. Bayley, "Development of Mental Abilities," in *Carmichael's Manual of Child Psychology*, ed.
P. Mussen (New York: John Wiley & Sons, 1970), pp. 1163–1209.

performance stabilized for most of them, fluctuating relatively little on subsequent tests. The same pattern is true for boys. By the time children are five or six years of age, their test scores indicate, at least in a general way, whether the children are likely to be average, high, or low scorers at later ages.

However, IQ fluctuation is also illustrated in Figure 3–1. Look at Case 13F. She had very high test scores at age 8, but her scores declined progressively until they were only average when she was 36. Why IQ scores remain relatively stable for some children but fluctuate for others is not clear. Emotional upsets or crises at home may be accompanied by marked drops in IQ for some children, but other children's test performance appears to be unaffected by similar events (Bayley, 1970).

The patterns illustrated in Figure 3–1 are based upon individually administered tests, which are among the best of the tests. Had the scores been based on group-administered tests—the sort usually given to children in schools—the picture would very likely have been of much greater fluctuation and less stability over time. When Hopkins and Bracht (1975) examined score stability over a 10-year period from 1st to 11th grade with the Stanford-Binet and with group-administered tests, the score stability of the Stanford-Binet was clearly highest. On the group administered tests, performance IQ scores were less stable than verbal IQ scores; and there was less stability in early than in later years of school—children's scores changed more on the average between grades two and four than, say, between grades seven and nine.

When it is observed, stability of test performance may reflect stability and continuity of environmental stimulation for intellectual performance as much as anything else. When young orphans whose IQ scores were so low that they were unadoptable were transferred from an unstimulating orphanage to an institution where they got a great deal of stimulation and attention, their IQ scores rose an average of 27.5 points. They were subsequently adopted and raised like other children, and as adults, they were not distinguishable from the general population in schooling, income, or emotional adjustment. A group of children who remained in the unstimulating orphanage showed an average IQ decline of 26.2 points; as adults they were far below the general population in schooling, income earned, and emotional adjustment (Skeels, 1966). In this study, a change in environment *sustained through the children's growing up* had marked consequences for intellectual development.

If stability of environmental influences is an important source of IQ stability, then the fact that IQ does not fluctuate much for many children suggests that environmental influences must remain fairly consistent for them. This appears to be the case. Hanson (1975) looked at a number of aspects of home environment assumed to be related to IQ for a group of children when they were infants (0–3), young children (4–6), and of school age (7–10). The home variables were consistent within each time period, meaning that they were highly correlated with one another; and they were stable across all three periods of childhood.

However, test scores can, and do, change for many children, especially test scores from group tests which most children take. This suggests that any attitude or practice which is based on the assumption that an IQ score says something permanent about a child is erroneous and may be unnecessarily limiting to the child. Parents who find out children's test scores may be as guilty as anyone else of forming expectations for them and treating them accordingly. Whether they think of a child as not very bright and expect little, or as very bright and expect a great deal, their expectations will influence the child. When the expectations are inappropriate, they may be a source of considerable stress for the child. (This is one reason why many schools are reluctant to release IQ information to parents.) The fact is that changes in intellectual performance pose difficulties for *any* classification of children based on such performance, including grouping school children by ability. Most educators are aware of this problem and make considerable effort to keep such assignment of children flexible, though it is often difficult to achieve complete flexibility in practice.

Correlates of IQ scores

IQ scores are correlated with a variety of environmental factors, any or all of which may influence—though not wholly determine—a child's test performance. One of these is *nutrition*. Severe protein deficiency can produce diseases accompanied by mental retardation; while lesser protein deficiencies and other dietary inadequacies may have less obvious overt signs but may still retard physical and mental development (Bengoa, 1970). At the very least, diet may affect the test performance of school-aged children through its impact on alertness, attentiveness, and health.

Family interactions also influence children's performance. Generally, children of warm and supportive parents are likely to perform relatively well and the children of hostile and rejecting parents are likely to perform relatively poorly. Whether parents hold punitive attitudes toward children, or use punitive disciplinary practices, depends to some extent on the parents' own education, intelligence, and social class. But Hurley (1967) found that even when such factors were controlled by studying social class groups separately, *parental "malevolence"*—by which he meant a combination of hostile and rejecting attitudes and punitive disciplinary practices—was still consistently associated with poor test performance in children.

There are, however, sex differences in how this general effect operates. Boys are likely to have higher scores if their relationships with their mothers are warm and accepting, and if their fathers are both occupationally successful themselves and at the same time close to and involved in their sons' lives—something unlikely to be the case if father is absent, or at home six or fewer hours per week (e.g., Honzik, 1967; Ferguson, 1970; Blanchard & Biller, 1971). Girls who have higher scores on the average are likely to have fathers who are accepting and supportive of their intellectual achievements. At the same time, their mothers are likely to be *less* nurturant than the mothers of other girls (e.g., Bayley & Schaefer, 1964; Crandall, Dewey, Katkovsky, & Preston, 1964; Moss & Kagan, 1958; Honzik, 1967). In addition, parental restrictiveness, criticism, and punitiveness, while associated with poor performance for both boys and girls, appears to have greater effects for girls than for boys (Hurley, 1967; Kagan & Freeman, 1963).

It is tempting to conclude that the differences among parents cause the differences in their children, but one must be careful about such conclusions. A child who is hard to handle, for example, may also have difficulties in school and test situations, and may require stricter behavior from parents. Attributes of both the children and the parents contribute to the effects discussed above.

Families also differ in the extent to which the *home environment* provides experiences which foster performance on IQ tests. In Hanson's (1975) study, cited earlier, 10 home environment variables were related to children's IQ scores. Although the patterns differed somewhat by age and sex, five or more of these variables were significantly correlated with IQ scores for both boys and girls at 5½ and 9½ years of age. Recall that Hanson also found that homes high on one of these variables were usually high on the others, and that they remained stable over the three age period studied. According to research reported by Marjoribanks in 1979, school environment is also correlated with test scores, although again the patterns of relationship differ somewhat for boys and girls.

Test scores are also affected by how many brothers and sisters a child has, how close in age they are, and where in the sibling hierarchy the child fits (e.g., eldest, second child, etc.). The smaller the family, the closer to first-born the child, and the greater the age-gap between siblings (especially for boys), the higher the average scores (e.g., Cicirelli, 1978). Results from one large study are shown in Figure 3–2. (Note that the differences, while systematic, are not large.) Zajonc and Markus (1975) suggest that the differences observed reflect, first, the amount of available adult intellectual stimulation, which is progressively diluted as more children are added to the family (parents can provide more stimulation apiece to two children than to five children). Second, older siblings have an advantage through their experience teaching younger children, which may be why first-borns in two-child families score higher on the average than only children. Other factors may operate as well, but it is clear that family size and spacing affect the home environment in which intellectual skills are expressed.

Personality characteristics are also associated with IQ score variations. *Anxiety* has little relationship to intellectual performance when children first start school, but in time children with high anxiety do less well on IQ tests—in fact, their IQ scores may even decline (Sontag, Baker, & Nelson, 1958). The debilitating effects of anxiety are clearest when tasks are complex. When tasks are simple and straightforward, children with high anxiety scores may actually do better then children with low anxiety scores. Since anxiety scores in earlier grades predict lower achievement in later grades, anxiety evidently does interfere with intellectual performance, rather than resulting from poor performance (Hill & Sarason, 1966). Ferguson (1970) suggests that poor intellectual performance associated with maternal hostility and punitiveness, discussed above, may be due in part to the fact that "rejecting and coercive maternal attitudes contribute to a chronic state of anxiety" (p. 133).

Children who are dependent and passive are likely to score lower on intellectual tests, especially if they are girls (e.g., Kagan & Moss, 1962). On the other hand, independence (together with competitiveness and motivation for intellectual mastery) characterized children who showed IQ gains between age 6

FIGURE 3–2 The smaller the family and the closer to first-born, the higher the average score on a test of intellectual ability.

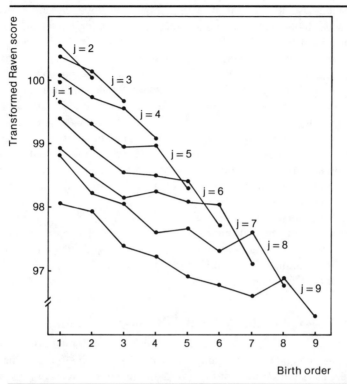

Source: R. B. Zajonc and G. B. Markus, "Birth Order and Intellectual Development," *Psychological Review* 82 (1975), pp. 74–88. p. 75.

and age 10 (Sontag et al., 1958). About twice as many boys as girls showed such IQ increases. Girls were more likely than boys to show IQ decreases over these years.

Achievement motivation refers to the desire to excel. Children with high achievement motivation typically have parents who have expected and encouraged their children to be independent and self-reliant from early in life, and have supported and encouraged their children's achievement strivings. Achievement motivation is often, but not always, associated with high intellectual performance, and one important determinant of whether it is so associated appears to be the area at which the individual wants to excel. Where intellectual mastery and academic achievement are important to the child, intellectual performance is likely to be good. Otherwise, there is no particular reason to expect achievement motivation to be related to intellectual performance. This may be one reason for the differences in academic achievement and intellectual performance between children from different social classes; achievement motivation in general, and motivation for academic achievement in particular, are strongest in the middle class.

Interestingly, both boys and girls who score high on tests of mental abilities show *cross-sex typing,* which is to say that the girls have more interests and activities usually thought of as masculine, and boys have more interests and activities thought of as feminine, than do other children (Oetzel, 1961, cited in Maccoby, 1966). For girls, it is tempting to attribute this relationship to the fact that intellectual competence and academic achievement are sex-typed as masculine. The fact that boys also show cross-sex typing, however, suggests either that there is some other, more general reason for the relationship or (as is entirely possible) that the effect arises for different reasons in boys than in girls. These high-scoring boys and girls do not necessarily have fewer interests and activities appropriate for their own sex; rather, they show the cross-sex interests *in addition to* appropriate like-sex interests. What may be happening, then, is that these children simply have wider ranges of interests than do other children, and that this is reflected in both their intellectual performance and their scores on measures of sex-typing.

Finally, there may be interrelationships among these different personality attributes and other attributes, such as self-confidence, self-reliance, persistence, self-control, and attentiveness, which suggests that a general pattern of interpersonal maturity or competence is associated with good intellectual performance (e.g., Ferguson, 1970).

Social class and ethnic group differences

Perhaps the most consistently found differences in intellectual performance occur when children from different social classes are compared. The higher the social class background of the group, the higher the average IQ score. Differences are also usually found when groups of children from different ethnic backgrounds are compared.

The relationship among social class, ethnic group, and patterns of performance on four different types of tests of mental ability (verbal, reasoning, number, and space) were investigated in a pair of particularly interesting studies. In the first of these (Lesser, Fifer, & Clark, 1965), groups of six- and seven-year-olds from New York City were tested. There were equal numbers of children from middle-class and lower-class homes; equal numbers of children from black, Jewish, Puerto Rican, and Chinese homes; and within each ethnic-social class subgroup, equal numbers of boys and girls. The authors were careful to choose test materials which would be familiar to children in all the groups; they also took care to ensure that each child was examined by a member of his or her own ethnic group who could speak to the child in the language of the child's home if need be (the three Chinese-speaking examiners, for instance, spoke a total of eight Chinese dialects, each of which was spoken by some of the Chinese children).

When the average scores of the children from each of the four subgroups were compared, there proved to be a characteristic pattern or profile of scores for each ethnic group. Subsequently, groups of black, Chinese, and Irish children in Boston were tested in the same way (Stodolsky & Lesser, 1967). No characteristic

FIGURE 3-3 Scores comparing lower- and middle-class black and Chinese children from Boston and New York on four tests of mental abilities.

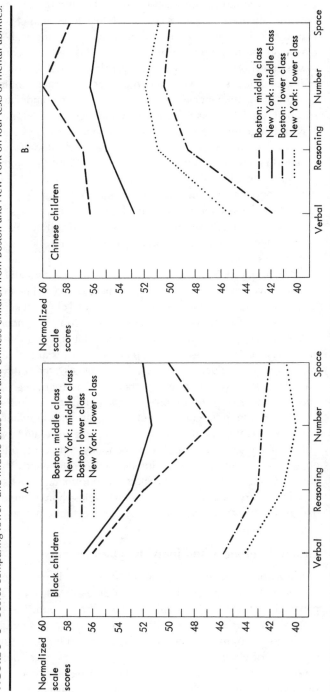

Source: S. S. Stodolsky and G. Lesser, "Learning Patterns in the Disadvantaged," *Harvard Educational Review* 37 (1967), pp. 546–93. Copyright © 1967 by President and Fellows of Harvard College.

profile was found for the Irish children. For the black and Chinese children, however, there were profiles very much like those of the New York City groups. Figure 3–3 shows the profiles for the black and Chinese children of both social classes in the two cities. In all instances, the average scores of children from lower-class homes are lower; but regardless of social class, the general pattern of high and low scores stays much the same for each ethnic group.

Why these differences among ethnic groups and among members of different social classes? There is the possibility that genetic differences operate in some way, although for reasons discussed later in this chapter such differences cannot be meaningfully assessed. On the other hand, Stodolsky and Lesser (1967) suggest that the observed patterns of mental abilities within ethnic groups are culturally determined. Families belonging to a relatively close-knit, coherent ethnic group may share not only ethnic traditions, but also attitudes toward child rearing, patterns of interaction with children, shared values, and other attributes which result in emphasis on particular skills and abilities. As a consequence, the development of some types of intellectual skills may be fostered over the development of others.

What about social class differences? Social class is a global concept, a label that is convenient for referring to a number of interrelated facts about individuals. By definition, children from different social class backgrounds have parents who differ in amount of education, level of occupation, income, and the type of neighborhood in which they live. But correlated with these defining attributes are others, such as types of child-rearing practices and attitudes; attitudes and values regarding education and academic success; the ability and willingness to provide children with toys, games, books, and experiences; and the knowledge and resources necessary for providing adequate nutrition. The life experiences of children from different social class backgrounds are likely to be different in many important ways. It is differences in these correlated experiences, and not differences in social class per se, which may contribute to the observed differences between the classes in intellectual performance. Think back over the environmental influences on intellectual performance that have been discussed. In almost every case, children from lower-class homes are more likely to have had experiences associated with poor intellectual functioning.

Group differences and individual performance

Throughout this chapter, comparisons have been made between average scores of children grouped together in different ways: by family variables, by personality attributes, by social class and ethnic group. These group differences are real. They are a source of information about kinds of influences which affect children's performance, and they may be useful for such purposes as planning programs for groups of children. But the *group averages do not tell us what to expect of individual children.* Even when the average scores of two groups differ significantly, some children in both groups will have high scores, some low; and many children in both groups will have similar scores. It is a serious error to think, for example, that because the average scores of children from lower-class homes are lower than the average scores of children from middle-class homes,

TABLE 3–1

Comparisons of patterns of mental ability scores of children from different ethnic-social class groups with the typical patterns for each group

Child's own group (40 children per group)	Pattern typical of group							
	M Ch	L Ch	M J	L J	M B	L B	M PR	L PR
Middle-class Chinese.......................	13	10	6	1	5	1	2	2
Lower-class Chinese	6	14	2	4	3	1	1	9
Middle-class Jewish.......................	4	0	32	4	0	0	0	0
Lower-class Jewish........................	0	1	9	18	7	4	0	1
Middle-class black........................	5	1	11	10	11	0	0	2
Lower-class black.........................	1	3	0	3	0	28	0	5
Middle-class Puerto Rican	6	6	3	6	4	0	3	12
Lower-class Puerto Rican	0	7	1	1	0	8	3	20

Read across the table. For instance, 13 of the 40 middle-class Chinese children had scores which matched the typical profile for middle-class Chinese children; 10 had scores more like the profile of lower-class Chinese children; 6 had scores more like the profile of middle-class Jewish children; and so on.

Source: S. S. Stodolsky and G. Lesser, "Learning Patterns in the Disadvantaged," *Harvard Educational Review* 37 (1967), pp. 546–93. Copyright © 1967 by President and Fellows of Harvard College.

all children from lower-class homes have lower scores than do children from middle-class homes. This type of error can have particularly negative effects when evaluative labels, such as "inferior" and "superior," are applied to group performance, and then generalized to individual children who happen to be members of the groups.

Some information from the study of patterns of mental abilities in different ethnic groups is instructive on this point. Remember that typical patterns of mental abilities were found for *groups* of black, Chinese, Jewish, and Puerto Rican children, with the patterns of scores—but not the level (high or low)—the same in different social classes. Table 3–1 shows the number of individual children within each group who actually showed the "typical" pattern of their ethnic group and social class (the italicized numbers) and the numbers of individual children whose patterns were actually more like those of some other group. In only three of the eight groups (middle-class Jewish, lower-class black, and lower-class Puerto Rican) did half or more of the individual children show the pattern "typical" of their own ethnic group and social class! In two instances (middle-class black and middle-class Puerto Rican) the profiles of over half of the children were actually more like those of children from other ethnic groups than like profiles "typical" of their own group in either social class. The typical patterns are the best descriptions *for the groups,* but if they were taken as the best descriptions for the individuals within the groups, they would be misleading more than half the time.

ISSUES AND CONTROVERSIES

Heredity and IQ scores

Contemporary theorists generally agree that intelligence depends upon both heredity and environment, in interaction with each other (as, in general, the psychobiological orientation requires recognizing the interaction of genetic and experiential influences). This means that each is continually modifying the effects of the other. Two hypothetical children having the same heredity but raised in different environments until they started school would enter school with differently developed intelligences (the same *genotype,* or hereditary background, may give rise to many different *phenotypes,* or observable expressions of the genotype). Even if these two children with identical genotypes now had identical experiences in school, the school experience would affect them differently because of the modifying influence of their earlier environments. Of course, the continuing interaction of heredity and environment is much more complex than this very simple illustration, and one of the major tasks facing psychologists is to begin to untangle the question of how these interactions proceed (Anastasi, 1958; Scarr-Salapatek, 1975).

In preceding sections, we have discussed many of the environmental influences found to be related to IQ test performance. The evidence for hereditary influences is equally strong. Studies of pairs of individuals whose genetic relationship to one another varies is one source of such evidence. From a large number of studies the correlation between scores of siblings is about .49, regardless of the sex of the siblings or their relative ages (Paul, 1980). The correlation between scores of monozygotic (identical) twins is substantially higher, with correlations in the .70s. In fact, there are sometimes striking resemblances between identical twins in personality and social attributes as well as IQ test scores even when they have been reared apart from early in life (e.g., Holden, 1980). In contrast, the scores of unrelated individuals cluster around zero.

Hereditary influences are also evident in studies of adopted children, their biological parents, their foster parents, and the biological children of the foster parents (e.g., Horn, Loehlin, & Willerman, 1979; Scarr & Weinberg, 1977). In these and other studies, the correlations between the IQ scores of children and their biological parents are substantially higher than are the correlations between the scores of adopted children and the foster parents who are raising them even when the children were given up by their biological parents at birth.

Although there is general agreement that heredity and environment interact to influence intelligence, there has been considerable controversy over estimates of heritability and their interpretation (for example, Jensen, 1969; Kamin, 1974). *Heritability* is the proportion of the total variation in an attribute which is due to heredity, for some particular group of population in a given setting. Estimates of heritability for IQ scores in white, Western populations are high—at least 50 to 75 percent (Scarr-Salapatek, 1975) and maybe even 80 percent or more of the variation in IQ scores may reflect genetic differences (Jensen, 1969). Jensen, arguing from his high heritability estimates, suggested that the role of environmental influences was probably minimal, and that therefore attempts to boost scholastic achievement through special programs, such as Head Start, were misguided and ineffective. The educational and social implications of such a position are considerable, especially if one generalizes across racial groups— and in light of the fact that when IQ scores of white and black children are compared, the average scores of white children are always higher than the average scores of black children, even when the children are from comparable social class backgrounds. Many have been tempted to conclude that since heritability is high, this racial difference must therefore reflect genetic differences between black and white groups.

However, heritability estimates apply only to the groups or populations on which they are based, in the settings in which the attribute was measured. Very little is known about the heritability of IQ scores in nonwhite, non-Western groups, though there is some evidence that the heritability of IQ scores is lower among blacks in the United States than among whites (Furby, 1973). Furthermore, regardless of whether heritabilities are high or low for these two groups, there is no way yet to tell whether an observed difference between two groups reflects heredity, environment, or both (Furby, 1973). As Scarr-Salapatek (1975) points out, unless one is willing to assume that members of two groups not only encounter the same environmental variables in the same way, but are developmentally influenced by them in the same way, there is no justifiable basis for making comparisons between racial groups.

Many of the concerns of the 1970s relate to the validity of the tests. We said above that validity is excellent when predicting scores on other tests or school grades, but what if one uses some other criterion, such as success in later life? One assumption which underlies much vocational counseling is that school grades (which are predicted by test scores) in turn predict adult occupational success. Yet McClelland (1973) points out that there is little support for that assumption. The relatively few studies that have looked for relationships between grades in school and later success find no evidence of any relationship, at least for individuals at a common level of education. And of the studies which have looked for relationships between job success and scores on the tests of mental abilities themselves, some large studies have found no evidence of any consistent relationship. Where some relationship is found, it tends to exist for high-status jobs, but not for low-status jobs, a pattern which McClelland (1973) points out could as easily mean that both job status and test scores reflect social class as it could mean that persons with higher scores are more intellectually competent.

Testing, bias, and social context

Criticisms of standardized intelligence testing are nothing new; they have recurred, in varying forms, over decades that tests have been in use. One can even view them as one index of the very considerable success of the testing movement—were the tests not successful, there would be no basis for concern (Haney, 1981).

What do the tests "really" measure?   Despite the above criticisms, the tests could still be of interest for what they might contribute to our understanding of mental abilities and developmental changes in such abilities. Yet here again, critics point out that the tests as used at present not only often fail to give us such information, but that they may even interfere with our understanding of mental abilities.

Most of these criticisms stem from the fact that children's scores on tests of mental abilities are gotten by adding up the number of correct answers they give, without any regard for how the children arrived at their answers. The tests count only the *products* of intelligence without considering the *processes* through which intelligence operates. One pitfall of this approach is illustrated by Sigel (1963). Before reading further, answer this item (from Guilford, 1959) by picking the one of the following four words which does not belong with the others: Clam Tree Oven Rose. This term is intended to tap classification skills: Does a person understand what kinds of objects can be grouped together and what kinds cannot? Of the four words given, most people pick *oven* because it is the only object listed which is not alive. Yet any one of the four items could be justified as a correct answer, depending on the basis one uses for classification. If one divided the items according to which were found on land and which in water, *clam* would be correct. This answer requires classification skills as much as the other does, yet would be scored incorrect. What usually happens is that the conventional answer—the answer most people are likely to give—is keyed as correct. Consequently, individuals who do not share the conventional wisdom of the majority—either because they have original ways of thinking or because they have grown up with a different conventional wisdom—are penalized. Here is one mechanism through which social class bias may be built into the tests.

Another criticism is that we really know very little either about the particular skills needed to solve the problems included in the tests or about the ways in which children apply those skills (see, for instance, Sigel, 1963; Farnham-Diggory, 1970; Bayley, 1970; Ginsburg, 1972). For example, a problem in verbal reasoning does not call upon some single skill; rather, it is likely to require the use and coordination of a complex aggregate of skills which might include recognition, memory, classification, and word comprehension. But little attention has been paid to such component skills and the ways in which they may be important for answering different types of test questions. Finally, a child's reasoning about a problem can reflect a good understanding of the problem and its requirements even when the final answer is incorrect. (Ginsberg [1972] describes some interesting instances of this in his chapter on "Intellect and the Schools.") We act as though right answers mean the child understands and wrong answers mean the child does not understand, but that is not necessarily true. The child giving the wrong answer *may* understand nearly as much as the child giving the right answer, but a test score will not tell us that.

One major set of concerns has to do with whether the tests are *culture fair* or not—whether IQ scores are equally valid for different cultural groups. There is evidence that they are not. Any test incorporates information, ideas, and attitudes likely to be most characteristic of the cultural group for which it was developed. When researchers working cross-culturally became aware of this problem, they attempted at first to develop tests which were *culture free*. But since intelligence always develops in a cultural environment, this proved to be impossible; so they tried instead to develop tests which were *culturally fair*—tests which do not penalize members of some cultural groups compared to others. Such attempts have not been very successful yet (Arvey, 1972). And when one compares performance on Stanford-Binet items for different national groups and at different points in time, there are substantial differences. Scores are always lower for groups other than the one for which the test was originally developed, and interestingly, scores on a given version of the test decline over time within cultural groups—which makes sense, since times change and cultures evolve. These differences appear to be inherent in the test itself, rather than a reflection of changes in intelligence (Smith, 1974).

Since IQ tests in the United States have usually been standardized on white middle-class groups, there are real questions as to their validity or usefulness for members of minority groups. Concerns over their validity, among other things, have led to challenges not only within the educational system but through the courts, with varying results; in the 1978 California case of *Larry P.* v. *Riles,* IQ tests were ruled to be racially biased and their use discriminatory, whereas in the 1980 Illinois case of *Pase* v. *Hannon* the court ruled that the tests are not culturally biased and so may be used to help determine which children should be given special education placement (for summaries of the two cases, see Armstrong, 1980; Exhibit A: IQ Trial, 1977; Exhibit B: IQ Trial, 1978).

Tests are too widely accepted and used to be dropped entirely in the immediately foreseeable future, although there are some advocates of this course. Rather, various courses of action have been recommended to minimize the difficulties encountered with tests as presently employed. First, misuses of the tests by examiners should not be confused with difficulties intrinsic to the tests themselves. There are documented cases, for example, of obvious abuses, such as children being placed in "slow" tracks in school on the basis of test scores when no one checked closely enough to discover that they were Spanish-speaking children who were examined in English. Abuses of this type can be minimized only by ensuring that those in positions to make placement decisions about children understand clearly the limits of the information provided by test scores. More subtly, children's academic performance and competence depends not only on "intellectual potential" (whatever that may be) but also upon motivational factors and adjustment (see correlates of IQ scores, above). It is probably true that decisions regarding children should never be made on the basis of information about intellectual performance alone, but should always incorporate motivational and other information about the child as well (e.g., Scarr, 1981). From a somewhat different perspective, one can argue that where a test has been shown to predict some criterion, use of the test for purposes relating to that criterion is legitimate since cultural differences affecting test performance are likely also to affect criterion performance (e.g., Anastasi, 1968). On the other hand, for some (perhaps all) purposes, it may be necessary to develop different tests, or at least different performance norms on given tests, for all different cultural groups with whom the test is to be used (e.g., Garcia, 1981).

INTELLIGENCE AS PROCESS AND INTELLIGENCE AS PRODUCT

We are now in a position to compare the *"process"* orientation of Piaget with the *"product"* orientation of researchers working with tests of mental abilities. There are both similarities and differences between the two orientations, as

Elkind (1969) points out. However, the fact that differences exist does not necessarily mean that one position is "right" and the other "wrong." The differences between the two orientations are such that they may very well complement rather than contradict each other.

Some of the major comparisons between the two orientations are summarized in Table 3–2. One theme which runs through several of these comparisons, beginning with the conceptualizations of intelligence, is the "product" orientation's emphasis on individual differences in intelligence compared to the "process" orientation's emphasis on commonalities in intelligence across individuals. Both orientations consider heredity a major determinant of intelligence, but they emphasize very different outcomes of heredity. The "process" orientation views human intelligence as a basic human attribute, comparable to having arms and legs instead of wings or fins, hair and skin instead of feathers or fur. But the "product" orientation, with its stress on individual differences in intelligence, is concerned with questions analogous to asking, not why individuals have arms and skin rather than wings and feathers, but why, given that individuals have arms and skin, one individual's arms are longer than the other's, or one individual's skin is black and the other's white. These are very different kinds of questions, though genetic determinants are important for both.

Likewise, both orientations consider experience important for intellectual development. But for Piaget, experience is important because without something to act on, intellectual structures do not develop; adaptation requires the intellectual stimulation derived from experience. Just as children draw the nourishment necessary for physical growth from the food they eat, so they draw the "aliment" or nourishment necessary for intellectual growth from experience. In comparison, the product theorists are more concerned with whether, given the common fact of growth in different settings, different environments might be associated with different rates or patterns of intellectual growth.

A second theme which relates to the characterization of the two orientations as "product" or "process" has to do with the interrelated issues of the type of performance assumed to reflect intelligence, how intelligence is measured and studied, and how it changes with development. The "product" orientation evolved with the development of standardized tests whose scores depend on numbers of correct answers—the products or outcomes of intellectual activity. This orientation has seen intellectual growth mostly as a matter of quantitative increases in the number of questions children can answer correctly, with little regard for whether there might also be qualitative changes in the children's performance (though the factor analytic studies mentioned in the preceding chapter are an exception to this statement). But the "process" orientation is concerned with children's reasoning, the processes by which they reach their answers. In this context, one could go so far as to argue that all children *always* give right answers, *given the way they think;* the question of interest is how children get from the information given them to the answer that is right to them. The processes which children use depend on the children's intellectual structures, and these structures develop both quantitatively and qualitatively—not

TABLE 3–2
"Product" and "process" orientations compared

Issue	"Product" orientation	"Process" orientation
Conception of intelligence	Attribute which differs from individual to individual	Universal attribute common to all human beings
Role of heredity	Major determinant	Major determinant
Consequence of heredity	Individual differences	Intelligence itself as universal human attribute
Role of experience	Major determinant	Major determinant
Consequence of experience	Individual differences fostered	Exercise of intellectual structures promoting intellectual growth
Changes with development	Amount known (number of right answers) increases	Mode of knowing (intellectual structures) changes qualitatively
Aims of research	Assessing and explaining individual differences	Describing and explaining changes in intellectual structures
Performance of interest	Correct answers (products)	Means of arriving at answers, right or wrong (processes)
Preferred means of measurement	Standardized tests of mental abilities	Flexible interview using standard materials

only can older children use given structures in more contexts than can younger children, but some intellectual structures available to older children are unavailable to younger children. Answers to questions by themselves cannot show the reasoning on which they are based, so Piaget developed the "clinical method" in which carefully trained researchers interview children about standard materials, using a flexible approach which permits each interview to be adapted to the notions expressed by each child. Many American psychologists have criticized the clinical method because it differs from child to child. However, as many of the phenomena described by Piaget have withstood experimental replication, these criticisms have abated somewhat.

For the most part, then, the differences between the two orientations do not represent disagreement over interpretations of fact. Rather, the orientations ask different kinds of questions and are concerned with different kinds of facts. Each orientation would undoubtedly be strengthened and enriched by incorporating some parts of the other. For instance, information from standardized tests might be richer if more attention were paid to children's reasoning as well as to their answers; and on the other hand, rigorous experimentational study of Piaget's ideas can clarify and strengthen understanding of the processes which he had the genius to identify. As for the issue of univerality versus individual differences, product theorists stressing differences may present a misleading picture by overlooking intellectual strengths shared by many individuals. But on the other hand, individuals do differ, regardless of common heritage or common strengths. Piaget himself acknowledges that individual differences are important, but prefers to focus his attention on the more universal attributes of development. As Bruner (1973) comments, both universalistic and individualistic types of theories have always been around, and both types are probably necessary. A really complete understanding of intellectual development will probably incorporate both points of view.

SUMMARY

Although there is still disagreement about what intelligence is, there are many different types of IQ tests which give comparable information about children's performance and which predict school grades reasonably well. Although children's IQ scores begin to stabilize at about the time they enter school, there is enough fluctuation to pose real problems for procedures that classify children by IQ scores, such as ability grouping.

Children's scores on IQ tests are correlated with a number of factors, including nutrition, family interaction patterns, home and school environment, sibling status, personality attributes, and social group membership. These are average relationships which hold for groups, but individual members of any group may have scores quite different from the group average.

Heredity influences intellectual functioning in interaction with environmental influence, but the issue of what this implies is still controversial. Heritability for IQ scores is probably high, but knowing this is not sufficient basis for making statements about the origin of differences between groups whose average scores differ. There is also ongoing controversy over the issue of bias in IQ tests with critics arguing that the tests are valid only for members of the social group for which they were standardized. And there are critics who maintain that because we look only at answers and not at the reasoning which produced them, test scores at best tell us little and at worst mislead us about children's intellectual competencies.

Comparisons of product and process orientations toward intelligence show both similarities and differences. In many ways the two orientations are more complementary than contradictory. Integration of the two orientations will probably be necessary before intellectual development is fully understood.

TERMS AND CONCEPTS

construct
IQ score
mental age
reliability
test-retest reliability
odd-even reliability
alternate form reliability
validity
parental "malevolence"
achievment motivation

genotype
phenotype
culture-free tests
culture-fair tests
heritability
process orientation toward intelligence
product orientation toward intelligence

SUGGESTED ADDITIONAL READING

Bayley, N. Development of mental abilities. In P. Mussen (Ed.), *Carmichael's manual of child psychology* (3rd ed.) (Vol. 1). New York: John Wiley & Sons, 1970.

Ginsburg, H. *The myth of the deprived child.* Englewood Cliffs, N. J.: Prentice-Hall, 1972.

Glaser, R., & Bond, L., (Eds.), Testing: Concepts, policy, practice, and research. *American Psychologist,* 1981, *36,* 997–1189.

Scarr-Salapatek, S. Genetics and the development of intelligence. In F. D. Harowitz (Ed.), *Review of child development research* (Vol. 4). Chicago: University of Chicago Press, 1975.

BOX 4 – 1
Study questions

What kind of researcher would be called a cognitive behaviorist?

What is the information-processing orientation toward human intelligence?

Distinguish between short-term memory and long-term memory and describe the major features of each.

How does children's use of memory strategies change during the school years?

Distinguish between differentiation and enrichment theories of perceptual learning.

Describe three trends in perceptual learning, with examples of each relevant for reading and learning.

What is phonological segmentation? Discuss reasons, including possible psycho-biological constraints, why many children find it difficult.

Define cerebral lateralization and discuss its implications for learning to read.

What are two major areas (beyond mechanical skills) essential to good reading? Give examples of each.

What are metacognitive experiences? What is metacognitive knowledge?

Describe the change in children's metacognitive skills over the school years and their relationship to performance.

CHAPTER 4

COGNITION APPLIED: READING AND LEARNING

The work on children's learning to be covered in this chapter differs sharply in its approach from the work influenced by Piaget's theory. It grew out of U.S. *behaviorism,* which dominated general psychology—and especially theories of learning—through the first half of this century. Behaviorists insisted that only observable behaviors—things people do which can be seen and counted—could legitimately be studied by psychologists. Such constructs as mind, thinking, or attention cannot be directly observed. Consequently, the behaviorists argued, one cannot study such constructs but must focus instead on what people do—their behavior—in relation to what leads up to it and what results it gets. Contemporary researchers influenced by this tradition, the *cognitive behaviorists,* are willing to make inferences about phenomena such as thinking or attention, but they still insist that the foundation for making such inferences must be variations in some observable phenomenon.

Behaviorism brought with it a number of characteristic orientations, many of which continue to influence cognitive behaviorists today. One of these was a tendency to take the environmentalists' position on heredity—environment issues—and many today still lean in this direction, although they are most likely to take an interactionist position officially. J. B. Watson, a major figure among early behaviorists who did pioneering work on children's learning and later applied his ideas to child development (Watson & Raynor, 1920; Watson, 1928) was an extreme environmentalist who argued that with appropriate conditioning any child could be raised to become any desired type of adult. He assumed that children are born essentially unformed (the blank slate or *tabula rasa* assumption) and that their subsequent development is shaped by the learning experiences which they encounter. (Note the contrast with the psychobiological orientation taken in this text.) A second characteristic orientation is that development is continuous, reflecting the cumulative effects of learning, rather than occurring in stages characterized by qualitatively different attributes—and despite Piaget's influence, researchers in traditions growing out of behaviorism still do not usually think in terms of stages of development.

There was also a tendency to conceptualize learners as passive, responding to environmental stimulation (these theories were called S-R, or Stimulus-Response, theories). In the face of evidence that children and adults are clearly active processors of information—some of which evidence will be described in this chapter—this tendency has diminished; but again, note the sharp contrast to Piaget's view of the active nature of children's intellectual growth, at least up to the 1970s. Other characteristic orientations relate to the research process itself. There must be experimental evidence for statements that one might want to make about behavior, and the quality of that evidence can only be as good as the research on which it is based. Consequently, research methods and experimental studies have been stressed more heavily in the United States than elsewhere.

Studies of children's learning in the S-R theory framework burgeoned during the 1950s and 1960s; good summaries of this work are available in Stevenson (1972). During these same decades, however, human information processing was also emerging as a framework for studying learning and remembering; we will be discussing this framework in more detail in the next section. During the 1970s the information processing framework largely supplanted the earlier S-R conceptualizations; but researchers in the field are still intellectual offspring of the earlier behaviorists, and the general behaviorist orientations just discussed remain characteristic of them.

The volume of work regarding children's learning is far too large to summarize readily in a single chapter. Learning to read is one of the major accomplishments of children in elementary school, so we have opted to focus our discussion by choosing topics relevant to reading. These topics will make up most of the rest of the chapter. First, though, let us look a little more closely at the information processing framework.

INFORMATION PROCESSING

Information processing refers more to an orientation toward human intellectual activity than to any specific theory (though there are specific theories within this tradition; e.g., Newell & Simon, 1972). The conception of humans as information processors originally developed when psychologists became intrigued with computer simulation of human intellectual functioning—that is, attempts to develop programs through which computers might match or simulate human intellectual skills. Computers must be given very specific instruction for what they do; so in order to develop a computer simulation, the entire sequence of events required to solve the problem or perform the skill must be analyzed in careful detail. In doing this one prepares not only a computer program, but also a detailed process analysis which may serve as a model of the human intellectual skill as well.

The information processing perspective does not require assuming that human beings are computers! But it does emphasize that human intellectual activity is a complex of processes with many interlinking components, engaged in by individuals who have particular processing capabilities and limits (one being that they can remember only so much at a time). Box 4–2 describes the range of interacting processes which Herbert Simon, an influential information processing theorist, believes constitutes the minimum for which a developmental theory of information processing must account—a demanding program, as you can see. In keeping with their programming emphasis, information processing theorists are likely to ask how information gets *encoded* (or translated) into some

---

BOX 4 – 2
What must an information processing theory take into account?

Information processing theorists generally agree that human performance depends on a variety of processes. To get some idea of the magnitude of the task of accounting for learning in children from an information processing point of view, consider the range of topics suggested as fundamental by one major information processing theorist—and remember that these processes may operate simultaneously, that they more often than not interact with each other, and furthermore, that they change with development.

1. At the sensory end—the eyes and the ears—the detail of physiological mechanism determines, to a great extent, the ways in which information is processed. The sensory organs and their central connections form a complex interface between man and his environment.

2. As we move through perception to cognition, we find that central processes are less affected by detailed features of the system's construction and seem to be shaped mainly by its broad architectural outlines and a few key parameters.

3. In describing this architecture, particularly as it affects development and learning processes, we need to give special prominence to these features:
   a. The short-term memory, limited in capacity to holding a few chunks [of information];
   b. The mechanisms of attention that determine what small fraction of the sensorily available information will be selected for central processing;
   c. The long-term memory, potentially unlimited in capacity: probably organized in terms of quite general systems of associations and directed associations; slow to store new information;
   d. Hemispheric specialization in long-term memory for storage of information relating to different modalities—visual and auditory, for example;
   e. The control of behavior, including the internal behavior of thinking, by stored, learnable and modifiable, strategies or programs.

Source: H. A. Simon, "On the Development of the Processor," in *Information Processing in Children*, ed. S. Farnham-Diggory (New York: Academic Press, 1972), p. 4.

storable form, what the characteristics of the storage system might be, and how the information is *decoded* and *retrieved* (gotten back out of storage) when it is needed. Furthermore, they are likely to speak about *decision rules, strategies, and programs for responding,* which have to do with when and how information is encoded or retrieved; and more recently, of *schemas, scripts, or plans for behavior,* concepts which deal with the organization or structure of behavioral sequences (e.g., see Brown, 1981).

The information processing orientation has proved to be a fruitful one. Researchers, especially those interested in human memory, have learned quite a bit about many of the features mentioned in Simon's list (Box 4–2). We shall return to some of them later in the chapter. To elaborate on some of the others, however, researchers do agree on the distinction between short-term and long-term memory. *Short-term memory* (STM) is working memory; it is where you first store new information, what you use every day when solving problems, keeping phone numbers in mind, studying, and so forth. You are usually aware of what it contains. However, not only is this form of memory limited in capacity, as Simon pointed out, but the length of time that information persists in STM is measured in seconds; the specific amount of time depends on factors such as the amount of new information coming in which may displace what is already there. Children retain less in STM than do adults, but this appears to be because it takes them longer to process a given bit of information (remember the time constraints) and because they use less effective processing strategies than do adults, rather than because their STM's "hold less" than do those of adults (Chi, 1976).

From short-term memory, some (but not all) information is encoded into *long-term memory* (LTM) where it may be stored for minutes or for years. Thus, LTM is one's intellectual storage system; Brown (1975) calls LTM *"memory as knowing"* to underscore the point that it consists of one's entire body of *semantic memory,* or meaningful information. One characteristic of semantic memory is that it is structured; that there is an organization or "filing system" is evident even in very young children. Both children and adults are likely to use categories based on meaning to organize or group what they know, though the meaning relationships on which they form their categories may change with age—young children, for example, are likely to use functional categories (ice cream is to eat, a ball is to play with), whereas older children and adults are more likely to use conceptual categories (foods, toys).

The particular categories used may differ in other ways, too; some semantic categories, such as the masculine or feminine connotations of items, are more salient to children than to adults (Nadelman, 1974). Some categories used infrequently by adults, such as sense impressions like "redness" or "roundness," may be used by older school-aged children but not by younger ones (Wagner, 1970, cited in Hagen et al., 1975). But the fact that LTM is organized by categories is true for both children and adults.

Similarly, both children and adults remember by means of *semantic integration*—incorporating new information to the context of what they already know. Even preschoolers remember the gist or meaning of new information rather than the exact word-for-word form in which they learned it. For example, if given related sentences such as "The book is on the table," and "The table is in front of the chair," then asked to pick out these "old" sentences from a longer set of sentences, children will identify as "old" those sentences which would be true given the information in the sentences originally seen ("The book is in front of the chair"), though they have not seen these sentences before. They have no difficulty in distinguishing as "new" those sentences which would be false, given the original sentences (for example, Paris & Mahoney, 1974; Paris & Carter, 1973). What they remember is *not* particular sentences but what the sentences mean. Even preschoolers demonstrate semantic integration. Changes which take place over the school years are primarily in improved use of semantic integration due to increasing knowledge and changing logical skills, rather than in the occurrence of integration itself (Paris, 1975).

If semantic memory includes all that children know, one might expect changes in the way children organize their memories which relate to change in the structure of intelligence (Brown, 1975; Piaget & Inhelder, 1973). Evidently such changes do take place. For instance, children entering concrete operations who are shown a display of same-length sticks arranged in ascending order like a staircase can draw them more accurately after six months than they can soon after seeing them (Piaget & Inhelder, 1973; Altemeyer, Fulton, & Birney, 1969). One interpretation of such memory improvement over time is that it reflects children's acquisition of the operation of seriation, which they can then bring to bear on their memory of the sticks.

Simon (Box 4–2) also mentioned strategies or programs for the control of behavior as a major feature of an information processing theory. Brown (1975) uses the term *memory as knowing how to know* to refer to the strategies an individual can call upon in order to remember more effectively. This aspect of memory changes dramatically during the school years. As preschoolers, children have few such skills and seem to lack much awareness that there might be need for them (we will discuss this change in awareness further in the section on metacognition). In fact, even when they know how to use a strategy, young children frequently show a *production deficiency*—they fail to use the strategy spontaneously but must be prompted or instructed to do so. By the end of the school years, however, children have a diversity of such strategic skills which they use spontaneously and upon which they draw flexibly depending upon the requirements of the situation.

As an illustration, children in one study (Keeney, Cannizzo, & Flavell, 1967) had to remember the sequence in which the experimenter pointed to animal pictures, all of which were familiar to the children. Rehearsing by naming the pictures should be a helpful mnemonic device (memory aid) on this task. Children whose lip movements indicated that they were labelling or naming remembered significantly more than did children whose lips did not move. On a second set of trials, these same children were all instructed to name the animals as the experimenter pointed to each one. The performance difference disappeared. On a third set of trials, when children were given the option of labelling or not, many of the children who did not spontaneously name the animals at the outset reverted to not naming them again, and once again they remembered significantly less than did the children who named the animals.

Good performance on this task clearly depended on the production of a strategy, specifically, naming the animals to be remembered. Performance was good whether the strategy, when used, was produced spontaneously or only in response to instructions. Other tasks, some of which permitted use of strategic aids such as manipulating paper cutouts to match items to be remembered, produced similar results. In fact, over several studies (reviewed along with others in Flavell, 1970) Flavell and his co-workers found a great deal of evidence of production deficiency. The age at which children began to use a strategy spontaneously depended on the task, although in many cases spontaneous production of mediators was clearly developing during the school years. For instance, the spontaneous naming of animals in the task described above occurred with virtually all of a group of fifth graders, about half of a group of second graders, and almost none of a kindergarten group.

In addition, there is evidence of *production inefficiencies*—partial but ineffective use of strategies such as lining up cutouts which might serve as memory aids but not doing so until after the objects they represented were already screened from view. It appears that children only gradually begin to produce appropriate strategies as they become experienced with effective strategic aids and learn to recognize their applicability to various tasks.

Similar changes in children's use of strategies to retrieve information they have learned are illustrated in a study by Kobasigawa (1974). First-, third-, and sixth-grade children were shown sets of three pictures from a given category, each set accompanied by a cue card: three animal pictures with a picture of a zoo, for instance, or three musical instruments with a picture of a music book. They were to remember the sets of three pictures. On recall, some children were given the cue cards and told they could use them to help remember if they thought this would help (cue condition); some children were shown the cue cards one by one, told there had been three pictures with the card, and asked to remember those three pictures (directed cue condition); and some were simply asked to remember the sets of pictures without any cue (free recall condition). As Figure 4–1 illustrates, having the cue cards available without being provided a strategy for using them (cue condition) was of no help at all to first graders. However, they could remember as much as older children when provided with a strategy (directed cue condition), so they had learned the information; but they did not know how to go about getting it back. By sixth grade the children knew how to do this; they could use the cue cards effectively, whether or not they were provided with a strategy, suggesting that they were producing appropriate strategies spontaneously.

These findings about children's learning and remembering, many of which either grew out of or are compatible with the information processing orientation, are clearly useful and relevant for understanding children's learning and remembering both in school and out. We will encounter other useful data from informa-

FIGURE 4–1 Mean number of items correctly recalled by first-, third-, and sixth-grade children as a function of grade and recall condition. First graders can remember as much as sixth graders if they are provided with an effective recall strategy (directed cue), but sixth graders can spontaneously use such a strategy (cue condition).

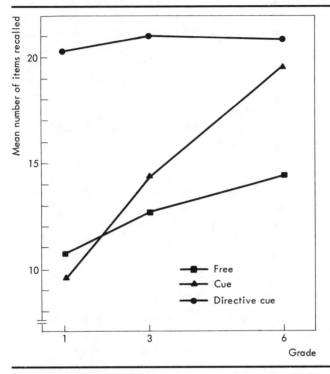

Source: A. Kobasigawa, "Utilization of Retrieval Cues by Children in Recall," *Child Development* 45 (1974), pp. 127–34. Copyright 1974 by The Society for Research in Child Development, Inc.

tion processing studies as we proceed with our discussion of reading, to which we turn next.

READING

What makes up good reading? What skills and abilities are required by reading? Gibson and Levin (1975) argue vigorously that in mature readers, reading is a multifaceted, adaptive, rule-governed process, the exact nature of which depends on the reasons for which the individual is reading—for entertainment? information? to pass an examination?—as well as the nature of the material which is being read—is it difficult? easy? well-organized? brand-new or already familiar to the reader? They criticize most theories of reading and, in particular, information processing theories, for focusing too narrowly on some single important reading process to the exclusion of other, equally important processes. Such criticisms are now being made by information processing theorists themselves; Carr (1981) summarizes evidence regarding four categories of factors each of which contributes to reading performance. All of them, accordingly, must be incorporated into any adequate theory of the reading process, though theories to date have dealt with only a single factor at a time.

If reading is multifaceted, what are some of the component skills on which it depends? At the very least, the list of relevant skills must include the following: (1) visual perceptual skills which permit the child to differentiate among letter shapes, word shapes, and other visual forms; (2) being able to translate from word patterns and spelling to sounds and meanings. In particular, many children have difficulty separating words into the phonemes or sound units of which they are made up; (3) integrating printed words with meanings in order to comprehend, which depends on both understanding language and on conceptual development; (4) being able to remember words and meanings long enough to permit them to be understood (short-term memory); (5) being able to make use of available knowledge to provide context for recognizing and comprehending words—you will understand a word more quickly in the context of a sentence than if you must deal with it by itself.

We shall make no attempt to discuss each of these skills exhaustively— research relevant to reading already fills whole books. However, let us look at a sampling of them.

Perception and perceptual learning

To begin to read, children must be able to distinguish between writing and other displays, such as pictures, as well as to distinguish between the shapes of different letters, among other things. They become able to do this through processes of *perceptual learning,* which refers to changes in children's performance on perceptual tasks as a result of experience. These changes are not a matter of changes in basic sensory capabilities such as visual acuity or the ability to detect differences between tones, though sensory capabilities do change with age (e.g., Pick & Pick, 1970). Instead, performance changes due to perceptual learning reflect changes in how children use the sensory capabilities they have: what they attend to, how they explore objects, how they apply what they perceive to the task at hand.

To take an example: letters that are the same except for a reversal in orientation (b,d; p,q) are often confusing for children learning to read and write. Early studies showed that many children tended to confuse such letter pairs until they were 7 or 7½ years old (for example, Davidson, 1935). However, when five-year-olds with no prior reading experience were trained to press a lever in the direction in which the letter was oriented (right for b, left for d), they quickly learned to distinguish the two, and they were subsequently able to transfer this learned distinction to another task (Hendrickson & Muehl, 1962). Obviously these children had the perceptual apparatus required to make this distinction, even though they might not have used that apparatus for another two years without the special training.

An even earlier skill that children must master is differentiation of words from other visual displays. Gibson and Levin (1975) cite a study in which 86 percent of three-year olds, 90 percent of four-year-olds, and 96 percent of five- and six-year-olds could already distinguish samples of writing from samples of other kinds of symbols, though they were nonreaders themselves. Evidently they use features such as whether the symbols were lined up (as letters are in words), whether the symbols were varied or repetitive (letters in words vary), and so forth (Lavine, 1972). These children were from literate environments in the United States; the importance of relevant experience for their high rates of recognition of writing is underscored by their much greater knowledge of the attributes of writing when compared with children of the same age in a rural Mexican community where writing and printing were rare.

By what processes do children learn to make such perceptual distinctions? *Differentiation theory* maintains that these changes are not a matter of learning new responses, but a matter of increasing sensitivity to the properties of stimuli, which children learn to differentiate with experience (Gibson, 1969). In the letter orientation example, young children do not differentiate letter orientation from other properties of the letters, and so, of course, they do not respond to it. Learning to differentiate the appropriate cue comes with experience in the form of encounters with that cue, which could occur in special training (as with the five-year-olds), training in reading, or other, more general experience. A basic principle here is that *stimuli always contain much more information than we are able to process.* Perception is necessarily selective, taking in only some small part of the information available. Through the experience which accrues with development, children make finer and finer differentiations among stimulus properties and become increasingly skilled at attending to those properties relevant for whatever task is at hand. Consequently, changes in perceptual learning performance result from changes in selectivity and in the direction of perception. There is no need to invoke some additional process, such as forming a new scheme, which someone in Piaget's tradition might suggest. Gibson calls such interpretations *"enrichment"* theories, since they assume that something—an association, a scheme—must be added to perception to explain the change in performance. It is not that schemes are never formed—only that they are not necessary to understand perceptual learning from the standpoint of differentiation theory.

Gibson (1969; Gibson & Levin, 1975) also suggests three developmental trends which may characterize perceptual learning. One of these trends is that with development, *information comes to be picked up from the environment with greater efficiency.* One way in which this occurs is that children become able to recognize and respond to *distinctive features*—particularly features of an object or an event which enable it to be readily discriminated from other objects or events. Once a set of distinctive features has been learned, children need only look for those features to identify the object or event. To identify letters, for example, children must attend to features such as break versus close (c and o), lines versus curves (u and v), rotations and reversals (p versus q, u versus n). In one well-known study, Gibson, Gibson, Pick and Osser (1962) studied children's errors in differentiating letter-like forms which were transformed in these different ways. They also included perspective transformations, which are the changes in appearance of objects depending on the perspective from which they are seen—the visual image of a dinner plate is round only when looked at head-on; as we usually see them from varying angles, the visual image is more elliptical or oval, though we still "know" they are round. Their results for four-through eight-year olds are shown in Figure 4–2. Confusions of line-to-curve, rotation-and-reversal, and break-and-close transformations decline steadily with increasing age, very likely because the children were learning to attend to the relevant distinctive features in the course of reading instruction at school. Perspective transformations, in contrast, ran high, most likely because we must learn to ignore these cues—we need to recognize that plate as a plate, or that door as a door, regardless of its changes in appearance as our perspective shifts; we need to recognize an o or an i as such regardless of whether our reading matter is held up or lying flat. A somewhat different example is the person who can listen to a running engine and not only tell whether or not it is running correctly, but pinpoint what is wrong if it is not running correctly. To most adults, the sound of an engine is a largely undifferentiated roar. Only if the cues are obvious—for instance, when an engine runs very rough—does the engine sound "different" to them. But persons with a great deal of experience in working with

FIGURE 4–2 Children's errors on different types of transformations of letterlike forms.

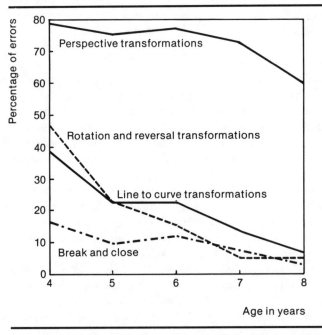

Source: E. J. Gibson, J. J. Gibson, A. D. Pick, and H. Osser, A Developmental Study of the Discrimination of Letter-like Forms, *Journal of Comparative and Physiological Psychology* 55 (1962), pp. 897–906.

and listening to engines learn to differentiate and respond to much finer cues—
cues which are there for everyone but can be differentiated only by those with
relevant experience.

In addition, with experience children become increasingly responsive to
perceptual invariants, that is, attributes of stimuli or relationships among stimuli
that remain the same under different conditions. The fact that forms remain
unchanged in spite of perspective transformations is one example of invariance.
As another, rhythms have properties in common regardless of whether they are
heard, seen (as in flashes of light), or felt (as might happen if a person tapped on
one's arm). In Morse code, for example, visual patterns of dots and dashes are
interchangeable with auditory patterns. Gibson suggests that children's increasing skill at *cross-modal transfer*—being able to visually identify something
that has been handled and vice versa, for example—reflects their increasing
sensitivity to higher-order invariants, that is, invariants such as rhythm which are
shared in common by different sensory modalities.

Another developmental trend which Gibson suggests is that perception
moves toward *increasing specificity of discrimination.* Older children not only
distinguish between, but also respond to as different, stimuli that younger children respond to as though they were the same. This can be seen in generalization
studies, where individuals are trained to respond in some way to a particular
stimulus; when the response is being made consistently, other stimuli of varying
degrees of dissimilarity to the original stimulus are presented to see whether they
elicit the same response. If they do, the response has generalized. Younger
children typically generalize to wider ranges of stimuli than do older children or
adults. The increasing specificity of response to letter-like forms—that is, the
decrease in errors which had indicated that the different transformations were
confused with one another—also illustrates this trend. Again, these findings do
not mean that younger children's perceptual apparatus is incapable of making
distinctions as sharp as those older children make. Given sufficient incentive for
more specificity of response, younger children can learn to perform as older
children do (Jeffrey & Skager, 1962).

Finally, Gibson suggests that children become more skilled at *"optimizing
attention"*—at directing attention toward relevant attributes and obtaining desired information from the environment. One important change here is in children's search strategies. Given an object to look at, preschool children may
spend most of their looking time focusing on one or two salient attributes of the
object, with little systematic looking at its other properties. Given an object to
explore haptically (by touch), they may grasp the object between their palms and
hold or squeeze it, but fail to trace the contours or to seek out distinctive features
that might help to identify the object later on. As they grow older and more
experienced, they begin to search more efficiently and systematically, looking
at contours or tracing them with fingertips, spending extra time on unusual
attributes, and so forth. This sort of improvement in search techniques extends
into the elementary school years and perhaps beyond, depending on the task.
Needless to say, even when younger and older children are given the same
stimuli, they will not wind up having the same information about those stimuli.

The younger children will know less because they have not sought out all the information.

Children also become better at directing or focusing their attention in a somewhat different sense—filtering out irrelevant information. Performance on *incidental learning tasks* provides one illustration of this change. Children might be shown different forms, each a different color, and required to respond to the forms. Later, they might be asked to recall not only the forms (the central, or intentional, task) but also the colors (the incidental task). In the early elementary school years, children are likely to remember both intentional and incidental cues equally well; but as they grow older, their memory for intentional cues improves, whereas their memory for incidental cues does not. By the end of elementary school those who are best on intentional memory are likely to do worst on incidental memory (Hagen, 1972). The older children are much better at filtering out and ignoring irrelevant information while attending to relevant information.

More explicitly reading-related, Gibson and Levin (1975) cite two studies by Willows and Mackinnon (1973) and Willows (1974) in which sixth-grade boys who were good and poor readers were asked to read stories the text of which, printed in black, was on alternate lines with text of a second story printed in red. Compared to boys who read the same text by itself, the poor readers made far more intrusion errors and took longer when asked to read orally. The good readers, in contrast, made more errors on a task of comprehension which reflected intrusion of meanings from the inserted lines. The two groups of readers were apparently affected in different ways: for the poor readers, the physical presence of the alternate lines was debilitating, while for the good readers, it was the meaning of the inserted material which made a difference. Adults who are skilled readers can usually ignore both the physical presence and the meanings of the inserted lines, selectively attending only to the target lines.

Being able to visually discriminate between different letters and different words is obviously fundamental to learning to read. Gibson and Levin discuss a number of pre-reading skills, many of which depend on changes in perceptual skills. Among them are development of writing-related skills such as scribbling and spontaneous "writing" which children with access to markers and paper often produce before starting school; differentiation of writing from other visual displays, as discussed earlier; learning to identify and discriminate letters— many children can tell you whether a symbol is a letter or not even before they know any letter names; overcoming the reversals and letter confusions which crop up in the letter-name learning and early word learning of many children. However, Gibson and Levin point out that most children manage to overcome these confusions with relative ease, and Carr (1981) concurs that individual differences in some types of visual discrimination ability, such as susceptibility to reversal errors, evidently do not distinguish between good and poor readers. Older children make fewer errors than younger children, but they are not made more often by poor than by good readers. Carr does point out, however, that other aspects of visual discrimination, as well as feedback mechanisms such as those which make use of regularities of spelling as an aid to identifying written words, may prove to distinguish between good and poor readers in important ways.

Phonological and semantic recoding

There is another skill that is not acquired with ease, however, and that is *phonological segmentation*—being able to differentiate and recognize phonemes, the basic sound units of words. *Call, fall,* and *ball* are all one-syllable words which vary only in their initial phoneme, but that difference alters their meaning. Our writing system is based on a phonetic alphabet; the letters and letter combinations with which words are spelled correspond to phonemes or sound units rather than to syllables, which are higher-order groupings of sounds—*syl' la ble,* as the dictionary shows it—or to whole words. There are writing systems in which units correspond to syllables; they are called *syllabaries.* There are also *logographic* writing systems in which symbols correspond to whole words. With a phonetic alphabet such as ours, however, children must be able to distinguish the separate sounds or they will not be able to match them to their corresponding spelling units. (See Figure 4–3 and Box 4–3 for examples of a logography and a syllabary designed to help children achieve phonetic segmentation in the context of a syllabary curriculum.) Children must have phonological segmentation skills if they are to recognize the correspondence between a letter or letter combination and a given sound; without it, they have no differentiated sound to match with a letter. They must become able to hear the sound segmentation in what is said—remember sounding out words from grade school days? Not until they can do this can they translate (or recode) from spelling to pronunciation (*phonological recoding*) and from spelling to meaning (*semantic recording*). Paradoxically, children master such sound segmentation early and easily in spoken language—without it they could not fluently recombine sounds into different words, which they can obviously do. Furthermore, they probably have good command of the phonological rules for what are acceptable sound combinations in their native language by sometime between ages four and six. If children in the United States are presented with sound combinations which are "illegal" by the rules of English phonology, even four-year olds can often say that the illegal combinations can not be words. (English words never begin with *Vm-* or *Bd-,* for example, nor do they ever end with *-tg* or *-sf.*) If asked to imitate or repeat such nonword combinations, children made more mistakes on illegal than legal combinations; furthermore, their mistakes tended to regularize the combinations—to make them more congruent with the phonological rules. So, when speaking, children clearly have considerable mastery over sound combinations, and the rules for making them, by the time they begin school.

But speaking is spontaneous; it does not require paying attention to the acoustic properties of words or deliberately manipulating sound combinations in particular ways, whereas this is necessary if one is to learn to read. Such *conscious* acoustic awareness and mastery comes to children late and with difficulty; and it is clearly associated with reading, being present or better developed in good than in poor readers. Before age six or so, few children are able to do the following tasks, each of which reflects mastery and voluntary control of sound segmentation: They cannot delete a sound from a given word and come up with another, different word (stand, sand; play, pay; Bruce, 1964). They cannot learn pig Latin, which requires that the initial phoneme be discriminated from the rest of the word, shifted to the end of the word, and followed with the syllable "ay"—as an illustration, the words "pig Latin" come out "igpay atin-lay." And they have trouble making rhymes, which also require segmenting out the end sounds of words and matching them to similar end sounds in other words (Savin, 1972).

What makes use of these skills in reading so difficult, and why do poor readers have so much more trouble with them than do good readers? The single-factor information processing models reviewed by Carr (1981) suggest several mechanisms that may differ in good and poor readers. One is that phonemic awareness—the ability to break speech down into its constituent sounds and then to connect those sounds to spelling patterns—is simply insufficiently developed in poor readers to allow them to master these connections. When Rozin and Gleitman (1977) gave children a syllabary—a writing system in which the meaning correspondence is to syllables or sound combinations rather than to individual phonemes as illustrated in Figure 4–3—even children who had great

FIGURE 4–3 Outline of a syllabary curriculum designed to introduce the phonetic alphabet through experience with nonphonetic writing systems. See also Box 4–3.

	Semasiography	Logography	Phoneticization	Syllabary	Introduction to the alphabet
Description	Reading for meaning through pictures	Mapping between spoken words and visual symbols	Focusing on sound rather than meaning by developing awareness of sound segmentation	Constructing and segmenting meaningful words and sentences in terms of syllables	Segmenting and blending initial consonant sounds
Activities	Interpretation of pictures. Reading material of the form: bee hit can / pen in hand	Reading material of the form: bee hit can / pen in hand	"Speaking slowly" game. Nonsense noise game. ϡ ∧ ∧ ϡ goo la la goo. Rebus homonyms: man can saw can. Concrete blends: = rainbow	Basic blends of meaningful syllables. = sandwich (sand witch). Addition of meaningless syllables (e.g., terminal y, er, ing): long er. Partial fading of segmentation cues: be • ing	Blends using initial consonant sounds: s • ing & s • and

Source: The Structure and Acquisition of Reading, II. The reading process and the acquisition of the alphabetic principle. In A. S. Reber and D. Scarborough (eds.), *Toward a Psychology of Reading.* Hillsdale, N.J.: Lawrence Erlbaum Associates, 1977. Reproduced as figure 5, p. 271, P. Rozin, "The Evolution of Intelligence and Access to the Cognitive Unconscious," in *Progress in Psychobiology and Physiological Psychology,* vol. 6 (New York: Academic Press, 1976), pp. 245–80.

BOX 4–3
What do the steps in the syllabary curriculum mean?

Paul Rozin describes the steps outlined in the syllabary curriculum (see Figure 4–3) as follows:

> In the first stage, semasiography, children learn to interpret pictures and thus to get meanings directly from the page. In the second step, logography, they learn picture-symbols that stand for words and construct simple sentences with them. In the third stage, phoneticization, direct orthographic representation of the sounds of speech rather than the meanings is introduced. Attention is called to sound segmentation of speech by a "speaking slowly" game, in which long words are broken into syllables and pronounced slowly (e.g. *hos-pi-tal*). The children must guess the word they hear. To exemplify the idea that symbols can represent sounds, they play a nonsense noise game. A few odd and entertaining noises (such as "clicking" with the tongue or whistles) are each given a symbol equivalent. Children then learn to read off symbol sequences by making the proper noise sequences. Rebuses (e.g., *can, saw*) are used to emphasize the use of words for their sound value. Blends of two words (syllables) that form new words are also introduced in a game format. In the fourth stage, an English syllabary, consisting of about 70 common English syllables and the words made by blending these syllables, is introduced. Wherever possible, pictorial symbols are provided along with the written form of each syllable to help in identifying and remembering them. However, for some of the more abstract items (e.g., *er, the*) no pictorial aids are provided for obvious reasons. Children progress through this syllabary primarily by playing and word construction games with the syllabic elements and reading 15 progressively more difficult story books. The segmentation cues separating the syllables are gradually made less salient. . . . Once some fluency in this syllabary is gained, the fifth stage, introduction to the alphabet, begins. Alphabetic (phonemic) elements are introduced gradually, beginning with initial *s,* a sound relatively easy to pronounce in isolation. It is blended onto the already learned syllabic elements.

Source: P. Rozin, "The Evolution of Intelligence and Access to the Cognitive Unconscious," in *Progress in Psychobiology and Physiological Psychology,* vol. 6. (New York: Academic Press, 1976), 270.

difficulty reading with a phonetic alphabet readily mastered reading with the syllabary. So the problem had to be with phonemes as units, not with matching sounds to visual patterns in general.

Another mechanism may have to do with demands on memory when children are first learning to connect phonemes and spelling (Perfetti & Lesgold, 1978). Relevant here is the finding that poor readers may not differ much from good readers when the words they are reading are familiar and much practiced, but they are much worse than good readers at pronouncing unfamiliar but orthographically "legal" letter combinations. If matching a sound with a spelling pattern demanded a great deal of attention and the capacity for attention were limited, making the match-up might use up so much of the available attention that little would be left over for putting the matched-up pairs together into words or relating them to meanings.

There are also models that suggest the problem lies in memory—poor readers may have greater difficulty gaining access to internal representations of printed words, or they may have greater difficulty maintaining letters and phonemes in short-term memory long enough to integrate them into a meaningful pattern. Carr, however, suggests that any such memory deficits—which may well exist— are probably secondary to the problem of grasping the concept of a phoneme and of learning to isolate phonemes within speech signals.

In addition to the mechanisms discussed here, there may be a psychobiological constraint on development of phonemic awareness. Let us turn to the theme of psychobiological constraints.

Psychobiological constraints and reading

Early in the chapter we noted that information processing approaches recognize that there are psychobiological constraints on information processing capacity. Rozin (1976) has suggested that children's great difficulty with phonemic segmentation may reflect such a constraint. Taking an evolutionary perspective, Rozin suggests that intelligence consists of *adaptive specializations,* which are programs or patterns of adaptive behavior that evolve initially as solutions to particular problems. As one example, he cites the food-finding capacities of honeybees, which are a remarkably complex, adaptable set of behaviors for which bees are "pre-wired"—that is, the basis for the behaviors is part of the bees' inherent genetic equipment. Another example might be some of the visual specializations in humans, such as spatial perception; people typically do not bump into things, and are able to judge relative size at varying distances. These skills are present very early in life and appear to require little learning, suggesting that they too are in part "pre-wired." Yet another example might be phonemic segmentation, as evident in oral speech; as indicated above, the fact that someone can speak fluently is evidence that that person can engage in highly complex processing of phonemes within the stream of speech.

However, adaptive specializations differ in their *accessibility*—the degree to which they can be separated from their original function and brought into conscious and deliberate application to other problems requiring a similar solution. In the present case, the question is to what extent the adaptive specialization of phonemic segmentation, evident in oral speech, can be separated from oral speech and made accessible for application to written speech and reading. We as humans have many such pre-wired capabilities to which we have little or no access; Rozin refers to such inaccessible machinery as the *cognitive unconscious.* However, access to adaptive specializations so that they can be applied to problems in addition to those for which they originally developed may be one of the main cognitive advances brought about by evolution. Learning processes such as forming associations between two events, or forming schemes, may be examples of adaptive specializations to which humans have gained considerable access. Even flatworms can form associations—and there is no basis for saying the process is different for them than it is for people—but in flatworms, accessibility is limited: associations can be formed only under narrow ranges of circumstances, whereas in people, there is considerable access to such processes.

What of phonemic segmentation? Rozin argues that over much of human evolution segmentation skills remained in the cognitive unconscious, accessible only for spoken language. What has happened in more recent eras is that accessibility for other purposes, and particularly for the voluntary use which is necessary for reading, has been evolving. Rozin notes that human beings have developed many different writing systems, but that all but one of these have been either logographies or systems of picture writing, where a picture stands for a whole word, or syllabaries (see Figure 4–3). As far as is known, a phonetic alphabet was developed only once; it has spread and evolved into the variety of alphabets we know today. Rozin also notes that in Japan, where children must learn to read not one but two syllabaries, along with assorted pictograms adapted from Chinese, reading problems are far *rarer* than they are in the United States where children must master a phonetic system. Both of these observations would be congruent with the notion that humans as yet have only limited access to the adaptive specialization of phonemic segmentation. If Rozin is right, the great difficulty that children have in bringing phonemic segmentation under voluntary control is not surprising; and a major task of education, as he points out, is to devise means that aid children in gaining access to this specialization. The syllabary curriculum by Rozin and Gleitman which is outlined in Figure 4–3 is one approach to providing such aid.

Hemispheric lateralization of the brain and reading

Probably few individuals outside of academic circles are familiar with Rozin's ideas regarding phonemic segmentation, adaptive specialization, and accessibility. In contrast, many readers will be familiar with currently popular ideas regarding the functioning of the "right brain" versus the "left brain." As popularly conceived, the left brain does verbal, linear thinking, whereas the right brain does wholistic, patterned thinking—a tidy dichotomy which if valid would have obvious implications for teaching and learning, including learning to read. Unfortunately, the dichotomy as stated is such an oversimplification that it is functionally untrue.

For those to whom these ideas are new, some background may be helpful. The human brain has two major halves or hemispheres which are connected in normal persons by a central commisure. Each hemisphere regulates action contralaterally, that is, on the opposite side of the body, except for the eyes; so the right hemisphere regulates the action of the right eye, the left arm, hand, leg, foot, and so forth; while the left hemisphere regulates the left eye, the right arm, hand, leg, foot, and so forth.

The two hemispheres do not have exactly corresponding functions, however. *Lateral assymmetry* refers to the differences in function between them. Lateral asymmetry has been known to exist since the mid-19th century when Broca reported observations identifying a speech center in the left hemisphere which had no analog in the right hemisphere. In the 1960s and 1970s, interest in the

differences between the two hemispheres was reinvigorated by a series of fascinating studies of individuals who, for treatment (usually successful) of epilepsy,
have had the commisure connecting their left and right hemispheres surgically
severed (e.g., Gazzaniga, 1970; Levy & Trevarthon, 1976; Levy, Trevarthon, &
Sperry, 1972; Sperry, 1974). In many ways such split-brain individuals are
indistinguishable from persons whose brains are intact. There are some dramatic
differences, however. If, for example, one shows them visual stimuli in such a
way that the right and left eyes see different things, questions about what is
shown to the left eye are answered verbally; but questions about what is shown
to the right eye may elicit "I don't know" verbal responses even as the left hand
is pointing to or otherwise indicating some nonverbal response.

As interest in issues of lateralization grew, researchers also developed techniques for comparing right and left hemispheres in normal, intact brains—there
are good reasons for questioning the applicability of results based upon atypical,
split-brain individuals to the functioning of the intact brain. On the basis of a
major review of such research, Bradshaw and Nettleton (1981) argue strongly
that the traditional assignment of verbal functions to the left hemisphere and
nonverbal functions to the right hemisphere (the oversimplification referred to
early in this section) is simply inadequate. If more speech processing does go on
in the left hemisphere, they suggest that it is not because of some speech center
or specialized mechanisms, but rather because the left hemisphere has capacities for sequential, time-dependent processing—which is obviously necessary
for speech and for reading since words can only be heard or read one at a time,
in sequence. On the other hand, the right hemisphere, which has capacities for
more wholistic, global processing, also has a considerable capacity for comprehension (if not production) for speech.

The best conclusion at this point, say Bradshaw and Nettleton, is that there
is a continuum of function between the two hemispheres, not a dichotomy; the
left hemisphere may be more active in verbal processing because of its time and
sequence analytical abilities, and the right hemisphere may be more active in
space and pattern processing because of its greater capacity for holistic processing, but one cannot make sharp distinctions between the functions of the
two. And if one cannot make sharp, clear-cut distinctions between the two, then
there is little foundation for programs or exercises for "teaching the right brain."
Harris (1982) points out that the current fad with its emphasis on right hemisphere functioning is the most recent wave in a series going back to the last
century. Initially, the "ambidextrous man" was idealized; then beginning in the
1930s, spurred by the work of Orton (1937) on reading and language, left
hemisphere functions were emphasized. Now the tendency is to emphasize right
hemisphere functions; according to some writers, this is necessary in order to
counterbalance the heavy emphasis on left hemisphere functions from previous
years. Unfortunately, as Harris points out and as should be evident from other
arguments in this section, there is at present simply insufficient evidence regarding actual brain hemisphere activities to provide a foundation for developing
programs of any sort. The programs may be perfectly good in their own right, but

it is for reasons other than any demonstrated relationship to specializations in brain functioning.

Coming back more specifically to reading, one of the major prevalent hypotheses about dyslexia, or reading disability, is that it reflects some sort of disorder of cerebral asymmetry—that, for example, the lateral asymmetries found in typical individuals are incomplete or inadequately established in the brains of children with reading difficulties. But here again there are serious difficulties, as Naylor (1980) suggests. One set of difficulties has to do with defining dyslexia; both Naylor and Carr (1981) point out that definitions of dyslexia are far from satisfactory, usually failing to specify clearly the nature of dyslexia or how it might be diagnosed. A second, related set of difficulties has to do with the multifaceted nature of the reading process itself. In preceding sections, we have barely touched on the range of skills which must be pulled together in successful reading. Deficiencies in any one or any combination of these skills could result in reading problems; which of these would qualify as "real" dyslexia? Or given their range, does it even make sense to think of dyslexia as a particular disorder rather than as a set of disorders which may have different foundations and which have in common only that they interfere with skilled reading performance? From his review of studies of lateralization in children with reading problems, Naylor concluded that there was no strong evidence that such children differ from other children in brain lateralization or that they have any particular left hemisphere deficit which might interfere with their reading. However, different components of the reading process and the modes of processing which those components require have not been distinguished in studies to date; when more detailed examination takes place, it may become possible to specify brain mechanisms basic to particular processing demands and their relationship to components of good and poor reading. But it is unlikely that such relationships will be simple or primarily related to the functioning of either hemisphere.

Other work besides that dealing with cerebral asymmetry reinforces the notion that the relation between brain functions and reading are complex and not easily indexed (that is, there are no magic signs which identify particular dysfunctions). Difficulties with finger localization, for example—being unable to identify a finger that was touched when it could not be seen—is an accepted index of brain dysfunction which has been associated with reading difficulties in several studies. But when Fletcher, Taylor, Morris, and Satz (1982) looked at the relationship between finger localization and reading performance of good and poor readers followed longitudinally from third to sixth grade, their main findings were that finger recognition neither provided a clear-cut or unitary measure of brain functioning, nor were there specific relationships with reading achievement. Evidently finger recognition was related to reading because of its relationship to other general developmental processes which, in turn, are important for reading.

Again, we must conclude on available evidence that there are some sort of relationships between variations in brain functioning and variations in reading skill, but that the relationships are indirect and complex, and that we are far from understanding them. From what is now known, a caveat to future parents and educators is in order; be very cautious and skeptical of any reading instruction programs which claim to be based on any single or direct neurophysiological function.

Comprehension

Ultimately, the goal of learning to read is to develop good comprehension— to be able to understand what one reads, to extract meaning easily from printed text. Most of us would agree that a good reader can grasp the meaning of written material with ease and skill, whereas poor readers are likely to struggle with the material and even then not grasp its meaning as fully, despite their greater effort.

Beyond this general description, what do we mean by comprehension? There is no single answer to this question, for good reasons. One is that what a person might consider good comprehension depends on the material and on one's goals, what one wants to get out of the material. Your criteria for comprehension will differ depending on whether you are scanning a newspaper, reading for recreation, or studying material on which you will be examined. So long as you get what you want or need from the material, no one criterion is "better" than another. In addition, remember that reading itself is not a unified process, but rather many different processes; it stands to reason that one's comprehension levels will depend on one's mastery of these diverse processes, any one of which may facilitate or interfere with ready understanding. In this sense, we have been dealing with processes important for comprehension throughout the preceding sections. Difficulties with any of the processes discussed above may prevent one from grasping the meaning of what is read; one's attention may be spent on dealing with the mechanics of reading rather than the content, or one's flow of information from the text may be disrupted by such difficulties.

Yet even though mastery of the mechanics of reading is clearly fundamental and necessary to understanding, such mastery by itself does not assure good comprehension. Good and poor readers may be equally good at identifying individual words; they may also be equally good at extracting meanings from nonverbal symbols, according to Gibson and Levin (1975), so the difficulties of some poorer readers must reside in processes other than these.

If two readers can be equally good with mechanics of reading such as vocabulary or word recognition and still differ in how well they comprehend, what does the good reader have that the poor reader does not? From the summaries of both Gibson and Levin (1975) and of Carr (1981), many of the differences appear to fall into one of two major, and interrelated, categories: first, sensitivity to and flexible use of structure inherent in the material; and second, sensitivity to and retention of the content of what is read and its implications, permitting inference of facts and arguments not directly expressed in the material itself.

Structure or organization at a number of levels may be fundamental to understanding—as Markman (1981) points out, it doesn't make sense to say that one understands something unstructured such as one's phone number. Structure at a variety of levels may affect reading comprehension. At a very specific level, there is sensitivity to the frequency of occurrence of letters (which occurs more often, t or j? a or z?) and of patterns of spelling (recall, for example, the earlier discussion of legal and illegal letter combinations). At perhaps the other extreme of generality, there is the higher-order organization of themes and ideas which comprise any written production—the major ideas, the subordinate ideas. Better readers, and more experienced readers, are much better at readily distinguishing between the major and minor points in what they read. At intermediate levels of generality there is sensitivity to syntactic or grammatical structure (could a noun like *hat* or *picture* complete the sentence, *The boy was going to . . .?* Why not?)

One important example of sensitivity to organization of what is read is that skilled readers appear to be more able to integrate meanings based on the relationships among words and phrases than are poor readers, who often appear to read word by word. An early illustration among nonreading novices of such failure to integrate meanings is evident in the difficulty experienced by children up to about age seven (and among some children having difficulty learning to read) in recognizing the equivalence between action sequences and symbolically presented "instructions" describing those sequences (Farnham-Diggory, 1972). Having been trained to "read" such symbols as ⟋ for jump, ⌒ for over, ☉ for around, and then given a sequence of symbols meaning something like "jump over block" and asked to do it, five-year olds tend to perform each part separately. They jump, they gesture or comment on "over," they point to a block on the floor. But they fail to integrate or synthesize the instruction into a coordinated action sequence of jumping over the block, even though they can follow such an instruction perfectly well if it is given orally. Part of the problem may be that successful performance on this task requires apprehending five or six chunks or units of information, whereas there is reason to believe that five-year olds can only apprehend about four chunks or units of information at a time (remember the issue of limits on the capacity of the information processor? Adults can apprehend or take in about seven chunks at a time, give or take a couple.) So Farnham-Diggory hypothesized that the children reduce the information to manageable size by simply pairing each symbol with part of the total action, which allows them to remember all of the components even though they lose the relationship among them.

A similar difficulty with integrating meanings of groups of words appears to characterize some experienced readers. Adult readers (junior college students) who had poor comprehension scores despite good verbal and word recognition skills, but who appeared to read word by word, were helped significantly when sentences which they read were spatially separated into meaningful phrases; conditions against which this one was compared included regularly presented sentences (only the usual breaks between words), sentences presented one word to a line, and sentences in which spatial separations broke up rather than emphasized meaningful groups of words (Cromer, 1970). Good readers showed good comprehensions under all sentence presentation conditions. Presumably they were able to do so because they spontaneously or automatically imposed organization upon the material as they read, integrating meanings appropriately. The poor readers evidently did not do this; so having the organization explicit in the material facilitated their performance. As with the children in the preceding example, this may again be a matter of the limits on how much can be attended to at once. Poor readers may use up so much attention focusing on meanings of individual words one at a time that little is left over for higher-order integration of meanings of groups of words.

When we turn to sensitivity to the content of what is read, a new phenomenon becomes important. To understand successfully, the reader must relate what is read to what is already known—the semantic store (remember the discussion of long-term memory?). If you do not already know what is meant by words such as metonomy or frangipani, seeing the words in print will not reveal their meaning to you no matter how easily you can sound them out. (Of course you can look them up, and from then on they are likely to become part of your available store.)

Given adequate knowledge, however, readers relate the meaning of what they read to what they know, in the process making inferences at different levels—going "beyond the information given." One level at which this takes place is that the meaning of what one reads sets up expectations for words or ideas to come, which can facilitate or interfere with one's comprehension of the following material depending on whether the upcoming material is congruous with what has been read or not. For example, Schwantes, Boesl, and Ritz (1980) were interested in readers' recognition speed for words in differing semantic contexts. To generate different contexts, they took nine-word sentences, separated off the last word and defined it as the target word, then presented the target words following either all eight prior words (the whole sentence), the last four words prior to the target, the last two words prior to the target, or no prior words at all. In these circumstances, more context should facilitate the speed at which the word is recognized. They also defined a set of incongruous targets and contexts by taking a similar set of sentences and target words but scrambling them, so that the target words were not mated with prior words from their own sentences. Under these circumstances, more context should *interfere* with word recognition—the more context, the slower the speeds. The reaction times of third-grade, sixth-grade, and college students in all of these circumstances are shown in Figure 4–4. At least for the four- and eight-word contexts, increasing congruous context was linked to faster word recognition while increasing incongruous context was linked to lower word recognition. This was true at all grade levels. Perhaps more striking, though, are two other findings. First, context effects were much greater among younger readers—compare the findings for the different age groups in Figure 4–4. Second, note the very dramatic decline in recognition speeds as reading experience increased—all college speeds are faster than any sixth-grade speed, and all sixth-grade speeds are faster than any third-grade speed. Looking at these results, along with other results from their own and others' studies, Schwantes et al. suggest that word recognition becomes increasingly automatic with experience and skill. The more automatic their responses, the less dependent readers are upon context effects and the more efficient and flexible their word recognition responses can be. So context effects still influence more experienced and better readers, but to nowhere near the degree that is true for less experienced or poorer readers.

FIGURE 4–4 Mean word recognition reaction times of third-grade, sixth-grade, and college-age students following contexts that differed in length and in congruity with target word. Open forms show times for congruous contexts, closed forms for incongruous contexts. See text for discussion.

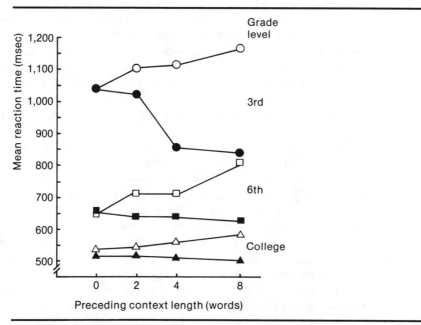

Source: F. M. Schwantes, S. L. Boesl, and E. G. Ritz, "Children's Use of Context in a Word Recognition: A Psycholinguistic Guessing Game," *Child Development* 55 (1980), pp. 730–36, figure 1, p. 733.

Good readers make more general inferences as well, going beyond facts and concepts explicitly stated in the text to conclusions not explicitly stated. Consider the sentence, "Alice picked up the small creature which had fallen from its nest." What kind of creature is it? What is its relative age? How do you know? In reading, to get an author's message it is often necessary to make inferences based not only on individual sentences, as in the example just given, but upon information different parts of which might have been presented in several locations in the text. Thus, it would be necessary both to remember points presented earlier and also to integrate them with the new information in order to be able to make an appropriate inference. As it happens, the likelihood that readers will do this increases as they become more experienced and skilled. In one study demonstrating this effect, Johnson and Smith (1981) had third and fifth graders read a story under different conditions, then questioned them about both material explicitly stated in the story and ideas that required inference. Not too surprisingly, children at both grade levels failed to make inferences if they did not remember the premise material. More interestingly, however, the fifth graders were much more likely to integrate and make inferences from premises presented in different paragraphs of the story, though the two grades did not differ in their ability to make inferences based on premises presented in contiguity. The difference between the grades did not reflect a difference in the capability to make inferences—given contiguously presented material, children from both grades made inferences with equal ease. In fact, there is increasing reason to believe that *capacity* to make inferences is present even in children as young as three and four, so long as they understand the causal relationships involved in the situation with which they are dealing (Gelman, Bullock, & Meck, 1980). Nor is the difference reducible to differences in memory—the third graders might remember both relevant pieces of information, but as isolated points which they did not put together. Rather, it appears that once again what characterizes the more skilled reader is the ability to integrate or put together information, in this case, information acquired at different times as reading progresses.

Even from this sampling, it is evident that good reading, as evidenced in good comprehension, depends on the orchestration of a variety of interrelated skills; several researchers emphasize that good readers are not only better at these skills when studied singly, but also can move flexibly among them and coordinate them smoothly as appropriate for the reading task at hand. Gibson and Levin have been emphasizing the multifaceted nature of reading since 1975; and information processing theorists such as Carr (1981) and Singer and Crouse (1981) have begun developing models of ways in which different components of the reading process may interrelate in influencing reading performance. It will be interesting to see how our knowledge and understanding of the processes involved in good reading progress over the next decade.

METACOGNITION AND COGNITIVE MONITORING

Cognition consists of all the forms of knowing—learning, perceiving, remembering, and so forth. But each of us also knows a good deal about how we (or others) learn, perceive, remember. *Metacognition* consists of all such knowledge about cognizing, one's own or others'; Brown (1975) calls it *knowing about knowing.* You might think of it as social cognition which deals with knowledge of persons as intelligent beings, in contrast to the work discussed in Chapter 2 which dealt with knowledge of persons as social beings (e.g., Flavell & Wellman, 1977).

Flavell (1979, 1981a, 1981b) distinguishes between metacognitive experiences and metacognitive knowledge. *Metacognitive experiences* occur whenever one becomes aware or conscious of some metacognition—you realize that something you just read didn't make sense, for example, or that you've finally integrated some set of ideas so that you understand them, or that there are different strategies for solving a problem among which you can choose. *Metacognitive knowledge* is everything that one knows or believes about cognizing. Metacognitive knowledge may be about *persons*—for instance, what makes people (including oneself) more or less competent on any intellectual task, or particular skills one may have or lack; about intellectual *tasks*—for example, that more material or more complexity makes a task more difficult, or that remembering the gist of something is easier than remembering word for word; or about *strategies*—how to go about working on different kinds of tasks, advantages or disadvantages of different strategies, and so forth. Finally, *cognitive monitoring* refers to keeping track of how one is doing with some task and regulating behavior accordingly. Suppose, for example, that you hold the metacognition that if you understand what you read you should be able to summarize the main points mentally. You may monitor your understanding by putting yourself through such a review, going back to re-read (or noting that you should do so) if your mental summary is not satisfactory.

In general, children about to start school have very limited metacognitive skills. Situations that would produce metacognitive experiences in older children or adults frequently do not do so in preschool and primary grade children. Markman, for example, cites studies in which children were presented with different types of material which included inconsistent and sometimes clearly contradictory content (Markman, 1981). Younger children were far less likely to notice inconsistencies or to seek clarification; in one study with third and sixth graders, this was true even when they were warned that something would not make sense and told that they were to find it (Markman, 1979). Markman suggests a number of processes through which readers or listeners may monitor their comprehension. In the case of detecting inconsistencies, it is necessary to integrate, and perhaps to apply inferential reasoning to, information given at different points in the material. We saw in the last section that younger children are less likely to integrate material presented in different sentences; that same deficiency may be in part responsible for Markman's results.

Metacognitive deficiencies and failures to monitor performance are evident in many areas of children's learning and problem-solving performance, including at least the following general areas identified by Brown and her co-workers (Brown, 1978, 1980):

1. Recognizing that problem difficulty has increased and that therefore there is a need for strategic intervention (Brown, 1975).
2. Using inferential reasoning to assess the probability that an assumption is true, given the information they already have (Brown, 1978).
3. Predicting the outcome of their attempts at strategy utilization both before and after the fact (Brown & Lawton, 1977).
4. Predicting the task difficulty in a variety of memory and problem-solving situations (Brown, 1978; Tenney, 1975);
5. Planning ahead in terms of strategic study-time appointments (Brown & Campione, 1977; Brown & Smiley, 1978).
6. Monitoring the success of attempts to learn so that termination of such activities can be made when they are successful (and no longer necessary) or unsuccessful, so that new activities can be tried (Brown & Barclay, 1976; Brown, Campione, & Barclay, 1978).

In general, children fail to consider their behavior against sensible criteria, they follow instructions blindly, and they are deficient in self-questioning skills that would enable them to determine these inadequacies (Brown, 1980, p. 457).

Obviously these deficiencies have implications for children's study skills and learning. Brown (1980) points out a number of specific areas where younger children are less effective learners because of their less well-developed metacognitive and monitoring skills. For one, they are less likely to distinguish between material they've mastered and material they have not; perhaps for this reason, when they spend time in studying they are less likely to spend extra time on what they don't know, or know less well. A related issue is that it is often difficult for younger children to distinguish what the main points of a passage may be. In fact, with long and complex passages students may not be able to consistently distinguish ideas at different levels of importance until junior high school age or later (Brown & Smiley, 1977). Of course, if one cannot tell which are the main ideas, one is not likely to spend extra study time on them! Also, when it comes to picking retrieval cues, cues to emphasize in order to help one to remember the material later on, even eighth graders apparently still have difficulty doing so in a flexible and effective manner. Further, younger children have difficulty estimating how ready they are for a test; even with simple materials, it is not until third grade or later that children become able to make such judgments about the state of their own knowledge with some accuracy, and with more complex materials—as they typically use in school in later grades—even older students may have difficulty making such judgments.

Children enter school, then, with little effective metacognitive knowledge and minimal skill at cognitive monitoring. Over the school years their skills in these areas improve dramatically. Their metacognitive knowledge increases enormously; they become familiar with a wider and wider range of strategies and problem-solving approaches. At least with simple materials, by the time they leave grade school they can gauge their own levels of knowledge, distribute study time reasonably effectively, use varying strategies for studying and remembering, and engage in other metacognitive and monitoring activites. At the same time, though, it is clear that metacognitions and their effective applications are far from fully developed when children leave elementary school for middle school or junior high school. As will be suggested below, it may not be until these later years that children really begin to integrate and apply their metacognitive knowledge and monitoring skills effectively when faced with intellectual tasks.

However, there are a number of unresolved issues regarding metacognition and cognitive monitoring, starting with definitional issues. For instance, does a child have to be able to put something into words for it to qualify as a metacognition, or is it sufficient that the child's behavior reflect some monitoring process (which presumably would not occur unless the child held some relevant metacognition?) If only verbally stated knowledge can qualify as metacognition, what are the implications both of changes in verbal skill and also of the considerable difficulty which exists in accurately observing and reporting on one's own behavior, or the behavior of others? Certainly there is no reason to assume that children would find it any easier to be sensitive to cues to intellectual behavior than they find it to be sensitive to cues to social and emotional behaviors (Chapter 2). Further, there are implicit assumptions which are frequently made about the relationship between metacognition and cognitive monitoring. One such assumption is stated above—that unless a child holds some metacognition, relevant cognitive monitoring will not occur. (The relationships does not necessarily work the other way—one could certainly know something without acting on it, and children often do so; production deficiencies could be one example.) So far, though, this is an assumption, and some authors such as Cavanaugh and Perlmutter (1982) insist that we must carefully distinguish between meta-cognition and cognitive monitoring if we are to be able to examine their relationship more closely.

Another issue has to do with the relationship about metacognition and behavior, especially learning behaviors. Authors often assume (as has been done in some of the discussion above) that the better children's metacognitions, the more effective their performance will be. But tests of this assumption for grade school children, which to date have mostly dealt with metamemory and performance on memory tasks, show moderate relationships at best. A good example of results from one carefully done study are shown in Table 4–1, from Cavanaugh and Borkowski (1980). Children included in this study were from kindergarten, first, third, and fifth grades. Metamemory clearly was better at each successive grade level. But the relationships between metamemory and actual remembering were not impressive. Note that while a substantial number of the correlations reported in Table 4–1 were significant (as indicated by asterisks), a substantial number were not; and of those which were significant, none of the correlations were very high. The results summarized in Table 4–1 are averaged across grades, but that apparently made little difference; Cavanaugh and Borkowski found no evidence that the connection between metamemory and memory performance increased between kindergarten and fifth grade.

TABLE 4–1
Correlations between 14 metamemory subtest scores and 8 memory measures

Metamemory subtest	Free sort			Cognitive cuing			Alphabet search	
	Strategy	Recall	Cluster-ing	Strategy	Recall	Cluster-ing	Recall	Cluster-ing
Study time	.31***	.30***	.28***	.19*	.28***	.28***	.19*	.14
Study plan	.30***	.32***	.32***	.32***	.37***	.33***	.28***	.29***
Retrieval: object	−.06	.11	.11	.02	.04	.10	.04	.14***
Retrieval: event.	−.32***	−.22**	−.10	−.19*	−.30***	−.22**	−.27***	−.04***
Memory ability	−.09	.03	.11	.01	−.05	.01	−.19*	−.01
Immediate–delay	−.05	.08	.10	.07	.06	.04	.08	.07
Story–list	−.29***	−.08	.03	−.04	−.09	−.03	−.29***	.02
Opposites–arbitrary	.32***	−.35***	.34***	.28***	.31***	.25***	.34***	.22**
Preparation: object	.41***	.34***	.34***	.20**	.22**	.20**	.24**	.13
Preparation: event	.21**	.24**	.20**	.12	.22**	.21**	.24**	.20**
Colored–uncolored spacing.	.08	.02	.03	.09	.03	−.01	.10	−.03
Savings	−.09	.04	.09	−.09	−.18*	−.16*	−.10	−.04
Retroactive interference	.20**	.32***	.27***	.15*	.20**	.16*	.20**	.09
Rote–paraphrase.	.37***	.37***	.34***	.38***	.36***	.35***	.22*	.10

* $p < .05$.
** $p < .01$.
*** $p < .001$.

Source: J. C. Cavanaugh and J. G. Borkowski, "Searching for Metamemory-Memory Connections: A Developmental Study," *Developmental Psychology* 16 (1980), pp. 441–453.

Why are the relationships between metamemory and memory performance so limited? Perhaps it is only when one looks at metacognitions about particular tasks and performance on those tasks that one finds connections; but analyses performed by Cavanaugh and Borkowski suggest that this explanation does not account for their findings. Or perhaps researchers are not yet asking the appropriate questions about the relationship between metacognition and performance; clarifying definitions as suggested above may be a necessary first step toward defining more appropriate questions. On the other hand, perhaps children having metacognitive knowledge do not put it to use because they do not integrate it into some more general plan which at once takes into account the performance goal to be reached, the strategies which might be used, and the effects of using such strategies. Again, the phenomenon of production deficiency would be congruent with such a suggestion. Such integration of metacognitions, strategies, and performance may be more characteristic of adolescents than of the grade school children with whom we are concerned. Waters (1982), studying 8th- and 10th-grade students, found strong relationships between knowledge of appropriate memory strategies, use of those strategies, and memory performance; comparing her results with the more equivocal results from younger children, she argues that the role of metamemory changes from middle childhood to adolescence. In middle childhood, metamemory, strategy use, and performance are not yet related in predictable ways, but in adolescence they become predictably related to one another. It may be that it is not until children approach adolescence that their metacognitions about people, about strategies, and about tasks and their demands become sufficiently well developed that they can begin to regularly and effectively coordinate them in a planful way. Note, though, that this is not to suggest something new and magical emerging with adolescence, but rather the fruits of cumulative experience with the school-related metacognitions which have been studied to date. Brown (1980) argues with some vigor that metacognitive deficiencies are not the province of children uniquely but are the province of the novice—anyone, child, adolescent, or adult, who is newly encountering some problem area will have to overcome the same kinds of metacognitive deficiencies as have been discussed here.

Finally, there is the question of how children acquire metacognitions and monitoring skills. At one level this question is about training; given that children who do use appropriate strategies generally perform better on a given task than children who do not use such strategies, can one teach the strategies to the nonusers? Results of such training attempts to date have not been especially encouraging. Taking Kramer and Engle's (1981) study as an example, children whose mental age was eight were trained in both the strategy of rehearsal—that is, they were trained to repeat material to be remembered to themselves—and in strategy awareness, which consisted of describing the strategy to themselves. Children trained to rehearse had better same-task recall scores; but strategy awareness training did not affect recall scores, and neither form of training showed much generalization to other similar tasks. Children trained in strategy awareness were more able to verbalize appropriate strategic behavior, but evidently they were not able to integrate this improved strategy knowledge into their performance in effective ways. A different result which may nonetheless be thematically similar is reported by Brown (1980) who comments that while students could be induced to use study aids such as note-taking, underlining, or highlighting which they did not use spontaneously, they typically used such aids less effectively than did students who used them spontaneously. To be helpful, such study strategies should emphasize the main points and concepts in the material being studied. Spontaneous users typically selected such major points for emphasis, but induced users appeared to use the aids more at random, as though they were not sensitive to the thematic organization of the material. In both of these cases, it appears that acquiring a metacognition or a new strategy by itself is insufficient—and if it is true that the crucial thing is integration of metacognitions and strategies into a more general planfulness, such results are just what one would expect. Training children on a specific strategy or meta-cognition would be a little like trying to get children to swim by teaching them to kick their feet. Of course, they will need to know how to kick their feet in order to swim. But to actually swim, they must also know how to move their hands and arms and how to hold their heads up in some way so as to breathe, and in particular how to do all of these things in coordination. Training in particular metacognitions or strategy awareness may contribute to improved performance in the long run, but not until it can be coordinated with other components of planful behavior in an articulated way.

At a more general level, there is the issue of what it is in children's ongoing experience that contributes to the changes in metacognitive skills which are observed over the school years. Little information is available on this question. However, Gardner and Rogoff (1982) suggest that a central role be assigned to shared cognitive activity that takes place whenever an adult (or more experienced problem solver) works with a child, providing assistance on some intellectual task. In order for the two to work together effectively, some common framework must be developed so that the information dealt with is intelligible to both participants; ordinarily the adult will translate concepts and events into terms which are comprehensible to the child. In the course of such mutual intellectual activity the adult structures the activity and also demonstrates both cognitive and metacognitive activities, often inviting the child to practice by repeating the same activities or initating similar ones. Parents will be the primary agents of such joint intellectual enterprises at least until the children are well embarked in school; the parent-child interactions to which Gardner and Rogoff turn to illustrate their points take place between mothers and primary grade children. Once in school, the range of agents with whom such shared intellectual work may take place expands rapidly; teachers undoubtedly provide many such experiences, especially to the extent that they spend time in one-to-one work with individual children. It seems likely too that once children begin to become sensitive to the relevance of metacognitive knowledge and activities, their own active participation in the many intellectual and problem-solving activities in which they engage would provide the basis for inference of relevant metacognitive principles.

SUMMARY

Though the behaviorist revolution in psychology has peaked and passed, contemporary cognitive behaviorists continue to be influenced by a number of orientations introduced by the earlier behaviorists. Among these are an insistence that theorizing about behavior, whether overt or covert, be rooted in variations in observable phenomena, and that the quality of one's observations depend on the quality of one's research methods.

Information processing is one orientation toward human intellectual activity which emphasizes that human intellectual activity is a complex of processes with many interlinking components, and that humans as information processors have both definable capacities and limits. Primarily (though not exclusively) from information processing theory have come contemporary conceptions of memory, including the distinctions between short-term or working memory and long-term or semantic memory; knowledge of the conceptual organization of semantic memory; and knowledge of strategies in memory performance, which change dramatically during the school years. Not only do younger children have fewer strategies, but they show production deficiencies in failing to use those that they do know.

Learning to read is also a complex and multifaceted process, the exact nature of which depends on many factors including the purpose for which one is reading. Among the processes important to reading, this chapter dealt first with prereading skills which are rooted in perception and perceptual learning, such as distinguishing between writing and other symbols or learning to differentiate the distinctive features which define letters. Three developmental trends characterize such perceptual learning. One is that information comes to be picked up from the environment with greater efficiency. A second is that perception moves toward increasing specificity of discrimination; and a third is that with development, children become more skilled at optimizing attention.

Another skill fundamental to reading is phonological segmentation, or being able to differentiate and recognize the phonemes of which words are composed. Many children have considerable difficulty mastering this skill at the conscious level necessary for learning to read, though they manage it fluently when speaking. Such difficulty could stem from insufficiently developed phonemic awareness, or from memory demands required of novices first matching spelling to sound. It may also reflect a psychobiological constraint, in that the adaptive specialization of phonemic segmentation may not be equally accessible to all children.

As for questions of hemispheric specialization and reading, there appears to be little good foundation for the contemporary emphasis on "teaching the right brain." There are indeed important and subtle differences between the right and left hemispheres of the brain, but the differences are not sharp and clear-cut as much of the popular work implies. In fact, at present there is relatively little that can be said with certainty about the relationship between brain functioning and reading skill.

Reading comprehension requires perceptual foundations and phonological segmentation, but it also requires sensitivity to and flexible use of the structure inherent in the material read, and also sensitivity to and retention of content which will permit inference of points not directly expressed in the material. Structure may be important at all levels from frequency of occurrence of letters to the hierarchical organization of themes and ideas. Especially important is the ability to integrate meanings based on the relationships among words and phrases, as opposed to being caught up by words one by one. As for content, good readers relate the meaning of what they read to what they know and in the process infer meanings which are not directly expressed. All of these skills, and others, must be simultaneously and flexibly brought into play if one is to read fluently and with good comprehension.

Finally, metacognition or knowing about knowing, and cognitive monitoring, which is keeping track of how some cognitive process is progressing, are generally only minimally available to preschool and primary grade children, but as the school years progress, metacognitive knowledge, strategy use, and monitoring all progress rapidly. However, even by the end of grade school children still typically do little monitoring of complex or lengthy material; and there is reason to suspect that while the different components of the process are developing rapidly during the school years, it may not be until adolescence that one sees the components being regularly integrated into a more general process of planfulness.

TERMS AND CONCEPTS

behaviorism
cognitive behaviorism
stimulus-response theories
information processing
encoding
decoding
retrieval
storage
short-term memory
long-term memory
semantic memory
semantic integration
strategies of programs for control of
    behavior
memory as knowing how to know
production deficiency
production inefficiency
perceptual learning
differentiation theory
enrichment theories

distinctive features
increasing economy in information
    pick-up
perceptual invariants
cross-modal transfer
increasing specificity of
    discrimination
optimizing attention
incidental learning
phonological segmentation
syllabaries
logographies
phonological recoding
semantic recoding
phonemic awareness
i.daptive specializations
accessibility
cognitive unconscious
hemispheric lateralization
lateral asymmetry of brain function

dyslexia

metacognition

metacognitive experiences

metacognitive knowledge

cognitive monitoring

SUGGESTED ADDITIONAL READING

Brown, A. L. Metacognitive development and reading. In R. J. Spiro, B. C. Bruce, & W. F. Brewer (Eds.), *Theoretical issues in reading comprehension.* Hillsdale, N. J.: Lawrence Erlbaum Associates, 1980.

Carr, T. H. Building theories of reading ability: On the relation between individual differences in cognitive skills and reading comprehension. *Cognition,* 1981, *9,* 73–114.

Gibson, E. J., & Levin, H. *The psychology of reading.* Cambridge, Mass.: MIT Press, 1975.

Harris, L. J. Teaching the right brain: Historical perspectives on a contemporary fad. In C. T. Best (Ed.), *Developmental neuropsychology and education.* New York: Academic Press, 1982.

BOX 5–1
Study questions

Explain why studies of the impact of schooling cannot be done in the United States.

What are formal and informal educational experiences and how do they influence one another?

What are the major differences between schooled and unschooled individuals?

Make some statement of your own educational philosophy and its implication for issues raised in this chapter.

How does participation in early education programs affect low-income children?

Why have comparisons of different educational programs produced equivocal results?

Describe outcomes for children of participation in open versus structured/traditional classrooms.

Define classroom climate, classroom management, and teacher expectations and discuss the outcomes of each for children.

What is the five-to-seven transition? Why is it important for schooling?

How do boys' and girls' school experiences differ?

What considerations must be taken into account when deciding whether and how to assign particular groups of children to programs?

CHAPTER 5

CHILDREN AND SCHOOLS

What difference does it make whether children go to school? Obviously, their social lives are substantially restructured; they spend a considerable amount of time away from home under the jurisdiction of nonparental adults and in the company of a more-or-less fixed group of other children. They are also exposed to a good deal of information which might or might not otherwise be part of their experience—it is hard, for instance, to imagine very many children learning the names of the presidents or the capitals of the 50 states, or even the multiplication tables, if it were not required at some point in school. But might not such social or informational acquisitions be gotten as readily outside of school? Do children who go to school differ intellectually from children who do not, and if so, what are these differences? If there are effects of schooling, can we distinguish further between the outcomes of different types of school programs? These questions are the starting point for the first section of this chapter. In the second section, the attributes of children and the differences such attributes make for school experience will be considered.

THE IMPACT OF SCHOOL

Cross-cultural studies: Does school affect cognition?

To find out whether going to school affects children's intellectual skills, the obvious strategy is to identify individuals who come from similar home and community backgrounds but who differ in whether they are going, or ever have gone, to school. Because schooling is so nearly universal in the United States and other industrialized countries, unschooled groups are nearly impossible to find. In poorer Third World countries, however, it is possible to find groups of individuals of about the same age who have similar backgrounds but who differ in whether or not they went to school. Such studies are complex and difficult to do well. One must control for a host of factors other than schooling which might affect children's intellectual performance, factors such as social class, urban-rural residence, age, presence of intellectually stimulating materials in the home, and so forth. There are also problems in developing materials—they must adequately tap some intellectual skill or capacity but not be unfamiliar or strange for the persons being tested; one cannot simply administer materials developed in the United States to children in rural Guatemala or Kenya and assume their meaning will be the same to all three groups of children. If such factors are not controlled, observable differences may be due to their effects rather than to the effects of schooling.

To illustrate some of the complexities of such studies, Stevenson (1982) describes a research project in which Peruvian children were studied. The children came from three quite different geographical areas; a major city, villages on a highland plain, and villages located in a rain forest. About half the children in each age group had had no schooling; the others were in grades one, two, or three. There were equal numbers of girls and boys. Each child completed a battery of tests which included achievement tests; a variety of memory tasks; learning by observation and learning by trial-and-error; use of analogies, seriation, and other conceptual tasks. Not surprisingly, the children in school outperformed the nonschooled children on most of these tasks.

Parent interviews revealed no systematic basis for keeping children home or sending them to school, so schooled and unschooled children did not differ systematically in this regard. However, a closer look at family characteristics revealed a number of ways in which the family experiences of children in school differed from that of nonschool children, despite their other apparent similarities. Fathers of school children had significantly more education than did fathers of children not in school (mothers had little education in general, and no similar effect was found for them). In the rural areas, fathers of school children were also more likely to be literate. (This comparison was irrelevant in the city where nearly all fathers were literate, but note the difference in backgrounds for urban and rural children.) Similarly, the likelihood that items such as electricity, books, radios, machines of any sort, toys, or any of five other such items were present in the home was significantly greater for children in school. So, too, was the likelihood that children had encountered out-of-school teaching at home, such as learning numbers, colors, money, and so forth. Further analyses showed that variables such as these were not only correlated with children's performance on individual cognitive tasks, but they accounted for a quarter to a half of the variance in children's performance; in other words, much of the difference between schooled and unschooled children was the result, not of their having been in school, but of home and background factors which were correlated with their being in school. Such results leave one wondering whether schooling per se was contributing anything to the difference between the schooled and unschooled groups. Stevenson and his co-workers, having evaluated the background factors, were then in a position to see whether there were still any differences after such factors were taken into account. The answer is a clear yes; the differences were not large, but there were highly significant correlations between schooling and performance on the different tasks.

What does such information suggest for our understanding of children in urbanized countries such as the United States? Many factors, such as parents' education, availability of books and other sources of intellectual stimulation in the home, parents as models for reading and engaging in intellectual activities, parents' participation with children in problem-solving activities, peers' involvement in school and intellectual interests, and other home and neighborhood factors, have been related to children's school aptitude and school performance in these countries as well, and such factors differ by socioeconomic class. They are more frequently present in middle- and upper- than in lower-socioeconomic status homes. Perhaps these and other out-of-school experiences, including informal instruction from parents, peers, and others, are as much a source of the intellectual changes taking place during the school years as are the formal school experiences to which we tend to attribute such changes. Greenfield and Lave (1982), discussing their own studies of informal instruction in weaving among rural Indian girls in Mexico and in tailoring among apprenticed boys in Monrovia, Liberia, came to the following conclusions when they compared their findings with information about formal classroom education.

1.   Instructional techniques in informal learning situations are quite varied, as are instructional techniques in formal situations. Language may be used more systematically and extensively in formal education, but verbal instructions and explanations are clearly important in informal learning as well.

2.   Learning by observation and by doing may be more central in informal than in formal learning settings, but "teachers" in informal learning situations provide a great deal of organization of learning experience, taking into account the attributes and level of skill of the learner with whom they are working. Imagine, for example, how the same mother might act when providing cooking lessons for a 5-year-old making her first batch of brownies and for her 11-year-old son who won a blue ribbon for his muffins at last year's 4-H fair. So informal learning experiences are not necessarily just haphazard, unstructured, untutored events from which children must glean what they can on their own.

3.   What is learned in either formal or informal educational settings will generalize to related problem situations that can be recognized as such. Children don't necessarily learn the same things in the two types of settings— although they may—but what is learned in either case can generalize in limited ways.

4.   Finally, there are the mutual influences of educational settings on each other within any culture, as was evident in Stevenson's study; and children are influenced by all of the forms of teaching to which they are exposed, whether it takes place in a formal school setting or not. Children in some cultural contexts may have little opportunity for formal schooling, but this is not to say that they will not learn a great deal by informal means; and in urbanized settings, children

have a wide variety of both formal and informal educational experiences, all of which influence their development.

However, Stevenson (1982) did also find effects of schooling per se on children's intellectual performance. Can anything further be said about such differences in intellectual functioning? If we look at older individuals—young adults, say—do those who have been to school still perform differently than those who have not, or was the difference observed only a temporary advantage with unschooled individuals "catching up" over time?

There are some differences that persist over time. Among those discussed by Rogoff (1981) in her comprehensive review are the following.

1. Schooled and unschooled groups differ in perceptual performance on tasks that involve perceptual analysis, such as disembedding figures from backgrounds or analyzing patterns, and on tasks that require interpreting cues for depth in two-dimensional representations. Unschooled children and adults are less likely to be familiar with Western conventions for two-dimensional representation of depth, which we are apt to take for granted.

2. On memory tasks that can be performed more efficiently by using organizational strategies, unschooled groups do not do as well as schooled groups, though they can perform just as well if some organizational strategy is provided for them. (It sounds as though unschooled individuals, even as adults, are more likely to show production deficiencies for such organizational strategies.) However, once something is learned, there is no difference between schooled and unschooled groups in how well it is retained over time.

3. Classification and concept formation tasks tend to be approached differently, with schooled subjects making use of taxonomic categories—foods, animals, having three angles—whereas unschooled subjects are more likely to group objects according to functional relationships—the *knife* peels the *potatoes* which go in the *pot* to cook; the *flour* and *butter* are mixed with the *spoon* to make bread. (How would a schooled participant group the six key items, which are underscored?) This difference seems to reflect differences in interpretation of the task, rather than differences in cognitive competencies; unschooled subjects can usually use taxonomic categories perfectly well if they can be induced to do so, but they do not find them especially meaningful.

4. When problems of logic, such as syllogisms (In the north, all bears are white. John is in the north. What color are the bears he sees?) are presented verbally, unschooled participants have great difficulty, often refusing to accept the hypothetical problem posed. They appear reluctant to accept such verbal premises unless they themselves have had some relevant personal experience. Schooled participants show no such reluctance, accepting the premises and reasoning hypothetically as though about matters of fact. Again, this difference appears to be one of style rather than ability; the disagreement appears to be over what type of evidence is necessary before one can make statements about some issue, with schooled subjects using *"theoretic"* reasons based on reasoning while unschooled individuals prefer *"empiric"* reasons based in their own experience (Scribner, 1975).

5. And, of course, there are the differences between schooled and un-schooled persons in performance on Piaget's tasks which suggest that formal operational thinking is associated with industrialized, urbanized settings; these studies were referred to in Chapter 1.

So schools do have some long-lasting impact on intellectual skills, influencing the ways in which children learn to apply basic cognitive processes (accepting hypothetical premises or not; producing strategies or not) though not necessarily on the processes themselves (both groups could remember equally well once something was learned; both groups could use taxonomic categories, though they were not equally likely to so do.) Perhaps because there is no point in studying causes until one can be sure there is some phenomenon to be studied, notions about the ways in which schools achieve such observed effects are still largely speculative. However, Rogoff (1981) identifies four such speculations that have been made. One is that the cognitive changes observed come about as a result of the emphasis in schools on searching for general rules, looking for the general reasons to explain why some specific instance is true. A second has to do with the effect of instruction in words, out of context; virtually all school instruction is done by the verbal medium. (Readers might consider their mode of learning about children with this text, as well as related class events such as lectures, in contrast to learning through interactions with children.)

A third proposed mechanism through which schooling might affect cognitive activities is through specific skills taught in schools. Tests of cognitive skills, such as memory tests or information tests, are not often encountered outside of schools; nor are many types of tasks such as classification tasks. So becoming proficient at strategies for such tasks may be a relatively school-specific achievement. And finally, there are those who argue that literacy itself may be responsible for the changes observed. Writing, for example, may require some analytical separation of thought from situational context (e.g., Greenfield, 1972); or literacy itself may be viewed as the mastery of a particular technology which extends cognitive activities in particular ways (Olson, 1976, 1977).

Educational programs and their effects

Having established that schooling does affect children's cognitive skills, let us turn to the question of educational programs and their effects. As you will see, this question is as complex and difficult to address as was the question of the effects of schooling per se.

Philosophies   One reason that evaluation of programs is difficult is that there is considerable disagreement about what schools should be like. What values or philosophies should they reflect? What classroom practices might be effective in implementing given desired outcomes? Should schools emphasize the "three Rs" or should they emphasize personal growth and self-worth? Should children follow a clearly structured academic plan, or should they decide for themselves what they study and when? Should schools be viewed as primarily custodial institutions whose main function is to keep children off the street, or should they be actively involved in all aspects of childrearing, including the development of morals and values? However questions like these are answered obviously determines the emphasis of any educational program.

Both educators and people in general (who frequently consider themselves knowledgeable about education) often have strong opinions on such questions. They hold deep-seated convictions—*Commitments,* as Dunkin and Biddle (1974) call them—that The Answer to more successful education lies in progressive education, or open classrooms, or behavior modification, or stricter discipline and emphasis on the three Rs. The intensity with which schools are criticized stems in large measure from such Commitments. The problem is how to resolve the differences among different Commitments—a problem complicated by the fact that many of the issues in question are matters of value rather than fact (for example, should schools explicitly teach morality, or is this usurping the rights of families?) as well as by the frequent unavailability of adequate evidence on which to judge the factual issues (which classroom practices are associated with which effects on which children)?

Issues such as these pervade research and discussion about school programs. Any given research or evaluation outcome may mean different things depending on the values and philosophies of the person considering that outcome. To anticipate a recurring theme, there are no simple answers regarding programs and their effectiveness.

Early education programs   One group of programs that has been extensively studied is early education programs intended to enhance the school performance of children from low-income homes. Such children are educationally at risk, being much more likely than children from middle-class homes to do poorly in school. There are many reasons for this; one is that the family backgrounds of such children do not provide them with school-related skills which would facilitate their school success. (One could argue that there is less connection between formal and informal education for them than for children from better-off families.) If this is the case, then perhaps early educational intervention could provide some of the skills low-income children are less likely to get through informal educational experiences. During the 1960s, such reasoning led to the institution of a variety of early education programs; many were under private auspices, but the largest and most familiar of such programs are those included in the U.S. government-sponsored Project Head Start.

Have such programs been effective? Box 5–2 shows a summary of outcomes based on research published between 1969 and 1976. From this summary it is clear that at least for children in full-year Head Start programs, there were significant gains not only in intellectual skills, but in social and family interactions as well. Critics argued that such gains were not always very large, that intellectual gains had often "washed out" by the time the children reached the later grades, and that in spite of interventions poor children were still doing less well in school than were better-off children. Yet, if intellectual functioning is flexible enough to be influenced by a year of special experiences, it should come as no surprise that that same flexibility results in re-adaptation once the special

BOX 5-2
Project Head Start: Its impact on children and families

What effects have research and evaluation studies found attributable to children's participation in Project Head Start? When research findings from national surveys, dissertations, and literature reviews published between 1969 and 1976 were summarized, Head Start was associated with the following outcomes.

Positive outcomes. These scores or effects were significantly greater for Head Start participants than for nonparticipants:

Intelligence test scores, for participants in full-year programs.

Academic achievement, for participants in full-year programs.

Cognitive development, for participants in full-year programs.

Socially mature behavior.

Physical health.

Attitudes of parents of participating children toward them.

Increased positive interaction of mothers with their children.

Neutral findings. No significant differences between Head Start participants and nonparticipants were found for these outcomes:

Cognitive development, for participants in summer programs only.

Intellectual performance of children enrolled in different types of Head Start Programs.

Self-concepts of participating children, unless their program included a high degree of parent involvement.

Source: Adapted from Ada Jo Mann, Adele Harrell, and Maure Hurt, Jr., *A Review of Head Start Research since 1969 and an Annotated Bibliography*, U.S. Department of Health, Education, and Welfare: DHEW Publication NO. (OHDS) 78-31102, 1977.

experience is no longer available. As Klaus and Gray (1968) point out, it isn't reasonable to expect a year's experience to act as an inoculation or "shot in the arm" which makes children's intellectual performance impervious to the effects of later experiences.

Furthermore, the critics may have been unduly pessimistic about longer-term effects of early education programs. In an unusual collaborative study reported by Lazar and Darlington (1982), low-income children who had participated in each of 12 different early education programs were followed up when they were between the ages of 9 and 19. Of those children participating in early programs, significantly more were able to meet their school's requirements, and significantly fewer were assigned to special education classes or retained in grade than were children in control groups that had not attended early education classes. In addition, children in the early education programs scored higher on IQ tests for several years following their participation in the program, and there was some evidence that they did better on achievement tests as well. Looking more specifically at one of the projects included in the collaborative study, the Perry

Preschool Project of Ypsilanti, Michigan (Schweinhart & Weikart, 1980), by age 15 students who had participated in this program had test scores a full grade higher than those of nonparticipant control children. Furthermore, only half as many of the program participants than of controls required special education services. There were other interesting effects as well: the proportion of preschool graduates showing antisocial or delinquent behavior was substantially lower than the proportion of nongraduates showing such behavior, and preschool graduates were more likely to hold afterschool jobs.

From these studies, early education experiences certainly appear to have some important long-range consequences not only for intellectual performance, but also for social behaviors. It is the case that early education graduates still do not, on the average, do as well in school as do children from middle-class backgrounds. If equal levels of performance for children from all socioeconomic backgrounds is a criterion, then early education programs have not succeeded. But such a criterion may be unrealistically demanding. Meanwhile, the real gains children have achieved through such programs are certainly of value. Not only are the children doing better in school, their success appears to persist to later grades; students' opportunities for satisfaction and pride in their school work are increased and occasions leading to frustration decreased. Furthermore, the reduction in need for costly special education services represents substantial financial savings for school districts that have such early educational programs. Early education programs may not be the magic key to achieving full educational equity for students from all backgrounds, but they are a step in that direction.

Comparing programs: Project Follow Through   In the preceding sections, we have dealt with formal schooling in general, making the case that schools do influence cognitive development and that early educational programs do have significant effects on the school performance and achievement of low-income children. But schools come in a variety of forms, reflecting the influence of different educational philosophies and modes of implementation of those philosophies. A program based on Piaget's theory, for example, might attempt to maximize children's opportunities for exploration and action on materials and ideas. Another kind of program might emphasize mastery of skills through drill and practice; yet another might also emphasize mastery of skills but use reinforcement techniques such as *performance contracting,* where teacher and child agree on a set of specific educational objectives and, on achieving those objectives, the child is reinforced by being allowed some special activity or other reward. Still other programs may be based on the assumption that social outcomes, such as self-expression, understanding of self and others, and working effectively with others, are at least as important outcomes of schooling as are the more traditional academic achievements.

Do such program variations make a difference? That is, do children learn better under one type of program than another? One difficulty should immediately be obvious. In dealing with programs based on such different philosophies, what is it that children should learn better? If such different programs are effective in accomplishing what they wish, then each might legitimately claim that it is most effective—and be correct for the outcomes valued in the philosophy the program reflects. It is at points like this that variations in philosophy, and the Commitments people hold, may become bases for intense disagreement and contention between different groups.

But all of this may be moot. Some critics argue that such program variations make no difference of any importance (e.g., Coleman, Campbell, Hobson, Mc-Portland, Mood, Weinfeld, & York, 1966; Jencks, 1972). One basis for such an argument is that children's school experience is so interlinked with their home and neighborhood experiences—their informal educational experiences—as to add little or nothing to them. Another basis rests in studies that suggest that children's school performance (given that socioeconomic status is controlled) shows little variation regardless of differences in school or program attributes such as physical plant, available facilities, teacher-pupil ratios, average length of teacher experience.

Comparison of these latter attributes may not provide a reasonable test of differences among programs, however. Knowing the type of physical resources does not indicate how they are used; knowing the teacher's years of experience tells nothing about what actually happens in teacher-pupil interchanges. If one wants to know what school personnel mean when they claim to have some particular type of program, one needs to know not only the philosophy, but the execution—how is the program implemented in actual classroom practices? What do children actually experience in such programs? To answer such questions, one must observe classrooms representing different types of programs. The observations can then be compared to see in what ways, if any, the programs differ in actual practice. If they differ, then one can try to find out whether the variations make a difference in outcomes, such as achievement test scores or other measures.

To conduct such a study is a truly gargantuan undertaking. However, comparisons of different primary grade programs participating in Project Follow Through do provide one such study. Project Follow Through was intended to be an extension of Project Head Start. Under the auspices of the U.S. government, a variety of education programs designed for children in kindergarten through third grade participated. The programs varied from highly structured to open or nonstructured; any given program was usually implemented in several sites or geographical locations. An early report by Stallings (1975) based on obser- vations of first- and third-grade classrooms representing seven programs as they were implemented in 36 different towns and cities was quite positive. Each of the seven programs proved to be distinctive; on the basis of the observations alone, raters could usually tell which program a given classroom represented and could also differentiate the Follow Through classrooms from the non-Follow Through classrooms that were observed for comparison purposes.

Not only were the programs distinguishable, according to the analyses re- ported by Stallings, they also influenced children in different ways. Achievement in reading and mathematics was greatest for both first- and third-grade children in programs providing systematic, structured instruction in these areas and where textbooks and programmed workbooks were used. Children enrolled in such programs also showed the greatest task persistence. However, children from such programs were also absent from school more often, an important point if increased absence reflects lower interest in school. In contrast, children from more flexible, less structured programs in which a wide variety of activities were available scored higher on Raven's Coloured Progressive Matrices, a test of nonverbal perceptual problem solving. They were also more independent, and they engaged in cooperative activity with one another more often. These outcomes seem reasonable; they appear to suggest that children's strengths in cognitive activities will reflect the emphasis of the programs in which they are enrolled.

These differences in children's performance were not simply a matter of the children's ability. Instructional practices accounted for about one third of first-grade children's achievement in math and for about one fourth of their achievement in reading, and the proportions were higher for third graders. So it appears (from this report) that the pessimistic statements of critics about the effectiveness of classroom practices were a result of looking at inappropriate evidence.

However, these positive conclusions may be premature. A later, more comprehensive analysis (Stebbins, St. Pierre, Proper, Anderson, & Cerva, 1977; Bock, Stebbins & Proper, 1977) set off a series of lively interchanges and disagreements. Points of contention ranged from problems in the way the study was originally conducted to the ways in which model programs were summarized and grouped for analysis to the conclusions that were drawn regarding program effectiveness. Most germane for this discussion is the observation that implementation of any given program varied enormously from site to site (even Stallings, 1975, reported considerable intersite variation). In fact, there was typically more difference between implementations of a given program at different sites than there was between the different programs themselves. Given this variation, whether programs could be reliably distinguished from one another was a point of disagreement, with the authors of the initial report (Stebbins et al., 1977) maintaining that they could, whereas authors of the criticism of the report (House, Glass, McLean, & Walker, 1978) suggesting that they could not. Thus it appears that even when educators accept some educational philosophy and teachers are trained in some program implementing that philosophy, what actually happens in the classroom depends at least as much and perhaps more upon local conditions—the particular school and teacher, the particular families and neighborhoods the program serves—than on the educational orientation per se.

The authors of the original report (Stebbins et al., 1977) suggested that not only could one find some reliable (if small) differences between programs despite their internal variation from site to site, but that such differences did not necessarily place pupils enrolled in Follow Through programs at an advantage compared with other similar children not enrolled in Follow Through. When such differences did favor Follow Through participants, the programs were likely to be those emphasizing basic skills, such as vocabulary, arithmetic computation, spelling and language (Stebbins et al., 1977; Anderson, St. Pierre, Proper & Stebbins, 1978). This latter conclusion was widely publicized in the national press as supporting the contention that "basics are best."

Critics (e.g., House et al., 1978) countered by arguing that if one grouped the Follow Through programs in other but equally defensible ways, the apparent superiority of programs emphasizing basic skills disappeared. They also challenged the definition of "basic skills"—why, they asked, are only the mechanical skills that require rote learning emphasized as basic, rather than those skills classed separately as cognitive-conceptual, such as "learning to learn" and problem-solving skills? Surely, these skills are also essential for children. (Note the role of educational philosophies here—different emphasis on what is important in education and what its outcome should be.) For these and other reasons, their conclusion is that there is no foundation for concluding that model programs emphasizing basic skills are superior in their effects to other types of programs. (Readers interested in further information about the different positions should read the papers cited above which appeared in *The Harvard Educational Review,* 1978).

At present, then, it appears that no firm conclusions about the effects of different programs can be drawn. It is true that individual programs within models are different from one locale to another, which is probably one important reason why overall comparisons of programs are so limited. If there are differences between programs, the limited evidence supports the contention that children do best at that which is stressed in the program they attend; children drilled in the mechanics of reading and arithmetic will score higher on achievement tests that tap those skills than will children not so prepared. But any such differences, if they exist, are small. Children clearly learn in all types of programs.

Open and structured classrooms   One of the dimensions on which all programs vary, and a dimension which has been a focus of considerable interest in recent decades, is their degree of openness versus structure. The general premise on which *open classrooms* are based is that of giving children freedom to learn in their own way. (There are some definitions of open classrooms that refer only to architectural structure, whether or not there are walls between defined classrooms. However, our concern is primarily with those definitions that involve the activities in which children and teachers engage.) *Structured or traditional classrooms,* with seats all in rows, children working on the same materials at the same time, and structured lesson plans, are claimed to be unduly restrictive, providing little opportunity for creativity or for personal development, and perhaps—by making the questionable assumption that all children in a classroom can learn the same thing at the same time in the same way—even interferring with effective learning (for example, see Ginsberg, 1972).

Do the more flexible practices in open classrooms in fact foster creativity and self-esteem as well as promote learning? The first complication in trying to answer this question is defining an open classroom or a traditional classroom: there is no single clear definition (Good, Biddle, & Brophy, 1975; Horwitz, 1979). A number of different attributes have been used to classify classrooms as open rather than traditional: children rather than teachers setting the educational objectives; greater diversity of materials and activities; flexible use of

FIGURE 5–1   A traditional classroom. Traditional classrooms reflect the philosophy that there is a body of academic knowledge which children learn best when it is presented in a structured way in a structured setting.

Photograph courtesy of Patricia Hollander Gross—Stock, Boston

FIGURE 5–2   An open classroom. Open classrooms reflect the philosophy that children not only learn best but develop best personally and socially when they are free to structure their own learning experiences according to their own interests in a flexible setting with many resources.

Photograph courtesy of Elizabeth Hamlin—Stock, Boston

space, including (but not requiring) the design of physical space so that chairs, tables, and room partitions are movable; pacing or timing of movement from one activity to the next made by the student rather than the teacher; little or no large-group instruction; classes grouped by interest rather than by age or achievement level; lessons and materials developed by students rather than teachers; student participation in rule making; activities selected by children on the basis of their own interests rather than by teachers; children rather than teachers initiating teacher-child interaction; children allowed to interact freely with one another (Traub, Weiss, Fisher, & Musella, 1973; Katz, 1972). Classrooms called open will have some of these attributes, but they may have any combination of them in varying degrees. Consequently, open classrooms may be very different from one another, and research has not yet made clear the extent to which their various attributes affect different outcomes for children. A similar point can be raised regarding classrooms described as "traditional." This is probably one reason why many studies comparing open and traditional classrooms have yielded mixed results—they have not looked explicitly enough at what was actually happening in these classrooms, so they may be lumping together classrooms in which very different things are happening.

Studies of open or informal programs in effect in the 1960s and earlier showed generally positive outcomes of such programs for children (Horwitz, 1979). For example, Minuchin, Biber, Shapiro, and Zimiles (1969) compared fourth-grade classrooms in four schools, two of which were open and two traditional. Children in the more structured classrooms had higher achievement test scores. Children from both types of programs did equally well on problem-solving tasks designed to require flexibility of thinking, while children from the open classrooms far outperformed children from the traditional classrooms on group problem-solving tasks that required effective intellectual cooperation. There were no systematic differences in self-concept between children from the two types of classrooms though there were suggestions that children from the two types of classrooms based their feelings about themselves on somewhat different criteria. And children in open classrooms—boys as well as girls—liked school better than did children from traditional classrooms.

Results of studies appearing in the 1960s and 1970s have not been as clear-cut, however. Horwitz (1979) located about 200 studies relating open versus structured classroom experience (however defined) to a number of different child outcomes. Of primary interest are effects related to academic achievement, which was examined in 102 of the studies Horwitz found. Of these, 14 favored open schools, 12 favored traditional schools; 29 found mixed results, and 47 found no significant differences. Clearly, children enrolled in either type of classroom are as likely to do well on measures of achievement as not.

What of other types of child outcomes? Results were also mixed for many of these. In 61 studies that measured self-concept, for example, children enrolled in open schools scored higher in 15 studies while children in traditional schools scored higher in two studies, 15 studies were mixed, and 29 found no significant differences. Studies of adjustment and of anxiety showed similar mixed patterns with no clear advantage for children in either type of classroom; so also did studies of locus of control (the extent that persons feel they have control over their own destinies). On several other outcomes, however, the results (though not unmixed) leaned in favor of children in open classrooms. These outcomes included attitude toward school, with 40 percent of 57 studies showing more positive attitudes among children in open schools, but only 4 percent showing more positive attitudes among children in traditional schools; creativity, where 36 percent of 33 studies found differences favoring open classrooms while none found differences favoring traditional classrooms; curiosity, where 43 percent (of 14 studies) found differences in favor of open classrooms while none showed differences in favor of traditional classrooms; and cooperation, where 67 percent of 9 studies found differences favoring open classrooms while none found differences favoring traditional classrooms. (In all cases, the remaining studies found either mixed results or no significant differences.) All of these differences that tend to favor open classrooms are in areas which their proponents claim that they foster.

Why were there not even any trends favoring one or the other type of classroom on measures of achievement? One major reason is likely that the questions are asked too globally. At a relatively superficial level, this is to suggest that different areas of academic achievement require different cognitive skills which may not be fostered by the same educational experiences. Reading comprehension, composition or writing skills, and mathematical achievement may be differently facilitated by a given program; the experiences that foster early learning of arithmetic facts and spelling may not be the same ones that foster reading comprehension and problem-solving skills in later grades.

Going further, however, it may not be sufficient to look at some criterion measure following completion of some educational program. Carr and Evans (1981) argue that it may be necessary instead to make much more fine-grained analyses of the learning conditions—just what transpires between teachers and children in actual classrooms; of the children's basic cognitive abilities, which after all are what they bring to bear on learning the task; and of the interrelationships among all of these. Carr and Evans applied this approach to evaluation of early reading instruction and found differences clearly favoring structured instruction for early reading achievement. The children were first graders enrolled in one of two groups of classrooms which were about the same in size and in student socioeconomic status. One group of classrooms was run along relatively traditional, teacher-centered lines; the other, along more open or student-centered lines. In both curricula the pupils spent about the same amounts of time in reading intact text. However, students in the traditional classes spent about three fifths of their time in teacher-supervised group instruction and desk activity, making use of basal readers, phonics drills, and practice at using context appropriately to aid in word recognition. Children in the open classrooms spent about three fifths of their time in tutorial or independent study; they engaged in more imaginative play and peer interaction, and reading was learned through self-generation of stories and making personal sight-word banks.

When Carr and Evans speak of measuring basic cognitive abilities, they do not mean scores from IQ or other ability tests. Rather, they are talking of specific abilities expected to be important for the cognitive task in question. Thus, in addition to two measures of reading skill, they measured three aspects of information processing ability, and three measures of language complexity. The two measures of reading skill were significantly higher for children in the traditional classrooms; there were no significant differences between instruction groups on the other measures, so the reading difference cannot simply be attributed to them. More tellingly, when patterns of intercorrelations among measures were examined, five of six of the correlations between information processing and reading were higher for children from teacher-directed classrooms, and the information processing measures were more closely related to one another in the teacher-directed classrooms. Apparently, this form of instruction facilitated the children's application of information processing skills to reading.

As for the intercorrelations among reading and language measures, four of the six correlations were significant and positive in traditional classrooms, but significantly *negative*—meaning that higher language skills were associated with *poorer* reading performance—among the open classrooms. Carr and Evans suggest that this apparently paradoxical finding reflects the fact that general language skills can be applied to reading only to the extent that one has good print-specific encoding mechanisms—such as are emphasized in the teacher-directed classrooms—and that such skills are learned most readily when there is systematic instruction and corrective feedback. Further, when print-specific mechanisms are not well-established but a child has good language skills, the likelihood of making errors based on interpretation from context is increased, thus producing the paradoxical negative relationship among these early readers. As the children's print-specific skills improve (which they will do; even in student-centered classrooms, children's reading skills eventually improve), this negative relationship should decline.

Carr and Evans' findings once again appear to support the general point made earlier: Children learn what they are taught. But they make their point much more explicitly: If what children are taught meets the task requirements with which they are faced, and makes it possible for them to use the relevant cognitive capabilities effectively, then their performance will be enhanced. But to make such analyses requires more finegrained measures of the educational process, of children's cognitive capacities, of the task requirements of skills children are to master, and of the outcomes of training in children's performance than has generally been done. Perhaps the inconclusive outcomes not only of much research on open and structured classrooms, but also on effects of different model programs reflect the global levels at which the research questions have been asked.

TEACHERS

Whatever the aims of an educational program, it is teachers who actually interact with children. Whatever outcomes appear for children necessarily reflect teachers and their activities in the classroom. This general point has been recognized for years, and a sizable body of information about teachers has developed. Unfortunately, it is only in the last decade or two that researchers have started to make the kind of detailed observation of what teachers actually do that can serve as a satisfactory basis for identifying good and poor teaching (for example, see Dunkin & Biddle, 1974; Good et al., 1975).

Classroom climate

Classroom climate refers to the social atmosphere a teacher generates in interaction with a given class of pupils. Is the teacher warm or cold? Directive (lecturing, giving instructions) or indirective (allowing flexibility, raising questions)? Democratic or authoritarian? Is instruction teacher-centered or learner-centered? The idea that children fare better in some climates than in others has been the source of a great deal of research, and there is what amounts to a Commitment in many circles that a good teacher creates a classroom climate characterized by such attributes as learner-centeredness, warmth, and democratic interchange with students.

However, Dunkin and Biddle (1974) reviewed more than 100 studies of classroom climate and the outcome was sobering. They focused on warmth and directiveness as two major themes running through several ways of classifying classroom climate. There was some agreement that teachers in U.S. classrooms are usually directive rather than nondirective, and that they tend to be emotionally neutral rather than warm or cold: they give relatively little praise, attention, or criticism. However, when efforts were made to determine the relationship between these variables and such outcomes as children's attitudes and achievement, the results were generally contradictory and inconclusive. It is likely that the questions have been asked in the wrong way; and Dunkin and Biddle point out a number of serious flaws in the studies done to date, beginning with inadequate definition—exactly what is meant by, or to be recorded as, warm behavior or directive behavior? It may also be that classroom climate really makes little difference for children's learning or attitudes. At this point the evidence is simply insufficient.

Classroom management

How to maintain discipline and regulate student behavior is an issue of considerable interest and concern to teachers. However, it is beginning to appear that how teachers handle discipline problems per se is less important than their *classroom management*—how they organize and structure the flow of classroom acitivities in order to keep students active and to minimize disruption. Kounin (1970) originally set out to compare the discipline practices of two groups of teachers, one group with classrooms which ran smoothly and another group with classrooms which were more or less chaotic. To his surprise, he was unable to find any consistent patterns of differences in the handling of disciplinary incidents by the two groups of teachers. Rather, he found that the two groups differed in their management of the flow of activities, their pacing of activities so as to keep students involved without "losing" them, the variety of activities they made available to students, and so forth. Disciplinary incidents were minimized in the classrooms of teachers who were good managers because the students were more involved in their work and less likely to act up. In particular, the good managers had an attribute which Kounin called *withitness* (yes, really!). They were alert to what was happening throughout their classrooms, so that if a child was between activities and getting bored (fertile ground for disruptive behavior) or a fracas was brewing in a corner of the room, they were often able to pick this up and redirect the children's activities, thus preventing disciplinary incidents.

Classroom management is related to children's academic achievement as well as their behavior in class. Brophy and Evertson (1976) observed second- and third-grade teachers whose classes had shown consistent gains (whether high or low) on achievement tests over a period of years. The effective teachers—those whose classes consistently showed high achievement gains—were also effective classroom managers. They set up systems to ensure that children knew what they were to do and when and how to get help if they needed it. The effective teachers also provided additional options for children who had finished assignments. They evidently matched assignments to individual children's levels of skill successfully, since children in their classrooms were much less likely either to finish quickly and have nothing to do or to give up in frustration. Much of this organization consists of what Brophy and Evertson called *proactive structuring:* before entering the classroom, the teachers planned and prepared materials and activities for a variety of contingencies which might materialize. Brophy and Evertson also point out that effective teaching is not a matter of mastering some basic set of "teaching skills," but of knowing and orchestrating a wide variety of different skills to match the requirements of the children in the classroom.

Teacher expectation

Does what a teacher expects of a child affect that child's school performance and test scores? One early study found significant increases in the IQ scores of first and second graders who had been identified to their teachers as "spurters" from whom rapid development could be expected during the school year. The children had actually been chosen at random (Rosenthal & Jacobson, 1968).

The idea is that teacher expectancies for children can become self-fulfilling prophecies. The teacher, perhaps by interacting differently with children for whom different expectancies are held, may elicit differential responses from the children so that they perform in the ways that the teacher expects. Needless to say, such an effect would indicate a source of considerable teacher influence over children—and one with some very sobering implications, given the widely held expectancies associated with sterotypes of boys and girls, of very poor children, of ethnic minority children, and so forth.

Such effects may exist, but they are not always found, are usually not very strong, may be greater for some groups of children than for others, and may affect other measures of performance more than they affect IQ scores (see Brophy &

Good, 1974). Some studies have found no effects of teacher expectancies (for example, Claiborn, 1969; José, 1971). At the beginning of the school year Fleming and Anttonen (1971) gave four kinds of test information to 39 second-grade teachers, none of whom knew the purpose of the study until after it was completed. For one group of children, actual IQ scores were given; for another group, inflated IQ scores; for a third group, mental ability profiles; and for the fourth group, no test information. The type of information given made no difference for children's achievement test scores, self-concept, or grades at the end of the year. In general, the teachers were sensitive to the children's actual performance and, in fact, often thought that the inflated IQ scores were inaccurate.

On the other hand, Sutherland and Goldschmid (1974) found that whether or not IQ change occurred depended on which subgroup of children one looked at. Rather than give the teachers IQ score information, they had second-grade teachers without test information rank children for estimated academic potential at the end of the second month of school. Overall, there was no relationship between teachers' expectations and change in IQ score over a five-month period. But when Sutherland and Goldschmid took children whose tests scores were high or low, and then compared the children for whom teachers' expectations were concordant with (matched) or discrepant from (did not match) the test scores, the picture changed (see Table 5–1). There was still no difference for the low-ability children, but there were significant declines in the IQ test scores of the high-ability children for whom teachers held the discordant expectation that their academic potential was average.

Even though the direct effects of teacher expectations on particular children may be small, there are more general effects of teachers' attitudes on children's performance. Fleming and Anttonen (1971) asked teachers how important they considered IQ and achievement tests. Children taught by teachers who held high

TABLE 5– 1

Changes in IQ scores of low-ability and high-ability children when teachers' expectations were concordant with or discrepant from the children's tested ability.

Group	N	Test	Expectation	Average IQ	Average IQ difference	t	df	p
Low-intelligence range (80–95)								
Concordant	8	WISC	Below average/poor	90.50	14.63⎫	0.75	14	N.S.
Discrepant	8	WISC	Average	89.25	18.88⎭			
Concordant	10	L–T	Below average/poor	86.60	11.90⎫	0.66	19	N.S.
Discrepant	11	L–T	Average	87.90	15.18⎭			
High-intelligence range (120–135)								
Concordant	10	WISC	Above average/superior	126.80	13.50⎫	2.85	18	.01
Discrepant	10	WISC	Average	125.00	3.40⎭			
Concordant	7	L–T	Above average/superior	127.29	0.14⎫	1.87	14	.05
Discrepant	9	L–T	Average	125.40	—8.56⎭			

WISC: Wechsler Intelligence Scale for Children
L–T: Lorge Thorndike Group Intelligence Test.
Source: From A. Sutherland and M. L. Goldschmid, "Negative Teacher Expectation and IQ Change in Children with Superior Intellectual Potential," *Child Development* 45 (1974), pp. 852–56. Copyright 1974 by The Society for Research in Child Development, Inc.

opinions of such tests had both higher class grades and higher achievement test scores than did children whose teachers did not think much of the tests—a fact reminiscent of Minuchin et al.'s (1969) finding that children in traditional class-rooms, where tests are considered important, had higher achievement test scores than did children in open classrooms where tests and test scores are played down. Brophy and Evertson (1976) argue that one important aspect of teacher effectiveness is the teacher's role definition, and that the teacher's role definition is related to the self-fulfilling prophecy effect. Here, however, the self-fulfilling prophecy seems to occur for teachers' expectations of themselves. Teachers who thought that their role was to teach children what they should learn, and who considered themselves able to do so, were more effective than were teachers who did not hold these self-perceptions.

A final comment. All of the studies discussed here were either limited to primary grade children or found effects mostly in the early grades. Since many studies have not included older children, it may be premature to say that all such expectancy effects are greater for younger children. Nonetheless, these studies suggest that primary grade children are different from other children, and that attributes of schools and teachers may influence primary grade children more than they influence older children.

CHILDREN IN SCHOOLS

The five-to-seven transition: From association to cognition?

A cross-cultural survey of ages at which children were considered ready to take on a number of different types of responsibilities produced some fascinating findings (Rogoff, Sellers, Pirotta, Fox & White, 1975). The primary finding for our purposes here is that it was at about five to seven years of age that children in most of these settings were first considered mature enough for schooling or training. Furthermore, this was just one of a disproportionate number of new responsibilities in regard to which children were judged competent, compared to either older or younger children. What is it about children that changes during this period? Especially—for our purposes here—what is it about the change that makes this a good age for most children to start school? White (1965) has suggested that many of the changes seen during these years appear to have a common theme: the change in performance appears to reflect a newly devel-oping ability to inhibit or withhold immediate responses to situations, permitting more thoughtful responses to be made. Children can be observed to inhibit or refrain from doing *particular* acts at earlier ages, sometimes as young as nine months to one year of age. What emerges at about ages five to seven is a *generalized capacity for inhibition* which children can apply in a variety of situations.

White suggests that a number of different responses might be made in any situation. Some of these, which White calls *associative responses,* are made very quickly and might be characterized as immediate or spontaneous responses. In many instances, they are also likely to be incorrect responses. Others, which

White calls *cognitive responses,* may require reflection, selection from among alternative strategies, and so on. Such responses have longer latencies; that is, it takes longer to arrive at them than is required for associative responses. Since it takes longer to arrive at a cognitive response than at an associative response, one must inhibit associative responses before cognitive responses can be made. White's argument is that children's ability to inhibit associative responses undergoes a major change at about five to seven years of age, permitting more cognitive responses to become evident. Some of the changes relevant to White's hypothesis have been discussed already. Conservation, discussed in Chapter 2, requires that children refrain from responding to obvious perceptual appearances, such as the height of water in containers, and that they respond instead to relationships among attributes. The production deficiencies of young children, and the fact that children don't usually begin to produce more effective strategies until after age seven or eight, may also reflect this transition.

White also mentions other changes. One of these is the ability to inhibit voluntary actions in response to instructions (Luria, 1961). From very early in life, children can *do* things in response to instructions; but it is not until about age five that they begin to be able to respond to instructions that they *stop* themselves from doing things, especially instructions they must remember. Many such instructions are given to children: "Don't slam the door; don't run in the halls; don't wipe your dirty hands on the clean towels." It is a frequent source of aggravation to parents and teachers that children who "know perfectly well" regularly violate such instructions. What this research on self-direction suggests, however, is that "knowing perfectly well" is not necessarily of much help to young children; they literally do not stop and think, but respond unreflectively to the immediate situation. At about age five, however, the ability to "stop and think" begins to become evident. There are antecedents of this ability in earlier years, to be sure (for example, Stayton, Hogan, & Ainsworth, 1971); and depending on the complexity of the task, restraint may be difficult until well after age five (for example, Strommen, 1973). Nonetheless, children do make major gains in this ability at about ages five to seven (e.g., Waters & Tinsley, 1981).

White (1965) also mentions research of his own in which he looked at the accuracy of responses on a learning task in relation to the amount of time children took to make their responses. White's model as described above would predict that children who respond immediately should make many errors, whereas children who take more time—suggesting that they are inhibiting associative responses—should be more likely to be correct. This was the case for five- and six-year-olds (see Figure 5–3). For four-year-olds, however, no such relationship was evident; they made about the same proportion of errors whether their response times were short or long. Again, the implication is that not until about age five is associative responding inhibited very successfully.

Why ability to inhibit immediate responses should increase between about age five and seven is not clear, though there are several possible reasons. Neurophysiological maturation could be one factor (see Chapter 1). Another could be the achievement of sufficient mastery of language to permit its effective

FIGURE 5–3 Relationship between proportion of errors on a discrimination task and time taken to make a response. There is little relationship for the "youngest" group (about 3½ to 4½), but fast responders were more likely to be wrong in the "middle" and "oldest" groups (about 4½ to 5½ and 5½ to 6½, respectively).

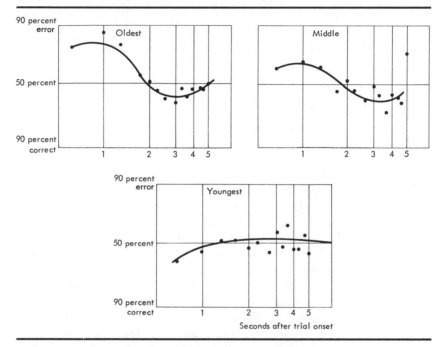

Source: S. H. White, "Evidence for a Hierarchical Arrangement of Learning Processes," in *Advances in Child Development and Behavior,* vol. 2, ed. L. Lipsitt and C. C. Spiker (New York: Academic Press, 1965), pp. 187–220.

use in planning and self-instruction, a hypothesis suggested by Soviet psychologists. Or it may be that by about this age other cognitive responses have become sufficiently strengthened through experience to compete effectively with the more immediate associative responses. Whatever the reason, if White is correct, the capacity for inhibition that appears at about this age may be a major foundation underlying the tremendous proliferation of skills and competencies over the school years.

While children may achieve a generalized capacity for inhibition and thus for learning more cognitive responses by the time they are six or seven, their attributes as learners at this age are nonetheless different from the attributes of older school children. For instance, when differences between open and traditional classrooms are found, they are likely to be greater for older elementary school children than for younger ones, especially as regards affective variables such as self-concept and enjoying school (for example, see Good et al., 1975). Evidently primary grade children need individualized contact and corrective feedback on assignments from teachers more than they need verbal discussion, opportunity to question, and pupil-to-pupil interaction (Brophy and Evertson, 1976). Regardless of social class background, children first entering school have fewer work skills and (obviously) less experience with school-related activities than do children who have attended school for some time. They also do not yet apply memory strategies to learning tasks efficiently (Chapter 4); and, as Brophy and Evertson (1976) point out, on entering school many children are still pre-operational, whereas older children are more likely to have concrete operations (Chapter 3). For all of these reasons, the modes of instruction that are most effective in the primary grades may be different from those that are most effective for older children.

Boys and girls in school

If it is true that the effects of school depend on child attributes and that teacher expectancies shape the interactions teachers have with children, it is not too surprising that the experiences of boys and girls at school differ in subtle ways and that much of the variation relates to sex-typing and sex-role standards.

From the children's point of view, school and what goes on there is generally seen as feminine (for example, see Kagan, 1964). Certainly it is true that much of the behavior required at school—being cooperative, obedient, quiet, polite, dependable—is much more in accord with the sex-role standards for girls than for boys. This differential match with sex-role standards has been taken as one reason why girls like school better than boys do, why girls get better marks than boys in elementary school (but not in the higher grades), why the average achievement of boys is lower than that of girls during these years, and why boys are much more likely to have learning problems, reading difficulties, and show problem behavior in the classroom. These differential effects for boys may be more a matter of mismatch between American boys and American schools than of maleness or such; in West Germany, for example, the average reading achievement of elementary-age boys exceeds that of girls (Preston, 1952), and boys in other countries do not have such a disproportionate share of school-related problems.

Frequently, the "feminine" quality of elementary classrooms has been attributed to the very high proportion of female teachers (88 percent in 1971, according to Sadker, 1972). When male teachers are examined, however, it turns out that their classroom demands and requirements are not that different from those of female teachers and that the achievement of boys with male teachers is not necessarily higher than that of boys with female teachers (Brophy & Good, 1973). If one considers the requirements of a classroom—or of any group working together—this is not surprising. Getting along and accomplishing what needs to be done require at least some degree of cooperation, politeness, dependability, and the like—though, of course, it is possible to overemphasize such attributes, and this may occur in many classrooms. Brophy and Good (1973) suggest that there is a *student role*—a set of behaviors required of students, whether boys or girls—which teachers require, regardless of their sex. It is the match or mismatch between the student role and the sex-role standards of boys and girls that is at issue, and not the teacher's sex per se.

This is not to say that there are no differences between male and female teachers. At least in preschools, teachers tend to favor children of their own sex for leadership assignments; male teachers relate more to male-typed activities, and boys are attracted more strongly to male teachers, whereas girls are attracted about equally to male and female teachers (Lee & Wolinsky, 1973). But simply getting more men into elementary school classrooms is not going to change the differential match of school activities to the sex-role standards for boys and girls. And while most attention has been paid to the mismatch for boys because of the negative effects that mismatch is assumed to have on them, one can also argue that there are less obvious, but equally important, hazards for girls if role-typed patterns are reinforced too strongly (see also Chapter 6).

Another source of difference in boys' and girls' experience at school is that teachers interact with them differently. Teachers of preschoolers interact more with boys even when the rate of the children's behavior is taken into account, which means that the effect does not occur simply because boys are more active and demanding (Serbin, O'Leary, Kent, & Tonick, 1973). This holds not only for disruptive and dependent behaviors (except for responding to the child's nearness), but for teachers' instructional activities—they spend more time teaching boys than girls. Why this should be true is not clear, and the degree to which it is true for teachers of older children is not yet known. But if boys are in fact receiving more attention, instruction, and direction than are girls, they are also very likely to be learning different things than girls both about school work and about themselves.

In the later grades, there is more disagreement over just what patterns of teacher-boy, teacher-girl interaction prevail in classrooms. Some studies suggest that teachers generally interact more with boys than with girls, that boys receive both more criticism and disapproval and also more praise (for example, see Dunkin & Biddle, 1974). Teachers may also attribute girls' and boys' performance to different child attributes; for example, Dweck, Davidson, Nelson, and Enna (1978), studying three fourth- and fifth-grade classrooms, found that nearly half of teacher criticisms of boys' work related to nonintellectual aspects of their performance, whereas nearly half of the criticism of girls' work was focused on intellectual inadequacies. Further, the teachers were much more likely to attribute the failure of boys than girls to lack of motivation or effort. Since attributions of failure to motivation or effort identify the problem as outside oneself and changeable, it is much easier to maintain a positive self-concept and to change (or vow to change) one's behavior (try harder) when criticism is couched in these terms than when failure is attributed to ability, which is internal to self and perceived as relatively unchangeable (such attributions and their effects will be discussed further in Chapter 6). However, Parsons, Kaczala, and Meece (1982) did not find the same patterns of teacher praise and criticism. They studied teacher-child interactions in 17 math classrooms for fifth through ninth grades. In general, as in earlier studies, they found that boys were sometimes more likely to receive praise and criticism than were girls; boys for whom teachers had low expectancies for performance received particularly high levels of teacher interaction, while girls for whom teachers had high expectancies received the lowest levels of teacher interaction. However, the relationship between teacher behaviors and children's self-concept of ability differed for boys and girls. Boys', but not girls', self-concept of ability was higher when there was relatively high levels of both praise and criticism from the teacher.

Why the discrepancies between these studies? Perhaps what happens in math classrooms is different from what happens in other classrooms; perhaps the ways in which teachers interact with children change from late elementary (fourth to fifth grades) to middle school or junior high (fifth to ninth grades); perhaps the results in one or the other study reflected "local conditions," something about the particular school system within which it was conducted. In both cases, however, those studies show that teacher behaviors do influence students' self-concepts of ability and their performance, and that relationships between teacher behavior and student attributes are different for girls and boys. However, more information is necessary before we can specify just what the relationships are and how they operate differently for boys and girls.

Different children, different programs?

So far, our discussion has mostly ignored the issue of whether different groups of children might learn better in different types of classrooms. Yet one would expect that children with very different home experiences, or children different in personal attributes, or children differing in other ways might react differently to given school programs, being more likely to do well in some kinds of programs than others.

Considerable attention has been paid to differences among children from different ethnic and social class backgrounds and, in particular, to the needs of those children, usually from minority ethnic groups and from lower social-class homes, who are less likely to do well in school. Earlier in the chapter, we suggested (as have many other authors) that the informal educational experiences of such children, while valuable in their own right, do not jibe with the demands of school in the same way as do the informal education experiences of majority culture, middle-class children.

One relevant contrast between such groups may be that middle-class families place greater stress on goal orientation, task completion, and tending to business (especially in relation to intellectual demands) than do lower-class families; and these differences may be evident long before children begin school. One study that compared the "work responses"—attempts to respond in some relevant way—which three-year-olds made to questions of an examiner in their homes found that lower-class children were only about half as likely as middle-class children to make such responses (Hertzig, Birch, Thomas & Mendez, 1968). Though both groups talked about the same amount, the lower-class children were also much less likely to apply language to the examiner's demands. Informal observations also suggested less distinction in general between task-oriented and social encounters in lower-class homes than in middle-class homes. Examiners in lower-class homes were treated like guests, offered coffee, engaged in conversation, even asked to watch the children for a few minutes. In addition, demands made on children by mothers were often not followed through. The middle-class homes were much more business-like. Mothers clearly viewed the examiners as there for the sole purpose of administering the examination, and focused their efforts toward accomplishing that purpose efficiently.

Other evidence that there is less emphasis on goal seeking in the environments of lower-class children is cited by Bruner (1973). In particular, Bruner mentions the work of Schoggen (1969), which shows that social agents in the environments of lower-class children perform far fewer acts aimed toward getting the children to seek goals than do social agents in the environments of middle-class children. More generally, Bruner points out that there is almost certainly a relationship between these differences in demands for goal seeking and mastery and the frequent finding that achievement motivation, which is fostered by such demands, is stronger in middle-class children than in lower-class children.

Effects of these differences in emphasis on task orientation may show up in performance as well as motivation. Gallimore and Au (1979), discussing their work with lower-class Hawaiian children, comment that often the same minority children who are at risk at school appear quite competent at home. They noticed that such children did not perform at relatively low levels on all school tasks, which one would expect if some "cognitive deficit" were characteristic of them. Rather, there was widespread inconsistency in their performance from one task to the next and from one setting to the next—much what one might expect if these children had about the same intellectual capabilities as middle-class children but were less experienced with requirements that these capabilities be applied to intellectual tasks. When a reading instruction program was instituted which encouraged more consistent application of the children's available cognitive strategies, the children's performance showed significant improvements.

In a somewhat different vein, Anderson, Teale, and Estrada (1980) observed the exposure of preschool children to *literacy events,* which they defined as "any action sequence, involving one or more persons, in which the production [writing] and/or comprehension [reading] of print plays a role" (p. 59). The children were from low-income black, Mexican-American, and Anglo families. Since the study was in its early stages, the authors caution against making firm conclusions based on the preliminary findings reported. Still, even from the preliminary data, it is clear that children's exposure to literacy events differed. In these particular observations, for example, Anglo children were less likely to engage in reading events by themselves but were more than twice as likely to engage in such activities with an adult than were black or Mexican-American children. Mexican-American children observed adults reading only a third as often as did children in the other two groups. As for writing events, Anglo children were much more likely to be involved in such events than were children from either of the other groups. Such variations in literacy experiences are bound to influence children's performance when they encounter related activities in school.

Reviewing relationships between learner characteristics and optimal instruction, Brophy (1978) suggests that, in general, lower-class students are likely to learn more if they are taught with smaller chunks of information at a time, with more repetition, and with more individualized, frequent opportunities for practice and for feedback. In contrast, children from middle-class homes do better when demands are high and when more difficult material is presented at a faster pace. Their performance is also less dependent on patience, encouragement, and warmth from teachers than is the performance of children from lower-class homes. An important theme here is the relationships between instructional content and pacing, on the one hand, and the students' learning histories and achievement levels, on the other hand. In the case of children from higher-class backgrounds, the best instructional treatment is similar to the treatment they receive from parents, whereas in the case of students from lower-class backgrounds the best instructional strategies may be those that counteract the motivational strategies and school-related experiences they encounter at home.

What of differences between children grouped on bases other than home background characteristics? Brophy (1978) cites evidence, for example, that students high in conceptual level, students high on some personality attributes such as anxiety or dogmatism, and students with external locus of control may perform better when instruction is more structured than open. He also discussed differences between introverted students, who are unlikely to ask questions or volunteer participation in discussion, and extroverted students, who enjoy speaking up in public situations; differences between individuals high in achievement motivation, who respond better to criticism than to praise and individuals low in achievement motivation, who respond better to praise than to criticism; and students differing on a number of other dimensions.

One interpretation that can be made of comparisons such as these is that the best instructional strategy should capitalize on the students' preferences or strengths and build from there. Thus children who find structured instruction more congenial should be placed in more structured settings; distribution of constructive criticism and of praise should differ from students high and low in achievement motivation; and so forth. As Brophy points out, however, there is a flaw in such reasoning. Especially for children in elementary school, teaching only to a child's preferences or strengths may deprive that child of opportunities to learn necessary skills in low-preferred or weak areas. No matter how much more comfortable children are with structure, there will be occasions when they will need to be able to cope with unstructured situations; no matter how shy or introverted a student, there will still be times when it is necessary to speak in front of others. Many would argue that it is important that schools provide not only exercise of strengths, but at least some minimal skills in areas of weakness. (Note the emergence of issues of philosophy again.) Such concerns are less with older students, especially college students, whose learning skills are more completely formed. But insofar as schooling in earlier grades is seen as having a shaping or socializing function, providing children with at least minimal skills for a wide range of situations, there is a strong basis for recommending that all children be exposed to educational experiences requiring a wide range of modes of performance, rather than being placed into programs which stress those modes with which they are already most comfortable.

So with placement of children in programs, it is once again clear that on issues important to education, there are no simple answers. One must consider not only the particular attributes of the child or group of children, but the outcomes which one considers important, the benefits likely to be achieved through a given eduational decision, and also the costs likely to be incurred by that decision for the students in question.

SUMMARY

To see whether children's intellectual development is shaped by going to school, it is necessary to turn to cross-cultural studies in which groups of individuals with and without school experience can be compared. Such studies show that children's school attendance is correlated with many features of their home environments, and that much of the difference between schooled and unschooled groups must be attributed to these background differences, rather than to schooling. Still, even when such differences are taken into account, significant (if small) differences remain which, though smaller than might have been thought, show significant effects of schooling on intellectual development. The ways in which schooled and unschooled groups differ include the performance on some perceptual tasks, especially those which require disembedding or interpreting cues for depth; use of organizational strategies on memory tasks when organization is not provided; likelihood of making use of taxonomic categories in classification and concept formation tasks; willingness to accept verbally stated premises for which the individual has no referent in personal experience; and performance on Piaget's tasks which require formal operations. These differences seem to reflect ways of applying basic intellectual skills, rather than differences in the basic skills themselves.

When looking at the consequences of particular educational programs, the evidence shows that early education programs designed for children from low-income homes clearly foster higher levels of school achievement in their graduates, although those levels still do not match those of children from middle-income homes. The higher achievement levels, as well as more positive feelings about school, are still evident in eighth grade, years after the early education experience. The results of comparisons of primary grade programs which differ in a number of ways are much less clear-cut. Long-term analyses of such programs, in general, comparable to those done for early education programs, have not yet been reported. But it has proved to be difficult to distinguish between different programs, in part because the within-program differences from one site to another are so great. Comparisons of classrooms on the more general dimension of whether they are open or structured/traditional have also been difficult, in part because both open and traditional classrooms have been defined in so many different ways. On presently available evidence (with all its weaknesses) there is no basis for claiming superiority for either type of classroom as far as outcomes of academic achievement, self-concept, adjustment or anxiety, or locus of control. On the other hand, there is some basis for stating that children in open classrooms are more likely to score higher on attitudes toward school, creativity, curiosity, and cooperation. However, the equivocal nature of the evidence regarding achievement may be in part because the questions were asked too globally. When beginning readers' performance was compared in relation to open versus structured classroom experience and in relation to specific cognitive abilities relevant for reading, the children with structured experience—which had features especially relevant for their level of learning—performed significantly better by several criteria.

Classroom climate has been assumed to be an important influence on children's learning and attitudes, but research evidence is so contradictory that it cannot be said what kind of a difference (if any) climate makes. Classroom management is clearly more important. Good classroom managers maintain a steady flow of activities matched to the children's requirements. Children in their classes are more involved in classwork, require fewer disciplinary measures, and show greater achievement than do children whose teachers are poor managers. Teachers' expectations about children's ability do not influence performance as strongly as early studies suggested, but teachers' attitudes about what is important, and their role definitions of themselves as teachers, do affect their influence on children.

As for child attributes being important for education, the transition from associative to cognitive responding which children undergo between the ages of approximately five to seven may be the basis for the cross-culturally found expectations that it is at about this time that children can be expected to profit from schooling or training. The capacity for inhibition which is hypothesized to underlie this transition can be seen not only in children's performance on cognitive tasks, such as conservation or memory tasks requiring strategy use, but in their day-to-day behavioral regulation as well. It is still true, however, that the most beneficial modes of instruction may be different for children entering school and children in the later grades. The experiences of boys and girls in school are also different; teachers do behave differently toward boys and girls, but exactly what the differences in such interaction patterns are is still a matter of controversy. As for the issue of whether instructional programs should be geared to the particular aptitudes or preferences of children from different groups, programs geared toward the particular learning histories and achievement levels of children from middle- and lower-income homes appear to be effective in optimizing achievement levels. Lower-income children may have less out-of-school experience involving goal orientation or task-directed application of their cognitive skills in consistent ways, as well as less experience with literacy-related materials and events. However, when it comes to making program decisions based on the preferences or strengths of some group of students rather than on their learning histories, it is important to consider what children might lose by not acquiring at least minimal skills in their nonpreferred learning mode as well as what they might gain by emphasizing their preference or strength. Here, as throughout all discussion of issues relating to education, philosophies of education—its goals, desired outcomes—are as important as are any research findings or facts.

TERMS AND CONCEPTS

informal education

formal education

theoretic reasons for logical
statements

empiric reasons for logical
statements

commitments (to educational
philosophies)

performance contracting

open classrooms

structured or traditional classrooms

classroom climate

classroom management

withitness

proactive structuring

five-to-seven transition

associative responses

cognitive responses

generalized capacity for inhibition

student role

literacy events

SUGGESTED ADDITIONAL READING

Brophy, J. E. Interactions between learner characteristics and optimal instruction. In D. Bar-tal and L. Saxe (Eds.), *Social psychology of education: Theory and research.* New York: Hemisphere Publishing, 1978.

Ginsburg, H. *The myth of the deprived child.* Englewood Cliffs, N.J.: Prentice-Hall, 1972.

Good, T. L., Biddle, B. J., & Brophy, J. E. *Teachers make a difference.* New York: Holt, Rinehart, and Winston, 1975.

Rogoff, B. Schooling and the development of cognitive skills. In H. C. Triandis & A. Heron (Eds.), *Handbook of cross-cultural psychology. Developmental psychology* (Vol. 4). Boston: Allyn & Bacon, 1981.

Wagner, D. A., & Stevenson, H. W., (Eds.). *Cultural perspectives on child development.* San Francisco: W. H. Freeman, 1982.

BOX 6-1
Study questions

Summarize the evidence regarding the relationships of heredity and personality.

Define temperament; how is temperament related to personality?

What basis is there for expecting, or not expecting, continuity of attributes over the school years and into later periods of life?

What factors influence the process of modeling or observational learning?

What relationships exist between television viewing and personality?

Define and describe the processes which together make up sex-role development.

What is psychological androgyny?

What are the major considerations that need to be taken into account when thinking about effectance or mastery motivation?

What are some of the major factors that influence intrinsic motivation, that is, working on some task for the pleasure of doing it?

What attributes characterize children who show learned helplessness?

CHAPTER 6

PERSONALITY AND SOCIALIZATION

Theories of personality development, and especially personality during the school years, were presented in Chapter 1. Now it is time to return to such issues, examining more closely what researchers have to say about personality development. In keeping with a psychobiological orientation, we assume that personality, like cognition, reflects both genetic and environmental influences in interaction with one another. We shall begin by looking at evidence regarding biological processes and personality. Then we shall consider imitation or modeling as a basic process through which personality may be influenced, television as a source of influence on children, sex-role development, and competence and achievement motivation.

BIOLOGY AND PERSONALITY

Heredity and personality

If heredity is one basis for personality, one should find, as one does for mental abilities, that individuals most closely related genetically are most similar, while individuals of more distant genetic relationships are less similar. In general, the evidence bears this out, though the patterns are not as strong nor as consistent as they are in the case of intellectual skills. Over a number of studies (e.g., see Loehlin, 1977) personality inventory scores of identical twins correlated about .5 while those of fraternal twins correlated about .3—but one study using behavioral observations found no tendency for the scores of identical twins to be more similar than the scores of fraternal twins (Plomin & Foch, 1980). Interestingly, the patterns of relationships obtained suggest that personality similarities may reflect *only* hereditary patterns, whereas environmental influences within families tend to make children different—for instance, children are treated differently by parents, have different positions in the family structure, may be differentially influenced by sources outside the family such as peers (Rowe & Plomin, 1981). This is an intriguing suggestion quite different from the more traditional position that children within a family share not only common genes, but a common environment which influences them in similar ways!

Likewise, in studies of adoptive families higher correlations of scores between adopted-away children and biological parents than of the children and their adoptive parents would reflect hereditary processes. These studies also provide support, but not strong support, for the influence of heredity on personality scores. In one such study Loehlin, Horn, and Willerman (1981) found little personality resemblance between family members whether biologically related or not. The exception occurred when they looked at a subgroup which had been studied with special care; there, they did find some evidence for heritability, especially for extraversion or outgoingness. Because the stronger results occurred when measurements had been done with special care, they suggest that part of the problem in other research (including some of their own) lies in the measurement techniques which have not been sufficiently sensitive to the information of interest.

From these studies, then, it appears that hereditary processes do have some influence on children's personality attributes, but the extent of such influence is still an open question.

Temperament and personality

A somewhat different approach to psychobiological foundations of personality is found in studies of temperament, characteristic patterns of reactivity and of self-regulation which are *constitutional*—rooted in an individual's biological makeup as influenced by heredity and experience (Rothbart & Derryberry, 1981; Thomas, Chess, & Birch, 1968; Thomas & Chess, 1977). *Reactivity* refers to the characteristic ways an individual reacts to new situations. Some may like new situations, some dislike them; some may react promptly and energetically; others may react cautiously and timidly. Note that temperament is *not* the same as personality. A person who reacts cautiously or timidly may be predisposed, i.e., more likely to become, shy—but whether that happens depends on the individual's history. *Self-regulation* refers to characteristic ways in which individuals moderate their reactivity to situations—paying attention or not, approaching or avoiding will make the individual's experience of a situation more or less intense, thus regulating its impact (Rothbart & Derryberry, 1981). Children differ in temperament from infancy, and in fact, the majority of studies of temperament have dealt with infants (e.g., see studies reviewed in Rothbart & Derryberry, 1981; Bates, 1980). Temperament also shows some stability over time, at least within given periods of life. However, whether there is continuity from one major life period to another is an open question (e.g., Sameroff, 1975; Rothbart

& Derryberry, 1981). Thus we can characterize school-aged children as showing particular patterns of temperament, but we can't be sure to what extent they showed the same patterns as infants or may show the same patterns as adolescents or as adults.

The major study of temperament to date that has dealt with school-aged children has been the longitudinal study begun in 1956 by Thomas, Chess, Birch, and their co-workers (Thomas, Chess, Birch, Hertzig & Korn, 1963; Thomas, Chess, & Birch, 1968; Thomas & Chess, 1977). They first identified the set of temperament characteristics described in Table 6–1. Subsequently, they

TABLE 6–1
Temperament characteristics or categories of reactivity which may be used to describe behavior

Characteristic	Definition	Illustration
Activy level	Amount of motor activity	High: Always on the move Low: Doesn't move around much
Rhythmicity	Regularity of repetitive biological functions	High: Eating, sleeping, active periods, and bowel and bladder functions occur at predictable times Low: Eating, sleeping, active periods, and bowel and bladder functions irregular and unpredictable
Approach-withdrawal	Characteristic *intial* response to a new situation	High: Approaches new situations, such as meeting people or starting school Low: Hangs back or initially refuses to enter new situations, such as meeting people or starting school
Adaptability	Ease with which child can change behavior to fit new situations, regardless of initial response	High: Readily adapts to change in schedule, even if there was initial resistance (withdrawal) Low: Actively resists changes in routines over continuing period of time
Intensity of reaction	How much energy the child puts into responding	High: Reacts intensely—laughs and cries long and hard, resists with vigor Low: Reacts mildly, smiles rather than laughs, cries softly, passive resistance
Threshold of responsiveness	How strong external stimulation must be before child responds	High: Does not smile, cry, or get frightened easily Low: Smiles readily, cries over minor events, is easily frightened
Quality of mood	Amount of pleasant, friendly behavior compared to amount of unpleasant, unfriendly behavior	High: Characteristically outgoing, friendly; takes pleasure in activities Low: Characteristically unfriendly; expresses displeasure or dislike of many activities
Distractibility	Ease with which child can be distracted from ongoing activity by interruptions	High: Does not concentrate well—other events disrupt activity Low: Can concentrate on ongoing activity despite interruptions or distractions
Persistence and attention span	Stick-to-itiveness—maintaining an activity despite obstacles	High: Continues activity over time or until finished—a distractible persistent child may be distracted but will continue to return to original activity until finished Low: Gives up readily; short attention span

Source: A. Thomas, S. Chess, and H. G. Birch, *Temperament and Behavior Disorders in Children* (New York: New York University Press, 1968).

identified three major patterns of early child temperament and related those patterns to children's behavioral adjustment. *Easy children* were just that. They were usually positive in mood; regular, low, or mild in the intensity of their reactions; usually positive in their approaches to new situations; and readily adaptable. *Slow-to-warm-up children* tended to withdraw initially from new situations rather than to approach them and to adapt slowly. They usually reacted with mild intensity. When they started school, children with such temperament characteristics were likely to be reluctant to participate in activities with other children, hanging back and watching before they got involved themselves. Once they got involved, however, and once the school situation and their new classmates became familiar, they were indistinguishable from the other children at school.

Finally, there were the *difficult children*. These children showed irregularity, mostly withdrawal responses to new events, predominantly intense reactions, frequent expressions of negative mood, and slowness in adapting to changes in the environment. The difficult children did not simply hold back when faced with new situations, as did the slow-to-warm-up children. They actively resisted, requiring their parents to undergo a long and difficult battle whenever changes were made.

These three temperament patterns characterized the majority of the children in the study. When the patterns were related to occurrence of behavioral disorders in the school years, difficult children were more likely to manifest such disorders (though Bates, 1980, argues that it may be caregivers' social perceptions of a child as difficult, rather than characteristics of the child, which are associated with poor adjustment outcomes). The difficult children were not necessarily predisposed to behavioral disorders in some way but rather were much more demanding of their parents than were other children. In the face of these demands, the parents were likely to respond in ways that interfered with, instead of fostering, the healthy development of the children. (Notice that the outcome depends on *both* parents and child.)

Although difficult children manifested relatively more later behavioral disorders than did easy or slow-to-warm-up children, there were instances of disorders among these other temperament groups as well. Thomas et al. (1968) suggest that whether or not behavioral disorders develop depends on the degree of match or mismatch between children's attributes and the situations in which the children find themselves. Where there is a good match, or *consonance*, development will proceed normally. Where there is a mismatch, or *dissonance*, however, the mismatch places stress on the child, and a behavior disorder is more likely to develop.

Dissonance may take a number of forms. Among the forms which Thomas et al. (1968) describe and illustrate with case histories are the following.

1. Dissonance between parental practices or demands and the child's temperament or capacities. Notice that this form of dissonance suggests that whether or not a particular parental practice "works" is not just a matter of the practice itself but also of how well it fits a particular child. This form of dissonance is illustrated in Box 6–2, which describes how two children of similar tem-

---

BOX 6 – 2
How the attributes of parent and child interact

The following paragraphs illustrate how two children with similar early temperament patterns may be very different persons by the time they reach school age, depending on how their parents interact with them.

The differences in the developmental courses of difficult children which result from differences in parent-child interactions are illustrated by the contrasting behavioral courses of two of the study children. Both youngsters, one a girl and the other a boy, showed similar characteristics of behavioral functioning in the early years of life, with irregular sleep patterns, constipation, and painful evacuations at times, slow acceptance of new foods, prolonged adjustment periods to new routines, and frequent and loud periods of crying. Adaptation to nursery school in the fourth year was also a problem for both children. Parental attitudes and practices, however, differed greatly. The girl's father was usually angry with her. In speaking of her, he gave the impression of disliking the youngster and was punitive and spent little or no recreational time with her. The mother was more concerned for the child, more understanding, and more permissive, but quite inconsistent. There was only one area in which there was firm but quiet parental consistency, namely, with regard to safety rules. The boy's parents, on the other hand, were unusually tolerant and consistent. The child's lengthy adjustment periods were accepted calmly; his strident altercations with his younger siblings were dealt with good-humoredly. The parents waited out his negative moods without getting angry. They tended to be very permissive, but set safety limits and consistently pointed out the needs and rights of his peers at play.

By the age of five and a half years, these two children, whose initial characteristics had been so similar, showed marked differences in behavior. The boy's initial difficulties in nursery school had disappeared, he was a constructive member of his class, had groups of friends with whom he exchanged visits, and functioned smoothly in most areas of daily living. The girl, on the other hand, had developed a number of symptoms of increasing severity. These included explosive anger, negativism, fear of the dark, encopresis [defecation in one's clothes], thumb-sucking, insatiable demands for toys and sweets, poor peer relationships, and protective lying. It is of interest that there was no symptomatology or negativism in the one area where parental practice had been firmly consistent, i.e., safety rules.

Source: A. Thomas, S. Chess, and H. G. Birch, *Temperament and Behavior Disorders in Children* (New York: New York University Press, 1968), pp. 82–83.

---

perament developed very differently because in one instance the parents' demands were dissonant, and in the other consonant, with the child's characteristics.

2.   Dissonance between values and behaviors developed at home and behavioral expectancies at school and with peers. Easy children who adapt readily to their home environments may experience this form of dissonance if the patterns to which they have adapted at home are considered weird or unacceptable at school.

3.   Inconsistencies in the patternings of parental practices and attitudes resulting in excessive stress for the child. Here the dissonance is not so much between the parents and the child as it is between what the parents demand at different times. Even a highly adaptable child may experience a great deal of stress if parents are inconsistent in what they expect their children to adapt to. One can imagine how much tension and stress would be generated if such inconsistent parents have difficult children, who do not adapt easily under the best of circumstances.

4.   Interparental dissonance and the use of the child's characteristics as a weapon in interparental conflict. This form of dissonance might occur if the intense and negative responses of a difficult child were blamed on the mother by the father as evidence of her poor handling of the child, rather than being recognized and dealt with by both parents as the child's characteristic response.

5.   Dissonance between parental feelings and behavior and the child's expectations of acceptance and affection. A mother who cannot accept the fact that her child is now in school and is no longer a baby may fail to provide the love and support which the child had come to expect from preschool interactions.

6.   Dissonance between a teacher's mode of functioning and the child's characteristics. The illustrative case presented by Thomas et al. (1968) concerns a child with a long attention span who did not like to shift activities until he had finished his current project. His parents and kindergarten teacher had recognized this pattern and made allowance for it. His first-grade teacher did not, however, and her insistence that he follow her schedule rather than his own precipitated temper tantrums which eventually became disruptive enough to require treatment.

One can also ask what relationship exists between patterns of temperament and performance in school. Thomas and Chess (1977) report comparisons of temperament measured at age five and indices of school performance (along with some results of related studies) which suggest that children who are low on adaptability and tend to withdraw in new situations (slow-to-warm up children) were likely to have lower achievement test scores than other children. These were not ability differences—there were no associations between temperament at age five and IQ scores.

Whether temperamental predispositions persist over different periods of life is an open question, as we indicated above (though there is at least evidence that activity level shows some continuity from preschool—2½, 3—to the primary grades at age 7 or 7½; see Halverson & Waldrop, 1973, 1976; Buss, Block, & Block, 1980. However, the idea that there are stable and persistent predispositions at least through the school years is backed up by information from other sources. Bronson (1969) analyzed data from a longitudinal study of children gathered between the time they were 5 and the time they were 16. Bronson was able to identify two dimensions of behavior that she believes reflect *central orientations,* or "characteristic and relatively unmodifiable predispositions to certain modes of interaction which play an important role in determining the nature of the individual's experience, his effectiveness in coping with devel-

opmental tasks, and the kinds of beliefs about himself and others that he eventually comes to maintain" (pp. 3–4). The first dimension, *emotional expressiveness—reserve*, was evident in measures that reflected whether a child typically showed high spirits or tended to show little affect (or emotion) and in
measures that reflected whether or not interactions with people were important
to the child. The second dimension, *placidity-explosiveness*, was evident in
measures that reflected a child's readiness to react in situations as well as
whether the child reacted belligerently or calmly.

The relative stability of these dimensions between the ages of 5 and 16
suggests that the orientations they reflect are indeed persistent and enduring over
these years. However, the behavioral expression of the dimensions did not
necessarily remain the same throughout the period. For instance, placidity-
explosiveness was linked to school-related activities during elementary school,
with placid children assessed by teachers as adjusting better to the classroom;
but this relationship did not hold in junior and senior high school. Also, although
the patterns of interrelationships were basically the same for boys and girls, there
were instances in which the same scores had different meanings, depending on
the sex of the child. High expressiveness, for example, implies social assertiveness, an attribute that is more in accordance with sex-role standards for boys
than with sex-role standards for girls. Perhaps for this reason, high-expressive
boys were usually admired and liked by others, whereas high-expressive girls
were often admired but not necessarily liked. The two dimensions themselves
were generally unrelated to each other. Placid children might be either expressive or reserved; expressive children might be either placid or explosive.

The two dimensions also showed different relationships with other factors,
such as patterns of parental behavior. Emotional expressiveness—reserve was
relatively independent of parental behavior, whereas placidity-explosiveness
was strongly related to parental behavior, especially for boys. Observations such
as this last one led Bronson to suggest that, though both dimensions are stable,
emotional expressiveness-reserve is more pervasive: It is easier to anger a placid
child or calm an explosive one than it is to squelch an expressive child or to get
a reserved child to open up.

The research on which Bronson's work is based is very different from that on
which the studies of temperament are based, and Bronson is careful to avoid
calling the dimensions identified in her analysis characteristics of temperament.
Notice, though, that both of Bronson's dimensions do describe variations in
reactivity, as do Thomas, Chess, and Birch's temperament characteristics. Taken
together, both bodies of work indicate that children have characteristic reac-
tivities that persist over the school years and that moderate their experience in
important ways.

IDENTIFICATION AND MODELING

Identification, the incorporation of another's attributes into one's own personality, is a central influence on personality development in both psychodynamic
and social learning theories (see Chapter 1). A variety of mechanisms have been

BOX 6–3
How does identification take place?

Some of the major ideas about how identification takes place are briefly described below. While reading them, notice that they are not necessarily mutually exclusive, but may well operate in complementary ways. Children may both love and fear their parents, may perceive similarities with them, and may recognize their power. During the school years, any or all of these processes may contribute to children's identification.

Theory	Description
Developmental identification	Identification results from fear of loss of love. Also called anaclitic identification. Freud described this as an early form of identification evident in infancy.
Defensive identification	Identification results from fear of punishment or physical harm from a powerful authority figure. Also called identification with the aggressor. Such identification is probably infrequent, occurring only when a parent is cold and dominant, no parent is supportive, and the home atmosphere is stressful (Hetherington & Frankie, 1967). Derived from Freud's theory of the Oedipus conflict.
Status envy theory	Children identify with persons who enjoy status and privileges the children would like for themselves. Derived from Freud's theory of the Oedipus conflict (Whiting, 1960).
Power theory	Children identify with persons they perceive as having power, or control over resources, including both rewards and punishments. It is the model's control over the resources that is important, not whether the child is actually rewarded or punished (Parsons, 1955).
Perceived similarity theory	Children who perceive a model as like themselves in one way may believe themselves to be like the model in other ways as well, and so imitate the model. Such identification is more likely to occur when the model is salient and the modeled action is congruent with the child's self-concept (Stotland, 1969; Kagan, 1964).
Cognitive-developmental theory	Children's developing concepts allow them to classify others as like or unlike themselves, resulting in identification as they selectively model after individuals classified as like themselves. General rules of conduct develop through induction from what similar and dissimilar models do (Kohlberg, 1969).
Reciprocal role theory	Children learn appropriate roles, not through imitation, but from persons who interact with them in role-differentiated ways. From this point of view, fathers are the main source of sex role learning for both boys and girls because they, more than mothers, act differently toward, and expect different behaviors from, their sons and daughters (Johnson, 1963).

suggested as basic to the formation of identifications (see Box 6–3). Of course, psychodynamic theorists and social learning theorists differ on the nature of identification. Psychodynamic theorists emphasize the emotional relationship between child and model. In the prototypical Oedipus conflict, for example, identification takes place because of the child's intense feelings toward parents and the repression resulting from his or her inability to resolve those feelings. In contrast, social learning theorists argue that since imitation or behavioral similarity is the only evidence one ever has that identification has taken place, identification cannot be distinguished in any important way from imitation and *modeling*. For them, "identificatory processes" are the factors influencing modeling, as summarized below (Bandura, 1969). Regardless of these differences, both types of theory say that children's most important identifications are likely to be with parents, peers, teachers. Children are emotionally involved with these groups of persons and also have long-lasting relationships with them through which continuing observational learning may take place.

Children first begin to identify with parents long before they enter school, and most research interest has focused on these early identifications. Just the same, identifications continue to shape personality development during the school years. One way in which this happens is through the continuing influence of identifications established earlier in life. Identification is not something that takes place once sometime before age five and then is over and done with. Children identified with parents will continue to internalize their parents' attributes throughout the school years and beyond.

In addition, on entering school children encounter new models—teachers, peers, perhaps other adults, such as club leaders or coaches—with whom new identifications may be formed. With the passage of time and increasing independence from the family, the influence of these new identifications gains in importance. New identifications are most likely to influence attributes and behaviors for which parents or other early models were inappropriate or inadequate models. For example, parents, being adults, can never be effective models for how to act appropriately as a 10-year old among age-mates. This can be learned only from other children.

Imitation and modeling

One major contribution of social learning theory has been the study of modeling or observational learning—learning by watching others. Children (and adults) obviously imitate others successfully, even when they have not been reinforced for the imitated behavior.

Children learn much more from observation than they ever actually do themselves; and it is important to distinguish between learning and performance. Boys and girls may learn equal amounts about applying makeup while watching their mothers, or about shaving while watching their fathers, but their likelihood of doing these things themselves is quite different. *Cognitive factors,* such as the classification of certain activities as appropriate for one's own sex, influence whether or not something learned through observation will be performed. *Vicar-*

144

ious reinforcement—seeing someone else rewarded or punished for doing something—also influences performance. In one study that illustrates this effect—and also the importance of distinguishing between learning and performance—the aggressive behavior of three groups of children in free play was compared (Bandura, 1965). All three groups saw a film in which the same model performed the same aggressive acts, but one group saw the model punished, the second saw the model rewarded, and the third saw neither punishment nor reinforcement (neutral outcome). The children who saw the model reinforced imitated most, whereas the children who saw the model punished imitated least, demonstrating the effects of vicarious reinforcement (see Figure 6–1, screened columns). Later, the same children were offered attractive incentives to act as the model had—and they all did. The differences between the reinforcement groups disappeared (Figure 6–1, solid columns). All three groups had clearly learned equal amounts about aggressive behavior from watching the model, even though their initial performance depended on whether the model was rewarded or punished.

FIGURE 6–1 When children were offered no incentive, whether or not they imitated an aggressive model depended on whether the model was rewarded, punished, or experienced no consequences following aggression (screened columns). But when these same children were offered an attractive incentive to act as the model had, they were equally able to do so (solid columns).

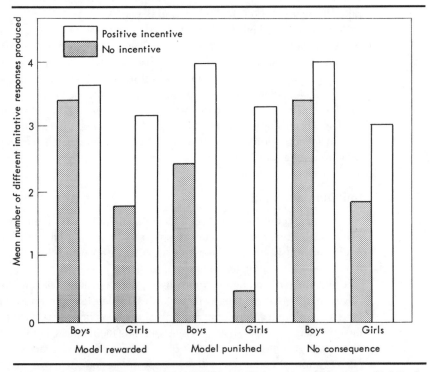

Source: A. Bandura, "Influences of Models' Reinforcement Contingencies on the Acquisition of Imitation Responses," *Journal of Personality and Social Psychology* 1 (1965), pp. 589–95. Copyright 1965 by the American Psychological Association. Reprinted by permission.

Observational learning also depends on *characteristics or attributes of the model*. Children are more likely to imitate some models than others, and this may reflect differences in learning as well as in performance. One especially important model attribute is *power*, defined as holding control over rewards and punishments (and, therefore, potentially over the child's behavior). The more powerful a child perceives a model to be the more likely it is that the child will imitate the model. Parents obviously have power relative to children, as do teachers, older siblings, and admired peers.

However, models need not be persons the child knows, or even human beings. Any admired figure, such as an athlete or an entertainer, may serve as a model. And in one laboratory study, children imitated cartoon characters as readily as they did either human characters on film or "live" models (Bandura, Ross, & Ross, 1963a).

Another important model attribute is whether the model is *warm and nurturant or cold and distant*. The warmer the model, the more likely a child is to imitate that model. This has been a consistent finding of studies whose models are persons with whom children have established and continuing relationships, such as their parents and teachers. It has been a less consistent finding of studies whose models are strangers to the children, suggesting that the importance of some model attributes depends on how long and how well the child and the model have known each other—and raising questions about whether studies whose models are strangers are relevant for understanding the influence of familiar, well-known models, such as parents and teachers (Hetherington & McIntrye, 1975).

The sex of the model and the sex of the child also influence the likelihood that a model will be imitated. Both boys and girls are more likely to imitate same-sex models, especially when the behavior modeled is perceived as appropriate for one's own sex. But this is truer for boys than for girls. Boys are more likely to imitate men than girls are to imitate women, and at the same time boys are less likely to imitate women than girls are to imitate men. This may be partly a matter of perception of males as more powerful than females. By age five, many children—both boys and girls—already hold this perception (for example, Bandura, Ross, & Ross, 1963b; Worell, 1981).

TELEVISION AND PERSONALITY DEVELOPMENT

The issue of whether and how television viewing may influence children's development has attracted increasing interest and concern in recent years. Such interest is well founded, given the amount of time that children spend watching television. By age five, children already watch about three hours of television a day, on the average, and the amount of time spent watching television increases steadily during the school years (Lyle & Hoffman, 1972a, 1972b). (Of course, there is enormous variation for individual children. Some may not watch at all on many days of the week, while others may watch as much as five or six hours a day.)

But noting that children watch television a lot is a far cry from demonstrating that television influences their development. Social learning studies show that children learn not only through imitation but also from cartoon and filmed models. But does this learning show up in what they do? Television characters cannot influence children directly, as real persons do, and television is only one of many potential influences on any aspect of children's behavior. Further, the early studies of observational learning were laboratory studies, and many critics questioned whether their results were relevant to whether children actually acted differently in real-life situations as a result of their television viewing. By now enough information has accumulated that researchers generally agree that television does affect children's behavior in a variety of ways, though there are many moderating factors which affect the strength and direction of that influence (e.g., Comstock, 1975). For general reviews, readers might look at Liebert, Neal, and Davidson, 1982.

Television violence and children's aggression

Perhaps the most intensely studied and argued issue, especially through the early 1970s, was the question of whether or not violence portrayed on television influenced children's aggressive behaviors. Although there are still critics, by now the weight of the evidence is such that most researchers agree: under the appropriate circumstances, children who see more violence on TV do, in fact, behave more aggressively. For example, in one longitudinal study, individuals who first participated as third graders (Eron, 1963) were followed up 10 years later, just after they had graduated from high school (grade 13). At both ages, viewing preferences were determined, and each person rated classmates for aggressiveness. Now one can examine the correlations not only between violent content and aggressiveness at each age, but also between preference for violence at grade 3 and aggression at grade 13, and rated aggression at grade 3 and preference for violent content at grade 13. If being aggressive results in choosing violent programs, then grade 3 aggression should have a high correlation with grade 13 preferences. But if watching violent content is a cause of aggression, then the strongest correlation should be between grade 3 program preferences and grade 13 aggression. This is the pattern that was found, supporting the interpretation that watching televised violence does increase aggressive behavior (Eron, Lefkowitz, Huesmann, & Walder, 1972).

A different kind of illustration is provided by a field study which compared the effects of aggressive content (Batman, Superman), prosocial content (Mister Rogers' Neighborhood) and neutral content (children's films) on preschool children's behavior in class and free play (Friedrich & Stein, 1973). Following two weeks of baseline observation (this established ongoing levels of behavior against which changes could be compared), the children were shown programs and then observed in regular preschool activities for the following hour. These observations continued over a four-week period, during which time any given child saw only one of the three types of programs. There were several clear changes in the ways the children acted depending on the type of program they viewed, and these changes were still evident (though not as strong) two weeks after the last program had been shown. Children who saw aggressive programs became less able to tolerate delay or to exercise self-control and less willing to obey rules than they had been during the baseline observations. There was also a clear increase in aggressive acts toward other people, but only for those children—both boys and girls—who were above average in aggressiveness initially.

In comparison, children who saw prosocial programs showed greater task persistence, rule obedience, and tolerance of delay than they had shown during the baseline observations. This was especially true for children whose IQ scores were above average. Among children from lower-class homes, there were also increases in prosocial behaviors, such as cooperativeness, nurturance, and expression of feelings. Children from middle-class homes showed no comparable change. The influence of social class most probably reflects differences in parental values and parent-child interactions in middle- and lower-class homes. For instance, when parents of a group of preschoolers were surveyed informally regarding their children's television viewing, nearly all of the middle-class parents said that they wanted their children to watch "Mister Rogers' Neighborhood," whereas nearly all of the lower-class parents preferred that their children *not* watch this program (Taran, 1975). The lower-class parents perceived Mister Rogers as effeminate and did not want their child exposed to such a model.

Television and other attributes

From the study just discussed, it is clear that television can induce not only aggression, but also *prosocial behaviors,* such as cooperativeness, nurturance, and self-control. Similarly, Poulos, Rubinstein, and Liebert (1975) found that for first graders, watching a "Lassie" episode which emphasized prosocial behaviors elicited more choice of helping reactions later on than did watching a neutral "Lassie" episode or watching an episode of "The Brady Bunch."

There is also evidence that male and female characters portrayed on television influence children's sex role stereotypes or standards, that is, their general perceptions of what men and women ought to be like. Children do accept television characters as role models; even when given an option not to nominate a character, 70 percent of 200 third to sixth graders nominated a character as someone they wanted to be like when they grew up (Miller & Reeves, 1976), and all children can make such nominations (Miller, 1975). Perhaps more convincing is the finding that children who see characters in counter-stereotypic roles are more likely to perceive those roles as appropriate and acceptable (Miller & Reevers, 1976; Atkin, 1975).

Television characters are certainly not the only models influencing children's sex-role stereotypes; they are probably not even the most important models. Yet given their influence on children's perceptions of the sterotypes, the ways in which men and women are portrayed on television becomes relevant. The evidence is remarkably consistent. Virtually all studies show that both men and women are portrayed in highly traditional, stereotyped, and unrealistic ways— which may be partly responsible for the findings that children from kindergarten through sixth grade who spend a great deal of time watching television show much stronger traditional sex-role development than do children who spend little time watching television (McGhee & Frueh, 1980).

Boys and girls receive very different messages from television about what they ought to be like, and what they see, though more or less congruent with traditional sex roles so far as it goes, is certainly not realistic. Busby commented in 1975 that the changing roles of women—as working mothers, single parents, professionals—were simply not depicted on television. There have been some improvements in intervening years, but the unrealistic portrayals still predominate.

Political socialization is another attribute influenced by watching television. Children from kindergarten to fifth grade who watch television news shows have greater knowledge of political events, are more likely to discuss news events with others, are more interested in public affairs, and are more likely to seek additional information about what they see in news shows (Atkin & Gantz, 1975). Comparative analyses made when some of the same children were followed up a year later indicated that the greater political interest of news watchers was probably a result of exposure to news shows and not just a choice of such shows by children already interested in political affairs. *Learning and cognitive development* can also be influenced by television, as evidenced by the successes of "Sesame Street" (for example, Ball & Bogatz, 1972), and such programs as "The Electric Company" are designed to provide similar learning experiences for school-aged children. However, though specific programs like these may foster learning, the effect of general viewing is less clear. One study designed to investigate the relationship between amount of viewing and language maturity found a generally negative relationship, especially for children between about 8 and 11 (Milkovitch, Miller, Bettinghaus, & Atkin, 1975). The more television the children watched, the *less* mature their language development—a suggestive finding which requires further study.

Finally, there is the issue of whether TV viewing is related to problem behavior in some children. *Media addicts* are children who are very heavy viewers, spending time with television to the exclusion of other activities. Such disproportionate involvement with television (or with other forms of the mass media, such as movies) is frequently associated with evidence of personal maladjustment. Media addicts are more likely to show signs of neurosis, and to have strong feelings of rejection and personal insecurity, than are children who spend less time with the media (Himmelweit, Oppenheim, & Vince, 1958). However, in contrast to the influences discussed previously, in which personality and other attributes appear to be influenced by television, media addiction appears to be a symptom resulting from already existing personality difficulties. Himmelweit et al. (1958) compared children before and after television came to their communities. The personal difficulties of children who became addicts once television was available were already evident *before* they were exposed to television. Evidently children suffering from personal difficulties withdraw from other activities and forms of personal contact and turn to the mass media instead.

Moderating factors

Enough qualifications have been made in the preceding sections to indicate that the outcomes of television viewing are not simple and direct, influencing children in the same way. Rather, television viewing interacts with other factors such as personality characteristics, cognitive characteristics, and family characteristics that moderate or influence the outcomes observed.

To illustrate, *family characteristics* that moderate outcomes of viewing what is perceived as violent, and whether violent acts are considered acceptable, depend partly on social class background (Greenberg & Gordon, 1972). Fifth grade boys from lower-class homes perceived less violence and considered it more acceptable than did fifth grade boys from middle-class homes who watched the same programs, probably because of differences in the amount of violence encountered by the two groups of children in their neighborhood environments. However, whether a particular child's family maintains clear norms or values regarding violent behavior as a way of resolving conflict is also important. Regardless of social class, children whose families maintain clear norms are less likely to consider aggression a good way of resolving conflict than are children whose families do not maintain clear norms (Dominick & Greenberg, 1972).

Cognitive development moderates children's understanding of what they watch in important ways; this is probably one reason why several researchers have found young children—preschool and primary grades—to be more influenced by what they view than older elementary children and adolescents (e.g., see Collins, 1975, 1978). For instance, when children of different ages were interviewed after viewing a televised episode to determine their comprehension of an aggressive sequence, most kindergartners were able to recount only the aggressive content of the episode; not until eighth grade were the largest number of children able to relate the aggressive sequence to the motives behind it and its consequences (see Figure 6–2) (Collins, Berndt, & Hess, 1974). Further, even third graders are less likely to understand the relationship between scenes if the scenes are separated by an interruption such as a commercial; so the connection between, say, negative consequences when the bad guy "gets it" at the end and unacceptable behavior earlier in the program is not likely to be made (Collins, 1973). These results are consistent with the themes that social sensitivity and awareness of others' feelings improve markedly over the school years, and that children become increasingly able to integrate different kinds of information during these years. At the same time the suggestion that younger children may have difficulty in relating observed actions to their consequences is sobering, given the importance of consequences to the model in social learning theory. If adults watching the same scenes provide commentaries on the meaning of scenes and relationships among them the children's comprehension improves substantially (Collins, Sobol, & Westby, 1981). Perhaps it is important that concerned parents not only monitor what children watch, but provide interpretive comments whenever possible.

FIGURE 6–2 Changes in comprehension of television violence over the school years. Kindergartners notice aggression but cannot explain why the aggression occurred (motive) or what happened to the aggressor because of it (consequences). Not until eighth grade could the largest number of children explain the relationships among motives, aggression, and consequences.

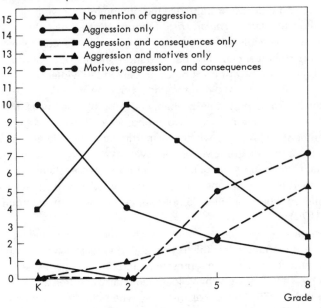

Source: W. A. Collins, T. J. Berndt, and V. L. Hess, "Observational Learning of Motives and Consequences for Television Aggression: A Developmental Study," *Child Development* 45 (1974), pp. 799–802. Copyright 1974 by The Society for Research in Child Development, Inc.

Children's age may also be important in influencing their choice of preferred characters. At least in Scandinavian studies, younger children identify with characters their own age, which older children were unlikely to do. Perhaps in part because of this, they frequently prefer children's programming until about age eight or nine, when their preferences shift to adult programming (Feilitzer and Linné, 1975).

Children's *personal attributes* are also important. We saw in a preceding section that children most influenced by watching aggressive content were those who were already rated as average or above in aggressiveness. As another example, children's reaction to sex-role information from television depends in part on their level of understanding that gender is constant, that is, one is a boy or a girl all of one's life and in all situations. When four- to six-year old children were shown commercials in which a toy was presented as appropriate for one sex, high gender constant children subsequently were willing to play with the toy only if it had been presented as appropriate for their own sex, whereas low gender constant children—who understood the commercial equally well—

were willing to play with the toys regardless of gender attribution (Ruble, Balaban, & Cooper, 1981).

SEX-ROLE DEVELOPMENT

Every culture has a set of *sex-role standards* or *sex-role stereotypes* which describe the standards of masculinity and femininity accepted in that culture. In the United States, the traditional stereotype of masculinity includes assertiveness, independence, orientation toward objects rather than toward persons or relationships, active sexuality, and emotional control. For women, the traditional stereotype includes passivity, dependence, orientation toward persons rather than objects, nurturance of others, passive sexuality, and emotional expressiveness. These traditional stereotypes have been challenged in recent years, but they definitely still persist.

Sex-role development, children's learning about and coming to terms with these standards in their own lives, has a number of components most of which have already begun to develop before children begin school. Sexual identity— one's sense of self as male or female, a cornerstone of identity—develops quite early, being established before children are three. *Gender constancy* is knowledge that one's sex does not change, nor does anyone else's. Little boys, for instance, do not grow up to be mommies who then grow up to be daddies. Gender constancy is also first becoming evident by three or four, but there is variation even up to age seven. Generally, children recognize their own gender constancy before they understand that others' gender is constant too, and gender constancy is more closely linked to intellectual development than it is to chronological age (e.g., Gouze & Nadelman, 1980; Marcus & Overton, 1978; Slaby & Frey, 1975).

Knowledge of sex-role stereotypes has also begun to develop before children start school; even preschool and kindergarten children can tell you things about what boys and girls are like, what mommies do and daddies do. Interestingly, their ideas are characteristically quite traditional, even though they may be growing up in nontraditional homes. Maccoby and Jacklin (1974) mention a four-year-old who insisted that only boys can be doctors. Her own mother was a surgeon. Such stories are not unusual. Children will say, for example, that it's daddies who drive cars, even though the parent they actually see at the wheel is mommy more often than not. Obviously, children's ideas about sex roles are not something simply and directly derived from their own immediate experience!

Finally, *sex-role identity* refers to the child's sense of self as masculine or feminine, the personal coming-to-terms with cultural prescriptions. To the extent that children accept the socially prescribed standards and incorporate them into their own behavior, they are said to be sex-typed. Katz (1979a) suggests that the years up to about age 12 constitute a first stage in sex-role development during which the main emphasis is on learning about sex roles and the main pressures are toward sex-role conformity. (During later stages in adolescence and adulthood other kinds of pressures come into play and sex-role demands may differ.) For children, the pressures toward conformity may already be under challenge by the end of the school years; among girls at least, 11-year-olds show less traditional stereotyping than do 7-year-olds (Meyer, 1980). This may reflect moderation of stereotypic notions through personal identifications (see below) or it may reflect the impact of an increasingly wide range of models and sources of information about sex roles at school and through the mass media.

Children do encounter a good deal of socialization pressure to behave in ways that are sex-typed. Sex roles are usually more clearly delineated among working-class groups than among middle-class groups, and this is reflected in earlier sex-typing among lower-class children than among middle-class children (Rabban, 1950). There is also more, and more consistent, pressure on boys to act in sex-appropriate ways than there is on girls (although the greater ambiguity in sex-typing for girls may cause them greater stress once they reach adolescence and young adulthood). Being a sissy is a shameful thing that boys try to avoid at all costs; being a tomboy is acceptable and, for some girls, even a matter of pride. Perhaps for these reasons, among others, girls are likely to be more flexible regarding sex roles and related behaviors (Worell, 1981). Regardless of sex or social class, however, by second or third grade, children of both sexes are usually strongly sex-typed in regard to their preferred activities; their preferred friends; achievement expectations (what girls can be good at, what boys can be good at); personality attributions for others; expected adult occupations; and so forth.

While children do begin school with some awareness of sex roles, the school years appear to be an important period for rapidly expanding knowledge about sex roles and for consolidation of sex-role behaviors into patterns that may persist into adulthood. When people's adult attributes were compared with measures of their attributes during earlier periods of life, Kagan and Moss (1962) found that ratings made between 6 and 10 years of age were the first to predict adult attributes on many of the personality variables studied. However, sex-role pressures clearly affected these relationships. Continuities were found primarily if the behaviors in question were sex-role appropriate. So, for example, passivity showed continuity for girls but not for boys; aggressiveness showed continuity for boys, but not girls. Behavior disorganization, which included mostly masculine-typed factors such as getting very angry and being unable to tolerate aggression, predicted adult aggression in boys but in contrast predicted intellectual mastery, dependency conflict, and masculine interests in girls—as though social pressures against the masculine-typed earlier pattern had transformed it into more culturally accepted patterns as the girls grew up.

What difference does sex-typing make?

Children's sex-typed preferences and expectations don't just sit in their heads but actively influence their choices and performance in a wide range of circumstances. Even children as young as two or three tend to choose toys categorized as sex-appropriate and to prefer to play with same-sex peers—though, of course, these preferences will be much stronger in the school years, reaching a peak in about second or third grade. Children will even resist pressure to play with cross-sex toys, though this effect may be moderated somewhat by teacher activities (e.g., Ross & Ross, 1972; Serbin, Connor, & Citron, 1981). Performance, including learning and memory performance, are also affected if activities are sex-types. On the same sex-neutral game, both boys and girls got higher scores if the game was presented to them as sex-appropriate rather than sex-inappropriate (Montemayor, 1974). And when asked to remember information that was consistent or inconsistent with traditional role expectations, children generally do better at remembering role-consistent information (e.g., Koblinsky, Cruse, & Sugawara, 1978; Liben & Signorella, 1980). Of course, there are variations. For instance, Liben and Signorella found that the gender-consistent information was remembered best only when the characters were males, which may reflect the lesser role flexibility allowed, and so greater incongruity of role-inconsistency, for males. The implications of findings like these are thought-provoking if one considers the sex-typing of school subjects, such as math, science, or literature.

Why should children show such sex-typed patterns of behavior? Martin and Halverson (1981) start by assuming that it is a normal human tendency to sterotype, that is, to group information into clusters or *schemas* which serve as "naive theories that guide information processing" (p. 1121). In the case of sex-role learning, they suggest that there are two important schemas. The first is an "in group, out group" schema which contains all the general information a child may have about categorizing objects, traits, roles, as appropriate for males or females. The second is an "own sex" schema, which is a narrower and more detailed specification of the attributes appropriate to the child's own sex. Items or behaviors categorized as own-sex appropriate will be acted on: information will be sought about them, learned, remembered. Items or behaviors categorized as opposite-sex appropriate will not be further pursued or will be actively rejected. Thus, both boys and girls know that fathers shave (usually) and mothers use makeup (usually), which is information at the "in group, out group" level. But boys will be more interested in, and learn more about, shaving, whereas girls will be more interested in, play at, and learn more about makeup. In these ways the sex-related schemas serve to regulate children's behavior choices, to organize and direct their attention to information, and other functions. (Note that, though much more elaborated, this model has some thematic similarities with cognitive developmental theory, Box 6–2) These sex-role schemas, according to Martin and Halverson, are *self-defining*—that is, they provide information relevant to how one resembles and differs from others. They also vary in *salience*, which refers to their availability or likelihood of use for encoding information about self and others. Two children may know sex-role standards equally well, but if one uses that information to make choices and guide behavior in many situations, whereas the other uses such information in relatively few situations, the standard has high salience for the first child but low salience for the second child. Thus one will find some children who seem very concerned about behaving in sex-appropriate ways, whereas for others, it does not seem especially important. Obviously children's sex-role related schemas will develop as they learn and understand more about gender constancy, sex-role standards, and the other components of sex-role identity discussed earlier.

The androgyny controversy

The concept of *psychological androgyny* is defined as having attributes and preferences stereotyped as *both* masculine and feminine. This may sound strange to you if you think of masculinity and femininity as the two poles on a single continuum, which would mean that masculinity and femininity are mutually exclusive—the more one has of one, the less one can have of the other. Beginning in the 1970s, however, psychologists began conceptualizing masculinity and femininity as separate dimensions. One could be high on both or *androgynous;* low on both, or *undifferentiated;* high on one, but low on the other, in which case one is *traditionally sex-typed* if high on the dimension consistent with one's sex or *cross-sex typed* if high on the dimension inconsistent with one's sex (e.g., Bem, 1975a, 1975b; Spence, Helmreich, & Stapp, 1975). When a children's measure for assessing these two dimensions was developed, the proportions of each of these groupings found in one sample of third- to sixth-grade children was, for boys, undifferentiated, 27 percent; female-typed, 13 percent; male-typed, 33 percent; and androgynous, 27 percent. The corresponding percentages for girls were 16 percent, 39 percent, 14 percent, and 32 percent (Hall & Halberstadt, 1980). These percentages are fairly similar to those found in older adolescent and young-adult groups (e.g., Spence & Helmreich, 1978).

Even before the androgyny concept was introduced, appropriate sex-typing had been linked with better personal adjustment, greater acceptance from peers, and other indices. However, increasing numbers of researchers have argued that traditional sex-roles are limiting and restrictive, preventing people from enjoying the full range of what are really human behaviors, rather than just masculine or just feminine behaviors. If this is so, then androgynous persons should show greater *sex-role flexibility*—be willing to engage in a variety of activities, able to perform them well, and feel comfortable about doing them—regardless of how the activities are sex-typed. By implication, such individuals should also be well-adjusted. There is some validity to this approach. Early studies with adults showed, for example, that androgynous individuals had highest self-esteem while the self-esteem of undifferentiated persons was lowest (Spence, Helmreich, & Stapp, 1975); and they also demonstrated that androgynous individuals ". . . could be independent and assertive when they needed to be, and warm and responsive in appropriate situations. It didn't matter, in other words whether a behavior was stereotypically masculine or feminine; they did equally well on both" (Bem, 1975b, p. 62).

However, it would not be the androgyny *controversy* if there were not dissenting voices. Some of the dissention is essentially intramural, over how best to conceptualize and to measure masculinity, femininity, and androgyny. Some of the controversy is substantive, however. One substantive issue is whether any observed advantages accrue from androgyny per se or from the generally more socially desirable masculine attributes shared by androgynous individuals of both sexes. Thus, in studies of young adults, Olds and Shaver (1980) found that the masculine cluster of traits was generally beneficial whether found in men or women, whereas femininity tended to be detrimental, at least for academic achievement and health, for both men and women. Similarly, Kelly and Worell (1977) and Jones, Chernovetz, and Hansson (1978) found that high self-esteem was associated with masculine attributes in individuals of either sex. On the other hand, Flaherty and Dusek (1980), when they used a more differentiated measurement, found androgynous individuals to be high on both masculine- and feminine-typed scales, as the concept of androgynous flexibility would suggest.

Perhaps more basic is the issue of whether couching these studies in terms of sex-typing may be misleading. Maybe it is whether or not one has certain attributes, regardless of whether one is male or female or whether the attribute is typed as masculine or feminine, which is important to one's personal success, self-esteem, adjustment, and flexibility (e.g., Olds and Shaver, 1980; Helmreich, Spence, & Holahan, 1979). We cannot resolve these controversies here, but we can make some observations about them. First, no one has said that androgyny is bad for children or adults; rather, they question what it is that is good about it and whether we ought not shift our attention to studying particular attributes rather than to the perhaps incidental sex-typing of those attributes. A second is that no matter how the current controversies are resolved, they have shown beyond doubt that the old simple view of masculinity and femininity as op-posites simply do not do justice to the complexity of sex-role related behaviors and understanding in children and adults. A third is that if a parent or teacher sees a child engaging in some activity usually thought of as cross-sex typed for that child, such an observation is *not* by itself a basis for concern that there is anything deviant or wrong with the child; in fact, such cross-sex behavior may very well be a sign of healthy flexibility on the part of the child.

How are sex-typed behaviors learned?

Three major processes influence sex-role development. One of these is cog-nitive development. Not only do children learn more information about sex roles and show general changes in the thinking skills they can apply to such informa-tion, there is also the formation of schemas with their consequences for behavior and preferences which we have already discussed above.

A second major process is direct shaping of behavior through rewards or punishments. Being praised for being "ladylike" or "a real man," or being laughed at by peers for doing things they consider sex-inappropriate, are exam-ples of this process. Parents are usually thought of as the main source of such rewards and punishments, but this may be a mistake. In fact, children may encounter more open socialization pressure for sex-typed behaviors from stran-gers and from persons outside the home, since strangers are more likely to react to children on the basis of expectations for their sex whereas parents are more likely to relate to them as individuals having their own interest and attributes (e.g., Maccoby & Jacklin, 1974).

Finally, there are the processes of identification with and imitation of like-sex models, as discussed earlier in this chapter. The importance of like-sex parents as models has been emphasized traditionally; this emphasis follows directly from Freud's theory of personality development (Chapter 1). But here again, the parental influence may have been emphasized disproportionately. Children learn from a variety of sources besides parents—other adults, peers, media, and teachers. Sex-role behaviors from other sources may be more easily discriminated than sex-role behaviors of parents; children may not see much of their own parents' role-differentiated behavior in comparison to the adult role-differentiated behavior they may see on television, for example. In one study of sex-role flexibility, a concept similar to androgyny, as much as 60 percent of the variation in children's scores could be attributed to peers and television (Katz, 1979a, 1979b). Another study mentioned previously found girls' sex roles to be more traditional and stereotypic at age 7 than at age 11, whereas the correlation between the girls' scores and measures completed by their mothers was greater at age 11 than it was at 7 (Meyer, 1980). This pattern of results suggests that children identify first with a general sex-role stereotype which only later begins to be moderated through personal identification with mother. Notice that this is not to say that parents are not important, only that for sex-role development in the school years other sources may be more influential than parents.

COMPETENCE AND MASTERY MOTIVATION

The concepts of competence and industry play an important role in some theories of personality, as we saw in Chapter 1. Certainly, with their entry into school themes of competence and industry become more central to children's lives; there are now school-based expectations for tending to business and performing well as well as for getting along with peers, and once in school parents' concern over competence also become stronger.

For several years Susan Harter has been developing a theory of children's competence and mastery motivation which, while rooted in White's theory (Chapter 1), expands and elaborates on it in thought-provoking ways (Harter, 1978, 1980, 1981). White's original proposal was quite simple. A child's attempts at mastery result in success; such success produces pleasurable feelings of efficacy which, in turn, maintain or increase effectance motivation; and the higher the effectance motivation, the greater the likelihood that the child will make mastery attempts. Central to this model is *effectance motivation,* which constitutes the intrinsic, built-in motivational process that keeps the cycle going. This is fine so far as it goes; but when Harter tried to apply this model to understand children's behavior more explicitly, she discovered that there are a number of issues with which it does not deal. Many of the elaborations Harter has developed are incorporated into the diagram of her "working model" shown in Figure 6–3. Among the major modifications are the following.

First, mastery and competence may develop differently in different realms of endeavor—we are all familiar with a child who is good at school but not at sports, or the child who makes friends easily but is only moderately good in

FIGURE 6–3   Harter's working model of effectance motivation.

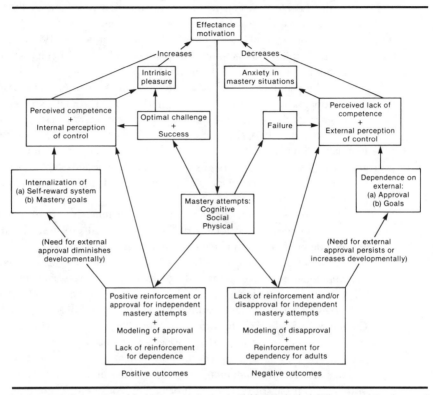

Source: S. Harter, "A Model of Mastery Motivation in Children: Individual Difference and Developmental Change," in *Minnesota Symposium on Child Psychology*, vol. 14 (Hillsdale, N. J.: Lawrence Erlbaum Associates, 1980).

class. Harter proposes that we distinguish children's perceived competence in these three realms: the cognitive, the social, and the physical.

Second, White's original formulation mentioned only success, yet it is clear that failures can influence effectance motivation as well. In Figure 6–3, influences related to successful mastery attempts—which produce an intrinsically oriented person—are shown on the left-hand side, while influences related to failures and likely to produce an extrinsically oriented person are shown on the right. (You will find the scheme of White's original formulation on the left, upper center of the figure.) Furthermore, not all successes are equal (and, by implication, neither are all failures equal). There appears to be a *level of optimal challenge or difficulty* at which a problem is hard enough that it is no longer any fun. For example, sixth graders who were given anagrams of four different difficulties preferred hard (but not very hard) anagrams, as indexed by smiling while they worked and by the difficulty level of new problems they would choose. Interestingly, when they thought the anagrams were school tasks for grades, rather than games, they chose easier ones on which to work (Harter, 1978). Similarly, 4- to 10-year olds assessed for level of classification skill (see

Chapter 2), when later given a choice of "learning centers" at which to work chose the "center" which featured classification problems at the level just beyond their present level of skill (Danner & Lonky, 1981).

Third, there is the issue of the child's socialization history—what has happened in a child's interactions with parents and other caregivers? These processes are incorporated in the outside loops of Figure 6–3. So, in the case of an intrinsically oriented child, mastery attempts lead to positive reinforcement from others, dependence is not rewarded, and so on. Through experiencing such consequences the child internalizes both a self-reward system and mastery goals, and as this happens, the child's need for external approval from others gradually diminishes. Notice, too, that these consequences apply to mastery *attempts* (That was a good try!) as well as to completed mastery efforts. A similar chain of negative consequences and their effects is diagrammed at the outside of the right-hand figure.

Harter points out that one's perceived competence and one's perception of control are important correlates of the motivational processes in the model. Perceived competence can be viewed as one subset of one's attributions regarding the causes of one's own behavior, and there is evidence that such attributions in competence-related settings undergo important changes between the primary grades and the later elementary grades. From Harter's work (1980) there are the outcomes of factor analytic studies of children's responses to her Perceived Competence Scale. For third to six graders, the factor analytic results clearly reflect the three separate domains of perceived competence. For younger children, however, this was not yet the case. There appears to be a general competence dimension which includes both cognitive and physical tasks—anything you have to try at, or can be good or bad at, goes here. Then there is a social acceptance dimension which includes both acceptance from peers and acceptance from mother. Evidently younger children do not conceptualize social interactions as involving skills; you are either liked or not liked.

Taking a somewhat different approach, Ruble, Boggiano, Feldman, and Loebl (1980) looked at children's use of *social comparison* information—information about their own performance relative to other children—as a basis for self-evaluation. Such a process may be an important basis for self-socialization by children; changes seen in it should be important both for how children understand and evaluate their own performance and for notions about how peer interactions may be important to children. Over two studies, they found no evidence that children in first and second grades make use of social comparison information in this way, although fourth graders clearly did so. This was not a matter of children not being interested in comparing their performance with others, or of children's being able to evaluate their own performance, both of which have been documented in five- or seven-year-olds. But the first and second graders did not put these two things together. Why they did not isn't clear. Still, it doesn't seem too out of line to suggest that there may be some link between emerging use of self-evaluation, emerging awareness that social interactions do require skill, and emerging social-cognitive awareness that one can assess and be assessed by peers (e.g., Chapter 2).

Ruble et al. also suggest that younger children may be so preoccupied with the tasks themselves that evaluation information, though present, isn't very salient to them, although many school practices—grades, teacher reactions, etc.—work to increase the salience of evaluation. These processes together with emerging social comparisons may also contribute to the differentiation of social, cognitive, and physical domains of competence.

Intrinsic versus extrinsic motivation

A central focus of Harter's model is on intrinsic motivation versus extrinsic motivation, with emphasis on intrinsic orientation in individuals—what processes make children more or less likely to find mastery attempts and activities interesting and fun for their own sake? A scale developed to measure children's intrinsic versus extrinsic orientation in classroom activities has produced some very interesting outcomes (Harter, 1981). When children's responses on the five subscales of the measure were analyzed, two clusters of subscales emerged. One cluster contained two subscales dealing with whether children feel able to make independent judgments about what to do versus relying on the teacher's direction of their activities, and knowing when they have succeeded or failed versus

FIGURE 6–4 Children's motivation for classroom activities may grow increasingly intrinsic over grades (bottom graphs) or increasingly extrinsic over grades (top graphs), depending upon which aspects of motivation one looks at.

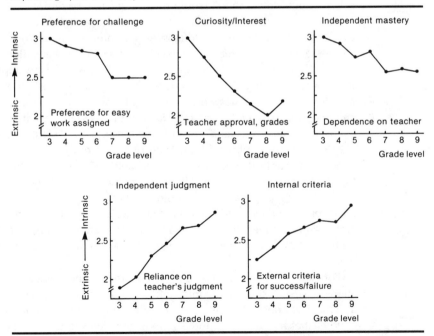

Note: Mean score by grade level for each subscale.
Source: S. Harter, "A New Self-Report Scale of Intrinsic Versus Extrinsic Orientation in the Classroom: Motivational and Informational Components," *Developmental Psychology* 17 (1981), pp. 300–12.

needing external evaluations such as grades, teacher feedback, and so forth. On these subscales, shown in the bottom of Figure 6–4, children's scores became increasingly intrinsic between grades three and nine. The second cluster showed the opposite pattern, however. This cluster, illustrated at the top of Figure 6–4, contains subscales dealing with children's preference for challenge versus preference for easy work; whether children work to satisfy their own curiosities and interest or to get the teacher's approval; and whether the children prefer to work things out for themselves or depend on the teacher for help in working out problems and assignments.

What to make of these divergent results? One point is that the two clusters seem to tap somewhat different areas. The first cluster, which shows increases over grades, seems to involve cognitive informational structures—knowing what to do, knowing criteria for evaluating performance. It makes sense that older children should know more about school, what to do there, and what the criteria are for good performance. The second cluster is more problematic, however. This cluster appears more clearly motivational, dealing with what children want to do, like to do, or prefer to do. Does the decline in scores suggest that over time schools gradually undermine children's intrinsic interest in school-based activities—which is, as Harter comments, the most value-laden possible interpretation? Or is it perhaps simply adaptation to school structure, which reinforces a relatively extrinsic orientation? In this latter case, it may well be that the results are very domain specific—that parallel sets of questions in physical and social domains, or even parallel questions regarding cognitive activities outside of school, would show a different pattern.

Intrinsic orientation is not just a matter of individual predispositions, however. No matter what an individual's level of intrinsic orientation, there will be circumstances under which it will be more or less likely that children will show intrinsic motivation, that is, engage in some activity without any apparent external reward for doing so. In an early study along these lines, young children's baseline rates of activities were observed in a preschool setting. Subsequently, children were induced to engage in a high base-rate activity in return for extrinsic reward, a "Good Player" certificate. When their subsequent free choices were again observed, the rates of choice of the rewarded activity declined significantly (Lepper, Greene, & Nisbett, 1973). Lepper (1980) comments that these and other similar results stirred a strong wave of interest, quite out of proportion to the limitations of the studies themselves. One cannot simply take these results and conclude that, for example, all extrinsic rewards—including grades—undermine intrinsic motivation, and therefore, through this mechanism schools stifle children's interest in learning. There is much, much more involved than that.

For example, coming back to more concrete issues of what it is about situations that may foster or undermine intrinsic motivation, Lepper (1980) discusses a number of considerations. One of these is the extent to which it is clear to children that an external reinforcer or motivator depends on the child's doing the activity. Two groups of children can be given the same award, but if one is told ahead of time that they'll get it for performing the task, whereas to the second group it is a surprise award following their performance, the first group will later show decrement in interest in the task but the second will not. The clearer the instrumental link between the activity and the reward, the more likely one will see decremental effects.

Another important issue is whether the reward is task-contingent or performance contingent. In the work-world, getting your paycheck is task-contingent—so long as you do your job, you get paid; but bonuses are performance contingent—you get them only if your performance has been above a certain standard. In relation to intrinsic motivation, it is task-contingent rewards that have the greatest decremental effect on children's subsequent interest. Lepper suggests that one likely reason for this is that performance-contingent rewards have an informational component—they tell an individual something about his or her performance which is likely to enhance perceived competence (back to intrinsic motivation in Harter's sense). In support of this interpretation, Lepper mentions other research which has shown quite consistently that verbal praise tends to increase subsequent intrinsic motivation, whereas tangible rewards for the same performance are less effective in doing so. Here again, however, verbal praise is likely to give children more information about their competence and ability at some task than does a tangible reward.

Obviously, we are dealing here with complex interactions of factors, but the issues are important enough to try to work our way through the complexities. On the one hand, one must obviously be quite clear about just what aspect of intrinsic motivation one is addressing: Are you talking about individual predispositions of children? Or are you concerned with characteristics of situations that are facilitory or detrimental to intrinsic motivation? If so, which characteristics of the situations? On the other hand, Lepper (1980) argues that showing decremental effects of rewards may be just one part of a larger phenomenon having to do with social constraint in general: Whenever there is a social constraint which is out of line or disproportionate to the issue at hand, it is likely to have decremental effects on subsequent performance. Examples of constraints besides rewards which have had such deleterious effects for children are close surveillance—"breathing down their necks"—and forcing them to do tasks which they might otherwise have done anyway. It is tempting to take individual portions of these findings and apply them directly to school and home situations, as was done with the early studies of the detrimental effects of reward on children's intrinsic motivation for activities. But in the long run, such overgeneralization is likely to be more misleading than informative. Meanwhile, as evident in the work reported above, we do know substantially more about intrinsic motivation in children and the situational factors which can influence it than we did 10 years ago!

Learned helplessness

We have had occasion previously to mention attribution theory, the study of people's inferences (attributions) about the causes of behavior and the consequences of such attributions. Some of the outcomes discussed in the preceding section can be seen in terms of attributions. Whether children see what they do as controlled by their own choices—intrinsic motivation, "I get to," or by external social constraints—external rewards or constraints, "I have to," are certainly attributions. Factors that increase "I have to" attributions are among those having detrimental effects on intrinsic motivation.

Another set of competence-related attributions that clearly affect children's behavior are those associated with *learned helplessness*—one's perception of oneself as unable to surmount failure. Learned helplessness is linked to the reasons children give for why they fail. Children high in learned helplessness attribute failures to unchanging factors over which they have little control, in particular ability (I'm just no good at this), whereas children low in learned helplessness attribute failure to controllable factors, especially effort, or to factors external to self (I didn't try hard enough; I should have done it that other way; I had bad luck; the teacher has it in for me). These differences in attributions are also linked to marked differences in performance when failure is encountered. Even when children have been carefully pretested to be sure they can do some task equally well, failure experiences are *much* more disruptive for learned helpless children. Their performance deteriorates following failure and they express negative feelings, whereas other children's performance does not deteriorate and may even improve (Dweck, 1975; Dweck and Repucci, 1973). This is true not only in cognitive problem-solving situations, but also in social situations. One study found that pretty much regardless of their popularity, learned helpless children faced with apparent rejection from a peer became socially less effective than they had been initially, whereas other children tried harder and often performed more effectively following apparent rejection (Goetz & Dweck, 1980).

Not only do children's attributions for failure differ depending on learned helplessness; so also do their strategies following failure—perhaps one reason the performance of low helpless children may actually improve. These differences are quite pronounced, as Table 6–2 shows (Diener & Dweck, 1978). Helpless children are likely to focus on the causes of failure (which, recall, are likely to be perceived as uncontrollable) and not on the tasks in question, so they make little change in their behavior or even quit trying. In contrast, low helpless or mastery oriented children are likely to focus on the task and its demands, monitoring their own strategies and modifying them in appropriate ways. Fur-

TABLE 6–2
Number of learned helpless and mastery-oriented children whose hypothesis-testing strategy improved, remained the same, or deteriorated following failure

Group	Improved study 1	2	Same study 1	2	Deteriorated study 1	2
Helpless	0	0	5	9	24	21
Mastery-Oriented	10	11	21	15	7	4

Source: C. I. Diener and C. S. Dweck, "An Analysis of Learned Helplessness: Continuous Changes in Performance, Strategy, and Achievement Cognitions Following Failure," *Journal of Personality and Social Psychology* 36 (1978), pp. 451–62. Fig. 2. p. 457.

thermore, when helpless children do encounter success, they are more likely than mastery oriented children to devalue it—underestimating their degree of success, stating that their successes do not reflect on their ability, and expecting their successes not to continue (Diener & Dweck, 1980). How many people do you know who despite consistently passing tests and good grades are nonetheless convinced that they haven't the ability to pass the upcoming test? Above, we mentioned that not all successes are equal because of characteristics of the tasks. Here again not all successes are equal, but in this case because objectively equivalent successes have very different meanings to helpless versus mastery oriented individuals.

What determines learned helplessness in children? For one thing, younger children are less vulnerable to helplessness than are older children. Kindergartners and first graders given puzzles to solve were less influenced by failure experiences than were third and fifth graders (Rholes, Blackwell, Jordan & Walters, 1981). Further, the attributions for success and failure of children in the first three grades tended to be positively correlated with each other and with outcomes, probably reflecting a *halo schema* in which outcome, effort, and ability are seen as related—If I get it right, I'm smart and lucky; if I get it wrong, I'm dumb and unlucky (Kun, 1977; Nicholls, 1978). For the fifth graders, in contrast, the correlations were negative, suggesting that children were using a *compensatory schema* in which ability and effort are negatively related—if I get it right, I'm smart, but if I get it wrong, I'm not lucky. (Learned helpless children would say, "If I get it wrong, I'm stupid.") Since learned helplessness is linked to ability attributions, children who use the "halo schema"—younger children —are less likely to fall into the helplessness pattern. (Note, too, that here is another example of a shift in how children construe themselves and their performance which changes from primary to later grades.)

The extent to which children's life experiences include failure also appears to influence learned helplessness, as one might predict from the right-hand side of Figure 6–3. (Learned helplessness is not the same thing as low effectance or low mastery motivation, but it can reasonably be thought of as one subcategory under this heading.) Retarded children inevitably experience more failure than do nonretarded children. When educable mentally retarded children who were mainstreamed were compared with nonretarded children from the same school system, not only did their use of strategies in a learning situation deteriorate substantially more following failure, but their teachers also rated them as significantly more helpless than other children on a variety of day-to-day behaviors (Weisz, 1981). In addition, there was some suggestion that these effects may be even greater for black retarded children, although more evidence on this point is needed.

There are also sex differences in learned helplessness, with girls likely to be more helpless than boys (e.g., Dweck & Bush, 1976; Dweck, Davidson, Nelson, & Enna, 1978). In one relevant study, Dweck, Goetz, and Strauss (1980) suggested that since girls are more likely to attribute failure to abilities that remain relatively consistent over situations and boys make attributions to motivational and situational factors that change from situation to situation, learned helplessness effects should be persistent for girls but attenuated for boys as one goes from one situation to another. They found this to be the case not only in a laboratory task, but in the "real life" situation of transferring from one grade to the next. As they point out, this may be one contributing factor to sex differences in math and verbal abilities which are little seen in the primary grades, but which become increasingly pronounced in the later grades and high school. Verbal skills like reading, once learned, need simply be reapplied to new material; changes are relatively gradual. Math, however, involves a succession of new domains and new concepts—arithmetic, algebra, and geometry—which may very well be perceived as different situations in ways that, say, seventh- and eighth-grade English or social studies are not. For boys, each of these "new situations" may present a new challenge relatively unencumbered by past history, but for girls with their tendency to overgeneralize ability attributions over situations, each new topic may simply be a new arena for more failures which accumulate over time. In this case, it is no surprise that even at equivalent achievement levels, girls are more likely to drop out of math!

Implicit in this discussion is the suggestion that for learned helpless children, each failure not only says something about the child's performance on the particular task, but also reinforces a more generalized expectancy or attribution that one is incompetent and incapable. Why should some children be so caught in such a trap whereas others seem to be relatively free of it? Life history experience is relevant: it certainly applies for retarded children who experience more failures. But there is no evidence that girls systematically fail more often than boys. Given that we are dealing with attributions—modes of cognitively construing or interpreting the world—perhaps systematically different messages to groups of children interact with actual failure and success experiences to produce some of the observed differences. For instance, what of messages regarding sex-appropriate behaviors from diverse sources, which tend to suggest that boys are competent and active, while girls are not? If a girl at some level believes the message that boys are competent, then her own competent performance is an objective success but a sex-role failure—a mixed message which would not occur for a boy, at least on this task.

And, of course, there is the issue of individual children's socialization histories, with the possibility that important processes that may contribute to later effectance motivation or learned helpless behavior may have roots as far back as infancy; there is evidence that supportive contingent stimulation in early years fosters not only specific performance, but also generalized expectancies for success (e.g., Lewis & Goldberg, 1968; Kodera, 1980; Fitzgerald, McKinney & Strommen, 1981). With the caution that the connecting links have not been examined, still it seems reasonable that some such connection should exist. Clearly, we have a good start but still have a great deal to learn before we fully understand children's competence and mastery motivation.

SUMMARY

The psychobiological foundations of personality are evident in topics covered in this chapter which deal, on the one hand, with hereditary patterns and early predispositions and, on the other hand, with processes and environmental influences that shape children's behavior over the school years. Evidence for heredity is not as strong as in the case of cognition, but there is reason to assume some hereditary influence in personality. Temperament refers to patterns of reactivity and self-regulation characteristic of an individual. Children already differ temperamentally in infancy, and differences among them show some stability over time—although one cannot assume that the same patterns seen in infancy will necessarily characterize that child eight years later. Of especial importance for understanding the role of temperament in development are the concepts of consonance, or match, and dissonance, or mismatch, between children's temperament patterns and the requirements of the situations in which they find themselves.

Identification and modeling, or observational learning, are two similar concepts which refer to processes whereby children come to take on the attributes of persons around them, especially persons important to them. Both psychodynamic theories and social learning theory consider such processes central to socialization. Observational learning depends on a number of factors: vicarious reinforcement, cognitive factors such as sex-role schemas, attributes of the child, and—especially important—attributes of the model, such as the model's power or nurturance toward the child.

Though learning from television is passive compared with direct interactions, children clearly are influenced by the television that they watch, at least in part, through observational learning. Watching violent programs does result in increased aggressive behavior, but other aspects of children's behavior are also influenced by television—prosocial behaviors, political awareness, learning. The effects of watching television are moderated by a number of factors such as family background, behavioral norms in the family, whether parents watch and discuss TV shows with their children; attributes of the children such as cognitive processing skills which improve with age; the initial levels of behaviors, such as aggressiveness; and so on. Very heavy viewers—media addicts—are often children who have psychological problems, but the evidence suggests that in this case, it is the problems that result in the heavy viewing and not the other way around.

Sex-role development consists of a child's coming to terms with a culture's sex-role prescriptions. Children must learn sex-role standards, establish sexual identities, establish sex-role identities, learn gender constancy. Children encounter pressures toward sex-role conformity; their ideas of sex roles are very traditional, especially in the early school years. Such pressures are more intense and one-sided for boys; girls show more flexibility. Sex roles may be beginning to consolidate during the school years in ways that may persist into later periods of life. Sex-role development does not occur in a vacuum, but is linked to children's processing of information, their preferences, what they will remember and learn. Psychological androgyny refers to having behaviors sex typed as both masculine and feminine. Early workers thought that androgynous individuals were better adjusted in a variety of ways. This may be true, though critics now are saying that it may be the presence of masculine-typed attributes that are really associated with the better adjustment, or, more radically, that we may be on a goose chase thinking of these things in terms of sex typing, rather than focusing on the attributes regardless of how they are typed.

Finally, the degree to which a child shows high levels of effectance or mastery motivation (is intrinsically oriented) reflects both factors about the child: predispositions, cumulative socialization history; and factors about the situation: whether the task is at an optimum level of difficulty, whether the task is in cognitive, social, or physical domains, whether there are external rewards or unwarranted social pressures on the child to perform such a task (in which case intrinsic motivation will decline). There are important changes in mastery related attributions from primary to later grades, as seen in changing factor structures of their perceived competence responses and in the changes in their use of social comparison information.

In contrast to mastery-oriented children, learned-helpless children believe that they are unable to overcome the effects of failure; they attribute their failures to their ability rather than to effort or external factors, and in fact, failure experience is much more disruptive to their performance than to the performance of other children. Younger children are less likely to be helpless than are older children. Children with greater histories of failure, such as retarded children, are more helpless, and girls are more helpless than boys. Such differences undoubtedly reflect the socialization histories of the children, especially their actual success and failures in interaction with social messages regarding the meaning of such successes and failures.

TERMS AND CONCEPTS

temperament
reactivity
self-regulation
constitutional patterns
easy children
slow-to-warm-up children
difficult children
consonance of child predispositions and situation
dissonance of child predispositions and situation
central orientation
emotional expressiveness-reserve
placidity-explosiveness-reserve
identification
modeling
observational learning
cognitive factors in observational learning
vicarious reinforcement

characteristics of models as factors influencing observational learning
prosocial behaviors
political socialization
media addicts
moderating factors in effects of TV viewing
sex-role standards or stereotypes
sex identity
sex-role identity
sex-role development
gender constancy
schemas for sex-role learning
self-defining schemas
salience and schemas
psychological androgyny
undifferentiated sex-typing
traditional sex-typing
cross-sex typing
sex-role flexibility

effectance motivation
level of optimal difficulty
social comparison
learned helplessness

halo schema in attributions of
success and failure
compensatory schema for
attributions success and failure

SUGGESTED ADDITIONAL READING

Thomas, A., & Chess, S. *Temperament and development*. New York: Brunner/Mazel, 1977.

Liebert, R. M., Neale, J. M., & Davidson, E. S. *The early window: Effects of television on children and youth* (2nd ed.). New York: Pergamon Press, 1982.

Maccoby, E., & Jacklin, C. N. *The psychology of sex differences*. Stanford, Calif.: Stanford University Press, 1975.

Harter, S. A model of intrinsic mastery motivation in children: Individual differences and developmental change. *Minnesota Symposia on child psychology* (Vol. 14). Hillsdale, N.J.: Lawrence Erlbaum Associates, 1980.

CHAPTER 7

MORAL DEVELOPMENT

Among the tasks facing children as they grow up is learning "ground rules" of their society. One major set of ground rules are the generally accepted moral standards by which people are judged as good or bad.

The specifics of what children learn to consider moral or immoral, as well as the particular attitudes and values to which they are exposed, depend very heavily on the social setting in which they grow up. There are few universal moral standards, and even those are likely to be expressed differently in different social groups. For example, all social groups regulate aggression among their own group members, and none condone murder. But if some group believes that only its own members are really human—and some groups do believe this— then killing an outsider is not murder. Or think of fighting and aggression among children; some groups condone little or no aggression, whereas others permit a great deal.

Likewise, all social groups regulate sexual relationships among their members in some way. But the degree to which sexual interest and exploration among children is considered natural, and the amount of freedom allowed them, differ considerably. The prevailing view in the United States is that sexual interest and curiosity among children should be strongly discouraged. Consequently, many children receive little or no information regarding sexuality until adolescence, if then. They are well aware of the adult disapproval, though this does not keep them from being curious.

Such attributes as striving for individual excellence and competitiveness tend to be highly valued in the United States. This is especially true for Anglo-American children. In several studies, Anglo-American children were consistently more competitive than were children from other cultural groups, enough so as to interfere with cooperative problem solving when working with another same-sex, same-age child (Kagan & Madsen, 1971, 1972; Madsen & Shapira, 1970). We also take for granted the related assumption that rewarding children for individual excellence is a valuable motivational device for learning (think of grades). However, among some American Indian tribes, cooperation, sharing, and group cohesiveness are highly valued, and competitiveness or striving for individual excellence is strongly discouraged. If children from these tribes are given special treats as reinforcements for good work, they simply share them with the other children—and this is true even among children young enough to be enrolled in a Head Start-type program. The reinforcement approach that works with most children in the United States did not work at all with such Indian children, somewhat to the bemusement of the program's developers. This example is instructive for its suggestion that behaviors and attributes which might easily be thought of as typical in children, such as difficulty in learning to share, or responding to special attention for individual achievement, may not be typical in the sense of being universal among children, but instead may reflect attributes fostered in children growing up where certain values, such as competitiveness, are taken for granted.

However, U.S. culture is our main concern here. The moral standards, attitudes, and values discussed in this chapter are likely to be widely encountered in the United States. This is not meant to imply that these are necessarily the best or the only standards children might learn. But they are standards that most children are likely to encounter, if not at home, then at school or among peers.

CONSCIENCE

Conscience is a concept familiar to most people as a sort of monitor that prevents one from doing wrong, as though there were some inner system that warned against forbidden acts or punished them if done (having a ''guilty conscience''). Preventing children from misbehavior and teaching them not to do wrong are areas of much concern to parents, and psychologists have spent more time in studying the conscience aspect of moral development than any other.

Freud's ideas influenced much of both psychological work and popular thinking on conscience. The pertinent part of Freud's theory begins at the end of the Oedipal period, when children are assumed to repress the conflicts and anxieties of that period while simultaneously beginning to identify with parents (see Chapter 1). Through identification, children are assumed to internalize their parents' standards and principles of conduct in much the same way that children are assumed to internalize other aspects of their parents' behavior. Such internalization presumes rapidly changing cognitive skills, including symbolization of meanings of events in the child's life, improved and increasingly conceptual memory organization, and differentiation of thoughts about fantasy from thoughts about reality (Tice, 1980). The internalization of adult standards results in the formation of the *superego*. Within the superego, the internalized prohibitions, or "thou shalt nots," make up the *conscience* whereas the internalized prescriptions, or "thou shalts," make up the *ego ideal.* Once the standards are internalized, either transgression or temptation to transgress against them is assumed to produce unpleasant feelings of guilt that may prevent giving in to temptation or may "punish" transgression. (For a recent review of this position in more depth, see Tice, 1980.)

However, the research evidence does not support this theory of conscience development very well. For one thing, the theory suggests that resistance to deviation should be related to the strength of conscience and to guilt. But no such relationship has been consistently demonstrated. However, moral conduct and resistance to deviation are related to such factors as intellectual development, self-esteem, and planning and decision-making capabilities (Kohlberg, 1964).

Furthermore, although children do learn rules of conduct, these rules do not appear to be internalized very well as general principles during middle childhood. In light of what is now known about cognitive development, this is not very surprising. Studies of the development of moral judgments (to be discussed in detail later) show little evidence of self-accepted moral principles until adolescence. In addition, it has been suggested that only at the beginning of the school years do children become able to inhibit immediate responses, even in situations where there is little emotional involvement (see Chapter 5). But temptations to transgress may be strongly felt and difficult to resist, making it much more difficult to refrain from forbidden acts. This is true at any age, but it may be especially true when children are first learning to apply their new capacity for inhibition.

Moreover, children do not appear to do much evaluating of their own behavior or impulses against rules of conduct, the process assumed to produce the guilt feelings that result in moral behavior. When sixth graders were asked to complete stories in which children had transgressed in some way, their story completions did include some self-evaluation, along with confession, making restitution, and other such outcomes (Aronfreed, 1961). But self-evaluation was relatively rare, and when it occurred, it did not typically lead to the other moral outcomes, such as confession and reparation. Aronfreed suggested that transgressions become associated with anxiety because they are often punished. Once this happens, any response which reduces the anxiety may be learned, and self-evaluation is just one of several types of responses that are learned in this way. This type of view is generally held by social learning theorists.

Finally, the process of identification with parents appears to play a less important role in moral development than has been believed (i.e., Hoffman, 1970). This is not too surprising if one stops and thinks for a moment. There is the matter of mixed messages which parents give to children, either because they hold one standard for themselves and another for their children, or because they themselves hold two standards but do not recognize the contradiction between them. The adult who smokes and drinks but punishes a child for doing so is one example of the "Do as I say, not as I do" category. Another example is the father who gets after his son for fighting or mischief-making but brags to friends about the son's spunk. The son is as likely to respond to the cues of his father's pride as to his father's expressed displeasure.

Parents may also be relatively invisible as models for moral standards, both because the activities of children and adults are separated and because much of adult moral consideration may be covert and therefore unobservable by children. Consequently, children do not see parents or other adults handling situations which the children themselves face, nor do they see the kinds of moral conflicts which adults face "out there" in the adult world. As for the adult moral behaviors that children do observe, the adults' feelings or reasons for acting as they do may not be made explicit, but may be detectable only through inference based on subtle cues. And, as we have already seen (Chapter 3), the capacity for this sort of interpersonal inference is not yet well developed in school-aged children, although it is increasing rapidly during the school years.

So identification with parents may be limited as a source of conscience development, not because identification is unimportant, but because parents are inaccessible as models. Parents undoubtedly differ in their accessibility, and it is likely that when parents are careful to "set a good example" by making their own moral standards explicit and by acting consistently in relation to them, as well as by pointing out similarities between their own moral decisions and those facing the children, identification as a basis for conscience development is strengthened. Parents may also become more salient as models as children grow older, in part as a consequence of children's improving social perception and in part because of children's increased interest and participation in adult concerns.

CONSISTENCY OF MORAL CONDUCT IN SCHOOL-AGED CHILDREN

To say that someone has a strong conscience is usually interpreted as meaning that that person has moral standards which are maintained regardless of the situation. The person is consistently honest, or trustworthy, or dependable. Do school-aged children show such consistency? The answer is, only to a small extent (Hartshorne & May, 1928; Burton, 1963). For the most part, whether or not children lie, or cheat, or steal, depends chiefly on the situation in which they find themselves. This is especially true in the primary grades. Among the important situational factors which may influence whether or not children violate codes of conduct are the likelihood of being caught, the severity of the perceived penalty if they are caught, and the importance to the child of the outcome that might be attained by violating some code of conduct. Children (adults too) are much more likely to transgress when they badly want some outcome, such as a good grade or special recognition, than when the outcome makes little difference to them. There may be sex differences in the factors influencing moral behavior. For example, one study of fifth graders found that girls are more likely to cheat if they have consistently negative self-perceptions, whereas situational factors, such as how badly they did on an exam, are more likely to influence boys (Johnson & Gormly, 1972).

In addition, there is the question of competition between the peer group's code and that of adults. In the child's eyes, humiliation or rejection by peers may be a much more serious outcome than punishment by parents or discipline by teachers, and the code of the peer group may be much more compelling than the "silly rules" laid down by grown-ups. So where the codes conflict, children may often go with the peer code.

However, inconsistent conduct across situations is not necessarily a bad thing. Different meaning and different demands are attached to different situations. The individual who is insensitive to such differences, or is unable to moderate behavior in relation to them, might well be called rigid or inflexible. A lie to avoid embarrassment may be a quite different matter than a lie to save another person's life. Stealing for the thrill of it may be quite different from stealing when that is one's only means of survival. Furthermore, before one can judge whether another individual observes a standard consistently, one must know the *other person's* interpretation of the standard. If, for instance, children think of cheating as something one does only on tests in school, whereas an experimenter also considers "fudging" one's score on a game as cheating, the children could behave completely consistently by their definition and yet be judged inconsistent by the experimenter. This issue of individual consistency in relation to situational demands is important not only in regard to moral behaviors but to personality attributes as well. Understanding what people do requires knowing something about both their individual attributes and the situations in which they find themselves (Bem & Allen, 1974).

If this is so, one might expect to find inconsistency in the moral conduct of both adults and children—and we do. It is likely that the incidence of transgression among adults is about as great as the incidence among children (Kohlberg, 1964). Adults do frequently lie, cheat, steal, or otherwise behave in proscribed ways. Petty thievery of office supplies and small equipment is widespread. So is cheating on income tax. The determinants mentioned for transgressions among children, including the likelihood of being caught, the consequences if caught, and the perceived seriousness of the transgression, influence many adults in much the same way that they influence children.

Nonetheless, transgressions may occur for different reasons or may reflect different processes among adults than among children. When children begin school, their definitions of lying, cheating, stealing, and other transgressions are likely to be tied to specific acts: lying is telling mom you did something when you didn't; stealing is taking Billy's bike. Such definitions are not only very concrete and specific; they are also idiosyncratic to each child. During the school years, children's definitions become more general—lying is saying something that's not true; stealing is taking anything that belongs to someone else—and also more similar to the definitions which most adults would hold. In addition, there is some evidence that consistency between stated standards and actual conduct does increase in the later years of grade school, at least for standards about which the children feel strongly. Henshel (1971) found that fourth-grade girls were equally likely to cheat, regardless of the value they expressed concerning cheating, whereas by seventh grade the girls who felt strongly that cheating was wrong were unlikely to do so when given the opportunity.

PARENTAL DISCIPLINE PATTERNS AND CONSCIENCE DEVELOPMENT

The role of parents as models for moral behavior has already been discussed. A second way in which parents influence the development of conscience is through their patterns of interacting with their children, through the kinds of consequences which parents provide for "good" and "bad" behavior.

Some interrelationships found between one classification of child-rearing practices and several indices of children's morality are shown in Tables 7–1 and 7–2 (adapted from Hoffman, 1970). These tables summarize the results of 11 studies, 9 of which dealt with children between about 4 and 13 years of age, the remainder with college students.

Hoffman's classification differentiates three major categories of childrearing practices. *Power assertion* refers to any technique whereby parents attempt to control children by exercising superior power, either physical power or the control of resources. Power assertion includes spankings and other physical punishments as well as deprivation of objects or privileges—making children go without dinner, "grounding," refusing permission to use desired materials or go to desired places.

TABLE 7–1
Mothers' child-rearing practices and children's conscience development

Child morality index*	Type of relationship	Type of child-rearing practice		
		Power assertion	Love withdrawal	Induction
Internal orientation	Positive	0	0	2
	Negative	3	1	0
	None evident	1	1	1
Guilt intensity	Positive	0	0	2
	Negative	2	0	0
	None evident	4	1	3
Resistance to temptation	Positive	0	1	2
	Negative	2	0	1
	None evident	3	3	2
Confession and acceptance of blame	Positive	0	2	3
	Negative	3	1	1
	None evident	2	3	4
Over all indices	Positive	0	3	9
	Negative	10	2	2
	None evident	10	8	10

* Internal orientation refers to accepting responsibility for one's own actions. Guilt intensity refers to the amount of guilt or self-criticism felt or expressed. Resistance to temptation, and confession and acceptance of blame, are self-explanatory.
Source: Adapted from M. L. Hoffman, "Moral Development, " in Carmichael's Manual of Child Psychology, ed. P. Mussen, 3d ed., vol. 2 (New York: John Wiley & Sons, 1970), pp. 261–359.

TABLE 7–2
Fathers' child-rearing practices and children's conscience development

Child morality index*	Type of relationship	Type of child-rearing practice		
		Power assertion	Love withdrawal	Induction
Internal orientation	Positive	0	0	0
	Negative	1	0	0
	None evident	1	1	1
Guilt intensity	Positive	0	0	0
	Negative	0	0	0
	None evident	2	1	2
Resistance to temptation	Positive	0	0	0
	Negative	1	0	0
	None evident	1	0	1
Confession and acceptance of blame	Positive	1	2	0
	Negative	1	0	0
	None evident	2	1	2
Over all indices	Positive	1	2	0
	Negative	3	0	0
	None evident	6	3	6

* Child morality indices are defined as in Table 7–1.
Source: Adapted from M. L. Hoffman, "Moral Development," in *Carmichael's Manual of Child Psychology*, ed. P. Mussen, 3d ed., vol. 2 (New York: John Wiley & Sons, 1970), pp. 261–359.

Power assertion includes the threat of such punishments as well as the punishments themselves.

Love withdrawal refers to any techniques in which parents express their anger and disapproval directly, but without relying on physical power or resource control. Parents who ignore or refuse to speak to their children, or who say they don't like their children, or who say they won't love their children unless they are "good," are using love-withdrawal techniques. Both power-assertion and love-withdrawal techniques are basically punitive, threatening children with negative consequences—material or emotional—unless the children behave as their parents wish.

Induction refers to techniques in which parents attempt to show their children why some behavior is desirable by providing reasons or explanations for choosing that behavior over another. Such techniques depend less on "Because I say so!" or "If you don't, you'll get it!" than on considerations relating to the kind of behavior in question. The parents attempt to show the child why one course of action may be better than another for the child's own well-being or because of effects on others.

Some, though not many, parents may use one or another of these techniques almost exclusively. Most parents, however, probably use some combination of the techniques. Consequently, parents classified into one of these three categories may range from those who nearly always use that technique, through those who use it most of the time, to those who use it only somewhat more than the others. In addition, the effects of these techniques almost certainly interact with other variables: The closeness and warmth between parent and child, the amount of discrepancy between parental codes and peer codes, the personal characteristics of particular children, to mention a few. In addition, some techniques may have more consistent effects than others on children's conscience development. For these reasons, one might expect somewhat mixed results when comparing the outcomes of different studies—and one does see this in Tables 7–1 and 7–2. Nonetheless, there are also some fairly consistent patterns over the studies. With one exception for fathers, power assertion is never positively related to conscience development. Where significant relationships are evident, they are always negative. Children whose parents regularly use physical punishment and deprivation techniques are less likely to show evidence of strong conscience development than are children whose parents typically use other techniques.

For induction, the pattern goes the other way. For mothers at least, where significant relationships are found they are mostly positive. For love withdrawal, in contrast, there does not appear to be any pattern of relationship. Love withdrawal does have other consequences. Children whose parents use this technique frequently are likely to be anxious children who have difficulty expressing anger toward others; they are also more susceptible to adult influence generally than are other children. And retrospective data from adults suggest that love withdrawal is one control technique associated with depression in adulthood (others include derision and negative evaluation, in contexts of parental rejection; Crook, Raskin, & Eliot, 1981). But their moral behavior does not appear to be consistently influenced one way or the other by love-withdrawal techniques.

Hoffman (1970) made a similar analysis of parental affection and the morality indices shown in Tables 7–1 and 7–2. Half of these comparisons showed significant relationships, and of those the large majority for both mothers and fathers showed a positive relationship between affection and conscience development. Both affection and induction thus appear to facilitate conscience development.

A comparison of Tables 7–1 and 7–2 also suggests differences between mothers and fathers as discipline agents. For instance, induction has positive relationships with conscience when used by mothers, but there is no evidence of any relationship when it is used by fathers. More generally, the tables suggest that mothers have the more potent influence on conscience development. More than half of the comparisons for mothers showed some significant relationships, whereas less than a fifth of the comparisons for fathers showed any significant relationship. However, fathers were included in far fewer of the studies—a problem that is consistently encountered in the literature of developmental psychology. It is also possible that fathers may have types of influence which are not assessed in these studies.

A reminder is in order here. Remember that children are not just passive objects of parental practice, but that their own attributes may shape their parents' practices. For instance, one would hardly expect induction to be effective if children did not pay attention to what parents say, or could not understand the point (as might be the case with young children). In fact, when four- and six-year-old children were distracted while mothers were giving them instructions, the mothers were more likely to use power-assertive commands rather than induction-style reasons (Chapman, 1979).

Punishment

When parents do use physical punishment and other power-assertive techniques, it is often with the intent of teaching the children to be "good." Yet for the indices of moral behavior discussed in the last section, the power-assertive techniques were the least effective for achieving this goal. Is there any reason for using punishment at all? This is a question of considerable concern and controversy among parents, who may hold viewpoints ranging from "Spare the rod and spoil the child," on the one hand, to deeply felt convictions that children should never be punished, on the other. It is also an important practical question, since most parents do punish their children at least occasionally; one study estimated that 98 percent of parents do so (Sears, Maccoby, & Levin, 1957).

Our concern here is primarily with physical punishment or power assertion. Can physical punishment be effective in stopping a child from forbidden activities? Research with animals is quite clear on this question: if the punishment is sufficiently intense, it may suppress behavior *temporarily*. Only when punishment is so severe as to be traumatic is there permanent suppression (Solomon, 1964). (The ethical reasons for not conducting research requiring such severe punishment of children should be obvious.) On the other hand, there can be permanent suppression of punished behavior in animals, and probably in human beings as well, if some rewarded alternative is provided. During the temporary suppression resulting from punishment, the individual may be able to learn other, more appropriate courses of action if such alternatives are available.

One group of experiments on the effects of punishment on children themselves was designed to study the effects on children's resistence to temptation of such variables as the timing of punishment, the intensity of punishment, and giving reasons for prohibitions. In these studies, children are typically shown pairs of toys—one large and attractive, the other small and unattractive. The children are told that they may touch or play with some toys but not others. The attractive toy of each pair is "prohibited." Whenever the children choose the attractive toy of a pair they are "punished" by such means as verbal reprimand (for example, "No, that's wrong"), a loud and unpleasant noise, and taking away candy previously given. The timing may be varied by "punishing" as soon as children reach for a forbidden toy or after they have picked it up; the intensity of punishment may be varied by changing the loudness of an unpleasant noise; and so forth. Once the children have learned to pick the unattractive toys consistently, the experimenter leaves the room. The children are then watched through one-way mirrors to see how well they resist the temptation to pick up or play with the "forbidden" toy.

These studies have shown that, in general, more intense punishments are more effective in suppressing the forbidden behavior, but that there is an interaction between the intensity of punishment and its timing. If punishments are mild, punishment given at the time the child makes the forbidden response is more effective than is punishment given some time afterward. But intense punishment is about equally effective whether it is administered immediately or following a delay (Parke, 1970). However, combining punishment with information about the prohibited act, or reasons why children should not perform it, is most effective of all. Not only do the children show more resistance to temptation, but their resistance is more likely to persist (Leizer & Rogers, 1974). Furthermore, the effectiveness of reasoning with the children increases during the school years.

Another source of concern is the question of whether punishment is psychologically damaging to children. The answer appears to be that punishment is not *necessarily* psychologically damaging so long as it is clearly related to the act being punished, but that if this is not the case, and if punishment is used frequently, there can indeed be negative effects. Studies of existing parental practices in relation to children's attributes do suggest that parents who are not abusive but who use predominantly power-assertive techniques are likely to have children who are submissive, dependent, compliant, and uncreative if the parents are warm toward the children; or neurotic, quarrelsome, socially withdrawn, and shy if the parents are hostile toward the children (Becker, 1964). In the case of abusive parents, punishment is arbitrary, intense, frequent, and not in any way easily related to any specific act—and the negative consequences of such abusive parental behavior have been of increasing concern to those interested in children's welfare over the past decade. Children who are abused are likely to learn behavior patterns such as uncontrolled aggression, inability to communicate effectively, fear of authority, avoidance of social interaction, inability to express positive emotions in social interactions, feelings of guilt, and low self-esteem. Social and intellectual—and even physical—development are often delayed. And if such children grow up to become parents, they are highly likely to abuse their own children (Gordon & Gordon, 1979). Obviously, abusive punishment has very high costs for children.

What this suggests is that if parents *must* punish a child, they should be very careful to be sure that the contingencies are clear to the child. With school-aged children, giving reasons may effectively do this. If parental punishment is arbitrary from the children's point of view, so that they do not understand the relationship between what they did and the punishment, or so that they do not understand why the act in question is not allowed, the children can make no connection between what they do and punishment. Consequently, they can neither avoid doing the same thing in the future nor figure out what they might do instead. Power assertion without reasons is likely to have these kinds of effects. Giving nonspecific reasons is also likely to have such effects. Telling children they are punished because they are "bad" may reinforce negative self-concepts, but give the child no way to avoid being "bad" another time. Similarly, "Because I told you to" is not a specific reason. Children may learn to submit to (or rebel against) adult authority, doing (or refusing to do) what they are told, but such a nonspecific statement gives no rationale for the adult command which could allow them to understand the prohibition and regulate their future behavior accordingly. However, an occasional punishment clearly linked to a specific act of the child may be an effective way of communicating with children.

Whether or not punishment is potentially damaging may also depend on how families known to the children look on punishment (Kagan, 1967). If the families with which a child is familiar do not believe in punishment and rarely use it, then even an occasional punishment may be felt by the child as a cruel and rejecting event. However, if the families with which a child is familiar believe that one expresses love and concern for children by punishing them when they are not good, then punishment may be felt as just an unpleasant fact of life, but not necessarily cruel or rejecting.

Discipline versus punishment

Some of the disagreements over the question of punishment arise because people do not distinguish between discipline and punishment. Discipline is the more general concept; it implies teaching or training, and it may or may not include punishment as a particular technique. The modes of discipline used by parents clearly influence their children in many ways.

Studies of parent practices—even cross-cultural studies—have repeatedly found at least two major dimensions of parental discipline (e.g., Schaefer, 1959; Bronstein-Burrows, 1981). One of these is the warmth versus hostility the parents show to the child; are they generally accepting and loving, or are they generally rejecting, cold, and hostile toward the child? That this dimension is relevant for moral behaviors (as well as other behaviors) is suggested by Hoffman's (1970) summary of studies of parental affection, mentioned above (pp. 174–175).

The other dimension involves style of controlling children, whether parents are permissive or restrictive, whether they allow and encourage autonomy or insist on controlling the child's actions. Probably the most familiar differentiation of parental styles along this dimension is that of Baumrind (1967, 1971, 1978) who differentiates between authoritarian, authoritative, and permissive parents. *Permissive parents* generally believe that children should be allowed to grow and develop without adult interference. There should be little or no discipline of any sort, let alone physical punishment. *Authoritarian parents* generally believe that children should be closely regulated and that discipline is essential. They are also likely to use power-assertive discipline. *Authoritative parents* are in between. They allow their children a great deal of freedom, but they do have some rules and standards of conduct about which they exercise firm control. They are also likely to use induction as a major discipline technique. When children of these types of parents were compared, the children from the authoritative homes were more likely to be independent and dominant (especially the girls) and socially responsive (especially the boys). When parents were authoritarian, the girls were more dependent and the boys less socially responsive than other children. And when parents were permissive, the boys were less competent and the girls were more resistant to adults.

Overall, Baumrind's findings indicate that children will be most socially competent when their parents use authoritative patterns of discipline (though she has also found that, among preschoolers, authoritarian parenting was associated with independence and dominance among black girls; and that a rarely-encountered harmonious pattern, in which parents appeared to have control—the children did as parents wished—but rarely exercised such control was also associated with social responsiveness and purposiveness for girls, but probably not for boys).

Again, though, we need to remember that parent-child influences are reciprocal—children influence their parents as well as the other way around. Lewis (1981), for example, commented that the outcomes associated with firm control by Baumrind and others appear to be at odds with what one would expect from attribution theory (see Chapter 6). Among other points, if researchers were to look at it from the children's end, they might find that it is children's willingness to obey rather than parents' firm control which generates the research findings. This consideration seems especially relevant in the case of the harmonious families, where children do as parents wish without parents exercising overt control.

Children's influence on their parents' discipline practices is evident in other ways as well. For instance, the actual misdeed a child has performed influences the choice of disciplinary action more than does any particular child-rearing philosophy of the parent. When mothers of four- to five-year-olds and seven- to eight-year-olds were played tapes of dramatized parent-child disciplinary encounters and asked what they would do, they did not consistently use similar practices from one misdeed to another but rather tended to agree with one another about what appropriate discipline should be for particular types of misdeeds (Grusec & Kiczynski, 1980). Where a child did something that caused psychological harm to others, they were likely to use reasoning or inductive techniques. Where mothers requested compliance but the children repeatedly refused, they were likely to use power-assertive techniques. Isolation or grounding was most likely to be used when the child caused physical damage to another person or object. It is also relevant to note that most mothers were likely to use multiple techniques, usually some combination of power assertion followed by reasoning. Not surprisingly, there are also interactions between characteristics of children and characteristics of adults in disciplinary situations. Bugental, Caporael, and Shennum (1980) trained four boys aged seven to nine to behave in ways that were responsive or unresponsive to adult control attempts. These boys then interacted in a toy-building task with 32 women, half of whom were mothers. The comparison of interest is between those women who were high in self-perception of control (internal locus of control) and those women who were low in self-perceptions of control (external locus of control). When the boys were unresponsive, these two groups of women showed opposite patterns of vocal assertiveness. The internally controlled women were more vocally assertive in unpleasant and pleasant interchange and less assertive in neutral interchanges, whereas the external women were more assertive in the neutral interchanges than they were in the others. Since a similar pattern had previously been observed with mothers interacting with their own "hard to control" children, this result was not just a by-product of unfamiliarity of these women with these children.

Similarly, adult *perceptual style* regarding children—whether the adult tends to perceive a standard (videotaped) child in positive, negative, or neutral ways—interacts with child characteristics (Messé, Stollak, Larson, & Michaels, 1979). For instance, an adult who perceives children negatively is likely to interact with a child in a more authoritarian manner than do other adults when engaged in some cooperative task; an adult who perceives children in very positive terms is likely to be ineffective in resolving conflict between a child and a peer. Undoubtedly there are other such interactions between child and adult attributes which will become known through further study. At this point, it is clear that while parental discipline patterns may depend in part upon parental philosophies and preferences, they also depend in important ways on the attributes of the children.

CONSIDERATION FOR OTHERS

Besides learning what they may not do, children must also learn prosocial behaviors—the moral prescriptions of their society, the "thou shalts" which specify the ways in which one should behave. Consideration for others has been the major focus of research on this aspect of moral development. It takes forms such as generosity, sharing, helping, and altruism—which implies aiding others at some cost to oneself and without expectation of personal reward. Bryan (1972), reviewing early studies many of which were concerned with the effects of models on children's willingness to make donations, identified several general themes in these studies. One of these is that even by the primary grades, children know the *"social responsibility norm."* They state that one should be generous, or help others in need. Not only do the children state the norm themselves; they also judge others by whether or not they accept the norm. There is a sense in which this is lip service, however, for it is according to whether others *say* they accept or reject the norm that children judge them, and children's statement of the norm is not necessarily related to their own sharing, especially in the primary grades (recall that standards and behavior are not necessarily related at that age).

A second theme is that what models *do* is much more important than what they *say*. Telling children that it's nice to share, or pointing out the virtues of sharing in various ways, has had little or no effect on children's willingness to donate. How much children donate is much more heavily influenced by how much the models donate themselves.

Other model attributes and behaviors also influence children's donations. For instance, models who express pleasure and enjoyment over their own donations are more effective than models who do not; and children usually donate more when models give them social approval for sharing (for example, "Good, that's a nice thing to do!"). However, there is one very interesting exception to this last point. After about the age of nine, social approval from a hypocritical model—one who preaches sharing but does not do so—actually *reduces* children's willingness to donate (Midlarsky, Bryan, & Brickman, 1973). Evidently, older school-aged children are becoming sensitive to moral inconsistency in others and responding to it negatively. If this is true in the lab, it is also likely to be true at home. Do parents who fail to practice what they preach also begin to forfeit some of their potential effectiveness as models? What effects does such inconsistency have on children's feelings about parents and on parent-child interactions?

As for children's own consistency in consideration for others, the evidence available suggests that in this regard the development of consideration for others is similar to the development of conscience. Consideration for others in various forms generally increases during the school years. In addition, at least for children in grades five through eight for whom several measures were available, there was about as much consistency as has been found for moral prohibitions (Dlugokinski & Firestone, 1973). More recently Payne (1980) observed fourth and sixth graders in different situations which called for donating, helping, sharing, and cooperating. As you can see in Table 7–3, donating and helping were moderately correlated (+.45) as were sharing and cooperating (+.41) but there was little correlation across these pairs. Interestingly, peer and teacher ratings of children's behavior were correlated much higher—evidently children are perceived as being much more consistent in their prosocial behaviors than they actually are. The actual amount of prosocial behavior depended on the situation, but where there were variations related to attributes of the children, such as sex or age, those relationships tended to be quite consistent. Girls, for example, behaved more prosocially than boys in four of the five situations; older children were more prosocial than younger children in all situations (and were so perceived by peers and teachers); children from higher socioeconomic status backgrounds were consistently more prosocial, and were so perceived by teachers; and children with higher academic ability were more prosocial in four of the five situations and were so perceived by both teachers and peers.

Naturalistic studies relating observations of children's consideration for others to parents' practices are rare. One pair of studies suggests that existing relationships are strengthened during the school years. Nursery school children's considerate actions showed little relationship to parental use of power-assertion, love-withdrawal, or induction techniques (Hoffman, 1963). By the seventh grade, however, there were significant relationships between peer judgments of children's consideration for others and these categories of parental

TABLE 7–3

Intercorrelations of prosocial behaviors of fourth- and sixth-grade children in different structure situations

	Correlations			
Situation	Donating services	Helping	Sharing	Cooperating
Donating goods...........	.40*	.37*	.14	.15
Donating services.........		.45*	.18	−.04
Helping.................			.04	−.04
Sharing				.41*

* p < .01

Source: F. D. Payne, "Children's Prosocial Conduct in Structured Situations and as Viewed by Others: Consistency, Convergence, and Relationships with Person Variables," *Child Development* 51 (1980) pp. 1252–59. Adapted from Table 1, p. 1255.

techniques (Hoffman & Saltzstein, 1967). For girls, the pattern was the same as that for moral prohibitions: Consideration for others was facilitated by induction and affection but negatively related to power assertion. For boys, however, the pattern was very different. Consideration was positively related to power assertion and affection, negatively related to love withdrawal, and showed no relationship with induction. Why there should be such differences between boys and girls is not at all clear. Consideration may be a more important norm for girls than for boys. More likely, the ways in which consideration is expected to be expressed may differ for boys and girls. Boys may be more likely to stand up for other children against a group, whereas girls may be more likely to help others and to show concern for others' feelings.

Parent practices can be categorized in other ways than those discussed earlier, and one other way proposed by McKinney (1980) is to look at whether parents emphasize doing good, in which case they use a *prescriptive value orientation,* or whether they emphasize doing bad, in which case they use *proscriptive value orientation* (see Table 7–4). The relevance of this categorization for prosocial behaviors is that at least for donation behavior, there are significant differences between four-year olds whose parents differ in value orientation (Olejnik & McKinney, 1973). Children whose parents held prescriptive value orientations donated more than did children whose parents held proscriptive value orientations. This was true for both boys and girls, and it was true regardless of whether parents were likely to use reward or punishment in disciplining their children. Very likely such relationships hold for other areas of moral behavior as well.

Changes in children's prosocial behaviors are probably related to cognitive changes which are taking place at the same time. Suls, Witenberg, and Gutkin (1981), for example, looked at children's and college students' evaluations of four situations: (1) *positive reciprocity,* where one does a favor for someone who did a favor first; (2) *altruism,* where one does a favor regardless of the other person's behavior; (3) *negative reciprocity,* where one refuses to do a favor because the other person previously refused to help; and (4) *ingratitude,* where one refuses to do a favor even when the other person had done one first. Third and fifth grade children distinguish between these situations and rank them in the order in which they are listed above. First graders responded similarly, but

TABLE 7– 4
Examples of prescriptive value orientations, which emphasize doing good, and of proscriptive value orientations, which emphasize doing bad

Parents with prescriptive value orientations	Parents with proscriptive value orientations
Reward doing good:	**Reward not doing bad:**
Good, you shared.	Good, you weren't stingy.
Be kind to others.	Don't be mean.
Punish not doing good:	**Punish doing bad:**
You didn't tell the truth.	You lied.
You should have done your own work.	You shouldn't cheat.

didn't distinguish between negative reciprocity and ingratitude. College students, however, ranked altruism as a more desirable than positive reciprocity, which may reflect their greater independence of immediate rewards and punishments as bases for judging moral situations (see moral judgments, below).

Similarly, when Grusec and Redler (1980) studied altruism (defined as willingness to make donations), they found that experimenter responses which enhanced personal attributions by emphasizing qualities of the child were most effective in enhancing prosocial behaviors of eight-year-olds. Eleven-year-olds were equally influenced by attribution responses and reinforcement responses, which praised the prosocial act. Neither type of response had much effect on five-year-olds. Grusec and Redler suggest that attribution-related responses may have their effect through altering the child's self-concept; in keeping with attribution theory, if one perceives oneself as likely to behave in prosocial ways, one will be more likely to do so. (It is for just this same reason that parents are given the opposite recommendation regarding misbehavior, that is, to criticize *not* the child, but the specific antisocial act. A child who attributes antisocial behaviors to something in the self is also more likely to continue to behave accordingly.)

MORAL JUDGMENTS

The study of *moral judgments* is concerned with how children decide that some action is good or bad. Piaget, who first inaugurated this line of inquiry with children, described major changes in children's moral reasoning during the school years. When children first enter school they hold rather rigid and inflexible ideas about what makes an action good or bad. They believe that rules of conduct are absolute, fixed, and unchangeable, and that these rules are determined by external authority. This is called *moral realism*. Whether they think an act is good or bad depends on its consequences. If it causes damage or results in punishment, it is bad. This is called *objective moral reasoning,* since the judgment is based on consequences external to the actor. However, by the time children reach the intermediate grades—and certainly by the time they leave elementary school—they are moving toward a conception of rules as alterable human conventions based on reciprocal agreement among the people who use them. This is called *moral relativism*. Whether these children think an act is good or bad depends more on the intentions of the actor than on the consequences of the act. Because the actor's subjective internal states are the basis for these judgments, this is called *subjective moral reasoning*.

To illustrate children's ideas about rules, here is part of what one 10-year-old Swiss boy had to say to Piaget when asked to invent a new rule for the game of marbles (Piaget, 1965, p. 63):

P: Invent a rule.
Ben: I couldn't invent one straight away like that.
P: Yes, you could . . . [Ben invents a rule.]
P: Good, would that come off with the others?
Ben: Oh, yes, they'd like to do that.

P: Then people would play that way?

Ben: Oh, no, because it would be cheating.

P: But all your pals would like to, wouldn't they?

Ben: Yes, they all would.

P: Then why would it be cheating?

Ben: Because I invented it; it isn't a rule! It's a wrong rule because it's outside of the rules. A fair rule is one that is in the game. . . .

P: When you are big, suppose everyone plays that way, will it be right or not?

Ben: It will be right then because there will be new children who will learn the rule.

P: And for you?

Ben: It will be wrong.

P: And what will it be "really and truly?"

Ben: It will really be wrong.

Ben is in between. He is beginning to realize that there could be different rules from those he knows (he does invent one) which could be accepted by others (new children who will learn the game). A younger child might have denied that there could be any different rules. But Ben's difficulty in accepting such rules as legitimate is obvious. Only the fixed set of rules that he knows (which are "in the game") can be fair. A more advanced child might have said that of course a new rule could be fair, so long as everyone agreed to it.

The shift from objective to subjective moral reasoning is more apparent when children are given stories in which they must judge which of two children has done a worse thing. One story might compare two children, one of whom broke 15 cups accidentally while helping mother, the other of whom broke only 1 cup by getting angry and throwing it. Another story might compare two children who are asked for directions by a stranger. The first child lies about the directions, but the stranger eventually finds the way. The second child tries to help, but doesn't remember correctly, so the stranger gets lost. To stories like these, in which one child causes a great deal of damage accidentally and the other has bad intentions, younger children will say that the child who broke 15 cups was worse because the other child only broke 1, or that the child who misremembered directions was worse because the stranger got lost. Older children will say that the child who had bad intentions—who threw the cup in anger, or who lied intentionally—was worse.

The shift from objective to subjective judgments takes place largely over the school years. Even kindergarten and first-grade children can discriminate intentions to some degree (Rule, Nesdale, & McAra, 1974). "You did that on purpose!" is a cry of outrage one frequently hears from children, by which they convey that what was done intentionally is worse than it would have been if it had happened by accident. When relatively little damage is done, young children make subjective judgments based on the intentions of the actors (Armsby, 1971; Gutkin, 1972) and when motives are made very explicit, even three-year-olds will make motive-based judgments (Nelson, 1980).

However, if the damage is great, and especially if the child with good intention causes a great deal of damage whereas the child with bad intentions causes little damage, children may not make subjective judgments consistently until the intermediate grades. The younger children may infer an actor's intentions as accurately as older children or adults, but they appear to have a production deficiency—they do not use the information in making their moral judgments (Walden, 1982). Other factors make a difference too. Children consider acts that cause personal injury worse than acts that cause material damage (Elkind & Dabek, 1977). When the actor in a story was hurt, children up to third grade judged that actor as worse than one who was unhurt, perhaps because of a belief in *immanent justice*—that consequences are intrinsically part of acts, so someone who is hurt must have done something to deserve it (Suls & Kalle, 1979).

Piaget's ideas about moral judgments have been expanded and elaborated by Kohlberg (1964, 1969). Kohlberg presented children with moral dilemmas, in which someone must decide between two actions, such as stealing a medicine versus letting someone die. On the basis of children's and adults' judgments of what the right thing to do would be, and why, Kohlberg proposes that there are three major levels of development of moral judgment, with two stages at each level. Descriptions of all six stages are given in Table 7–5.

In one of his studies, Kohlberg compared the moral reasoning of boys of 7, 10, 13, and 16 years of age. As Figure 7–1 shows, preconventional judgments, which predominate for the seven-year-olds, gradually decline over the school years, whereas conventional judgments increase, until by 13 years of age the

TABLE 7–5
Kohlberg's classification of levels of moral judgments

Level I. Pre-conventional level . . . . Judgments based on external consequences.	*Stage 1. Obedience and punishment orientation* One should do what one is told and keep out of trouble. Objective responsibility.
	Stage 2. Naive egoistic orientation One should satisfy one's own needs. If it feels good, it's good. If it doesn't feel good, it's not good. Reciprocity of the sort "I'll scratch your back if you'll scratch mine."
Level II. Conventional level . . . . Judgments based on doing the "right thing," as prescribed by social convention.	*Stage 3. Good-boy good-girl orientation* What is right pleases and helps others. Conformity to sterotyped images of role behavior. Judgment by intentions.
	Stage 4. Authority- and social-order-maintaining orientation Maintenance of law and order, respect for authority, and doing one's duty determine what is right.
Level III. Post-conventional level . . . . Judgments based on self-accepted moral principles.	*Stage 5. Contractual-legalistic orientation* What is right depends on principles arrived at by consensus with others, with respect for the relativism of personal values, and for the rights and welfare of others.
	Stage 6. Conscience or principle orientation What is right depends on self-defined general principles of conscience which are logically universal. Emphasis on mutual respect and trust.

majority of the children's judgments are at the conventional level. This trend continues for the 16-year-olds, though the change is not as great as that between earlier age levels. Even at 16, a minority of judgments are at the post-conventional level. This remains true in adulthood. The evidence is that most of the moral judgments made by adults in the United States are at the conventional level.

Children go through the stages in order and without skipping, although they may reach a given stage at different ages. For instance, 13-year-old boys in isolated villages of Turkey and Yucatan responded to Kohlberg's stories like 10-year olds in the United States (Kohlberg, 1969). Within the United States, children with high IQ scores, and children of higher social classes, regularly make more advanced moral judgments than do children of the same age with lower IQ scores or of lower social classes. In this regard, moral judgments resemble moral conduct, since resistance to deviation and other measures show similar relations to IQ and social class.

FIGURE 7–1   Mean percent of total moral statements of each of six moral judgment types made by 7-, 10-, 13-, and 16-year-old boys.

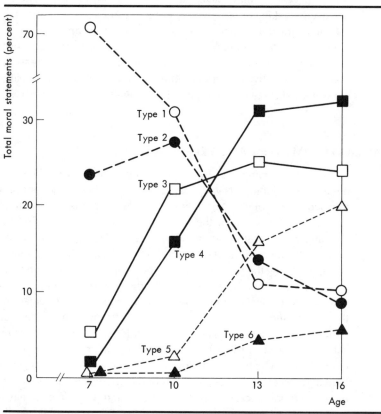

Source: L. Kohlberg, "Development of Moral Character and Moral Ideology," in Review of Child Development Research, vol. 1, ed. M. L. Hoffman and L. W. Hoffman (New York: Russell Sage Foundation, 1964), p. 403.

The reasons for these relationships may be different for moral judgments than for moral conduct, however. Parental discipline practices, which do relate to moral conduct, show no clear relationship to levels of moral judgment. On the other hand, exposure to moral reasoning at levels different from one's own does influence moral judgment at least in some circumstances (Crockenberg & Nicolayev, 1979). The adults in children's lives do not necessarily provide exposure to higher levels of reasonings. Olejnik (1980) found that only those adults whose own moral reasoning was at postconventional levels were very likely to use conventional reasoning with children; others used preconventional reasoning similar to the children's own.

Change in level of judgment following exposure to a higher level of reasoning may in part be a matter of modeling—children will shift their level of reasoning one stage up or down if they hear or see models reinforced for such judgments. But shifts to the level above their own are made more readily and are more likely to persist (Cowan, Langer, Heavenrich & Nathanson, 1969; LeFurgy & Woloshin, 1969) while exposure to reasoning two stages from their own has little effect (Turiel, 1966). Apparently, children most readily assimilate types of judgments just a little more advanced than their own, perhaps because those are the levels for which they have reached the requisite levels of cognitive and perspective-taking skills—which Kohlberg argues are necessary, though not sufficient, for developmental change to occur. In one study in which fourth through seventh graders were exposed to reasoning more advanced than their own, only those children who were approaching formal reasoning and had reached perspective taking stage three (Chapter 2) made the transition to the first conventional stage of moral judgment, stage three (Walker, 1980).

MORAL DEVELOPMENT: MANY PROCESSES

Moral development is obviously a complex process in which different forces are at work. Hoffman (1970) suggests that moral development proceeds along four separate, though interrelated, tracks. A brief look at these tracks may help to pull together some of the ideas discussed above. The first track is *social learning,* which best fits early moral development and results in behavior conformity. The moral attributes which children show at the beginning of the school years, including the rules they know, their capacity for resistance to temptation, and very likely their objective moral judgments, reflect children's experiences with reinforcements, punishments, and models. Social learning continues throughout life, and for some individuals it may remain the major basis for morality. As adults, such individuals would care little about moral principles, acting instead according to hedonistic principles based on the rewards and punishments which might follow their behavior. With changes in children's thinking, however, they begin to respond in more generalized ways to situations requiring moral decisions, so that rewards and punishments may become less important as determinants of their actions. For many children this begins to happen during the grade school years, with inductive discipline becoming effective as children's comprehension increases (Baumrind, 1978). By the end of the school years, children may be beginning to integrate cognitions, affects or feel-ings, and behaviors into moral belief systems, as Henshel's study (p. 173) suggests.

The second track is experience in taking the role of authority. The outcome of this process is perception of authority as rational. Taking the role of authority means participating in making decisions about how to act. Children gain experi-ence of this sort in games and other activities with peers, and also at home to the extent that parents include children in decision-making processes. Of the par-enting styles discussed earlier, authoritative parents are most likely to provide such opportunity for participation for their children (Baumrind, 1978). It is very likely that such participation contributes to the shift from moral realism to moral relativism in children's perceptions of rules, and to their acceptance of a con-ventional basis for moral judgments. Participation in decision making may also contribute to children's evaluations of moral standards, with children who have more decision-making experience being more likely to value moral standards highly and to behave accordingly. As a related point, Baumrind (1978) reported that in families of eight- and nine-year-olds, where there is *argumentative discourse*—parents openly challenging moral positions held by children or by each other and discussing the differences between them—children showed the most differentiation in reasoning about such issues. Since children from lower-class homes often have less opportunity to participate in roles of authority, this experience difference has been offered as one explanation for the social class differences frequently found in moral conduct and moral judgments.

The third process has to do with emotions, and its outcome is impulse control. As adults important to the child express displeasure or withhold love when children misbehave, such misbehavior and the impulses leading to it become associated with anxiety. The unpleasant feeling of anxiety, in turn, inhibits the misbehavior in question. As a result, children develop self-control in the sense that they stop themselves from prohibited acts even when authority figures are absent. This process may contribute to the importance or value which children place on different moral standards, or at least to consistency of behavior as standards and emotions are integrated—and again, the process seems to take place in the later years of middle childhood. However, children differ a great deal in the amount of love withdrawal to which they are exposed, and very likely in their responsiveness to it as well. If children experience a great deal of love withdrawal, they may become anxiety-ridden, overconforming, or even seri-ously depressed adults.

The fourth process is the integration of children's capacity for empathy with induction experiences through which children can be helped to understand the effects of their behavior on others. This process results in consideration for others. Since children's capacities for empathy are developing rapidly during the school years, induction experiences may be increasingly important in influ-encing consideration over those years. In addition, Baumrind (1978) suggests that parents who give children responsibility for others' welfare—and make very clear the positive consequences of their actions in caring for another—may enhance the reinforcing properties of such behavior and thus foster such pro-social behavior in their children.

SUMMARY

Children begin the school years as individuals who can say many of the rules and can follow them in some circumstances, but who show little evidence of integrating the rules into their behavior on any consistent basis, and who evaluate behavior by its consequences. By the end of the school years, they have become individuals who can state more general moral principles, who do follow those principles if they feel strongly about them, and who evaluate behavior on the basis of intentions and social convention.

Many factors feed into these changes, in particular, the nature of the interactions which exist between parent and child, as determined by *both* parent *and* child.

Moral development does not end with the school years. What happens in adolescence and adulthood may contribute in important ways to changes in moral standards, moral behaviors, and moral judgments. Nonetheless, it is during the school years that children may first begin to integrate thinking, emotions, and behavior, and it is on this foundation that the later developments will build.

TERMS AND CONCEPTS

conscience

superego

ego ideal

power assertion

love withdrawal

induction

discipline versus punishment

permissive pattern of child rearing

authoritarian pattern of child rearing

authoritative pattern of child rearing

social responsibility norm

prescriptive value orientation

proscriptive value orientation

moral judgments

moral realism

moral relativism

objective moral reasoning

subjective moral reasoning

prosocial behaviors

immanent justice

argumentative discourse

SUGGESTED ADDITIONAL READING

Baumrind, D. Parental disciplinary patterns and social competence in children. *Youth and Society,* 1978, *9,* 239–276.

Hoffman, M. L. Moral development. In P. Mussen (Ed.), *Carmichael's manual of child psychology* (Vol. 2). New York: John Wiley & Sons, 1970.

Windmiller, M., Lambert, N., & Turiel, E. (Eds.). *Moral development and socialization.* Boston: Allyn & Bacon, 1980.

CHAPTER 8

FAMILIES

At birth, children are completely dependent on their parents. By sometime in late adolescence, the developmental tasks facing them include achieving independence, separation from families, becoming self-sufficient, and transferring major emotional ties to persons outside the family (See McKinney, Fitzgerald, & Strommen, 1982.)

The transition from dependence to self-sufficiency takes place gradually, although there are some clear transition points. Starting school is one such transition. From the children's point of view, up until they start school they are with their families most of the time and are influenced primarily by them. Once they start school, they are away from their families a good part of the time, and relationships with others, especially peers, become increasingly important. From the parents' point of view, having school-aged children is neither as intensely satisfying nor as intensely frustrating as having preschoolers, who are seen as both much more demanding of parental time and attention and more rewarding; nor is having school-agers as worrisome as having teenagers, who are seen as being least demanding, but much more worrisome than younger children. (However, all parents, including parents of school-aged children, were most likely to answer a question about the best age for children to be by saying that the best age was their own children's current age; Hoffman & Manis, 1978). Perhaps this is another reason school-aged children have received rather less attention than children of other ages—their attributes and developmental tasks are such that they do not require caregiver attention nearly as much, whether in the form of supervision or of worry and concern.

In earlier chapters we have discussed many of the ways in which parental attributes are related to child attributes. Children enter school with characteristics already shaped by years of interaction with their parents, in the course of which patterns of mutual accommodation have been established. Correlations between parents' behavior and children's attributes, such as achievement motivation, anxiety, and dependence, are already evident before children start school, as are differences among children whose parents are authoritarian, authoritative, or permissive (Chapter 7; Baumrind, 1971). Also evident are differences between the children of warm and accepting parents and the children of cold and rejecting parents. These variations continue to be important through the school years and on into adolescence, when having or not having parents who are warm and accepting, and who set reasonable limits while allowing young people freedom, is an important factor in determining how well adolescents cope with the task of separation (McKinney et al., 1982; Conger, 1977). In general, early interactions continue to influence children as they go through school, partly because of the way children's behaviors have already been shaped by these interactions, and partly because in some important sense the same child continues to interact with the same parents.

In this chapter, rather than summarize additional information about how children's attributes are related to parents' attributes, we wish to take a somewhat different perspective. Families are not simply aggregates of people who happen to live under the same roof. Rather, they are *social systems,* each of which has unique patterns of interaction among its members. These patterns of interaction reflect the attributes of all the persons in the family, both parents and children. The patterns are also affected by *family structure,* or who the members of the family are—whether one or both parents are present, the number and sex of siblings, and so forth. Once patterns of family interaction are established they tend to persist, while gradually changing as family members change. We will begin by examining ways in which both children and parents may influence patterns of family interactions during the school years. Then we shall look at family structure and at some of the ways in which children's experience may be affected by the type of family with which they live.

PARENT-CHILD INTERACTIONS DURING THE SCHOOL YEARS

The concept of attachment

Attachment refers to the close reciprocal bond which may develop between two individuals. Initially, the concept was applied almost exclusively to the special bond that forms between an infant and its caregiver (see Fitzgerald, Strommen, & McKinney, 1982, Chapter 9). However, life-span theorists point out that attachment is relevant not only in infancy but in later periods of life as well.

The concept of attachment has been defined in a variety of ways. Lerner and Ryff (1978) propose a "definitional consensus" which incorporates the following five points:

1.   A person who is attached seeks to obtain and/or maintain proximity and contact with the object of attachment. For an infant or toddler this may mean following mother around and wanting to be held. In older children and adults, distal (or remote) modes of contact become more prevalent—even telephoning (recall the Bell Telephone advertising campaign of 1981 and 1982, "Reach out, reach out and touch someone"). Of course physical contact is still important. A child may run into the house to greet mom and get a quick hug; or visualize a group of 11-year-old girls walking in a group so close to one another that there is actual physical contact, while anyone even momentarily outdistanced hollers, "Wait up, you guys!" and rushes to close the distance.

2.   A child (or adult) shows attachment behaviors toward only one or a very few specific other individuals.

3.   The attached person's behavior elicits reciprocal behavior from the other person; signs of attachment or closeness are exchanged.

4.   If the other person doesn't reciprocate, the child (or adult) will act distressed. Nonreciprocation may well indicate rejection, never pleasant, but especially painful from someone about whom one cares.

5.   If such nonreciprocation persists, the attached person may seek alternative attachment opportunities from whatever broader social network is available.

To these five we would add the following:

6.   Persons attached to one another have strong affective involvement toward each other, that is, they like each other a lot. Attachment theorists don't usually mention love, but it lurks not far under the surface (Kalish and Knutson, 1976).

7.   There is a very good possibility that human beings have some innate predisposition to form attachments as part of their psychobiological heritage. At least for infants, by far the prevalent theory of infant-mother attachment is that of John Bowlby, a human ethologist who emphasizes the biological foundations and probable evolutionary advantage of the early formation of close mother-infant bonds (Bowlby, 1969; Ainsworth, 1973). Are there innate predispositions for attachment in later life as well? Certainly it is possible, though theorists are more likely to talk about patterns established through a child's interpersonal experience—and it should be pointed out that there are alternative points of view in regard to infancy as well (e.g. see Fitzgerald et al., 1982). Whatever the innate predispositions may be in infancy, it is pretty clear that attachments are increasingly regulated by social and cultural processes as children get older (Lerner & Ryff, 1978; Kahn & Antonucci, 1980).

In extending the concept to later periods of life, theorists raise a number of points. For one, the attachments formed in infancy are important as *precursors* of later behavior. The infant bonds persist over time; most people retain some fairly close or intense relationship with their parents throughout their lives. The quality of the attachment between a particular infant and its caregiver may influence that child's behavior in a number of ways, including the degree to which the child may later be influenced by that caregiver. Second, the early attachments may also serve as *prototypes* for later patterns of interpersonal development (Kahn & Antonucci, 1980). Thus, the strengths and weaknesses of the early attachment bond shape not only the continuing relationship with the caregiver but also subsequent relationships. A child may acquire behavior patterns and beliefs in the course of the early interpersonal relationships which later extend to peers, teachers, and others; if the early experience was warm, encouraging, and responsive, the child may enter later relationships with behavior patterns that tend to recreate such warm and responsive relationships, leaving that child in "an expanded universe from which to seek support in coping with the increasing problems and challenges of maturation" (Kahn and Antonucci, 1980, p. 260).

Kahn and Antonucci also argue that as children approach maturity, patterns of attachment behavior become linked to systems of social support, and they cite research indicating that in later life, those individuals who have at least one individual to whom they are close and from whom they receive personal support are better off psychologically in a variety of situations than are those who do not have someone to whom they are close. Does this mean that the child who is insecurely attached in infancy is likely to have no one close in adulthood and thus be less well-off psychologically? No, not necessarily. Even without any good evidence showing the course of attachment patterns over time for different groups of children, we can be sure that there are too many intervening events and patterns of interpersonal experiences which may modify any direction initially established in infancy. For instance, there is some reason to believe that children whose parents divorce may be somewhat more likely to experience loneliness as adults than do children whose parents do not divorce because of disruptive effects of the divorce on their attachment to parents (Shaver & Rubinstein, 1980). Other interpersonal experiences within and outside of the family may also affect a child's attachment patterns in positive as well as negative ways. Still, the early relationships may establish directions of development which tend to persist unless later experiences are such as to change them.

Thus for school-aged children, we should expect to see continuing close relationships with parents which are strongly influenced by the nature of the early attachment but moderated by what has happened between child and parents since infancy. In addition we would expect that the children's patterns of interaction with peers and others would vary depending on the nature of the early, prototypic attachment.

The concept of reciprocity

The patterns of interaction which develop between parents and children are not just a matter of parents influencing children. There is *reciprocity* in parent-child interactions: parents and children mutually influence one another (Bell, 1968, 1979; Lerner & Spanier, 1978). How parents act toward their children depends to a great extent on what kinds of persons the children are. Even in infancy there are differences among children which may influence the emerging patterns of parent-child interaction (see Fitzgerald, Strommen, & McKinney, 1982). If a parent is strict and controlling with a child, this may be because the parent holds a basically authoritarian view of child rearing and acts accordingly; but it could just as easily be because the particular child requires more parental regulation than do other children. Or if a child appears overly dependent on his or her parents, reluctant to enter new situations and uneasy about interacting with strangers, this may be because the parents have encouraged dependence by failing to allow the child to explore independently; but it could just as well be because of slow-to-warm-up temperament attributes of the child (Chapter 6).

For instance, in the case of independent and dependent behaviors, parents of five- to seven-year-olds who were shown videotapes of children the same age as their own expressed more encouragement of dependence and gave more direction when children acted dependent. When the children acted independent, however, the same parents showed more encouragement of independence and showed more nondirectiveness (Marcus 1975). A similar effect was found when mothers and fathers reacted to their daughters' behavior while the daughters worked on difficult problems, which elicited such dependent behavior, and easy problems which did not elicit dependent behavior since the girls could solve the problems themselves (Osofsky & Oldfield, 1972). Of course parental attributes are still important; Mondell and Tyler (1981) observed parents and their 4½- to 6-year-old children in semistructured play and problem- solving tasks and found that the more competent parents—those with high self-efficacy, high optimism and interpersonal trust, and an active, planful coping style—also treated their children as more capable and resourceful, were generally warm and positive toward them, and were more helpful with problem solving. Though Mondell and Tyler did not study the children's behavior, it seems likely that such a parental style would be associated with greater independence and competence on the part of the children, which in turn should elicit encouragement and nondirection from parents, and so forth. Such continuing reciprocity of ongoing mutual influence in the domains of competence and independent mastery may well be an important component of the socialization histories of competent children (Chapter 6). Bates and Pettit (1981), summarizing experimental research on child effects, suggest that "such research can be very briefly summarized as having established that portrayals of various children's socially positive behavior will produce directly reciprocal, positively responsive, and benignly controlling adult behavior" (p. 330).

How parents respond to children may depend not only on how they behave but on other attributes such as whether they are boys or girls—and here again we may see interactions between parent attributes and child attributes. Summarizing a number of studies of ways in which men and women differ in their responsiveness to children, Bates and Pettit (1981) suggest that the bulk of the evidence—though not quite all of it—indicates that men and women behave more indulgently toward children of the opposite sex than they do toward same-sex children if the children act aggressively, dependently, or in nonverbally rejecting ways. Perhaps, Bates and Pettit speculate, adults feel more responsible for teaching same-sex children responsible adult-like behavior while they see their role with opposite sex children as one of providing emotional support. Dealing more generally with the question of parents' positive and negative reactions to sons and daughters, Margolin and Patterson (1975) made home observations of interactions between parents and their 5- to 12-year-old children. When the proportion of positive and negative reactions was compared with what the children did, it was found that fathers provided almost twice as many positive reactions to their sons as to their daughters, whereas mothers showed about the same proportion of positive reactions to both sons and daughters. There were no differences in the proportions of negative reactions in this study.

However, proportions show the relative incidence of something, regardless of how often it occurs. When simple frequencies of occurrence were compared, it was found that boys were punished more often than girls, and that they probably also received more praise and encouragement (Maccoby & Jacklin, 1974). Boys also receive more intense pressure from parents to avoid behavior classed as sex-inappropriate. However, Maccoby and Jacklin's review of related studies, although showing the differences mentioned here, led them to conclude that on the whole parents and other adults actually treat boys and girls more similarly than differently.

Not only do child attributes influence adult actions, these child influences interact with adult characteristics. That is, a given child characteristic may have different effects depending upon the characteristics of the adult (e.g., see Bates and Pettit, 1981). We saw one illustration of such an interaction in Chapter 7, when women with internal and external locus of control were influenced in different ways by responsive and unresponsive behaviors in seven- to nine-year-old boys (Bugental, Caporael, & Shennum, 1980). Likewise, Type A and Type B mothers, where Type A is characterized by impatience and competetive achievement striving while Type B is characterized by the absence of these characteristics, responded differently to school-aged boys who were also either Type A or Type B (Matthews, 1977). Type A children elicited more pushing and more positive evaluation than did Type B children, but this happened consistently only for the Type B mothers; the Type A mothers tended not to differentiate behaviorally between the two types of children. This difference in mothers may be related to a more general tendency for Type Bs to be more responsive to variations in their environment than are Type As. And adults' perceptual style—whether they tend to conceptualize children's behavior as positive or negative—also interacts with what the child does in determining the adults' behavior (Messe, Stollak, Larson, & Michaels, 1979). A major task facing us is to continue to unravel these reciprocal relationships between adults' and children's behavior.

Continuity and change during the school years

What these observations imply is that to understand parent-child interactions it is not enough to categorize parents in some way and then compare their children's attributes, though such studies do provide useful information. Rather, a complex situation exists in which there is a child (or children) who has some relatively enduring attributes, but who is also changing with development; and there are parents with relatively enduring attributes, who must accommodate to the changes in the child and who may be changing themselves—development does not necessarily end with adolescence. Together, these participants constitute a family social system, members of which are linked together in a network of subsystems (parent-child, child-child, father-mother) which is characterized by processes of stability and change (Feiring & Lewis, 1978). Let us now to consider some of the sources of continuity and change in both parents and their school-aged children.

The children: Continuities   In what ways do children's behaviors remain consistent over time despite the obvious changes with development? In Chapter 6 we discussed the concept of temperament at some length, and pointed out that whatever temperament attributes a child shows on entering school are likely to persist at least throughout the school years. We also pointed out that sex-role related behaviors appear to be consolidating during these years, leading to an increasing consistency of role-related behaviors.

There are also the patterns of attachment and its expression initially established in the early interaction between parent and child, as discussed earlier in this chapter. The attachment feelings with which children enter the school years are likely to persist; a relationship that has historically been a troubled one may change over time, but usually will not magically become smooth when the child starts school. Likewise, the patterns of expressing attachment which the child shows on entering school may change in form as the child matures, but will not usually shift in nature—a child who has shown a pattern of loving, expressive, responsive behavior will not suddenly begin to show a rejecting, hostile pattern, for example. While behavior patterns do evolve, and while particular precipitating expericenes may sometimes have dramatic impacts, in general temperament styles and patterns of attachment behaviors will tend to persist, contributing to continuity and stability between parent and child.

The children: Sources of change   School-aged children may bring stable personal orientations to situations over the school years, but entering school itself, which defines the beginning of this period of life, is a major situational change to which children must adapt. Parents often recognize that starting school has implications for changes in their children, and may experience varying degrees of sadness or regret (or, sometimes, relief) that their children have ended one era of their lives and entered a new one.

Increasingly, not only the children's time but also their attention and interpersonal involvement center on matters related to school and to peers. New habits, words, and ideas learned from peers may be tried out at home, happily if they are congruent with family standards, but unhappily if they are not. Now, too, children can begin comparing their own homes with the homes of their peers, and from their new knowledge of the diversity of family ways can begin to press their own parents for freedoms and privileges permitted other children ("Tommy's mother says he can; how come you won't let me?"). Of course, the comparisons can show them not only negative but positive contrasts. Children may feel sorry for peers whose families do not share some strength or activity that is meaningful to them, and may even wish to share their own family activity with such friends.

Children are also changing and developing in the varieties of ways discussed in earlier chapters. One relevant change is in characteristic forms of egocentrism (Chapter 2). The form of egocentrism that is becoming prevalent in the thinking of school-aged children consists of failures to distinguish hypotheses from facts. Elkind (1981) labeled such failures *assumptive realities,* and suggested some manifestations which may relate directly to children's interactions with their parents. For instance, there is a particularly pervasive and long-lasting assumptive reality which Elkind calls *cognitive conceit.* Cognitive conceit is the assumption that adults aren't very bright, though children are ("Grown-ups don't know nothin'!"). This assumption develops when, using the new reasoning skills at their command, children inevitably catch adults in errors of reasoning or fact, and in this way discover that adults are not all-knowing, as the children had originally believed. Having discovered that an adult doesn't know something that *everybody* knows (since the child knows it), the child concludes that anyone who doesn't know that particular fact must not be very bright. Since this conclusion is an assumptive reality, evidence to the contrary has little effect on it.

Cognitive conceit is not often overt, Elkind points out, and in fact children more often act as though parents and other adults know more than children do. Certainly children recognize the fact of adult power relative to themselves! Yet cognitive conceit is an underlying theme which may show up in many forms— childhood traditions, jokes about stupid adults, games, parodies of adults, attitudes toward adult rules, even common childhood fantasies.

Assumptive realities may also show up in short-term situations. Elkind (1981) mentions children who have come up with some reason for a misbehavior, on the basis of which they convince themselves that they are innocent. In subsequently denying their guilt, they may anger their parents, who "know" from different reasoning that the children are guilty. Elkind comments, "At such times the parent fails to appreciate that for the child an assumptive reality is the truth" (p. 62). This is not to say that parents should go along with everything their children say! But there can be a great difference between parental reactions depending on whether parents think their child is telling brazen lies or being insolent and stubborn, or whether they recognize that the child is expressing a different reality which must be brought into touch with their own.

Another relevant set of changes is the rapidly expanding competence of school-aged children, which has been a recurrent theme of this book. Recall the studies cited earlier in which dependence was encouraged when the children acted dependent, whereas independence was encouraged when the children acted independent. Assuming that these findings apply more generally, one would expect that the more competent the child, the more independence the parents would allow. Parents must indeed gradually "let go" of their children (the process concurrent with the children's moving toward separation from their parents). Much of parents' letting go may be elicited by children's increasingly evident abilities to handle things on their own.

The parents: Continuities and changes   The studies of temperament and of enduring orientations in children cannot be extrapolated directly to adults, who have undergone much longer development and are coping with very different life demands and situations than are the children. Yet it seems likely that adults too would show characteristic patterns that would persist at least during the period when their children are in school, barring disruptive events or intervention. Parents can be classified by temperament characteristics or central orientations similar to those found for children, whether or not such attributes characterized the parents earlier in life. The question of the types of matches or mismatches that might exist between parents' attributes and their children's attributes, and of the ways in which such matches and mismatches may facilitate or interfere with positive parent-child interactions, is certainly one which merits study.

In addition, there should be continuities in attachment on the part of parents as there is on the part of children—attachment is a reciprocal process, remember. So their feelings for their children and their modes of expressing attachment to the children are likely to show some continuity and persistence during the school years, even while moderating to some extent in response to the changes in the children themselves. Further, parental practices and outlooks held when children enter school are likely to show some persistence over the school years. Parents who believe in physical punishment, and use it, are likely to continue doing so. Parents who believe in giving their children some voice in decisions that affect the children, or who try to reason and talk with their children, are likely to continue to do so.

At the same time, though, the ways in which such parental attitudes and practices are realized are likely to change over the course of the school years as the children themselves change. When children start school, parental concerns about their children show a predictable increase in emphasis on the children's competence, achievement, and school performance (Ferguson, 1976). Parents using physical punishment may punish both 6- and 12-year-olds, but what the children are punished for is likely to be different, and so are the ways in which the children are punished. The decisions in which 6- and 12-year-olds might be given a voice, and the topics which they might discuss with parents, are likely to differ. Thus, changes in the children themselves are an important factor influencing changes in the specific forms of interactions which may take place between the children and their parents. Parents who cannot accept the changes in their children, or who are too inflexible to change their own patterns as the children develop, may seriously hinder their children's psychological growth.

Of course, parents may change in other ways that influence their interactions with their children. A father may become increasingly preoccupied with his work, spending less and less time at home. Or he may realize that although he has said all along that his family holds high priority with him, he has not acted accordingly, and may change his priorities so as to participate more actively in interactions with his children. A mother, realizing that, much as she values her family, involvement outside the family is also important to her, may choose to go to work. Or she may realize that although she spends most of her time at home with her children, she actually spends little time on them aside from basic caretaking, and therefore restructures her activities so that she can spend some time each day with each child. Changes like these obviously have direct effects on children.

There are also many different kinds of situations to which both parents and children must adapt. Moving to a new community; the birth of a new child; a death in the family; parental discord resulting in a decision to divorce; the prolonged illness of a child—these and many other such changes must be dealt with by both parents and children and may result in a restructuring of parent-child interaction patterns.

There is also the point mentioned earlier that, once established, patterns of interaction among family members tend to persist over time. Some children must get well into adolescence or adulthood before they can overcome "childish" patterns of interacting with family members which are the habit of a lifetime. Parents may persist in expecting childish behavior from their children. When family interaction patterns are essentially healthy, providing support, warmth, and mutual satisfaction for family members, persisting patterns are a good thing. But when family interaction patterns are not healthy, persisting patterns may seriously hamper children. Because it is family interactions that are at issue, increasing numbers of therapists insist on working with the entire family rather than with a single child who has been referred for treatment.

So over the school years there are pressures toward continuity in family interaction patterns—ways in which children stay the same, ways in which parents stay the same, the persistence of established patterns of interaction. There are also pressures toward change—developmental changes in children, changes in parents, new situations which require modifications in family patterns. Under the impact of these conflicting pressures, interaction patterns in most families retain many qualities over the school years while at the same time gradually evolving in ways reflecting changes in both parents and children.

FAMILY STRUCTURE

Children's experiences in their families are influenced by *family structure*—that is, by the membership and organization of the family with whom the child lives and interacts on a day-to-day basis. Are there just parent(s) and child(ren)—a nuclear family—or do other kin live there too (extended family)? Are there two parents or just one, both natural parents or one a stepparent? Is the child first, last, or middle born? Boy or girl? Has the family experienced divorce? Does mother work? In view of recent social changes, these latter two factors have been the subject of especially strong interest.

All of these and other variations in family structure influence children's lives, but some points should be made clear from the outset. First, outcomes associated with different family structures are most likely caused, *not* by the structures in themselves, but by other associated processes which may become more or less likely with a given family format. It's harder, for instance, for parents to spend a lot of personal time with children when there are six children than when there are two, but some parents with six will spend more time per child than do some parents with two. If we compared on the basis of time-per-child regardless of family size, we would probably find that some of the outcomes associated with large families really reflect amount of time spent with each child rather than family size itself.

A second related point is that given family structures are not themselves intrinsically "good" or "bad" for children. There is nothing magical about, for example, two-parent families that makes them necessarily better than single-parent families or communal families; families of any type may be good or bad depending on a host of other factors, though it may be easier to provide supports for "good" outcomes and avoid fostering "bad" outcomes in some family structures than in others. And finally, children have a great deal of flexibility; they can grow and thrive in a variety of circumstances. If this were not true, we would find much the same family organization wherever we find human beings—but we don't; and we would not find characteristic forms of families changing over time as economic and social-cultural-attitudinal context change—but we do.

With these general points in mind, let us look at some family structure variations and their correlates.

Divorce

That substantial changes in family structure associated with divorce have taken place since 1960 is evident in Figure 8–1, which shows proportions of children living in different family groupings at different points in time. Note that in the projections for 1990, 60 percent or fewer of children under 18 will be living with two natural parents; 40 percent or more will have experienced divorce.

Divorce is, among other things, a change in family structure or organization which is itself a complex, multifaceted process. Not surprisingly, its outcomes for children are also complex and multifaceted, affected by processes at several levels (Kurdek, 1981). At the most general level are culture-based belief systems and values about family life; how likely parents are to divorce, and the amount of social stigma a child experiences if parents do divorce, are among factors influenced by such beliefs. (Though divorce is not considered the shameful event now that it was in the 1940s, there is still some stigma attached to it, and children may still encounter some prejudicial reactions and some associated shame and embarrassment when their parents divorce.)

Then there are social factors that affect the settings in which children find themselves—the changes from the pre-divorce family environment to the post-divorce environment. Post-divorce financial stresses can be especially disruptive. Settings also change in regard to interaction patterns with both parents, amount of parental stability and emotional support, location—some families move, so that children are having to deal with not only a new family structure, but also a new neighborhood and new school. Some evidence suggests that the greater the environmental change following the divorce, the harder the children's adjustment will be; for this reason some recommend that, whenever

FIGURE 8–1 Living arrangements of children under 18 in the United States from 1960 to 1990 (projected).

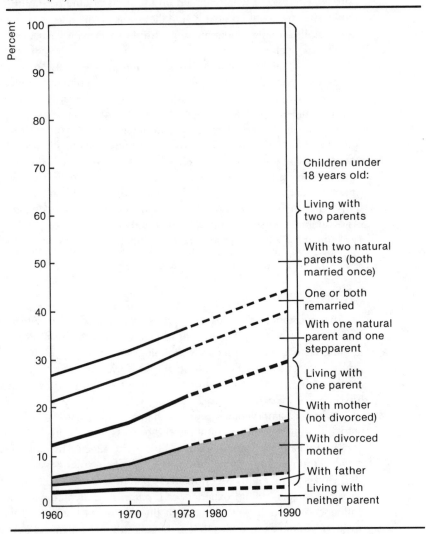

Source: P. Glick, "Children of Divorced Parents in Demographic Perspective," in T. E. Levitin, ed., "Children of Divorce," *Journal of Social Issues,* 35 (1979), pp. 170–82.

possible, families not move in the period immediately following divorce. However, there are qualifications, as usual. One study by Hetherington, Cox, and Cox (1978, 1979) followed families of children who were four at the time their parents separated; all children were in their mothers' custody. The year immediately following the divorce was difficult for *everyone,* parents and children. But the boys had the most problems, and their problems were still evident, though diminished, at the end of two years (by that time the girls were pretty much readjusted). However, the boys' reputations with teachers and peers as problem children were worse than was warranted by their actual behavior at the two-year follow-up, suggesting that the perceptions of others were in part sustaining the problem behaviors. The fact that boys who transferred schools were adjusting better after two years supports this interpretation. So for young boys in mothers' custody who show a lot of behavioral disruption following divorce, there may be an advantage in moving in the second year when the problem behaviors are no longer so great as to re-establish a reputation as trouble-makers in the new setting.

At a third level, there are changes in the patterns of interactions within the families themselves. Parents are under stress in the year following a divorce, and probably for this reason, their parenting competence declines (Hetherington, Cox & Cox, 1978; Wallerstein & Kelly, 1980). They are unable to provide as much emotional support for children. Custodial mothers are likely to become more restrictive of their children while fathers become more indulgent, but less available. There is less expression of affection, greater inconsistency of discipline. And this is happening during a period that children experience as painful. No wonder that Hetherington, Cox, and Cox found that children show increased problems with parents, poorer cognitive and school performance, and disrupted play and social interaction in the year or two following divorce!

What can help minimize such painful outcomes? Kurdek (1981) cites studies that show that adjustment problems are eased by the following circumstances: financial resources are not too strained; parents have low interpersonal conflict and hostility toward one another both before and after the divorce; the parents agree about childrearing and discipline; both parents show love and approval for the child; the custodial parent uses authoritative discipline; relationships between the ex-spouses are cordial and visitation is regular; parents are willing and able to discuss children's divorce-related concerns with them. Notice that these circumstances involve the active, caring, continuing interactions of *both* parents with children following divorce. For this and other reasons, joint custody agreements, where parents have children for equal periods of time and work out child-rearing issues collaboratively, may prove to be good practice where possible.

And re-emphasizing our earlier point that it is not the structure change per se but associated processes that are important for children, Hess and Camara (1979) demonstrated that the quality of relationships among family members was at least as important for children's behavior as was marital status itself. As Table 8–1 shows, child outcomes of stress, aggressiveness, social relations, and work effectiveness at school were more strongly affected by parental harmony and mother-child or father-child relationships, regardless of family type, than they were to family type itself. While it may be harder to maintain high-quality relationships while adjusting to divorce, many of the divorced families observed by Hess and Camara had better relationships than did many nondivorced families—there was more difference between families within either group than there was between the two groups.

Finally, the child's own qualities and competencies influence children's responses to and adjustment following divorce. Kurdek (1981) suggests that pre-

TABLE 8–1

Correlations of family type and process variables with child outcomes (Divorced and nondivorced groups combined)

Child outcomes	Family type (divorced or intact)	Parental harmony	Mother-child relation-ship	Father-child relation-ship	Frequency of father visits (divorced)	Duration of father visits (divorced)
Stress.............	−.41†	−.55‡	−.43†	−.44†	.22	−.35
Aggression	−.26	−.38*	−.47†	−.41†	−.06	.13
Social relations	−.03	.18	−.05	.54‡	−.19	.35
Work effective-ness at school	.36*	.24	.37*	.40†	−.09	−.16

Note. Divorced and nondivorced families were coded with values of 1 and 2 respectively. Hence, positive correlations between family type and child outcomes indicate higher mean values for intact families.
* p < .05
† p < .01
‡ p < .001
Source: R. D. Hess and K. A. Camara, "Post-divorce Family Relationships as Mediating Factors in the Consequences of Divorce for Children," in T. E. Levitin, ed., "Children of Divorce," *Journal of Social Issues* 35 (1979) pp. 79–96.

schoolers may be most vulnerable to disruption because they have the least cognitive and personal coping skills with which to understand and deal with the divorce and also because their parents are likely to be young and so to have more limited financial resources. For school-aged children, loss of noncustodial parent is experienced as a deep, personal loss which is often followed by patterns that resemble grieving—depression, withdrawal from social activities, decline in school performance, and repeated insistent requests for explanations. Adolescents have most cognitive and personal maturity and so may be less affected developmentally though they certainly may experience strong feelings about the divorce. For children between 8 and 17, Kurdek, Blisk, and Siesky (1981) found divorce adjustment to be moderately correlated with internal locus of control and with interpersonal reasoning, a composite measure they developed based on perspective taking (Chapter 2), assessment of others' intentions, and social cognitions regarding friendship (Chapter 9). Developmental changes in capacities such as these are very likely one reason for the age-related changes in vulnerability to divorce described above.

Single-parent families

From Figure 8–1 you can see that the number of children living with just one parent has risen sharply, from about 9 percent in 1960 (just under 8 percent with mothers) to around 19 percent in 1978 (17 percent with mother); the projection for 1990 is that about 25 percent of children, one in four, will be living with just one parent, and the majority of those still will be with the mother. Unless patterns of custody decisions change so as to give more fathers custody of their children, the proportion of father-headed, single-parent families will continue to be a very small proportion of such families. So discussions of single-parent families means primarily families headed by mothers. When such families are the aftermath of divorce, and to some extent when a parent is single for other reasons such as death or personal choice, many of the resulting problems are more severe for single mothers than for single fathers. Both men and women experience loneliness—but it is still easier for men to meet and date new partners, especially if they are unencumbered by child care. Economic problems are usually greater for mothers, who typically cannot command as high-paying jobs as their ex-spouses or who may have had little or no experience in the labor force. For either parent, the fact that there is no other back-up adult with whom to share chores and supervision substantially increases the complications and difficulty of running a household.

Given these and other problems they face, it is remarkable that so many single-parent families do so well—and they do. Depending on the parent, single-parent families can be close, cohesive units even in the face of adverse conditions (for example, Lewis, 1967; Hess & Camara, 1979; Weiss, 1979). Likewise, single-parent families can provide adequate supervision and good alternative care for children, and concerned parents can find ways of locating adults of the opposite sex to interact with their children and to serve as role models. Of course if a single mother is bitter and resentful toward the father, blames the children for living with the father, fails to supervise the children or provide emotional support, there will be negative consequences for the children—but this would be equally true in a two-parent family.

The fact that there is no second adult to share responsibilities leads to reorganization in single-parent families which typically results in children becoming more like "junior partners" in the family enterprise (Weiss, 1979). Compared to children in two-parent homes, these children become more independent, more responsible, take greater part in family decision making, and become more attuned to adult values and concerns. On the basis of interviews with children and parents, Weiss concludes that this experience is not only helpful to the parent and essential to family functioning, but probably more beneficial than not for the children. They become more mature than others their own age in many ways, and take pride in their contributions and capabilities—though they may also wish they hadn't had to be so responsible and could have had a more carefree, childlike time. Weiss does also suggest that preadolescents may be more vulnerable than adolescents because they may still have needs for parental support which the parent simply cannot meet. So they may learn to suppress such needs, and as a consequence may become unable to request such support even when the parent can be open enough to provide it. Note though that this also is a process which, while more likely to occur in single-parent families because of their reduced personnel resources in stressful times, could happen in *any* family when parents are preoccupied or under severe stress.

Though father custody is far rarer than mother custody, there is one study by Santrock and Warshak (1979) that compared the post-divorce adjustments of children 6 to 11 years of age, an equal number of whom were from divorced families in custody of their father, from divorced families in custody of their mothers, and from two-parent families. The researchers observed families in interaction and rated child and parent behavior on a number of dimensions.

These observations took place nearly three years following the divorce on the average, so the early disruption of the first year or two described above should have largely been past. A little to their surprise, Santrock and Warshak found that not only did children being raised by same-sex parents show greater social competence than children being raised by opposite sex parents, but that when comparing children from divorced and intact families the boys being raised by their fathers actually showed significantly *greater* social competence than did the boys growing up in intact families! Further, they generally found little, if any, overall difference between children from intact and divorced homes; such differences as were observed were interactions, meaning that it made a difference whether one was looking at sons or daughters, as well as what kind of family structure and what aspect of behavior. Why the "good showing" of boys in father custody? Santrock and Warshak point out that early disruptions in behavior might have presented a different picture had their families been closer to the time of the family break-up. However, they also point out that those few fathers who do seek and obtain custody may be an exceptional group of men whose general competence at fathering is higher than average. In any case, it clearly makes a difference whether the single parent is mother or father as well as whether the child is a boy or a girl. The greater difficulties of boys discussed earlier may have reflected in part their placement in mothers' custody.

Problems facing single-parent families are typically greater than those facing two-parent families; the problems aren't helped by the declining, but still widespread, tendency to devalue such families as inferior substitutes, rather than recognizing them as a functional family form in their own right. Herzog and Sudia (1973) advocated giving such families full recognition and working toward providing more support for them in forms such as counseling, housekeeping, and child-care services—recommendations which still are sound. Many single parents have turned for support to organizations such as Parents Without Partners, which are the result of a spontaneous social response to the special problems of single parents. Helping single parents to be aware of some of the pitfalls that face them and of ways in which they can cope with those pitfalls is also important (Lynn, 1974).

Absent fathers

For many of the same reasons that single parents are likely to be mothers, absent or missing parents are likely to be fathers. Fathers as noncustodial parents may move away or fail to exercise visitation rights; fathers are more likely than mothers to die before children are grown; and if a parent is gone for periods of time for military, professional, or business reasons, that parent is more likely to be the father than the mother.

The conventional wisdom is that father absence is bad for children, especially sons; that when no father is present, children are more likely to become juvenile delinquents; that there are negative effects on children's cognitive development; and that sex-role development is hampered, especially for boys who have no parental sex-role model. Unfortunately, the studies on which such conclusions are based only too often fail to take into account the host of factors affecting children's experiences in their families. In general, there are issues such as: How long has father been absent? Why (death, divorce, other reason)? How old was the child when father left? Are there other male figures in the child's life? Taking juvenile delinquency as a specific case, Herzog and Sudia's (1973) critical review pointed out that studies didn't differentiate delinquency of public record from delinquent behavior—yet children from some social groups (lower class, black, broken homes) are more likely to be caught, and once caught, prosecuted. Neither did the studies usually differentiate social class or community norms, yet lower-class and middle-class children may grow up with very different norms. Among family interaction factors, the quality of maternal supervision proves to be more important than does father absence per se (some similar effect almost certainly holds for quality of paternal supervision when mother is absent). The same is true for *family climate,* which is the amount of cohesiveness and harmony among family members. From their review, Herzog and Sudia conclude that while there may be a relationship between father absence and delinquency, it is probably so small as to be of little practical significance; and what relationship does exist is probably due less to father absence per se than to stress within the home occasioned by his absence, the mother's reaction to the separation, her ability to exercise adequate supervision, and depressed living and income conditions. Problems similar to these are found in research on other consequences of father absence as well. In general, father absence—like any variation in family structure—is so closely interwoven with other relevent factors that simply correlating father presence or absence with some child attribute is meaningless unless other factors are considered simultaneously.

As for father absence and cognitive development, Herzog and Sudia (1973) found the evidence too weak to support any strong conclusions, but more recent and better-controlled studies reviewed by Shinn (1978) do suggest that father absence has detrimental effects on children's intellectual performance. Further, there is suggestive evidence that absence during the preschool years may have greater effects than later absence, but that such effects may not show up fully until children start school—perhaps because cognitive skills become so much more salient then. Not surprisingly, factors such as length of absence and whether or not there are father surrogates available make a difference. Interestingly, there is clearer evidence that the *pattern* of abilities is influenced— children whose fathers are absent are likely to have poorer quantitative skills and better verbal skills than other children. Among possible reasons for these findings, Shinn reviews evidence suggesting that financial stress, high anxiety levels, and limited or poor quality of parent-child interaction—all of which may be heightened in single-parent families, as we saw above—may be among the processes responsible for the cognitive differences.

Prevalent theories have stressed the importance of father for sex-role learning in boys (though as we saw in Chapter 6, nonfamily processes influence sex-role learning more than we used to think). Many studies, though not all, do find that father-absent boys show less masculine orientation than do father-present boys (e.g., see Lynn, 1974; Herzog & Sudia, 1973).

The pattern of effects for separations because of father's death are somewhat different from, and usually less severe than, effects due to divorce. The very different context of father loss through death compared to father loss through divorce or desertion may be responsible for these differences. Divorce or desertion, but not death, is likely to occur in a family context of tension, stress, and discord which precedes the loss and may continue after the loss. In fact, where there is discord in the home, it may be better for children if the parents split up. Under these circumstances, any advantages of having both parents at home are outweighed by the effects of bad family climate (e.g., Nye, 1957).

How father absence affects girls has gotten far less attention. In general, girls' scholastic performance and mathematical skills are less affected by father absence than are boys' though some studies have reported such associations (Lynn, 1974; Shinn, 1978). Similarly, father absence is less likely to affect the traditional sex-role attributes of girls. This does not mean that there are no effects; it is quite possible that the right issues are not yet being studied. Looking at the ways that girls interact with men during adolescence (rather than at traditional feminine attributes), Hetherington (1972) showed that girls whose fathers had died were likely to be extremely shy, anxious, and uncomfortable around men and male peers, whereas girls whose parents had been divorced tended to be inappropriately assertive around men and male peers. Evidently, interactions with fathers are important in teaching girls to interact with members of the opposite sex.

In this section we have emphasized that interacting factors moderate the effects of father absence, and may in fact be more important than father absence per se. It would be easy to jump to the unjustified conclusion that if father absence makes little difference, then father presence must also make little difference. Not so. Father presence and father absence are not simple opposites, psychologically speaking. Fathers have an important influence on their children's development which may differ in important ways from the influence of mothers (Lamb, 1981), but is no less real. Lynn (1974) has written an excellent and interesting overview documenting the ways in which fathers contribute to their children's development. The question is, if father is not available, can the contributions he would ordinarily make be compensated for by other means? If so, then variations in the compensating factors should be the determinants of the development of father-absence children—as appears to be the case.

Working mothers

According to 1977 figures from the U.S. Department of Labor Women's Bureau, participation of women, and especially of mothers, in the labor force has risen dramatically over the past three decades. In 1946, 18 percent of mothers and 31 percent of all women were working; by 1976, the percent of mothers working, 49 percent, actually exceeded the percent of all women working, 47 percent. There is every reason to assume that these figures have continued to rise in the years since 1977.

As was the case for divorce, the impact of mothers' working depends on context at multiple levels: the cultural acceptability of working (which has been increasing as incidence increased); the mother's feelings about working; the meaning of her working to the family; the father's attitude if he is present; whether or not mother is a professional; whether the family is lower or middle class; and so forth.

Hoffman reviewed information regarding working mothers in 1974. There has been work in intervening years, but by and large her summary is still applicable. Her review is organized around five prevalent hypotheses. The first hypothesis is that working mothers provide a different role model than do non-working mothers, so that their children develop different ideas of what the female sex role is. The evidence supports this hypothesis. Both sons and daughters of working mothers are more likely to approve of women working, are likely to have less traditional sex-role stereotypes, and are likely to evaluate women's competence more highly than are children whose mothers do not work. In addition, daughters of working women show more independence and have higher achievement aspirations than do daughters of nonworking women. Of course, these differences do not stem solely from the fact that mother works. The division of labor in homes where mothers work tends to be less traditional and more egalitarian, so the differences may reflect children's perceptions of both parents (and the associated process difference, rather than the structure difference itself).

The second hypothesis is that mothers are affected emotionally if they work, and that this in turn affects their interactions with their children. This can indeed happen. On the one hand, a mother who feels excessive guilt about working may overcompensate, doing too much for her children. A mother who dislikes working, or whose job is such that juggling work and home responsibilities creates real strain, may react in ways that place stress on her children. On the other hand, satisfaction with work may improve a mother's morale, with corresponding improvements in her interactions with her family. In general, if a mother enjoys her work, has arranged matters so that handling the dual sets of responsibilities is not too great a strain, and does not overcompensate because of guilt feelings about working, her children will be as well adjusted and happy as the children of nonworking mothers, and sometimes more so.

The third hypothesis is that because of situational differences created when mothers work, working mothers use different child-rearing practices than do nonworking mothers. Working mothers stress independence training more than do nonworking mothers, and children whose mothers work generally have more household responsibilities than do other children—unless the working mothers have school-aged children and are better educated or enjoy working. However, these are the same mothers who are most likely to feel guilty and to overcompensate for working, so they may also be reluctant to press for independence or request household help from their children. Such mothers may try to live up to an overidealized view of what nonworking mothers do, actually spending more time with their children and doing more for them than do many nonworking mothers—trying to be "superwoman." However, encouraging independence in children and requesting help at home can be seen as an adaptive way to reduce the strain of dual responsibilities on the mother, and so lessen the effects of that strain on the family, while the emphasis on independence may facilitate the children's growing self-sufficiency and their eventual separation from the family.

The fourth hypothesis is that working mothers provide inadequate supervision for their children, and that the children are therefore more likely to become delinquent. In lower-class families, inadequate supervision is related to children's delinquent behavior *whether or not* the mother works, but relevant studies have provided no evidence linking delinquency to maternal employment. In middle-class families, children of working mothers are somewhat more likely to be delinquent, but there is insufficient evidence on supervision in such families to say whether or not maternal employment is the reason.

Finally, it has been hypothesized that the children of working mothers are deprived emotionally and intellectually, or that they feel rejected because their mothers work. There is no support for these contentions so far as school-aged children are concerned. Working mothers do not necessarily reject their children any more than nonworking mothers do. In fact, working mothers are likely to try to make up for their time away from home by making a point of spending time with their children. As long as this tendency does not become overcompensation, it evidently provides an effective counterbalance to any adverse effects of the mothers' time away from home. Further, now that working mothers are typical rather than deviant, children may be more likely to perceive working as something mothers usually do, rather than in personal terms as signalling rejection.

Clearly there are a number of dimensions along which children's experience differs if their mothers work. But there is no evidence of adverse effects associated with these differences in experience. Again, the important issue seems to be not the variation in family structure itself, but the whole network of structure dimensions and processes in which it is embedded.

Siblings

A final dimension of family structure is *sibling status*—what difference does it make if one is first or later born, in a large or small family, has brothers or sisters? Despite widespread popular acceptance, there is little evidence for the idea that sibling status and personal qualities are directly linked. The one exception is that first-borns are more often high achievers than are later-borns—but even this much-replicated finding has been challenged. Schooler (1972) pointed out that there are always more first-borns in the population than any other status, and studies showing more first-borns in positions of prominence haven't taken into account the relatively greater proportions of first-borns in the population. And Sutton-Smith and Rosenberg (1970) found, when they compared first- and second-borns in two-child families, that first-borns did have higher achievement—but only if the younger sibling was a brother.

Given the complexity of the situation it isn't surprising that that direct links are not found more often. Take two-child families, for example. By the time you consider brothers and sisters who are first- or second-born, you have eight possible sibling statuses (first-born boy with brother, first-born boy with sister, first-born girl with brother, and so forth). Adding just one more child, the number of such statuses jumps to 24. And this is *before* one takes into account other factors that make a difference, such as the spacing between children (Koch, 1955; Hoffman & Teyber, 1979); or temperamental and other attributes of the particular children themselves.

This is not to say that sibling status makes no difference, however. Parents learn with experience, and there is evidence that they systematically treat later-borns differently from first-borns, with whom they tend to be more strict, controlling, and concerned. Thus when mothers of 8- and 14-year-old boys were asked to react to hypothetical cases of problem behavior, mothers of first-borns were more likely to say that they would seek outside help for problems of moderate severity than were mothers of later-borns (for severe problems, all mothers considered seeking help; Abrams & Coie, 1981). Similarly, the mothers of first-borns were likely to attribute the problem behaviors to parental mishandling whereas mothers of later-borns were more likely to attribute the problem to social skill deficits in the boys. Clearly mothers of first- and later-borns differ in how they perceive problem behaviors and their sources—and as we saw earlier in the chapter, parent perceptions are one source of variation in parent-child interactions. Other studies have also found more concern over, and more intense socialization of, first-born than later-born children (e.g., Sutton-Smith & Rosenberg, 1970; Martin, 1975).

In a somewhat different vein, Rosenberg and Sutton-Smith (1974) argue that children in different sibling statuses learn different styles of interaction with others which they then tend to recreate in later life. (Note the resemblance between this notion that early interaction patterns within the family serve as prototypes of later relationships, and the notion discussed earlier that early attachments similarly serve as prototypes.) For instance, one can argue that the more intense socialization of first-borns by parents results in first-borns experiencing early interactions which are predominantly hierarchical in nature, from parental authority to child. Later-borns, however, are born into a setting in which, first, there are more children close to one's own age who do not have authority in the way that parents do, and second, parental socialization is less intense; so they are more likely to learn egalitarian modes of interacting with others. Sutton-Smith and Rosenberg (1970) predicted, and found, that first-borns are more likely later to enter occupations which are hierarchically organized, such as teaching or police work, whereas later-borns are more likely to enter occupations that involve more egalitarian interactions with others, such as sales.

Rosenberg and Sutton-Smith (1973) also found some fascinating associations between sibling status and later life choices such as choice of a spouse and family size. Table 8–2 shows the significant associations found for a sample of parents whose families of orgin had been two-child families. (Empty cells mean no systematic association was found.) Each row shows the choices most likely

TABLE 8–2

Effects of birth order and sibling status of mothers and fathers from two-child families on choice of mate

Sibling status	Mothers			
	Offspring	FFS	FBO	FSS
Elder of two sisters	Have large families	Trend to marry SFS man	Marry early-born	Marry man with male sibling
Younger of two sisters	Have small families	Marry only son SFS man	Marry early-born	
Elder sister with brother		Marry LFS man	Marry late-born	Marry man with female sibling
Younger sister with brother		Trend to marry LFS man		

Sibling status	Fathers			
	Offspring	MFS	MBO	MSS
Elder of two brothers	Trend to have large families	Marry LFS woman	Marry late-born	
Younger of two brothers	Trend to have small families	Marry SFS woman	Marry early-born	Marry woman with female sibling
Elder brother with sister			Marry late-born	Marry woman with male sibling
Younger brother with sister		Marry SFS woman	Marry early-born	Marry woman with male sibling

Note: FS refers to family size, BO to birth order, and SS to sibling status. Thus, FFS refers to father's family size, MFS to mother's family size, FBO to father's birth order, etc. SFS: Small family size. LFS: Large family size.

Source: B. G. Rosenberg and B. Sutton-Smith, "Family Structure and Sex-Role Variations," in *Nebraska Symposium on Motivation, 1973* (Lincoln: University of Nebraska Press, 1974).

to be made by individuals having the sibling status indicated at the beginning of the row. Note that, in general, where associations exist, early-borns are likely to marry later-borns who presumably have learned roles complementary to their own in early family life; and early-borns, whose experience included having younger siblings around, are more likely to have large families than are later-borns who grew up without younger children around. Of course, these early family experiences are not the only determinants of one's adult life choices! At the same time, the associations found by Rosenberg and Sutton-Smith certainly indicate that they are one important set of influences. Evidently all those years we spend growing up in our particular sibling status, whatever it might be, establishes predispositions which make us more comfortable and at ease with others whose experience established patterns complementary to our own.

SUMMARY

Over the school years, as over any period of development, there are both continuities and changes in children's relationships with their parents. The unique patterns that characterize each family system tend to persist over time. Attachments initially formed in infancy have persisting effects, and may also form a foundation and model for later attachments which children will form outside of their families. To the extent that child attributes and parent attributes remain consistent over the school years, their contribution to the reciprocal interaction between child and parent will continue do be the same.

At the same time, there are changes. Children grow up—become more independent, more competent—and these changes very likely elicit changes in parents' behavior as the parents allow freedom and independence commensurate with the children's developing competencies. Further, the new social worlds of school and peers become increasingly important to the children. Parents too may be undergoing changes in their own lives which contribute to alternations in the pattern of interactions between their children and themselves.

Families also vary in structure, that is, in membership and organization. Certainly children's experiences differ depending upon the structure of their families, but such differences in experience are probably due to the likelihood that given processes will occur or not rather than to effects of the structures in themselves. In the case of divorce, for example, the impact on a child will depend on a complex network of factors ranging from cultural attitudes through situational circumstances to the child's personal attributes. Though the period following the breakup of a family is hard on all family members, families of divorce can and often do maintain as good relationships for children as do nondivorced families—there is more difference within either type of family than there is between the two. Of course it is more difficult when there is only one parent available to the children; and this may be especially true for mothers raising sons. Most children are still placed in mothers' custody, through evidence suggests that children adapt best when placed in the custody of the same-sex parent. Further, father absence does affect children's cognitive performance and sex-role development, especially for boys.

Mother's working outside the home has become a fact of contemporary family life. Again, the consequences of mother's working are not intrinsically good or bad but depend on a host of factors. Certainly for school-aged children, their family experience may be somewhat different if mother works, but there is no reason to believe they do not develop any less well than if mother stays at home.

Finally, studies of sibling status suggest that, though there are no simple connections between sibling status and personal qualities as such, children do learn styles of interacting with others within their particular families which they then tend to replicate in later life choices such as vocation or selection of spouse.

TERMS AND CONCEPTS

families as social systems

family structure

attachment as precursor of later
  behavior

attachment as prototype of later
  behavior

reciprocity in parent-child relations

assumptive reality

cognitive conceit

family climate

sibling status

SUGGESTED ADDITIONAL READING

Hoffman, L. W. Effects of maternal employment on the child—a review of the research. *Development Psychology,* 1974, *10,* 204–228.

Kahn, R. L., & Antonucci, T. C. Convoys over the life course; Attachment, roles, and social support. In *Life span development and behavior* (Vol. 3). New York: Academic Press, 1980.

Kurdek, L. A. An integrative perspective on children's divorce adjustment. *American Psychologist,* 1981, *36,* 856–866.

Lerner, R. M., and Sapanier, G. B. (Eds.). *Child influence on marital and family interaction: A life-span perspective.* New York: Academic Press, 1978.

Levitin, T. E. (Ed.). Children of divorce. *Journal of Social Issues,* 1979, *35,* 1–25.

Rosenberg, B., & Sutton-Smith, B. Family structure and sex-role variation. In J. K. Cole and R. Dienstbier (Eds.), Human sexuality. *Nebraska Symposium on Motivation,* 1973. Lincoln: University of Nebraska Press, 1974.

BOX 9–1
Study questions

Describe Sullivan's theory of interpersonal interactions as applied to the school
     years.

What is the culture of childhood?

What are three influences of play on children's development?

Why are peer relationships important *to* children and *for* children?

Define sociometric statuses of star, rejected, isolate, and average child.

What are the correlates of popularity?

What is the physical attractiveness sterotype? How does it relate to children's
     acceptance by peers?

Define the three major body builds or somatotypes, describe the stereotypes asso-
     ciated with each, and summarize evidence showing how the stereotypes influ-
     ence children.

What are three kinds of evidence of the role of nonverbal cues in regulating
     children's social interactions and status hierarchies?

Distinguish friendship from popularity.

What are some of the major trends in children's expectations for friendship over the
     school years?

Summarize research evidence regarding the friendship skills of children younger
     than age eight and older than age eight.

What are some of the changes in friendship patterns from the primary grades to the
     later grades?

CHAPTER 9

FRIENDS AND PEER RELATIONSHIPS

Perhaps the greatest change in the social organization of children's lives once they begin school is the greatly increased amount of time they spend with peers. There are the formal classroom relationships with a large and relatively stable group of other children which now take up several hours of each child's day. In addition, informal peer contacts outside school hours absorb increasing proportions of schoolchildren's time. Children play, form clubs, embark on projects, squabble, state opinions, jockey for social position, and engage in a host of other activities with one another. In the course of these activities, they learn a great deal about others and about themselves.

SULLIVAN'S THEORY

Harry Stack Sullivan (1953) was a personality theorist who believed that the school years play a crucial formative role in personality development because of the changed relationships they bring with others—with adults but especially with peers. As Sullivan saw it, the school years are the period in life when children first really begin to become social. Children's relationships with adults change once they are in school because now they come in contact with a much wider range of authority figures than do younger children, whose contact is primarily with their parents. Furthermore, the children interact with a number of different adults in similar positions of authority—teachers, for instance—each of whom has particular characteristics. Through these contacts, children learn to interact with authority in diverse forms. They also learn that persons in authority

219

positions are individuals, a discovery that may ultimately lead them to discover that their parents are also individuals.

It is the new relationships with peers that are especially important, however. Peers, by definition, are equals. They are also persons similar to oneself in many ways, but with their own idiosyncrasies, attitudes, interests, wishes, and ideas about what is fair or fun to do. Encountering such differences, children must learn to come to terms with one another through their own actions. In addition, they must do so on their own in a way that is not true in authority-based relationships. Whether or not children are accepted, and how well they get along, depends on their own attributes and not on their relationships with someone else. At home their acceptance is partly a matter of being their parent's child; at school, of being a given teacher's pupil. But among peers they are nobody unless they can prove themselves on the peer group's terms.

What children learn in these relationships is *social accommodation* to other persons. They must learn about the many ways in which other children differ from themselves, and also how to cope with or accommodate those differences. The learning is not necessarily smooth or easy. Especially in the early school years, children do not have much awareness of others' feelings or many skills in relating to such feelings. Any observant parent or teacher can testify to the frequency with which school children's feelings and egos are bruised, even among children who usually get along well together. Yet painful though such incidents are when they occur, they are a major crucible through which awareness and responsiveness to others are learned.

Sullivan divides the school years into two parts: the *juvenile era* and *preadolescence*. The juvenile era begins when children first start school, bringing with it the changed interpersonal interactions described above. It is a period of rapid (and sometimes painful) learning about how to get along with, and make a position for oneself among, other children. Confrontations are direct, immediate, and lacking in what adults call tact; as Friedenberg says, "Juvenile politics are dirty, but they work" (1959, p. 45).

However, at some point—never before 8½ to 10, Sullivan believed—a new form of interpersonal interaction begins to develop. Children begin to show interest in a particular friend or chum, demonstrating real sensitivity to the chum as a person. The two become able to share not only activities but also triumphs and failures, joys and depressions. They show signs of caring about each other in ways that they have not shown toward others before. When children form such friendships, they have moved out of the juvenile era into preadolescence.

In this chapter we shall deal with a number of topics, many of which are relevant to Sullivan's ideas. Sullivan's work has not necessarily been the inspiration for this research, especially for the great burst of interest in children's friendships and peer relationships which has emerged over the past few years. Still, his ideas have been influential and are often cited; at a general descriptive level, the great increase in diversity of social contact and children's increasing skill in social accommodation clearly takes place. It is less clear whether some of his more specific points—such as that the character of children's friendships changes sometime after eight or nine years of age—are valid, as we shall see in later sections of the chapter.

THE CULTURE OF CHILDHOOD

Not only do children learn about getting along with others through interactions with peers, they are also introduced by peers into a social world which, though coexisting with the social world that children share with adults, differs from it in many ways. The social world of childhood has its own rituals, activities, traditions, and social codes, all of which children learn from one another. Adults play little direct role in the activities of that social world or in the transmission of its culture from one generation of children to another.

Adults rarely take much note of this children's world. They have outgrown it themselves; what they do notice may seem familiar and innocuous; and children tend to keep much of what goes on there to themselves. ("Where did you go? Out. What did you do? Nothing.") Sometimes this is because children engage in activities that are forbidden by adults. Adults have often forgotten, but if they were honest with themselves, they could describe many such activities from their own childhood—going to forbidden places; trying a cigarette; telling "dirty" jokes; raiding gardens or ringing doorbells; sex play; shoplifting.

It is entirely possible that many children view adult prohibitions of such activities as silly or unimportant. Elkind (1981) suggests that the assumptive reality of cognitive conceit (Chapter 8) may affect children's view of rules laid down by adults. Recall that cognitive conceit refers to children's perceptions of adults as stupid and themselves as clever. If adults are stupid, then the rules they make are probably stupid too. To break such rules and get away with it may even be a challenge through which children reinforce their perception of their own intellectual superiority. Of course, Elkind points out, children are realists about adult power in relation to themselves, so they are usually careful not to draw adult attention to such "cleverness" on their part.

But forbidden activities make up only a portion of what children do together. Mostly they play. Studying what they play turns out to provide an unexpected and fascinating picture of the continuity of children's traditions over time and space, and of the effectiveness of communication from one group of children to another (Opie & Opie, 1969, 1959).

There is a great deal of conservatism and tradition in what children learn from one another. The same game, with minor local variations, may be described throughout the British Isles, as well as in a variety of locations in the United States and elsewhere. Tag, Statue, Kick the Can, and Red Rover are among the dozens of games described by the Opies (1969). One also finds wide distribution of chants, rhymes, and signal calls which remain recognizable variations of some original version, though they may have been modified over time or they may vary in different localities (Opie & Opie, 1959). Where variations evolve they appear to be accidental, reflecting a misunderstanding or mishearing of an original version which the children then learn and transmit in the altered form.

An example of such a misunderstanding from the childhood of one of the authors was the substitution of "Ole Ole Olson Free" for "All the, All the, Outs in Free" when playing hiding games.

Not only do children of a given era play many of the same games, but when games are traced historically, they often prove to have been handed down over a surprising number of generations of children. The game of jacks, for instance, dates back at least to Roman times, when it was played with the vertebrae of small animals (look at a jack the next time you're in a toy store). The game of paper-scissors-stone, in which two players simultaneously flash an extended palm (paper), two extended fingers (scissors), or a fist (stone), has been played for centuries and is found worldwide. Blind Man's Buff, a rowdy game for adults a few centuries back, became a game for children in a cleaned-up version. London Bridge has its origins in historical events that took place several centuries ago. The historical connection has long been lost, but the game continues.

A similar phenomenon occurs for some of the verses and rhymes that children pass on from one to another, such as nursery rhymes or the rhymes to which children jump rope. Despite the modernization of content over time, it has been possible to trace some verses of this kind heard in the 20th century to verses going back at least as far as the 1700s (Opie & Opie, 1959). Then there is the taunting singsong used by children worldwide, although the continuity of this sound pattern may have a different basis. The tune we mean is the one that would go with "*Billy* has a *girl* friend," or with "*Susan* is a *show*- off." However, the universality of this melody may be as much a matter of the physics of musical sound and the physiology of the vocal cords, which are universal for human beings, as of cultural transmission over generations of children (Bernstein, 1973).

Within a given locality, games, chants, and customs show remarkable durability, persisting largely unchanged over many generations of children. Such local customs regulate many of children's transactions with one another—what one says to protect oneself from attack, how the leader or the "it" player is selected, how particular games are played, what one says to claim first choice. The equivalent customs may be quite different in other localities—a fact which children moving from one locality to another must discover the hard way when the codes to which they are accustomed not only do not work but are considered weird or dumb by their new playmates. The newcomers bring with them games and lore, some of which may "catch on" and be adopted by their new peers, but for the most part they must learn the local customs of their new community.

In addition to these deep-rooted and durable traditions, children also often transmit relatively transitory songs, jokes, and stories to one another. Current political events, popular songs, and fads may provide bases for rhymes or verses—often impolite or improper—which spread with great rapidity only to disappear again within a few months or years. The Opies (1959) cite a verse inspired by the abdication of King Edward VIII of England in 1936 to marry the divorcee Wallis Simpson:

> Hark the Herald Angels sing
> Mrs. Simpson's pinched our King.

News of the abdication did not become public until November 1936, yet this verse was sung by children throughout England by Christmas 1936, when it could not have been more than three or four weeks old. Likewise, the "Ballad of Davy Crockett" of the mid-1950s was the source of a variety of unofficial verses. One such verse originating in an identifiable town in England was reported within a matter of two or three months not only from many other towns in England, but even from Australia. Such rapid transmission of information across communities and even countries suggests the existence of a remarkably effective grapevine among children's groups.

The importance of play

At this point, some readers may wonder why anyone would bother to discuss children's games, when after all they are "just play." Such a question would reflect an attitude widely found in the United States, that play is trivial because it is for fun. As it happens, however, this attitude is a serious underestimation of play. Having fun—being able to enjoy living—is itself a valuable human attribute, and Sutton-Smith (1971) suggests that this may be the most important thing children learn through play.

But in addition, games and other play activities provide a situation in which children can test themselves, experiment with roles, work out feelings, and practice skills important for adult life in their society, under circumstances in which there is little risk or cost to them for doing so. Sutton-Smith and Roberts (1981) suggest, on the basis of cross-cultural studies of play, that not only does play provide practice in adult roles prototypic of those in which a child may engage in later life, it may also provide practice in dealing with novel situations and thus become an important factor in facilitating social change. Children's games and spontaneous play are not deliberately designed with such sober purposes in mind, of course, and not all play is necessarily "functional" in these senses. But apparently many games and play activities evolve in ways that reflect the attributes of societies and the demands societies place on the people living within them. Cross-culturally, games of strategy, such as chess and checkers, are associated with complexity of social organization as well as with emphasis on obedience training in child rearing. Games of chance, such as bingo and dice, are associated with stress on responsibility and anxiety about achievement, especially when survival conditions are uncertain. Games of physical skill, such as racing and bowling, are associated with emphasis on achievement. These contrasts are evident within our own culture. Girls, whose socialization tends to emphasize obedience and responsibility, prefer games of strategy and games of chance; boys, whose socialization emphasizes achievement, prefer games of physical skill (Roberts & Sutton-Smith, 1962). Likewise, areas of behavior that are taboo or are associated with intense socialization within a culture, so that they may be sources of emotional conflict for children, are also evident in play. This is probably one reason why much of children's humor—a verbal form of play—has sexual or aggressive content (as documented by Wolfenstein, 1954).

Testing play is a form of play which allows children to test themselves—their physical skills, their emotional reactions, their ability to cope with a variety of situations (Sutton-Smith, 1971). When children enter school, their testing play is already quite complex and varied, and it continues to become more so as they progress through the elementary grades. One major form of testing play during the school years is games of the sort discussed earlier. Sutton-Smith points out that most such testing games are contests dealing with some major feature of emotional life—fear and protection in hiding games; anger and destruction in games of attack, such as dodge ball; impulse control in games where surprise, stopping, or orientation is important, such as Priest of the Parish and Statue. Testing games provide important self-validation experiences for children as they try out their steadily increasing competencies in competition with other children near their own level. This is one of the ways in which the peer group defines the terms in which children must prove themselves.

Why peers are important

Let us return now to the question of why peers are important to children—a fact that everyone accepts. Sullivan (1953) argued that as children approach school age they begin to feel a need for companions about their own age and to seek them out. Many children begin to invent imaginary playmates at about this age, and Sullivan suggests that the children who do so are those who have less contact with other children, and so provide themselves with a playmate in order to meet this new social need. He may be right, although there is no adequate documentation of the point.

The culture of childhood suggests another reason why peer acceptance is so important. Only when children are accepted do they gain access to this unique social world where there are so many interesting things to learn and do, and where they can gain self-validation through their own participation. (From a social learning point of view, the control of access to the world of childhood gives peers great power.) In addition, only peers can serve as effective models for how to act among other children. And they can be very effective models indeed.

Peer relationships are not only important *to* children, they are also important *for* children. In addition to being influenced by what they see other children do, once accepted by peers, children become subject to other forms of influence as well. Peers provide a great deal of direct reinforcement to one another for such behaviors as assertiveness and cooperation. This is already true for preschool children; it becomes increasingly true when children enter school (Charlesworth & Hartup, 1967; Kohn, 1966; Patterson, Littman, & Bricker, 1967). In addition, as groups interact over time, group norms—shared values, goals, and motivations—develop. Such norms are not in much evidence among pre-schoolers. Hartup (1970) suggests that the early school years are the transition period during which group norms begin to become an important component of peer interactions (an argument which is congruent with Sullivan's description of the juvenile era). And there is the cognate matter of children's relative status within the peer group as it evolves, and the expectations which the group may form. Once established, a given child's status may remain fairly stable, though it is certainly not fixed or unitary—the same child may have high status in one activity or situation, but not in others. Once status is established, however, group norms and expectations may continue to elicit behavior congruent with that status from the child. A child who is considered a leader may be turned to for leadership; a child who is seen as the group clown may be expected to clown and may comply by doing so, thus further reinforcing the group expectation.

With all of these forms of influence, it is no wonder that peer relationships make an important difference in children's lives. Good peer relationships may even compensate for some of the negative effects of poor relationships at home, so that processes that might otherwise develop into personality or social deficits are overcome (Sullivan, 1953; Hartup, 1970). Experiments on people cannot be done, for obvious reasons. But it does appear likely that for some children, there are such compensatory effects (see, for instance, Freud & Dann, 1951).

On the other hand, poor peer relationships are consistently found to be related to general measures of maladjustment both during childhood and in later life (Hartup, 1970; Asher, Markell, & Hymel, 1981). When the earlier histories of children identified as delinquents in adolescence were compared with those of nondelinquent children who were otherwise similar, poor peer relationships were one of the distinquishing characteristics of the delinquent children as far back as third grade (Conger & Miller, 1966). And disproportionate numbers of adults who were unpopular in childhood are found in community-wide psychiatric registers (Cowen, Pederson, Babigan, Izzo, & Trost, 1973). At a lesser level of severity, men and women who had low intimacy scores as adults were likely to say that they had been bored and lonely as children (8 to 12 years of age); it appeared that they may have been isolated or rejected by their peers. For men, the evidence suggested in addition that as children they had been more critical of, and less sensitive to, their friends (Maas, 1968). Of course, one cannot say whether the poor peer relationships are part of the reason for the mal-adjustments, or vice versa. Furthermore, in such studies the less well-adjusted children may—and often do—have poor family relationships as well as poor peer relationships. Nonetheless, the quality of children's peer relationships are clearly associated with their general adjustment.

Obviously there are good reasons for being interested in children's re-lationships with their peers. We will look next at children's status in their peer groups—popularity and its correlates, physical attractiveness and acceptance, nonverbal cues and conflict. Then we will look at friendships—children's spe-cific relationships with another child.

PEER GROUP STATUS AND ACCEPTANCE

One main approach to investigating children's peer group status is to use *sociometric techniques*—instruments that ask children in some identifiable group (a classroom, for example) to nominate the child or children who best fit some description, such as best friend, meanest, liked by everybody, and so forth.

(Obviously, the relationships revealed depend in part on the particular questions asked.) The children's choices can then be tabulated to see who was nominated by many, who by few; which choices were reciprocal (two children name one another); and so forth. Simple frequencies of choice have been used in much research, but in recent years investigators have proposed more sophisticated (and, probably more meaningful) indices based on both positive and negative nominations (e.g., Peery, 1979; Newcomb & Bukowski, in press, 1983). Both very-well-liked and much-disliked children are social forces to be reckoned with in a group of children; both have high *social impact.* But they differ in *social preference*—other children like to be with the popular children but prefer *not* to be with the rejected children. Using these dimensions, one can differentiate *stars,* popular children who are high on both social impact and social preference; *rejected children,* disliked children who are high on social impact, but low on social preference; *isolates,* the socially "invisible" children who are low on both impact and preference; and *average children,* who are "in the middle" on both impact and preference.

Most of the available information still rests on the older, less-differentiated classifications, however. In this work, what characteristics are associated with being popular or rejected? Many studies overall show that there is no magical property which makes a child popular or unpopular; no single attribute has more than a modest relationship with acceptance, though there are many attributes which show moderate correlations. In the studies reviewed by Hartup (1970, 1978), popular children were consistently found to be more outgoing, sociable, and friendly than other children. They interact more with others, both initiating and receiving more interactions than less-well-liked children. Many of these

FIGURE 9–1 A sociogram showing patterns of choices of "best friend" within a classroom. Double arrows are reciprocated choices; single arrows are unreciprocated choices. Notice the sex cleavage: Both boys and girls are more likely to make same-sex choices than cross-sex choices.

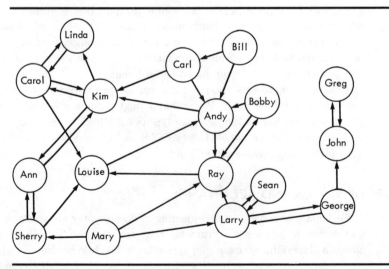

interactions are positive in tone, but Masters and Furman (1981) suggest that neutral acts—those which neither punish nor reinforce their recipient—may be at least equally important. Rejected children are not necessarily unsociable, however (remember social impact?), though their interaction bids may be more negative. Masters and Furman found that unpopular children gave and received punishment, but not reinforcement or neutral acts, more frequently than other children.

Popular children are also more socially sensitive and accepting of others, and show more compliance and cooperativeness than do less-well-liked children. Popularity is related to IQ and academic achievement, with brighter children being more popular. Physical factors, such as body build and attractiveness, are also related to popularity; we will return to this point later.

Self-esteem, dependence, and aggression are also related to acceptance, but in more complex ways. One would expect popular children to have higher self-esteem, but this may not be so. One study found that the most popular children had moderate self-esteem, whereas children with high and low self-esteem were less well liked (Reese, 1961). If children with high scores on self-esteem scales come across to peers as "stuck-up" or snobbish they would be less well liked.

In evaluating the effects of dependence and aggression on acceptance, one must distinguish between the styles in which these attributes are expressed. Children may act dependent toward peers in socially appropriate, mature ways such as seeking advice or requesting help when it is reasonable to do so; or in socially inappropriate, immature ways, such as seeking attention by negative means. Popular children make mature dependent gestures toward peers, whereas less popular children make immature dependence gestures. Whether a child is dependent on peers or on adults may also make a difference. Among younger children, those who are dependent on adults are less well liked by peers. This may still be true among school-aged children.

Aggression may also be expressed in mature, appropriate ways, such as sticking up for one's rights and defending oneself against attack, or in immature, inappropriate ways, such as unprovoked aggression, indirect aggression and hostility, and bullying. There may be a positive relationship between socially appropriate aggression and popularity, but if so, it is a weak one. But socially inappropriate aggression is clearly related to social rejection by peers. Note that rejection is not simply the opposite of acceptance; each is related to different patterns of attributes.

In addition to these personal attributes, some status attributes are related to peer acceptance. Social class is one. In groups which include children from different social class backgrounds, lower-class children are less popular than children from middle-class backgrounds. Race and ethnic group membership is another. Children of different ethnic background tend to stick to members of their own group, resulting in a cleavage between the groups when they are mixed. Birth order is yet another, with youngest and only children being more popular than oldest and middle children. Age has been assumed to be another, the notion being that children's social contacts, at least in Western cultures, are *age-segregated*—they are largely limited to same-age children. Obviously this is true in classroom, child-care facilities, recreation groups, and other children's institutions (e.g., Hartup, 1978). But when Ellis, Rogoff, and Cromer (1981) observed children's social encounters at home and outdoors, they found that children interacted with cross-age playmates—children two or more years different from themselves in age—as often, if not more often, than they interacted with near-age playmates. This was true regardless of whether an adult was present or not; it was especially likely to be true for children who were related to one another. This study corroborated other earlier work which had suggested that the age-segregation that children experience is primarily confined to school. Surprisingly, even children's names make a difference. Children who have names that other children rank low in social desirability are likely to be less popular, even when the names are ranked by a separate group who do not know the children personally (McDavid & Harari, 1966).

Finally, there is the sex cleavage which is so evident in the peer relationships of school-aged children. Even children as young as three years of age tend to prefer same-sex peers (e.g., Wasserman & Stern, 1978), but this tendency intensifies as they grow older, peaking during preadolescence. Girls play with girls, and boys play with boys, with only occasional crossovers (except, perhaps, for such events as large-group neighborhood games). In addition, sex differences in the patterning of peer contacts are already evident by the time children begin school (Waldrop & Halverson, 1975). Boys' play patterns are *extensive*—they tend to play together in large groups. Girls' play patterns are *intensive*—they tend to play with just one or two other girls. This tendency of boys to group together in gangs while girls form smaller groups persists through the school years, and is still characteristic in adolescence (for example, Douvan & Adelson, 1966).

Physical attractiveness

That physical attributes should be related to psychological or behavioral measures is just what one would expect if physical-biological and psychological processes interact as the psychobiological orientation suggests. In the case of peer interactions, the correlation between physical attractiveness and popularity is one such relationship. The more attractive others find a child, the more popular the child is likely to be; and this is true from at least about age six or seven on (Staffieri, 1967; Cavior & Lombardi, 1973; Cavior & Dokecki, 1973). Attractive children have a distinct social advantage with their peers.

The social advantage of attractive children holds up even when children know one another well, although knowing does make some difference. In the study by Cavior and Dokecki (1973), photographs of 5th and 11th graders were judged for physical attractiveness both by classmates (knowers) and by agemates who did not know the children (nonknowers). The attractiveness ratings made by knowers and nonknowers were very similar for 5th grade boys and 11th graders of both sexes, and this was especially true for children rated most and least attractive. For children of average attractiveness, the ratings were less similar, indicating that knowing did make a difference for these children. The photographs were also rated by classmates for popularity and for perceived attitude similarity—whether the raters thought the pictured child shared their ideas or not. Attractiveness, popularity, and perceived attitude similarity were all highly correlated: Children are more apt to like, and to think that they agree with, other children whom they consider attractive. One might argue that this relationship exists because we tend to see people we like as attractive and people we dislike as unattractive, but if this were the whole case, there should have been little agreement between the attractiveness ratings of knowers and non-knowers.

Why should attractiveness and popularity be related in this way? Actually, it is part of a more general phenomenon. Both children and adults generally respond to physically attractive persons more favorably than they respond to unattractive persons (despite fairly strong socialization not to do so—"don't judge a book by its cover"). That there is a *physical attractiveness stereotype*—that people both as children and as adults attribute more socially desirable attributes to attractive than to unattractive persons—is supported by a number of studies (e.g., see Berscheid & Walster, 1974). Among those reviewed by Adams (1977) were studies showing that teachers rate physically attractive children more positively than they do unattractive children, as well as other studies (such as those mentioned above) which show that children prefer physically attractive peers to unattractive peers. One study which compared 10- and 12-year-olds to 26-year-olds actually found that the girls' evaluations were more stereotyped than the adult women's! (Boys and men did not differ; Dushenko, Perry, Schilling, & Smolarski, 1978).

Adams (1977) goes on to argue that since the physical attractiveness stereotype affects the kind of social exchanges one receives from others—attractive individuals receive positive exchanges and unattractive individuals receive less positive exchanges—children differing in physical attractiveness will internalize different self-images, expectations for themselves, and interpersonal personality styles. As a result of their greater positive social experience, physically attractive people will be more likely to show self-confidence in interpersonal situations, and perhaps in other positive attributes as well. Most of the supportive evidence for this scheme is based on responses of adolescents and adults, but where school-aged children have been studied, the phenomena are clearly applicable to them as well.

Body build   One contributor to ratings of physical attractiveness which has gotten a lot of attention is physique or body build. Not only do different body builds vary in attractiveness, but there has been a long-continuing fascination with the idea that different body builds are associated with characteristic temperaments. Sheldon (1940, 1942) thought that there were three basic body builds, or *somatotypes,* each associated with different temperament types. *Endomorphs* are short, stocky, and likely to be fat; their associated temperament type is called *viscerotonic* and includes such attributes as pleasure-loving, warm, forgiving, calm, and dependent. *Ectomorphs* are tall and thin; their temperament type was called *cerebrotonic,* and included attributes such as detached, anxious, cool, self-centered. *Mesomorphs* are muscular and, compared to the other types, broad-shouldered and thin-hipped; their temperament type is *somatotonic* and includes attributes such as dominant, active, self-assured, reckless, and risk taking. (Note that all three hypothetical temperaments have both positive and negative features; this is not true of the stereotypes people actually hold.) Sheldon thought that the relationship between temperament and body type was constitutionally determined, that is, that the temperamental qualities are as much a direct effect of an individual's genetic makeup as is body build. This hypothesis is not generally accepted today, although the question is still open. Nowadays researchers are more likely to attribute any such relationships to indirect effects, mediated usually by social stereotypes and expectations. A physical attribute such as body build, which itself may directly reflect hereditary influences, elicits social reactions from others; these reactions in turn shape the developing individual. Adams' arguments about the effects of physical attractiveness via social stereotypes, summarized above, are one example of such an. hypothesized indirect effect.

Coming back to bodies, if widespread and consistent stereotypes are associated with different body builds, then children with different body builds will elicit different reactions from others. These differing reactions may, in turn, shape the children's behavior in quite different ways. What this suggests is that children having different body builds have quite different social environments, even when the same people make up those social environments.

Are consistently held stereotypes in fact associated with different body builds? They are, and the general results are consistent. (See Figure 9–2) In our culture, mesomorphs elicit a strong positive stereotype. Such attributes as leadership, most preferred by others as a friend, least dependent upon the friendship of others but having the most friends, best athlete, most assertive, outgoing, and active are ascribed to them. Endomorphs, in comparison, elicit a negative stereo-

FIGURE 9–2 Schematizations of three basic body builds and brief descriptions of the social stereotypes of each found in the United States.

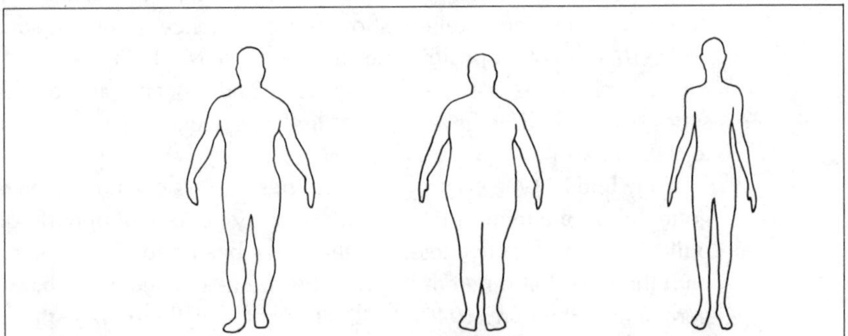

	Mesomorph: Muscular	Endomorph: Stocky	Ectomorph: Tall and thin
Name of body build Associated stereotype	Positive—leader, most friendly, outgoing, active	Negative—not a leader, fewest friends, self-interested, lazy	Neutral to negative—nervous, shy, needs friends, easily upset

type. They are seen as least likely to be leaders, least aggressive, least preferred as friends, putting their own interests before the interests of others, lazy. The stereotype of the ectomorph is somewhere in between the other two in desirability. Ectomorphs are described as nervous, shy, needing friends the most, vulnerable to emotional distress.

Not only are such stereotypes consistent; they are held by both children and adults. They have been found for both black and white male college students (Brodsky, 1954); 4- to 10-year-old boys in the Midwest (Staffieri, 1967); New York City boys at three age levels—5 to 6, 14 to 15, and 19 to 20 (Lerner & Korn, 1972); 6- to 10-year-old boys and girls in the Midwest (Hassan, cited in McCandless, 1970); and girls between 7 and 11 from a low to middle-income urban area (Staffieri, 1972). Stereotypes were least clearly delineated, though present, in Staffieri's (1967) preschool children, and the tendency to attribute good qualities to the mesomorph and bad qualities to the endomorph does increase with age (Lerner & Korn, 1972). But the stereotypes are clearly present and operating by kindergarten and first grade, and they are held equally strongly by children who themselves have different body builds (Lerner & Korn, 1972). So throughout middle childhood, both boys and girls encounter stereotypes based on their body builds not only from adults, but also—probably more importantly—from their peers. And children who are "tubbies," "lardos," or "stringbeans," are clearly at a disadvantage compared to their mesomorphic peers.

Children also act differently toward one another depending upon body build. Asked to place silhouette figures on a flannel board, school-aged children from kindergarten on consistently put more distance between endomorphs and other figures than between ectomorphs or mesomorphs and other figures—and the flannel board technique reflects what they do in actual interaction with other children (Lerner, Venning & Knapp, 1975; Lerner, Karabenick, & Meisels, 1975). Such differential treatment would be one means whereby "messages" regarding body build are conveyed; the children having less attractive body builds are, in fact, treated less positively by peers, as Adams (1977) suggests. If, in addition, peers persist in regarding children with certain body builds as lazy or assertive regardless of what they do, these children are likely to begin thinking of themselves as lazy or assertive. The way they behave may change as well, either as a result of others' consistent reactions to them or as a result of their own self-perception. If this happens, the stereotype becomes a self-fulfilling prophecy.

On the other hand, children might reject the applicability of the stereotype to themselves, especially when the stereotype is negative. Since the stereotypes are negative for the endomorph, and also for the ectomorph to some degree, one might expect children having these body types to be more likely to misperceive their own body type or to deny the applicability of the stereotype to themselves more frequently than do mesomorphs.

Children's self-perceptions do show these effects, so the prevailing stereotypes have some impact on self-concept. Hassan (cited in McCandless, 1970) tested the realism of self-concept, or the accuracy of identifying one's own body type, in her 5- to 10-year-old boys and girls. Older children were more accurate than younger children, and girls were more accurate than boys, but mesomorphs of all ages and both sexes were more accurate than were either endomorphs or ectomorphs. Lerner and Korn (1972) asked their groups of boys to identify their own body type and to state which body build they preferred. Half the boys at each age level were "chubby" (endomorphs), and half were "average" (mesomorphs). Table 9–1 shows the self-identifications and body build preferences of the chubby and average boys at age 5 and age 15. The 5-year-old endomorphs were especially likely to misidentify their body type: more than half identified themselves as mesomorphs. The older boys were more accurate, but about a third of the chubbies still identified themselves as mesomorphs. Almost none of the average boys at either age thought that they were endomorphs. A similar pattern holds for the body build preferences. Similar effects probably occur for girls. Staffieri (1972) reports that of his 60 girls ages 7 to 11, 40 wanted to look like the mesomorph and 20 wanted to look like the ectomorph. Ectomorphic body build evidently has somewhat different meanings for girls than for boys. Girls see the ectomorph as weak and quiet, which may fit with the sex role expectations for girls; and ectomorphy may even be desirable for some women, as in fashion modeling. Boys, however, see the ectomorph in more neurotic and negative terms, as socially submissive, lonely, nervous. But neither boys nor girls want to be endomorphs.

So the stereotypes affect self-perceptions; do they then influence behavior as well? We have no clear data yet, though it is likely that there is some effect. As we have seen in other chapters, what children do is influenced by how they think of themselves. At the same time, one should not expect large relationships between stereotypes and behavior for at least the following reasons: first, when the stereotype is negative, children may deny the behavioral stereotype as applying to themselves much as they deny their less-desirable body build. Second, these influences are but one part of the complex of factors which are influencing children's self-concept and behavior development. Third, children's body builds are often mixed in type, so that they would not necessarily elicit a single stereotype consistently; in this case, there would be no reason to expect consistent

TABLE 9–1
Body build self-identifications and body build preferences of "chubby" and "average" boys early in middle childhood (age 5) and after middle childhood (age 15)

Age and body build of boys	Body build identification*			Body build preference†		
	Endomorph	Mesomorph	Ectomorph	Endomorph	Mesomorph	Ectomorph
5:						
Chubby......	26.7%	60.0%	13.3%	0.0%	53.5%	46.7%
Average......	3.3%	63.3%	33.3%	10.0%	63.3%	26.7%
15:						
Chubby......	60.0%	36.7%	3.3%	0.0%	96.7%	3.3%
Average......	0.0%	83.3%	16.7%	0.0%	96.7%	3.3%

The accuracy of identification of one's own body type improves with age, and preference for the mesomorphic body build increases with age. However, even at age five "chubbies" are less accurate than "average" boys, and the endomorphic body build is almost never preferred.

* Accurate identification of own body type italicized.

† Preference for own body type italicized.

Source: R. M. Lerner and S. J. Korn, "The Development of Body-Build Stereotypes in Males," *Child Development* 43 (1972), pp. 908–20.

effects. And fourth, for many children body build changes over time (so does facial attractiveness, but not nearly so much so; e.g., Adams, 1977).

Nonverbal cues, social interactions, and status hierarchies

Among the issues which have interested ethologists—scientists who study animal behavior—are the status hierarchies one can observe in many animal groups, and the behavioral signals such as facial expressions, postures, or gestures by means of which animals signal threat, attack, submission, or other behavioral intentions to one another. Human ethologists, in turn, have asked similar questions about human beings, and especially about children.

Nonverbal cues do play an important part in regulating social interactions. Facial expressions, gestures, postural cues all provide us with information about others' reactions, feelings, and intentions; we react to such cues often without realizing what they are, just as we provide such cues to others often without realizing that we do so. By the time they reach school age, children already respond to many such cues from others. They can, for example, recognize and classify correctly the emotions indicated by many facial expressions (e.g., Ekman & Oster, 1979; recall too the discussion of empathy in Chapter 2). Not only that, but they act differently, and others act differently toward them, depending on the nonverbal cues they exhibit.

Most of our available illustrations come from studies of children in conflict situations, in part reflecting a strong interest on the part of ethologists in issues of dominance—who prevails in cases of conflict, what happens that influences that outcome? Camras (1977) suggested that children use facial expressions as part of a system of nonverbal communication which is brought to bear on the process of conflict resolutions. She observed pairs of previously unacquainted same-sex kindergartners in a situation in which they had to compete for a toy with which only one could play. If a child in possession of the toy had a facial expression that was rated by observers as aggressive (lowered brows, stare, face thrust forward, and so forth) that child was likely to resist giving up the toy, and the other child was subsequently more hesitant about making a new attempt to get a turn with the toy. Interestingly, she also found that if a child playing with the toy looked sad (had a facial expression with oblique brows) the partner was more likely to let the child play for a relatively long time. Were the partners perhaps being nice or sympathetic to a child perceived as experiencing distress? Camras (1980) later showed that kindergartners could also pick out from photos those facial expressions that would be seen in a conflict situation, and could relate components of facial expressions to the emotions which they typically express with reasonable accuracy. Children may not use such inferential skills in this form in actual conflict situations, but they are at least capable of them.

Another intriguing example comes from Zivin (1977) who had identified an expression which she called the "plus face" in preschoolers. This face is characterized by raised brows, raised chin, and firmly set neck. Children who use a plus face early in encounters with other children are highly likely to prevail in those encounters. In her 1977 study, Zivin compared incidence of plus faces and their outcomes for 4- to 5-year-olds and for 7- to 10-year-olds as they interacted in natural school settings. She also obtained children's rankings of their peers on "toughness," then divided each group into quarters from the toughest in the top quarter to the least tough in the lowest quarter. The relationships between toughness rank and use of plus faces for the two age groups are shown in Figure 9–3A and 9–3B. Note that at both ages, the tougher the child, the greater the use of plus faces; note too that this association is much more marked for the 7- to 10-year-olds than for the younger children.

There were also interesting differences in the distributions over ranks of who makes plus faces to whom. Among the younger children, there was a fair amount of plus faces across toughness ranks, but among the older children, there was a strong tendency for the plus faces to be made only to children in the same or adjacent ranks—in fact, no higher ranking child was observed making a plus face to a child in the bottom quarter on toughness, nor did any child in this bottom quarter make a plus face to a child in any of the higher ranks. (Children in ranks 2 and 3 did, however, make plus faces to top-ranking children.) Zivin suggests that this age difference in part reflects increasing cognitive control over use of the plus face as dictated culturally; that is, the older (and the higher in rank) the child, the more likely that the child both knows what it means to look challenging or threatening to another child and also has encountered training that it isn't nice to boss or threaten other children, especially children weaker than one's self. The age difference very likely also reflects older children's greater awareness of the status hierarchies in the groups of which they are members and their own place in them. For example, the more children are aware of the toughness hierarchy in their group, the greater the amount of agreement they should show with one another about who ranks where in the group. That is just what was found in one study where the percent agreement between

FIGURE 9–3 Average rate of "plus faces" per five minutes for children of different toughness rankings, divided into quarters. Note the much more pronounced contrast between ranks for the older children.

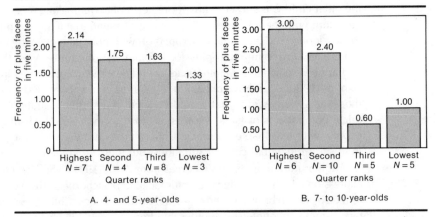

A. 4- and 5-year-olds

B. 7- to 10-year-olds

Source: G. Zivin, "On Becoming Subtle: Age and Social Rank Changes in the Use of a Facial Gesture," *Child Development* 48 (1977), pp. 1314–21. Figures 2 and 3, p. 1317.

children about toughness rankings in their classrooms went from 40 percent among preschoolers to 60 percent among kindergartners, 66 percent among first graders, and over 70 percent among second, third, and fourth graders (Edelman & Omark, 1973).

Nonverbal cues not only help to regulate conflict encounters, they may also be important in eliciting altruism when children intervene to help out another child in such an encounter. Ginsburg (1977) videotaped fights between third- to sixth-grade boys. Typically, fights ended when one boy showed nonverbal cues of submission—bowed head, slumped shoulders, lying still on the ground, or even shoe tying, all of which are behaviors which involve an appearance of diminution of stature. Ginsburg referred to such cessation of fighting in response to submission as a "biosocial norm," by which he meant that not only among children, but over many species, some submissive gesture is the signal for a fight or attack to end. What happened where a boy signalled submission but the other child kept on fighting? Interestingly, those were the cases where other children stepped in to stop the fight. Ginsburg later showed videotapes of both types of fights, with the endings edited out, to third- and fourth-grade boys and girls to see whether they could predict when fights should end and when some other child might intervene to try to help. In most cases, they were able to predict the ending correctly. They could not say why they made their prediction, however, except for very general statements such as "He looked like he needed help," which do not identify the particular cues which led to the judgment.

What should we make of studies like these? Rajecki and Flanery (1981) reviewing such studies, point out that their results parallel in interesting ways studies of dominance behavior in nonhuman primates. From this observation (and with much more sophisticated arguments than can be briefly summarized here) they argue that these behavioral similarities between humans and non-human primates are attributable to genetic similarity which results from some common ancestry. From this perspective, the fact that children's groups become organized into social hierarchies in which some children are dominant over others, as well as many of the behavioral cues and regulators which influence the formation and maintenance of such hierarchies, reflect children's nature as human beings.

Of course many do not accept such a strong psychobiological interpretation (as Rajecki and Flanery themselves are clearly aware). Learning processes are obviously important, as shown, for example, by the increase in sophistication of use of the plus face with age. It does appear to be the case that there are some inherently human cues in facial expressions, gestures, and so forth that are recognized not only by children, but agreed upon cross-culturally as well (e.g., Ekman & Oster, 1979); but children also become increasingly proficient in recognizing, interpreting, and sending such cues with age. Hartup (1978) says that children's peer group relations change from simple organizations with loosely differentiated interchanges and relatively primitive awareness of others, to complex hierarchies with clearly differentiated interaction and with recip-rocal and sophisticated attributions regarding others. Children's increasing fa-miliarity and skill with the kinds of cues discussed here and their meaning for hierarchical relationships with one another are probably one important factor contributing to these changes.

FRIENDSHIP

Friendship is a special relationship between two particular people. Information about popularity and status within peer hierarchies tells us about a child's general standing in a group; but it does not tell us about the quality of specific children's relationships with one another. Many people think that being popular means having lots of friends, but this isn't necessarily so. A child may be well liked and chosen by many other children, but not have a close, mutual relationship with any one of them. Yet a child chosen by only one other child may have a close, reciprocal friendship with that one other child.

Popularity and friendship are related to somewhat different social and personal characteristics, and they affect personal and social development in different ways. Some such differences are already evident in the relationships of four- and five-year olds; for example, Masters and Furman (1981) found that popular children interacted more (that is, engaged in both more positive and more neutral behavioral exchanges) with other children overall, but whether two given children were friends depended only on the interchanges between those two, regardless of their rates of interchange with the group as a whole.

At least through 1970 the bulk of our information about children's interactions with one another dealt with their status in groups (e.g., Hartup, 1970). In the last decade, however, this has changed. Researchers have studied both children's social cognitions—their conceptions of and expectations for friendship, and also their behavior patterns, that is, how they act with friends. At least in the early part of the decade, there was a strong tendency to describe young children's friendship skills negatively, in terms of skills they didn't have (cf. Chapter 2). More recently, it has become clear that while there are important changes in children's friendships over the school years, young children just entering school are much more socially competent than had been thought. Let us turn to the research to see what it tells us about both the early competencies and the changes with age.

Friendship expectations

As adults, we hold ideas about and expectations for friendship which are generally shared. We typically expect that friends feel mutual affection and trust; that they reciprocally help and share with one another and provide support in the face of trouble; that they are psychologically intimate, or "close;" that they admire and are loyal to one another (e.g., Berndt, 1981c; Strommen, 1977).

Children also hold expectations for friendship, which researchers have studied by asking them questions such as what makes someone a friend, or why some person is their friend. From what we know of social cognition (Chapter 2) we might expect that young children's friendship expectations are relatively external and superficial, but that over the school years, they become more internal, personal, and psychological in nature. This does indeed characterize much of the developmental change which takes place. Berndt, for example, asked boys and girls in kindergarten, third, and sixth grade questions such as, "How do you know that someone is your friend?" or, "What would make you decide not to be friends with someone anymore?" (Berndt, 1981c). The children's responses could be divided into eight different categories. The categories, and the mean scores of children in each of the grades in two separate studies, are shown in Table 9–2. Of the eight types of response, only one—play or association—did not change with age; it was a frequent response at all ages studied. One category, defining features, declined with age; responses sorted into this category simply reiterated that the children were friends but gave no reasons (S/he is my friend; I like him/her.) All the remaining categories increased significantly with age in one or both studies. Of particular interest are the categories of intimacy and loyal support, which are important defining criteria of friendship for adults. In both studies these categories showed sharp age changes, being rarely mentioned by kindergartners or third graders, but frequently mentioned by sixth graders.

Other researchers have conceptualized children's friendship expectations in somewhat different ways. Selman and his co-workers, for example, argue that children's ideas about friendship, along with their ideas about the individual and about the peer group, are all subcategories within the larger conception of *interpersonal awareness* and that interpersonal awareness develops in stages paralleling those proposed for role-taking ability by Selman and Byrne (Chapter 2; e.g., Cooney & Selman, 1978; Selman & Jaquette, 1978). As applied to friendship, Cooney and Selman suggest that friendship conceptions at each stage can be characterized as follows: Stage 0, momentary physical playmates (physical nearness, no recognition of thoughts or feelings); Stage 1, one-way assistance (my friend helps me); Stage 2, fair-weather cooperation (I help her and she helps me); Stage 3, intimate-mutual sharing (we work it out so we both feel good about it); Stage 4, autonomous interdependence (Stage 4 isn't usually seen until late adolescence; it was not discussed in Chapter 2). Cooney & Selman report

TABLE 9–2

Categories of friendship expectations used by kindergarten, third,- and sixth-grade children (mean scores by grade in two studies)

	Study 1			Study 2		
Category	Kindergarten	Third	Sixth	Kindergarten	Third	Sixth
Defining features...........	.97	1.06	.59	.72	.35	.25
Attributes	.16	.06	.34	.19	.17	.25
Play or association	1.31	1.47	1.22	.90	1.08	.97
Prosocial behavior	.38	.88	.91	.22	.44	.81
Aggressive behavior........	.56	1.00	1.00	.75	1.06	1.06
Intimacy or trust	.03	.03	.69	.00	.24	.50
Loyal support..............	.03	.19	.94	.03	.03	.34
Faithfulness	.31	.16	.44	.00	.25	.28

Source: T. J. Berndt, "Relations Between Social Cognition, Nonsocial Cognition, and Social Behavior: The Case of Friendship," in *Social Cognitive Development: Frontiers and Possible Futures*, ed. J. H. Flavell and L. Ross (Cambridge: Cambridge University Press, 1981), Table 8.1, p. 178.

that some children reach Stage 3 by about age 11, which fits well with Berndt's finding that intimacy becomes important in the late elementary grades.

Youniss and Volpe (1978), taking a perspective influenced by Piaget and Sullivan, point to the role of rules regulating friendship interactions, in particular shared rules of conduct such as that friends are nice to one another, share with one another (Berndt's category of prosocial behavior, Table 9–2, also deals with sharing and helping between friends.) According to Youniss and Volpe, the main change between age 6 and age 9 or 10 is that these rules become increasingly particularized to the specific friend—one doesn't just share in general, one shares what the friend doesn't have. And as children approach adolescence, they become increasingly likely to mention the friends' feelings or emotional state as well. Again, there is increasing recognition of, and response to, another child's internal needs, thoughts, or feelings.

Still another scheme was proposed by Bigelow and LaGaipa (1975), who suggested three stages in development of friendship conceptions. The first stage, which they described as situational, included dimensions such as common activities, liking and propinquity, and so forth. Stage II they described as contractual; it included the dimension of character admiration. Stage III they called internal/psychological; among dimensions located here were acceptance, loyalty, and commitment, genuineness, common interest, and intimacy potential. However, Bigelow and LaGaipa did also find that a number of friendship dimensions changed with age but did not fit into the stages, and that still other dimensions did not change with age. From a later analysis, Bigelow (1982) concluded that while the proposed stage sequence did describe the development of friendship expectations in a general way, the stages did not help much when it came to understanding the development of particular friendship expectations. So the question of the nature and usefulness of stage conceptions of friendship expectations is still open.

Nonetheless, across these bodies of research there is consensus that children's expectations do change in some predictable ways, and in particular there is consensus that conceptions and expectations for intimacy, loyalty, and other internal/personal attributes are not evident in young children's statements but develop during the school years. Studies of other related concepts also show increasing reliance on more internal attributes. For example, Rotenberg (1980), studying children's ideas about trust, told stories in which protagonists did or did not keep promises to kindergarteners, second, and fourth graders. The youngest children said that you trust someone who does nice things and who says or promises nice things—they based their judgment on simple external behavior. By fourth grade, however, the children judged trust on the basis of consistency between saying and doing; you trust someone if what is promised matches what is done.

However, there is also consensus that there are friendship expectations which, though they may evolve further with development, are already present and important when children start school. Play and association, expectations that friends share with one another, and reciprocal liking were all found in young children by at least two of the researchers cited. Obviously, while it is true that children's expectations become more subtle and more internal/psychological with age, it would be quite misleading to say that they have no reasonable friendship expectations when they start school.

Upon what is the establishment and development of friendship expectations based? Like any social cognitions, they necessarily are influenced by children's social experience. One important form of social experience is cumulative exposure to and knowledge of the norms for friendship held in their culture. Berndt (1981c) points out that the substantial increase in emphasis on intimacy and loyalty observed over the school years very likely reflects in part the children's internalization of the cultural valuation of these attributes as basic to friendship.

A second major form of social experience is children's direct personal experience with friends, to which we turn next.

Interactions with friends

Surprisingly, few studies have examined children's friendship expectations and their behaviors with friends at the same time. There have been a few exceptions; Cooney and Selman (1978), for example, report instances of relationship between levels of interpersonal awareness in disturbed children and their "reasoning-in-action"—their actual social behavior in different situations. In some instances, the quality of the social interaction seemed clearly linked to interpersonal awareness, as in the case of a boy who had great difficulty making friends at all until he began to act in ways more congruent with Stage 1 than with Stage 0. In other instances, disruptive influences such as fearfulness or anxiety appeared to keep children from acting at levels in accordance with the reasoning of which they were capable, as in the case of a boy who used Stage 2 interpersonal reasoning consistently when talking with examiners, but whose reasoning-in-action suggested Stage 1 when he was given an opportunity to be class leader.

Still, we are left with very limited information about the relationships between expectations for friendship and behavior with friends. The fact that kindergarten and primary-grade children are not yet able to state some expectation does not necessarily mean that they cannot show related behaviors. If experience with friends is one base for development of expectations, one should expect to see important friendship dimensions in children's actions before the children can talk about or describe them. There are other issues, too. Gottman and Parkhurst (1980), for example, point out that children's responses to questions about friendship expectations could just as well reflect vocabulary growth or ability to answer abstract questions as increased understanding of interpersonal relationships. They also point out that young children may not understand what the examiner is trying to ask, even though they are clear in their own minds about the issue of interest. And even when they do answer questions, what they say in a test situation may or may not have anything to do with what they think about when face-to-face with another person (this issue applies at any age). Remember too that even kindergarten children already have some well-established friendship expectations in common with older children.

So we should not be surprised to find that even young children have some impressive social skills as revealed in their interactions with friends—and they do. Gottman and Parkhurst (1980) videotaped children aged 2 to 6 (average age a little over 4½) as they played at home with either a best friend or a stranger. Interestingly, the younger children (under 4½!) exhibited more social skills than did the older children in several comparisons. Whether with friends or acquaintances, younger children were more likely to clarify communications to one another; they engaged in more fantasy, and the younger host child was more likely to explain reasons when there were disagreements with the guest child. Among friends specifically, the younger children were more likely to engage in social comparisons, expecially those which emphasized solidarity between the two children ("Me too!"); to comply with a wider range of control attempts by the other child; and to try to explain disagreements and avoid protracted disagreement, though they had more difficulty de-escalating squabbles than did the older children. Gottman and Parkhurst suggest that these differences reflect the older children's greater skill at resolving disagreement as well as their greater tolerance of it, which makes sense. It is striking, however, that the younger children were sufficiently skilled socially to effectively create "climates of agreement" in which likelihood of disagreements were reduced. Findings like these are in sharp contrast to views of young children as "egocentric" and lacking social skills.

What about other differences in behavior between friends and nonfriends which are already evident in young children? Newcomb and Brady (1982) found that mutuality was greater between friends than between acquaintances, as evidenced by more conversation, paying more attention to one another, sharing information more, showing more feelings and matching one another's feelings more often, and showing more synchronized cooperative effort on a problem-solving task. However, these differences were as prevalent among second-grade boys as they were among sixth-grade boys, leading Newcomb and Brady to suggest that "intimate social interaction is an important aspect of friendship that emerges early in childhood and remains fairly stable." Similarly, Masters and Furman (1981) note that behavioral reciprocity is already important in the friendships of four- and five-year olds, as illustrated in the finding mentioned earlier that friends both receive and dispense more rewards, neutral acts, and—for boys only—punishments to one another, in particular. And Berndt (1981b), working with first and fourth graders, found that the strength and stability of friendship choices from fall to spring was about the same for both grades.

However, Berndt also found that the older children were more likely to say that they would help and share with friends, as well as to actually do so, especially in the spring—the first-graders' willingness to help actually declined over the year. Interestingly, Berndt also found that, contrary to expectation, children were not more responsive to the expectations of their friends than the expectations of others in regard to helping and sharing. Apparently at issue is the conflict between freedom, helping because one chooses to do so, and responsiveness, helping because one ought or because the friend expects it. The conflict was less apparent for older children, not because they were more sensitive to one another, but because they entered into more mutual accommodation —"I'll help him more if he'll ask for less from me."

Of course, there are differences among different groups of children in their friendship patterns. Sex differences have been reported in several studies. In a different study of prosocial intentions and behaviors from that discussed in the last paragraph, Berndt (1981a) found that girls were both more likely both to say that they would help friends more than acquaintances and to actually do so. In fact, boys in this study helped friends *less* than they helped acquaintances. This may reflect the greater role of competitiveness in boys' relationships. Ahlgren and Johnson (1979) compared boys' and girls' preferences for cooperation and competition from 2nd through 12th grade and found that girls consistently preferred cooperation while boys consistently preferred competition. The difference was greatest between 8th and 10th grades, but it was clearly present in the elementary years. Shigetomi, Hartmann, and Gelfand (1981) similarly found that among fifth and sixth graders, girls both had better reputations for altruism (defined as helping others) and actually helped more, though there was a greater difference between boys' and girls' reputations than between the actual amount of helping they did.

Some studies also report more intimacy in the friendships of girls than boys, especially from preadolescence on. Figure 9–4 shows the changes in intimacy scores for same- and opposite-sex friendships from 5th grade to 11th grade (Sharabany, Gershoni, & Hofman, 1981). Note the pronounced sex cleavage in fifth grade which, though diminishing, is still present in seventh and ninth grades. Close boy-girl friendships are rare before late adolescence. Note, too, that girls describe their same-sex friendships as more intimate than do boys at all ages tested (though there was some fluctuation in the nature of the actual dimensions of friendship which contributed to the intimacy scores at different ages). A somewhat different line of research examined the similarity in interests and values of fifth-grade friends and nonfriends (Bukowski & Newcomb, 1982). The results showed not only that friends were more similar than were nonfriends, but that pairs of girl friends were more similar than were pairs of boy friends. This finding also suggests a greater intensity in the friendships of preadolescent girls than boys.

Popularity may not be the same thing as friendship, but this is not to say that there are no associations between the two. In fact, there is evidence that the friendship attributes of children varying in sociometric status differ in consistent ways. For one, the social reputations of star, average, isolated, and rejected children with their classmates differ, as one would expect, and some of these differences increase as one goes from first to fifth graders; the reputations of rejected children, in particular, are much more negative among fifth graders than among first graders (Rogosch & Newcomb, 1982). These reputations may interfere with subsequent friendship formation, making it increasingly more difficult for rejected than for isolated children to gain access to peer groups. Further, when matched with a stranger of the same sex and sociometric status and placed in a situation where they had to get acquainted, star children showed a reason-

FIGURE 9–4 Mean intimacy scores of boys and girls referring to their same-sex friendships (boys-boys, girls-girls) and their opposite-sex friendships (boys-girls, girls-boys).

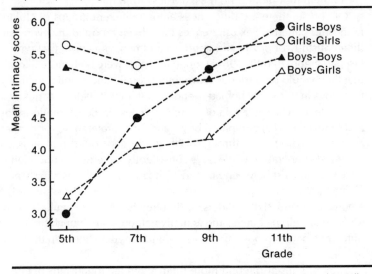

Source: R. Sharabany, R. Gershoni, and J. E. Hofman, "Girlfriend, Boyfriend: Age and Sex Differences in Intimate Friendships," *Developmental Psychology,* 17 (1981), pp. 800–808. Figure 1, p. 804.

able and effective sequence of social exchange, whereas isolated and rejected children had difficulties getting acquainted with one another (Newcomb, Jeunemann, & Meister, 1982). When pairs of same- and different-status children were compared while getting acquainted, popular pairs—especially boys—exchanged more personal information while low popular pairs exchanged information about play activities. Interestingly, though, it was the mixed-status pairs, especially of girls, who engaged in most exchange in relation to both personal information and play (Newcomb & Meister, 1982).

Undoubtedly there are other attributes that are related to individual differences in friendship skills which will become more evident as our knowledge of friendship expands.

Was Sullivan right? We began this chapter with a brief summary of Sullivan's ideas about children's social interactions during the school years. In light of the research that has been appearing, what can be said about the aptness or inappropriateness of Sullivan's ideas? One obvious problem is that Sullivan's position, like that of Piaget, makes it easy to undervalue the social skills and friendships of children younger than eight or nine years of age. As should be amply clear, such young children do have friends toward whom they behave in special ways and about whom they have some cognitions and expectations which they share with older children.

But this can be true and at the same time there can be important changes in the friendships of older children. In a helpful review article, Berndt (1982) summarizes evidence (much of it overlapping with studies discussed above) relevant to early adolescent friendships. In regard to the idea that intimacy and closeness begin to become important in preadolescence, the evidence generally supports Sullivan. As we saw, expectations regarding intimacy were much stronger among sixth graders than among younger children in the studies cited here. Berndt (1982) also cited unpublished data indicating that eighth graders know more intimate and personal information about their friends than do fourth graders, though there is no difference between children in the two grades in which is known about public, impersonal information.

As for mutual responsiveness—helping and sharing—the evidence is more mixed. Norms and expectations for helping and sharing are evident even in first graders, though they increase in strength with age; and in Newcomb and Brady's (1982) study, mutuality was as great with second graders as it was with sixth graders, though other studies have found greater sharing and helpfulness among older children. It may be that what one finds regarding mutual responsiveness depends on the particular contexts and situations which one studies, as Berndt points out.

Finally, if friendship becomes more important in preadolescence as Sullivan claims, one would expect that friendships would become more stable and more long-lasting than in early years; and the evidence cited by Berndt is more corroborative of this point than not.

Overall, then, not only the theory but the research suggest that there are important changes in children's friendships between the primary and later elementary grades. These changes are in addition to friendship skills which children already have, and some of them may be situation dependent, but they are important changes nonetheless.

SUMMARY

When entering school, frequent and lengthy contact with other children on a regular basis begins. Through this contact, children can gain access to the culture of childhood, the special world of children's games, rituals, information, and activities. Many of these games and rituals have persisted within this child's world for decades and even centuries; at the same time, current fads sweep the children's network with an efficiency that can be startling. At play within this world, children have a good time; they also, incidentally, learn about themselves and practice skills that may stand them in good stead as adults in their own culture.

Children's success within this world, their ability to become accepted and to form friendships, makes a difference in their current happiness and also has implications for later life. Those who have difficulties with peer relationships may be at risk for adjustment problems or psychological problems in later years. Some children, the stars, are very popular; others, the isolates and the rejected, are not sought out by other children, though rejected children have a negative social impact which isolates do not have. Average children are in between these extremes in acceptance. Many attributes are moderately related to acceptance or popularity—personality attributes such as outgoingness or dependence, status attributes such as sex, ethnic group membership, or age, and physical attributes such as attractiveness.

The relationship between attractiveness and popularity is probably mediated indirectly, by way of general expectations elicited by different body builds or other physical attributes. In particular, there is the physical attractiveness stereotype, the widely-held notion that people who are attractive physically are probably more attractive or good in other ways as well. Body build stereotypes are also widespead, with endomorphic, fat children (and adults) being at a particular social disadvantage while mesomorphic, muscular children are at a social advantage with their more acceptable body builds.

Children's social interactions are regulated in some important ways by gestures, facial expressions, and other nonverbal cues which children become increasingly adept at recognizing and using as they grow older. Some cues, such as the plus face, appear to be dominance bids; other cues, such as postures that diminish apparent body size, indicate submission. Children can often recognize and respond to such cues even when they cannot say what they are.

In view of the evidence, Sullivan's view that the school years can be divided into the juvenile era, when children first interact regularly with groups of peers, and preadolescence, when children first begin to form intimate, caring friendships with a particular friend, was both right and wrong. Children already know a lot about friendships, and behave in different ways with friends and nonfriends, by the time they begin to start school. Some of their ideas and expectations—as for reciprocity, mutuality, helpfulness, and so forth—may become stronger over time, but they do already show them. On the other hand, it is also clear that there are important changes in children's friendship as they grow older, some of which are much what Sullivan suggested. There is greatly increased emphasis on intimacy, loyalty, and other personal/psychological attributes among older children, clearly in their expectations for friendships and apparently in their friendship behaviors as well.

TERMS AND CONCEPTS

peers
social accommodation
juvenile era
preadolescence
culture of childhood
testing play
play as prototypic behavior
sociometric techniques
social impact
social preference
stars
rejected children
isolates

mature versus immature dependency
mature versus immature aggression
extensive versus intensive play
   patterns
age segregation of peers
perceived attitude similarity
physical attractiveness stereotype
somatotypes
endomorph
ectomorph
mesomorph
dominance hierarchy
plus face

biosocial norm submissive gestures   **interpersonal awareness**
and aggression   **freedom versus responsiveness and**
friendship versus popularity   **friendship expectations**
expectations for friendship

SUGGESTED ADDITIONAL READING

Adams, G. R. Physical attractiveness research: Toward a developmental social psychology of beauty. *Human Development,* 1977, 20, 217–239.

Berndt, T. J. The features and effects of friendship in early adolescence. *Child Development,* in press, 1982.

Hartup, W. W. Children and their friends. In H. McGurk (Ed.), *Issues in childhood social development.* London: Methuen, 1978.

Rajecki, D. W., & Flanery, R. C. Social conflict and dominance in children: A case for a primate homology. *Minnesota Symposia on Child Psychology, Vol. 14,* 1980.

CHAPTER 10

ATTITUDES, VALUES, AND SOCIETY

In addition to learning about their society's moral codes during the school years (Chapter 7), children also learn about its other social institutions: money and business, politics and power distribution, occupations and work, attitudes toward members of different cultural groups. Certainly it is true that school-aged children are years away from formal participation in political activities or from occupational choice, and there are senses in which they are simply not concerned about these issues.

But even though they may not be immediately concerned, they nonetheless live in a political world, among people who work; they are themselves members of racial and ethnic groups, and they are exposed to diverse stereotypes and prejudices toward different groups. Being active and curious, they begin to form impressions, attitudes, and even behavior patterns which may not be well articulated or understood but which nonetheless may shape the directions they will take through adolescence and into adulthood. In this chapter, we shall look, in particular, at children's development in regard to politics, occupations, and different cultural groups.

POLITICS

One does not usually think of school-aged children as political beings (in fact, Beuf [1977, p. 80] suggests that contemporary adults may resist recognition of children as political beings in much the same way that adults in Freud's times resisted recognition of children as sexual beings). In one sense, of course, children aren't political—they don't vote, belong to political parties, or otherwise participate in the political system directly.

But such formal participation is only one subcategory of political behavior. One can take much broader perspectives. For example, Charlesworth (1982) takes a psychosociobiological position in which he views political behavior as one subcategory of human social behaviors; social behaviors themselves, from an evolutionary perspective, are behaviors in which people engage so as to satisfy needs that they cannot satisfy individually, thus enhancing their chances for survival. He defines political behavior as "... a distinctively human behavior engaged in to deal with a competitive situation involving resource availability and utilization" (p. 279). At least from childhood, aggressive behavior is usually not viewed as an acceptable way of settling such competitive situations (which is not to say that it does not occur!). The things one does instead of hitting or forcing the other person—cooperation, manipulation, and so forth—are political behaviors.

Official political behaviors are those making up usual political practice, such as the voting, party membership, and so forth, mentioned above. However, there are also *unofficial political behaviors* which are not usually thought of nor recognized as part of traditional political practice, but which serve similar purposes of negotiation for resources when there is competition for them. Table 10–1 shows the sequence of development of political behavior over the life course as

TABLE 10–1
Development of political behavior over the life span

Ontogenetic phases	Major ontogenetic tasks	Task agents of competition and support	Competition behaviors	Political behavior categories
Infancy	Physical-psycho-logical survival Socialization	Parents Sibs Relatives	Aggression Intimidation	Proto
Childhood	Socialization Enculturation	Parents Sibs Teachers Peers Relatives	Intimidation Cooperation Aggression Manipulation Concealment	Unofficial Proto
Adolescence	Enculturation Reproduction	Peers Opposite-sex peers Teachers Parents Sibs	Cooperation Manipulation Concealment Intimidation	Unofficial
Adulthood	Reproduction	Spouse Employer Offspring Peers Relatives	Cooperation Manipulation Concealment Intimidation	Unofficial Official
Senescence	Physical-psycho-logical survival	Spouse Offspring Relatives Peers Service personnel	Cooperation Concealment Manipulation Intimidation	Official

Note: Individual cell entries are ordered from top to bottom in approximate descending order of importance.
Source: W. R. Charlesworth, "The Ontogeny of Political Behavior," *American Behavioral Scientist* 25 (1982), pp. 273–93. Figure 3, p. 286.

Charlesworth conceptualizes it. From this perspective, prototypic competitive struggles may occur even between infant and parent. In childhood, however, unofficial political behaviors are increasingly learned and practiced as children deal with a widening range of competitors—not just parents, but peers and teachers as well—and as they negotiate their way through the intense socialization and enculturation pressure with which they are faced during this period of life. In this larger sense, children's increasing social competence in holding their own with a group, or learning to negotiate privileges or discipline with parents or teachers, would be examples of their rapidly increasing prowess in unofficial political behavior.

On more familiar grounds, adult participation in official political behavior rests on a broad base of political socialization which includes the development of attitudes and feelings toward one's country; attitudes and information concerning our particular government structure and governing officials; attitudes and information concerning political parties and the political process; comprehension and thinking about such concepts as law, justice, and government itself; and the general skills and attributes of a "good citizen." A great deal of this political socialization takes place during the school years. In fact, one of the major studies of children's political knowledge was undertaken because earlier work with high school students found that ninth graders responded much as seniors did. Much of their political information had been acquired before they reached high school (Hess & Torney, 1967).

Knowledge about politics

In the primary grades, children's knowledge and understanding of official politics—of government, political processes, and political figures—are minimal. Government may be confused with highly visible national symbols, such as the flag and the Statue of Liberty, or with salient political figures such as the president. Many children know about the president, though they have little idea of what a president does. To many questions concerning political issues, they answer, "I don't know." When they do answer, their accounts are typically personalized, as though they cope with political abstractions by translating them into human terms already familiar to them from personal experience. The president is apt to be described as a benevolent, kind, and honest person who takes care of people. And, asked what government is, one unusually articulate and knowledgeable second grader answered in part:

> The government is like the President, but he isn't actually a president.
> . . . The sidewalks and streets are the government's property and he lets people walk in them. . . .
> "I've got it! The government is boss of all the governors, probably. Like the President is boss of all the senators. Senators are people from all different states. . . ." (Hess & Torney, 1967, p. 2).

Their information may be minimal, but children in these early school years already show emotional involvement in the form of attachment to their country and in their evaluation of concepts or institutions as good or bad. They may not yet be able to say what a nation is, but they say unhesitatingly and spontaneously that the United States is the best country in the world, or that it is the only country in which they would want to live. They have no idea what communism or democracy means, but they are very clear and definite on the notion that communism is bad. In many instances, affective and evaluative aspects of attitudes and values are evident long before there is comprehension of what they mean. These early evaluations reflect family influences, with children adopting the feelings they hear expressed by the adults around them.

As children grow older, their information increases and their views of government and related processes become more sophisticated. These changes partly reflect school experiences; by the intermediate grades, many schools include units on civics and government as part of the curriculum. The changes also reflect extracurricular experiences, as children accumulate information and points of view from discussions among adults, with peers, and from television. By the time children reach eighth grade, their information concerning politicians and government is becoming comparable to that of their teachers (Hess & Torney, 1967)—which is not to say they are well informed; many adults in the U.S. are not especially well informed or interested in political issues.

Not only does the children's information increase, but they show an increasing ability to differentiate political institutions and processes. In the primary grades, not only do children think of the president in personal terms, but they equate the office of the presidency with the person holding that office. Similarly, children in primary grades pretty much equate national government with the president. They may also know their mayor, but are otherwise unfamiliar with state and local government. In the intermediate grades, children begin to distinguish between the executive and legislative branches of the national government, though they continue to think of Congress as subordinate to the president. They also begin to become familiar with state government, though never as much as with national government (Greenstein, 1965).

Awareness of political parties and statements of party affiliation usually begin to appear during the intermediate grades, though this can happen earlier depending on circumstances such as the timing of presidential elections. One of the authors was in third grade during a presidential election year. By far the majority of the children in the class aligned themselves with one of the major parties, and feelings ran high as children argued with one another, shouted slogans, and praised their "own" party and candidate and put down the other. Of course, no one could have said what the difference was between Democrats and Republicans. And, typically, the children's choices reflected those of their families, especially their fathers. Note again, though, that lack of information or comprehension did not prevent strong feelings of identification with parties and candidates.

Comprehension of political issues

Children's comprehension (as separate from information or factual knowledge) of political issues and principles, and of other societal concepts as well, is also changing over these years (e.g., Furth, 1978). For example, children's conceptions of the law and its functions progress from a preconventional view-point which stresses obedience to the law, through a conventional viewpoint which stresses maintaining the law, to a post-conventional position which stresses the making and changing of laws in the service of the governed (Tapp & Kohlberg, 1971). The shift from preconventional to conventional thinking takes place between the school years and adolescence, as does the parallel shift for moral judgments (Chapter 7).

At the same time, as we would expect from cognitive development, elementary school children's understanding still tends to be concrete, simplistic, legalistic, authoritarian, pragmatic, and even just plain confused when compared to the thinking of adolescents. Gallatin (1980) defined three levels of responses regarding political issues. Level 1 included attributes such as those just mentioned. Level 2 consisted of transitional responses; and Level 3 consisted of conceptual responses which were framed in terms of a political principle or ideal, such as individual rights. Among 6th graders, 63 percent were at Level 1 and only 12 percent were at Level 3; among 8th graders, 46 percent were at Level 1 and 21 percent at Level 3; whereas among 10th and 12th graders, 32 and 21 percent respectively were at Level 1, and 33 and 46 percent respectively were at Level 3. Some sixth and eighth graders are already thinking conceptually about such issues, but most have a long way to go.

Political attitudes and experience

One major difference between the political attitudes expressed by children and those expressed by adults is that children's attitudes rarely evidence the cynicism about or distrust of government institutions and officials which are frequently expressed by adults. Young children view government and political figures as benevolent and, often, infallible. These views decline with age, but even by the end of the intermediate grades, the prevailing attitudes expressed by children are much more positive than are those of adults (see Figure 10–1). The socializing influences to which children are exposed are clearly edited to present a view of government in idealistic terms. On the one hand, such social-ization to think in ideal terms may facilitate strong attachment to the nation, its institutions, and its ideals, which may be important to continuing feelings of patriotism and continuing political interest in later years. On the other hand, the same ideal presentation may be a source of the cynicism observed in adults, once children begin to discover that political institutions and political figures are not infallible and do not achieve the ideals the children implicitly expect.

Another issue is the relationship between learning the prevalent civil ideals and learning to realize those ideals in practice. Children uniformly agree that all citizens should vote, and undoubtedly they carry this ideal with them to adult-hood. Yet many adults do not vote. Of greater concern are issues relating to civil liberties. By far the majority of U.S. citizens agree with the abstract proposition that all human beings are created equal, or with statements of the basic freedoms embodied in the Bill of Rights: freedom of speech, freedom of religion, and so

FIGURE 10–1 Mean responses of children in grades four through eight and their teachers when asked about the fallibility of public figures.

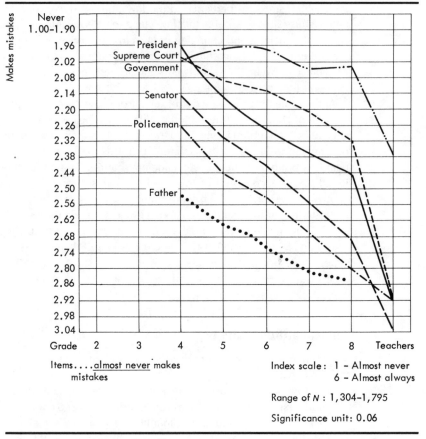

Items....almost never makes mistakes

Index scale: 1 – Almost never
6 – Almost always

Range of N : 1,304–1,795

Significance unit: 0.06

Source: R. D. Hess and J. V. Torney, *The Development of Political Attitudes in Children* (Garden City, N.Y.: Anchor Books, 1967), p. 58.

forth. Yet many U.S. citizens are unwilling to act in accordance with these beliefs in concrete situations, and may even fail to recognize the discrepancy between their abstract views and their concrete actions.

Such additudinal discrepancies may also go back to childhood. A case in point is the relationship between the ideal of free speech for all and its realization in willingness to allow individuals holding dissenting positions the right to be heard (Zellman & Sears, 1971). When children in grades five through nine were questioned about free speech in the abstract—"I believe in free speech for all, no matter what their views might be"—a majority of the children in all grades agreed. Yet when asked parallel questions about concrete situations—whether a communist should be allowed to speak in their city, saying that communism is good, or whether police should give the head of the American Nazi Party permission to have a meeting on a street corner—a majority of these same children disapproved. Whether or not children showed tolerance depended chiefly on their attitudes toward the group in question. The more they disagreed with or disliked the dissenting group, the more likely they were to be intolerant toward it. And there was little difference in the general outcomes between the younger and older children; these discrepant attitudes were already evident in the fifth graders. The democratic ideal was indeed learned, but it was learned as a slogan, not as an operational principle. The " 'message' that young children normally get about nonconforming minorities is that they should be repressed" (Zellman & Sears, 1971, p. 134).

Perhaps one direction that might help to resolve some of these difficulties is to make children more aware of the inevitability of conflict in any country incorporating diverse economic, social, and political views. The idealized picture of government held even by eighth graders contained little element of conflict; majority rule seemed to be interpreted as requiring unanimity (Hess & Torney, 1967). Yet good government or good politics is at least partly a matter of working out conflicts among various constituencies, as children may know already through their experience with unofficial political encounters. If children were also taught formally about the inevitability (and even desirability) of such conflicts, as well as some of the ways in which conflict can be managed, their views might be more realistic and might also provide a firmer foundation for their later political behavior (Hess & Torney, 1967; Zellman & Sears, 1971).

Early political socialization and later political beliefs

The idea that political orientations learned during childhood shape later political learning, and that such later modifications are relatively minor—which means that one's adolescent and adult political orientations are pretty much what one learned in childhood—is called the *primacy principle of political socialization*. According to one recent review which challenges it (Peterson & Somit, 1982), the primacy principle has been implicit in a great deal of political socialization research, including the work of Hess and Torney (1967) cited above. Peterson and Somit argue that there is little evidence that really supports the primacy principle, and that given children's limited comprehension of political principles along with the large amount of new learning that is encountered in adolescence and adulthood, there is little reason to expect continuity from childhood to adulthood in, say, political party preference, or some ideological principle.

Generally, we agree. A little-understood political preference or principle stated in third grade, perhaps in direct modeling on parental statements, is not likely to still be held in adulthood. At the same time, however, we suspect that there are nonetheless some important continuing influences. For one thing, there are many political orientations which children incorporate from their social environments which are never challenged in later years; until and unless they are challenged one may not even realize that one is taking them for granted. (This principle of nonconscious ideology will come up again in the last section of this chapter.) For another, the early evaluative learning which precedes understanding in many instances may also tend to restrict later choices in that it may restrict the range of alternatives which may "feel" good or right to an individual.

So even after a period of questioning, such as may occur in adolescence or adulthood, a person may come back to some position more similar to that held earlier than might otherwise have been the case.

OCCUPATIONS AND WORK

Separated as they are from the adult work world, school-aged children usually have little idea of the range of possible occupations or of what these occupations might demand. If asked what they want to be when they grow up (as children often are), they are likely to name one of a few highly visible occupations, which often have an aura of excitement or glamour about them from the children's point of view. Younger children may tell you that they want to be cowboys, firemen, nurses; older children may tell you that they would like to be pilots, doctors, athletes, movie stars, nurses, airline stewardesses. There is a fantasylike quality to these early choices, and they do not often persist for long (Ginzberg, 1951).

Yet during the school years, children are developing attitudes, interests, and expectations, both about themselves and about occupations, which will influence later occupational choices and work patterns. At the most general level, school children are acquiring behavioral characteristics which will provide a basis for work performance in later years. Independence and personal autonomy in dealing with everyday tasks, the development of internal controls over impulses and behavior, competence or effectance motivation, and achievement motivation all fall into this category (Osipow, 1970). Erikson's (1950) conception of those years in terms of development or industry is clearly relevant. One might also think of such attributes as persistence at tasks, responsibility, and dependability. Furthermore, through trying out and practicing many different types of skills, school-aged children are also developing concepts of themselves as good at some things and not at others, or as liking some things and not others. To the extent that occupational choices reflect some matching of one's own interests and abilities with occupational demands, these developing skills and self-perceptions will serve as important raw material for later occupational decisions.

If we speak in terms analogous to those we used for political development, these categories of skills might be seen as unofficial occupational participation, as distinct from official occupational participation involving actual job choices and work experience.

In addition, children are learning social evaluations—attitudes and values concerning the prestige of different occupations. Some occupations, such as lawyer or scientists, are generally highly regarded in the United States, whereas others, such as garbage collector or soda fountain clerk, are not. Especially for low-prestige occupations, rankings are fairly stable over time. The exact rank orders of occupations as rated by adults may change—for instance, nuclear physicists were ranked in 18th place (out of 90 occupations) in 1947 but jumped to 3rd place in 1963, an unusually large change. However, such shifts rarely result in the reclassification of a high-prestige occupation to low status, or vice versa (Hodge, Siegel, & Rossi, 1968).

During the school years, children's values regarding occupations begin to incorporate and reflect the prestige accorded them by adults. When children 5, 8, 11, and 14 years of age were asked what jobs they would really like to have as adults, or what was the best job anyone could have as an adult, the number of high-prestige choices increased steadily with age (Lounsbury, 1973). When these children were asked what occupations they might reasonably expect to have, their answers indicated that the children were also beginning to internalize perceived limitations based on group membership (see Figures 10–2 and 10–3). As they grew older, working-class boys were increasingly likely to say that they

FIGURE 10–2 Differences between ideal occupations and reasonably expected occupations as perceived by working-class and middle-class boys and girls at four age levels. A positive score means that the ideal occupations have higher prestige than do the occupations the children think they can reasonably expect to have.

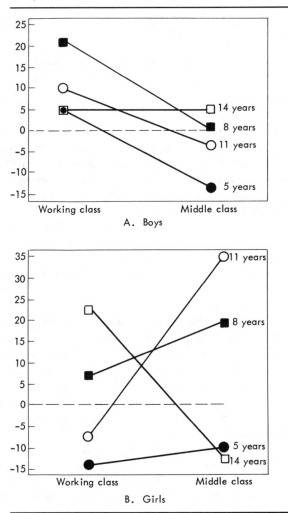

A. Boys

B. Girls

Source: K. R. Lounsbury, "Age Changes in Occupational Prestige: A Perceptual Model," unpublished doctoral dissertation, Michigan State University, 1973, p. 34.

FIGURE 10–3 Mean occupational prestige scores of occupations which middle-class and working-class boys and girls predict that they will hold as adults.

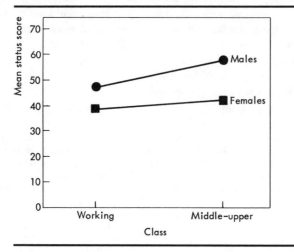

Source: K. R. Lounsbury, "Age Changes in Occupational Prestige: A Perceptual Model," unpublished doctoral dissertation, Michigan State University, 1973, p. 22.

could reasonably expect to have only occupations having lower prestige than those they would really like to have; no such limitation was evident in the responses of middle-class boys. In contrast, girls' responses did not differ consistently by social class (Figure 10–2). But at all ages, girls expected to be in lower-prestige occupations than did either working-class or middle-class boys (see Figure 10–3), and even at age five their choices were more likely to be drawn from those sex-typed as appropriate for girls. Middle-class and working-class girls and working-class boys did not appear to recognize the range of occupations that might be appropriate for them.

Other studies have reported similar findings. Reviewing relevant studies, MacKay and Miller (1982) note that in general school-aged children's level of occupational aspirations is related to their parents' socioeconomic status, and that this is more true for boys than girls. In addition, they identified five other sex-related trends in occupational choices during these years: (1) girls choose fewer types of occupations than boys; (2) girls more often select traditional sex-role stereotyped occupations than do boys; (3) among black children at least, girls are more likely to prefer male-typed occupations if they see a woman in such an occupation in a television ad, for example; (4) boys make choices at a wider range of levels than do girls; and (5) on the average, boys' occupational aspirations are higher than are girls'. In their own research, MacKay and Miller examined third- and fifth-graders' occupational choices in relation to worker functions, that is, the complexity of worker behavior required in interacting with each of the three areas of data (or information), people, and things for any given job. (In general, the greater the complexity of worker function, the higher the occupational prestige is likely to be.) Not too surprisingly, MacKay and Miller found that children from middle-income homes chose jobs of higher complexity than did children from lower-income homes, and boys chose jobs of higher complexity—especially complexity of interactions required with things—than did girls. These differences were already clear in the third graders.

Premature occupational foreclosure

Deciding against an occupation before one has sufficient information or experience to evaluate it realistically is called *premature occupational foreclosure*. Attitudes toward occupations developing during grade school may result in premature foreclosure, with the result that in later years children may never consider a variety of occupations that might suit them well, or will do so only after overcoming the earlier attitudes. Sometimes such foreclosure may come about because of idiosyncratic personal experiences or preferences, such as getting sick at the sight of blood, being bored at math, or loving to experiment.

However, premature foreclosure may also result from stereotyped images of what is appropriate or attainable, such as those described above. Children from lower-class homes, or from minority ethnic and racial groups, may develop expectations that many of the occupations they see depicted on TV or in school readers are not open to them. The research cited above suggests that this is already happening early in the grade school years. Developing attitudes toward education may reinforce this effect, given that many occupations may require education beyond high school. A major factor determining whether young people enter and continue in college, as important as ability and more important than social class or finances, is motivation or interest. High school seniors who later entered and stayed in college said that going to college was important to them, that their parents wanted them to go to college, and that they either had always assumed that they would go to college or had decided to do so before 10th grade (Trent & Medsker, 1968). Again, the suggestion is that attitudes important to educational and career decisions have roots in the years *before* adolescence.

Sex stereotyping of occupations has similar effects, and here it is girls in particular who experience premature foreclosure. Grade school girls are likely to say such things as, "I'll be a nurse because only boys can be doctors"—and this is still true in the 1980s, even for many girls whose parents are trying to minimize sex-role stereotyping in bringing them up. Sex stereotyping of occupations begins early; it is already evident in kindergartners. Riley (1981) asked more than 500 kindergarten children to draw a picture of what they would like to be when they grew up. When they finished that picture, boys were asked to pretend to be girls and girls to be boys; then they drew a picture of what they would like to be in the reversed roles. Choices made were then compared against the occupational sex ratios, or proportions of men and women actually working in that occupation. The children were able to do this with considerable consistency, as you can see from Table 10–2; a clear majority of both boys and girls, though a significantly higher proportion of boys, chose occupations predominantly performed by adults of their own sex. Both boys and girls could also

TABLE 10–2

Average percentage of men in occupations selected by kindergarten children, by sex of child and by own-sex and sex-reversal conditions

Condition	Boys (percentage)	Girls (percentage)
Self........	88.0	13.3[*]
Reversal	27.0	84.0[†]

[*] p<.05
[†] p<.001
Source: P. J. Riley, "The Influence of Gender on Occupational Aspirations of Kindergarten Children," *Journal of Vocational Behavior* 19 (1981), pp. 244–250. p. 247, Table 1.

reverse successfully, though over 8 percent of the boys (less than 2 percent of the girls) found this reversal upsetting and distasteful.

Unless there are dramatic and unexpected reversals in the social changes taking place over the past few decades, 50 percent or more of current school-aged girls will probably work as adults, and at least 10 percent of them will be heads of household at some point in their lives. Under these circumstances, it is important that girls be encouraged to consider as wide a range of occupations as do boys. Yet girls see far fewer models for a range of occupations than do boys, either among women they know or in sources such as textbooks and TV. Take textbooks. Far fewer women than men appear at all; of all women who do appear, by far the majority are wives and mothers. One analysis of 134 elementary textbooks from 14 different companies, all in use in the early 1970s, found 147 different occupational roles depicted for boys, but only 25 for girls. In addition, only three working mothers were depicted over all 134 textbooks, despite the fact that at that time 38 percent of working women had children under 18 (Women on Words and Images, 1972). (The figures are higher now; see Chapter 8).

Girls whose own mothers work accept a wider range of choices as appropriate for women than do girls whose mothers do not work (for example, Hartley, 1959; Douvan & Adelson, 1966; there is a similar effect for boys' acceptance of women in a range of roles). But the prevailing message on which girls' developing attitudes are based is that they should become wives and mothers, or choose from a relatively small set of alternatives. The majority of girls will marry and have families when they grow up, so depicting women as wives and mothers is reasonable. Depicting them as *only* or primarily wives and mothers is another matter. Failure to depict women, including mothers, in a range of occupational roles fosters premature foreclosure which may seriously handicap girls once they become adults.

SOCIAL GROUP MEMBERSHIP AND PREJUDICE

Even young children are members of social groups defined in various ways— racial, ethnic, religious—and at least from preschool or kindergarten, children are likely to have some contact or exposure to other groups than their own. Young children do learn to discriminate, in the sense of distinguishing between, members of these different groups. They may in addition develop stereotyped ideas of what members of different groups are like, develop likes or dislikes for some groups, and learn to act differently toward members of those groups: They may become prejudiced.

By the time children reach school, prejudiced attitudes are often already developing. Very early, children begin to pick up their parents' evaluations of other groups. They also begin to learn labels—terms like *nigger, wop, honky, kike,* as well as the more accepted names of racial, ethnic, and religious groups. The evaluations become attached to the labels, even though the children have little idea of what the labels mean. Allport (1954) calls this *pregeneralized learning,* because the evaluations precede clear understanding of what the labels mean.

Through pregeneralized learning, children are often primed to have negative feelings about the label once it is learned, and about the group to which it referes once they learn to distinguish members of that group. Since members of different racial groups can be distinguished by visible physical characteristics, in the case of racial prejudice this may begin to happen even before children enter school. Even three- and four-year olds are aware of racial differences (for example, Clark & Clark, 1947; Goodman, 1952; Porter, 1971), and they already show some behavioral differentiation. As children grow older, however, they stick increasingly to members of their own race, and are increasingly likely to act in negative ways toward children of other races.

Other prejudices are less likely to be evident in behavior so early, partly because it is much more difficult to tell which persons one ought to be prejudiced against. One cannot easily tell whether persons are Catholics, Jews, or Protestants—or Poles, Italians, or Irish—just by looking at them. So even when children have learned negative evaluations of such groups, they are less likely to apply those evaluations to their classmates until they do learn these less obvious distinctions. However, in all such instances the negative feelings precede any understanding of the differences among the groups. Prejudiced children do not ask why other groups are bad; they just "know" that they are.

Attitudes toward one's own social group

Obviously children learn different things about their own ethnic or racial group depending upon whether they are members of majority or minority, positively-perceived or negatively-perceived groups. Early studies suggested that both black and white children were more likely to attribute negative traits and characteristics to black dolls or drawings of black children, though this tendency may be diminishing as overt prejudice declines in general. Bingham (1974), for example, found that both black and white children were likely to attribute desirable characteristics to figures of their *own* race, and that this tendency was actually stronger among the black children!

Prejudiced attitudes may have been declining and becoming less socially acceptable among adults than in earlier decades, but they are still very much alive—especially in covert forms (e.g., see review by Crosby, Bromley, & Saxe,

1980). And current studies of children are still finding differential perceptions of members of different racial groups. Sagar and Schofield (1980), for example, found that among sixth grade boys, *both* black and white boys rated the same aggressive acts as more threatening and meaner when they are done by black than by white characters (though personal characteristics were rated more in accord with individual behavior than with group stereotypes). Evidently the black boys, like the white boys, were internalizing some stereotyped negative conceptions regarding the behavior of black children. And Beuf (1977), working with native American and white four- to six-year-olds, found that the native American children were much more likely to identify themselves as white and were as likely to do this at six as at four, whereas such misidentifications among white children were lower to start with and declined from age four to age six.

On the basis of her own and others' findings, Beuf (1977) suggested that development of perceptions of social groups proceeds primarily through cognitive-developmental processes, with such processes heavily influenced by parents, peers, media, and the social setting in which the children grow up. Some of the main components of her theory, and the ways they change with age, are shown in Table 10–3. That children by five and six are becoming aware of institutional racism and the relative hierarchical standing of different racial groups was evident in the doll play dramas enacted by the children with whom Beuf worked. For instance, one five-year-old Native American boy enacting a school scene chose a white adult doll for the teacher. When shown a brown

TABLE 10–3
Age of child and presence or absence of the factors associated with perceptions of racial dimensions of social life

Age	Perception of institutional racism; Understanding of racial hierarchies	Absorption of non-conscious ideology	Understanding of constancy of racial status	Association of race with other unrelated traits
3–4	Little awareness	Some exposure from television, but limited absorption	No	Yes
5–6	Exposure increased through broadening of social experience: perceives hierarchy	Peak time for absorbing messages the culture conveys	No	Yes
7–10	Exposure levels off, understands societal arrangements and racial hierarchy	Absorbs a good deal, but peers and activist parents can drive a wedge in the consistency of the ideology through counter-ideology	Yes	No

Source: A. Beuf, *Red Children in White America* (Pittsburgh: University of Pennsylvania Press, 1977). Table 14, p. 120.

adult doll and asked if it could be the teacher, the child replied emphatically, "No way! Her's just a *aide*" (p. 80). As Beuf comments, insofar as appointment of members of children's racial group as aides or to other visible, but non-powerful, positions is intended to provide high-status models for children, such strategies may not be working as planned. This child—and doubtless others as well—are clearly aware of the actual power hierarchy that exists.

Nonconscious ideology refers to "... a set of beliefs and attitudes which [the individual] accepts implicitly, but which remains outside ... awareness because alternative conceptions of the world remain unimaginable" (Bem, 1970, p. 89). Nonconscious ideology develops to the extent that all of a child's reference groups—parents, peers, others—present the same "message." Alternative conceptions are unimaginable because there has been no contradiction, no counter-message which could make the child recognize the nature of the ideology which has been taken for granted. Allport's pregeneralized learnings would be related to nonconscious ideology, as one subcategory.

Understanding of constancy of racial status means recognizing that one's racial identity, like one's sex, is something that will never change. As we saw in Chapter 6, constancy of gender identity is becoming evident at three and four but is still developing at older ages as well. Race is not salient to children as early as sex, in most instances, so constancy of racial identity should develop somewhat later, as Beuf suggests.

Finally by *associatedness* Beuf means children's "... tendency to combine two factors which are unrelated from an adult, logical point of view" (p. 108). As an illustration, Beuf tells of Tim, a middle-class white four-year-old whose sole contact with black persons was a 70-year-old woman friend who spent a lot of time with him. When a same-age friend of Tim's came back from vacation with a suntan, Tim got all upset because his friend had come back "all old" and so would not be able to play with him anymore. To Tim, brown skin and being old were associated.

Note that all of these important developments precede comprehension of the social system in the sense of being able to discuss it conceptually. Young children understand power hierarchies among social groups in the sense that they clearly recognize who has power, but it will not be until they approach and enter adolescence that their conceptual understanding will catch up.

Obviously parents are important in this learning process, but peers play a role which may be greater than we used to think. For example, in a white family known to one of the authors, the parents sought out an integrated school so that their two children could learn to practice the unprejudiced attitudes which they were being taught at home. To the parents' dismay, within a very short time the children were making very negative and prejudiced statements about their black classmates.

Two things appeared to be happening. One was that many children within the school held prejudiced attitudes, and there was some tension and rivalry between the black children and the white children. Naturally, the black children were not going to take a new white child on faith. Having initially encountered rejection and suspicion on the part of their black classmates, the two new children found it easy to accept the prejudices of their white classmates as correct.

The other thing that was happening was that their first contact with black children had shattered the new children's idealized view of what black children were like. The newcomers were unprepared for the fact that, regardless of race or other group membership, some people are nice and others are not, some are individuals one can like and others are not. Again, the prevailing attitudes of their classmates made it easy for the two new children to generalize from their negative experiences with *individual* black children to statements about all black children. Had the parents not been alert and continued to work with the children, the views of the peers rather than of the parents might have prevailed.

Another example comes from observations made by Beuf (1977) when, in order that older children (age seven and up) not feel left out, she allowed them to observe while younger children went through her experimental dollplay procedure. Unexpectedly, the older children exerted clear pressure on younger children to make positive same-race choices, either actively—by telling the child, correcting "errors," or even snatching a doll away and replacing it with the one they deemed appropriate—or through what Beuf called "subtle-intimidative" behaviors, through gasps or indrawn breaths at "wrong" choices, or through grins, sighs of relief, or bodily relaxation to "right" choices. As for changes in attitudes, Aboud (1980) examined black and white Canadian children's responses to members of Canadian ethnic groups depicted in picture books for children. Children's preferences for their own group stayed stable from kindergarten to first grade, but first graders were more likely to know the social labels for their own racial group and had clearer perceptions of similarity and dissimilarity between their own and other groups. Interestingly, the older children of both races were more likely to express positive attitudes toward members of other groups, leading Aboud to suggest that perhaps ethnocentrism, or preference for one's own ethnic group, represents an affective form of differentiation from others and as such is a necessary first step as children acquire affiliation with their own group.

Attitudes toward other social groups

Looking more explicitly at attitudes towards other groups than one's own, and especially at the usually negative, stereotyped attitudes which are labeled prejudice, there is an important distinction which must be made between *endemic prejudice* and *pathological prejudice*. Endemic prejudice refers to prejudiced attitudes that are widely held, and largely taken for granted, by any group of people—a widely-shared nonconscious ideology. Needless to say, there is a great deal of endemic prejudice in the United States, especially in regard to different racial groups. Children growing up in the context of endemic prejudice learn prejudiced attitudes much as they learn a host of other attitudes; such learning is, in effect, part of their socialization into their culture. The children may not even be aware of the ways in which they have adopted endemic attitudes.

In contrast, pathological prejudice refers to prejudiced attitudes that are part of an individual's personality structure. These are not just isolated attitudes which the individual has learned and can unlearn, but are an integral part of a much larger network of attitudes and personality attributes. Prejudice is generalized in such individuals. They are not prejudiced against some one group, but against many groups—other racial groups, other religious groups, communists, in fact any group other than their own. (When you hear someone raving about the Jew communist international bankers who are enemies of our American way of life, you are probably listening to an individual of this kind.) Originally called authoritarian personalities (Adorno, Frenkel-Brunswik, Levinson, & Sanford, 1950), such individuals tend to be rigid, anxious, conforming, authoritarian, and moralistic. They have difficulty coping with ambiguity either in social situations or in problem-solving situations. They may function very well if the demands of a situation are clear and concrete, but very poorly if the demands are not clear. They think categorically. There is good and bad, right and wrong, us and them, but little in between. (Since authoritarian personalities were first studied, they have been shown to be just one end, the right-wing or conservative end, of a more general dimension of dogmatism. There are also left-wing or liberal dogmatics, who hold rigidly to liberal views [Rokeach, 1960]. However, we know much less about liberal dogmatic children or adults.)

Prejudiced children already show many authoritarian attributes. Compared to more tolerant children, they are likely to reject anything they believe to be weak or different, to have rigid conceptions of sex roles, to show strict conformity to social values; they appear fearful and suspicious of others, and lack confidence in themselves (Frenkel-Brunswik, 1948). Even as young as age seven, they do less well on unstructured problem-solving tasks than do more tolerant children (Kutner, 1958).

Usually, authoritarian children have authoritarian parents. Prejudiced children are likely to describe their parents as stern, strict, and punitive (Frenkel-Brunswik, 1948). The parents themselves (at least the mothers) describe their child-rearing practices as more authoritarian and rigid, and less permissive and affectionate, than do the mothers of tolerant children (Harris, Gough, & Martin, 1950). McCandless (1967) has speculated that the rigidity and other attributes may develop because from the children's point of view, authoritarian practices are both intense and unpredictable. Since authoritarian parents do little reasoning with their children, the children are often punished for no reason that they can see. To cope with the resulting fear and anxiety, and to avoid future punishments, the children grasp at any rule or code and adhere to it rigidly. They want to know exactly what is expected of them. Hence, the rigidity, conformity, and difficulty in coping with ambiguity. At the same time, the unpredictability of their early experiences, and the intensity with which their punishments were experienced, leave them never quite sure of others or of themselves. Hence the proneness to distrust and suspicion of others and the lack of self-confidence.

What can be done to reduce prejudice? Can children who have already acquired prejudiced attitudes learn to be more tolerant? The answer is yes: Prejudiced children can learn to be more tolerant, but the ways in which this may be achieved are complex and do not work equally well with all children or in all situations. There are no simple solutions.

Prejudiced attitudes can be reduced by contact between members of different racial groups, depending on a number of contingencies. One contingency is basic: The groups must function as equals and in cooperation with one another. Where the groups do not function as equals, or where they are in conflict with one another, contact is likely to maintain or even increase prejudice. (See Proshansky, 1966, for a review of related research.) Among children, the attitudes of the adults in authority may mediate this effect. Children in a biracial summer camp gained most in tolerance when their counselors treated them as equals and expected them to treat one another similarly. This was especially true when the counselors were warm and worked well with the children, possibly because these attributes fostered the children's willingness to accept the adults as models (Yarrow, Campbell, & Yarrow, 1958). In integrated classrooms, some studies have found prejudiced attitudes to increase, some to decrease, following integration. It is very likely that the variable effects of integration on children's attitudes reflect variations in the degree to which teachers and school personnel believe in racial equality, as well as variations in the degree to which the local community supports integration.

The effects of contact on prejudiced attitudes also depend on the personality characteristics of the children themselves. Here, the evidence suggests that the more prejudiced an individual is, and the more pathological that individual's prejudice is, the more likely it is that prejudice will increase following contact. However, to the degree that prejudice is endemic rather than pathological, contact is likely to decrease prejudiced attitudes. For instance, following a four-week interracial camp for boys between 8 and 14 years of age, prejudice increased for some boys but decreased for others. Boys whose prejudice increased tended to be defiant, hostile toward their parents and defensive toward others generally. They saw themselves as frequent victims of unjustified aggression in a generally cruel and unsafe world. In contrast, boys whose prejudice decreased were much less hostile, defiant, or defensive. They had positive attitudes toward their parents and toward the social world in general (Mussen, 1960).

Where tolerance does increase following contact, it may do so because in these circumstances children must learn to deal with individual members of some racial or ethnic group, and hence to appreciate something of their differences, rather than lump them all together in a faceless aggregate. Children (or adults) who learn to apply a single label to a set of persons (or objects) tend to treat those persons or objects as more alike than do children who have not learned the common label. This is a well-documented phenomenon of learning called *acquired equivalence of cues.* The person who thinks in terms of a group label rather than in terms of individual persons may actually show less perceptual differentiation of the group's members. The greater the prejudice, the greater the likelihood that someone will say, "I don't know how you can tell them apart—they all look alike to me." And in fact, prejudiced schoolchildren do perceive the faces of individuals of another race as more alike than do more tolerant children (Katz, Johnson, & Parker, 1970). Following up on this finding, Katz (1973) hypothesized that if prejudiced children were given training in the differentiation of a series of faces, either by learning a different given name (Alice, Robin, Janet, Margie) for each of four faces, or by judging whether pairs of photographs of the faces were the same or different, their expressed attitudes might become more tolerant. The participants in the study were second- and sixth-grade black and white children at an integrated school, all of whom had expressed high prejudice on a battery of tests. Overall, the children who were given differentiation training of either type expressed less prejudice on follow-up tests than did other children who simply looked at pictures of the faces an equivalent amount of time.

This study suggests that materials or programs designed to give children practice in differentiating individuals within different racial or ethnic groups might be at least a minimum means of reducing some prejudiced attitudes. This might be especially important for children who have little or no contact with racial or ethnic groups other than their own, though the relevant comparative research has not yet been done. On a different level, the increasing incidence of regular characters of different ethnic and racial groups on prime-time TV shows and newscasts, where their recurrent appearances make it likely that they will be recognized and responded to as individuals, may foster differentiation of individuals in children (and in adults, for that matter). These changes, along with such other changes as increased racial and ethnic diversity in magazine advertising, may also be helping children to "take for granted" that blacks, or Orientals, or Chicanos, or even women, have the same feelings and concerns and do many of the same things as members of their own particular group.

However, Katz's study—and the others discussed as well—have some serious limitations which necessitate caution in applying their results. Where some experience has reduced prejudice, the decline observed is rarely, if ever, complete. Children who initially wanted no contact with members of another group may come to say that they would accept a child of another race or ethnic group as best friends at school, but may still be unwilling to say that they would invite the child home to dinner. In addition, where reductions in prejudice have been found, there is little information about the duration or persistence of such effects. And there is the recurrent difficulty in attitude research of the relationship between what people say and what they do: Do children who come to express different attitudes also act differently than they did before?

Obviously, changing prejudiced attitudes is a highly complex issue. Yet the difficulties of changing prejudiced attitudes are not surprising when one considers what such training must overcome. Endemic racial and ethnic prejudice is widespread and widely accepted. Removing it will require massive social change, perhaps comparable in scale to changing the prevailing definitions of masculinity and femininity, or changing the attitudes of most U.S. citizens about capitalistic economics. So long as endemic prejudice exists, social support for prejudiced rather than tolerant attitudes will continue.

In addition, there is the matter of parents as sources of prejudiced attitudes. So long as the parents themselves are prejudiced, they would find it difficult to hide their own feelings and ideas even if they tried to do so. However, they may not only decide not to do so, but may insist on their right to teach their children what they consider to be important truths. And here we encounter an ethical dilemma. We generally subscribe to the value that parents have both the right and the obligation to bring up their children as they see fit, to teach the children their own standards and values. Parents are often zealous in defending this right, as is evident in parental resistance to sex education in schools, in parental insistence on religious instruction in schools, and in parental opposition to textbooks approved by school boards or teachers, but not meeting with the parents' approval.

If parents hold the strong conviction that blacks are inferior and dangerous, that Jews are Christ-killers, that The Man is a blue-eyed devil, who is to tell them that they have no right to transmit those convictions to their children?

Difficulties also arise because emotional learning—the learning of evaluations—precedes either the information or the experience which might allow that learning to be put into any sort of context, and because emotional learning begins early in children's lives. Early learning is more difficult to change than later learning, and feelings are often more difficult to change than ideas. Finally, pathological prejudice is by definition integrated into personality structure. To the extent that prejudiced attitudes are pathological in this sense, changing them requires changing personality, which is possible but difficult.

With these constraints, it is no wonder that prejudiced attitudes change only slowly. Yet slow change, and small changes, are better than no change at all.

SUMMARY

Children are active participants in the world in which they live; domains such as politics, work, and intergroup attitudes are no exceptions. Since children are members of ethnic and racial groups from birth, it is not surprising to find emerging attitudes about their own and others' groups; but even in those domains where adult, formal participation is years in the future, we find evidence of emerging perceptions as early as the kindergarten years.

Over the three domains discussed in this chapter—and probably in other domains as well—children learn evaluative or affective responses early, often before they have much information about or comprehension of that which they are evaluating. Thus they learn early which ethnic or racial groups, which political parties, which occupations are OK or of high prestige and which are not OK or of low prestige. Negative and positive stereotypes learned as part of nonconscious ideology are examples of such early learning. Of course such learning isn't detailed, nor is it based on knowledge or comprehension. Over the school years, children's knowledge increases rapidly through their exposure to both formal (school) and informal (media, other) sources of learning. Toward the end of the school years, comprehension of principles important to the particular domain is beginning to emerge, and—as was the case for moral development— children are beginning to integrate cognitions, feelings, and behaviors.

Of course many of the specific attitudes expressed by school-agers are likely to change over time, as they are exposed to alternative ideas and new information; one would not wish to predict a child's specific occupational choice or political stance, or even attitude toward some racial group on the basis of statements made in fourth grade. At the same time the feelings learned early in life may be difficult to change in later years, and there may be many areas of nonconscious ideology that are never challenged or contradicted. There is also the range of learning through unofficial participation in political and other social systems; we do not know much yet about the relationship between unofficial and official participation, but the foundation established in the school years in unofficial behaviors—learning about conflict resolution, work habits—is likely to persist. Further, there may be active social reinforcements for maintaining many attitudes which were established early; the same general consensus of those around the child which is basic to establishment of a nonconscious ideology may later serve to reinforce continuation of that ideology when, through experience, it becomes the focus of conscious attention. So there are good reasons for expecting that much of the learning about social institutions established during the school years will continue to have some influence on the children's continuing development.

TERMS AND CONCEPTS

political behavior from a
   psychosociobiological perspective
official political behaviors
unofficial political behaviors
primacy principle in political
   socialization
premature occupational foreclosure
occupational prestige

pregeneralized learning
nonconscious ideology
associatedness of racial and other
   attributes
endemic prejudice
pathological prejudice
authoritarian personality
acquired equivalence of cues

SUGGESTED ADDITIONAL READING

Beuf, A. *Red children in white America.* Philadephia: University of Pennsylvania Press, 1977.

Peterson, S. A., & Somit, A. Cognitive development and childhood political socialization. *American Behavioral Scientist,* 1982, 25, 313–334.

GLOSSARY

Accessibility (of adaptive specializations) The degree to which an adaptive specialization in intellectual functioning can be separated from its original function and brought into conscious, deliberate application to other problems for which a similar solution is appropriate. See Adaptive specializations.

Accommodation (intellectual) Changes in intellectual structures which allow them to handle new information or events; the process of intellectual adaptation complementary to assimilation (Piaget). See also Adaptation; Assimilation.

Achievement motivation The desire to excel, to meet or surpass some standard of performance.

Acquired equivalence of cues The tendency to treat persons or objects in the same way if they are called by the same name.

Adaptation A universal attribute of biological characteristics allowing adjustment to new or different circumstances. As used by Piaget in the case of intelligence, change of intellectual organization through the complementary processes of accommodation and assimilation. See also Organization; Accommodation; Assimilation.

Adaptive specializations Programs or patterns of adaptive behavior which evolve initially as solutions to particular problems.

Androgyny See Psychological androgyny.

Argumentative discourse A form of family interaction wherein parents openly challenge moral positions held by their children and by each other, discussing the differences between the positions.

Assimilation (intellectual)   Incorporation of new information into intellectual structures; the process of intellectual adaptation complementary to accommodation (Piaget). See also Accommodation; Adaptation.

Associatedness of race and other attributes   In development of awareness of racial dimensions of social life, preschool children's tendency to connect race and attributes unrelated to race.

Associative responses   In mental tasks, the first (frequently incorrect) responses which may spring to mind. Contrast with cognitive responses.

Assumptive reality   Failure to distinguish hypothesis from fact, characteristic of the egocentrism associated with concrete operations. See also Cognitive conceit; Egocentrism.

Attachment   The close reciprocal bond which may develop between two individuals. Attachments formed in infancy between infant and caregiver may serve both as precursors of and prototypes for attachments which may form in later life.

Attribution theory   The study of people's inferences or attributions about the causes of behavior and the consequences of such attributions.

Authoritarian parents   Parents who believe children's behavior should be closely regulated and who are likely to use power-assertive discipline techniques. See also Permissive parents; Authoritative parents.

Authoritarian personality   A cluster of personality attributes that tend to be found in the same individuals, including rigidity, conventional outlook, obedience to authority, and scapegoating of members of minority groups.

Authoritative parents   Parents who allow their children a great deal of freedom but at the same time consistently enforce some rules and standards of conduct. See also Permissive parents; Authoritarian parents.

Axon   Part of the neuron (nerve cell) that carries the nerve impulse away from the body of the cell.

Behaviorism   The orientations within psychology which define psychology as the study of overt, observable behavior; at its peak in the 1940s and 1950s but still an influential force in much psychological work.

Behavior modification   The application of learning and reinforcement principles to change behavior in everyday situations.

Biosocial norm   Some behavior pattern for which one finds evidence of biological preparedness across many species including human beings.

Castration anxiety   In Freudian theory, the fear of harm from fathers assumed to be felt by boys during the Oedipus conflict. See also Oedipus conflict.

Catch-up phenomenon   Unusually rapid growth following interference with growth (as from serious illness) in the course of which a child regains some or all of the ground lost during the period of interference.

Central orientation   Characteristic and relatively unchangeable predispositions to interact in certain ways which shape an individual's development. See also Emotional expressiveness-reserve; Placidity-explosiveness.

Centration (Piaget)   Thinking which is focused (centered) on one perceptually obvious feature of a problem to the exclusion of other relevant features, so that changes in that feature are not conceptualized in relation to changes in other features, and the child is misled. General characteristic of children in Piaget's preoperational period. See also Conservation; Egocentrism.

Cerebrotonic   The temperament originally assumed to be associated with an ectomorphic body build; described as detached, anxious, cool, and self-centered. See also Ectomorph.

Classroom climate   The social atmosphere a teacher generates; for example, being directive or indirective, democratic or authoritarian; assumed to influence children's learning and attitudes, though research does not yet support this assumption.

Classroom management   How teachers organize and structure the flow of activity in their classrooms in order to both keep the students active and minimize disruptions. See also Withitness.

Cognitive conceit   A common assumptive reality among children that adults are not very bright although the children themselves are. See also Assumptive reality.

Cognitive developmental theory of identification   The theory that identification with same-sex models is a result of conceptualizing oneself as feminine or masculine, rather than a cause of such conceptualization.

Cognitive monitoring   That aspect of metacognition which consists of keeping track of how one is doing on some task and regulating one's behavior accordingly.

Cognitive psychology   The study of knowledge and awareness, including such topics as perception, attention, and information processing. Contrast with S-R learning theories.

Cognitive response   Responses to a situation which may require reflection, selection from among strategies, and so forth; by hypothesis, children must learn to inhibit faster-occuring associative responses (q.v.) before they can consistently make cognitive responses.

Cognitive unconscious   All of those adaptive specializations for which an organism is prepared which are specific to a particular function and not accessible (q.v.) for use for other purposes.

Cognitive universals   The basic attributes of organization and adaptation which apply to all biological characteristics and therefore to intelligence as a biological characteristic of human beings (Piaget). See also Organization; Adaptation.

Cohort   Generation; all of those individuals, and only those individuals, born at some particular point in historical time.

Competence   Degree of mastery over one's world. See also Effectance motivation.

Compulsivity   The tendency to be systematic and controlled, to cling to familiar routines, to avoid spontaneity and ambiguity.

Concrete operations, period of   Piaget's third major period of intellectual growth, when children first become capable of using intellectual operations which allow them to think logically about problems that have concrete (but not formal or propositional) content. Characteristic of most school-aged children in the United States. See also Operations; Formal operations, period of.

Conditioning   The establishment of learned associations between a stimulus and a response. See also Classical conditioning; Operant conditioning.

Conscience   In Freudian theory, that part of the superego consisting of internalized prohibitions or "thou shalt nots." See also Superego.

Conservation   Recognition that properties of objects (number, length, quantity) remain the same unless something is added or taken away, in spite of rearrangements, disalignments, or deformations which change the objects' appearance. A major achievement of Piaget's period of concrete operations.

Consonance of child attributes with situation   A close match between a child's attributes and situational features, such as parent attributes or teacher attributes. See also Dissonance of child attributes.

Constitutional predisposition   A tendency to develop some behavioral attributes more readily than others, perhaps reflecting genetic influences.

Construct   An abstract conceptualization, such as intelligence, creativity, or dependence, which is inferred from what people do.

Conventional level of moral reasoning   Kohlberg's second level of development of moral reasoning in which judgements are based on doing the "right" thing as prescribed by social convention.

Correlation   An association between two variables such that changes in one are accompanied by (but not necessarily caused by) changes in the other. If changes are in the same direction (either up or down) the correlation is positive; if changes are in the opposite direction, (one up, one down) the correlation is negative. Early in life, age and height are positively correlated; the older the child, the taller the child. In aging, age and height are negatively correlated; older individuals are likely to be somewhat shorter. Correlation coefficients, indices of the degree of relatedness, range from $+1.0$ (perfect positive correlation) to -1.0 (perfect negative correlation). The closer the correlation coefficient is to 0.0 (no correlation), the less the relationship between the two variables.

Cross-modal transfer   Being able to make use of information gained through one sensory modality (sight, touch, etc.) to solve some problem in another sensory modality; being able, for example, to pick out by touch alone some object previously seen but not felt.

Cross-sex typing   Having interest and attributes stereotypically classed as appropriate for the opposite sex.

Culture fair tests   Tests designed to be valid for individuals from different cultural groups.

Culture free tests   Tests to which individuals' responses are presumed to be a fair indicator of their "abilities" regardless of their cultural background; in view of the now-recognized interaction of intellect and culture, no longer considered to be a reasonable goal of test development.

Culture of childhood   The rich repertoire of rituals, activities, games, traditions and social codes which children learn from one another rather than from adults.

Decoding   In information processing, the processes whereby information in storage is retrieved.

Defensive identification   Identification based on fear of physical harm; derived from Freud's theory.

Dendrite   Part of the neuron (nerve cell) which carries the nerve impulse toward the body of the cell.

Developmental identification   Identification based on fear of loss of love; called "anaclitic identification" in Freud's theory.

Developmental tasks   Tasks which children are required to master, such as bowel and bladder control, control of aggression, control of sexuality; when and how they are mastered depends on the setting in which a child grows up.

Differentiation theory   A theory of perceptual learning which attributes change to increasing sensitivity to properties of stimuli which children learn to differentiate with experience, rather than to learning new responses.

Difficult children   Children whose temperament patterns include irregularity of timing, withdrawal from new events, unusually intense reactions, frequent expressions of negative mood, and slow adaptability.

Discipline   A broad concept of control implying teaching or training, which may or may not include physical punishment as a technique.

Discrimination learning tasks   Tasks designed to study the processes by which children learn to distinguish among categories of objects.

Dissonance of child attributes and situation   Mismatch between a child's attributes and situational features, such as parent or teacher attributes. See also Consonance of child attributes.

Distinctive features   Particular features of objects or events which enable them to be readily discriminated from other objects or events.

Dominance hierarchy   In social groups, the dominance ranking of their members.

Dyslexia   Reading disability.

Easy children   Children whose temperament patterns include a positive mood, low to mild intensity of reaction, a positive approach to new events, and adaptability; "sunny" children who are easy to raise.

Ectomorph   One of the basic body builds; described as tall and thin. See also Cerebrotonic; Somatotypes.

Effectance motivation   The satisfaction intrinsic to gaining mastery over one's world. See also Competence.

Ego ideal   In Freudian theory, that part of the superego consisting of internalized prescriptions or "thou shalts." See also Superego.

Egocentrism Failure to differentiate self from experience, manifested in different forms at different stages of intellectual functioning. Preoperational egocentrism can be viewed as inability to recognize a perspective or point of view different from one's own; concrete operational egocentrism, as failure to distinguish fact from hypothesis (Piaget).

Electra conflict A conflict Freud thought girls go through during the phallic period, characterized by close attachment to father and jealousy of mother, and resolved by repression of the conflict and identification with mother. See also Repression; Identification; Penis envy; Phallic stage.

Emotional expressiveness-reserve A central orientation characterized by how much affect or feeling children typically express and by how important interactions with other people are to them. See also Central orientation; Placidity-explosiveness.

Empathy The ability to understand how other people feel.

Encoding In information processing, the processes whereby information is translated into some storable form and transferred into long-term store (memory).

Endemic prejudice Prejudiced attitudes that are widely held and mostly taken for granted within some cultural group, which children learn and which they may also unlearn. Contrast with Pathological prejudice.

Endomorph One of the basic body builds; described as short, stocky, and likely to be fat. See also Viscerotonic; Somatotype.

Equilibration As used by Piaget, a self-regulatory process in intellectual growth in which encounters with new or discrepant information result in adaptation of intellectual structures so that they can handle the new information. See also Adaptation.

Factor analysis A statistical technique which identifies patterns of relationships among test scores or other types of data.

Family climate The degree of cohesiveness and harmony among family members characteristic of any given family.

Family structure How a family is composed, who its members are; for instance, One parent? Both parents? How many children? Boys or girls? What ages? and so forth.

Five-to-seven transition The shift from associative to cognitive responding assumed to take place for many children at about the ages of five to seven, in conjunction with emergence of a generalized capacity for inhibition.

Formal education Education received in schools separate from other aspects of children's daily lives, by teachers trained for that purpose, with emphasis on verbal analysis and comprehension.

Formal operations, Period of Piaget's fourth major period of intellectual growth, when children become capable of applying operational thinking to problems presented formally or propositionally. Usually not achieved until adolescence. See also Concrete operations, period of.

g factor of intelligence   A general or unitary factor of intelligence which pervades all types of intellectual activity, according to some views of intelligence. See also *s* factors of intelligence.

Gender constancy   Recognitions that one's gender (male or female) does not change as one grows older.

Generalization   Transfer of a response learned to one particular stimulus to other, similar stimuli; the greater the similarity, the more likely it is that generalization will occur.

Generalized capacity for inhibition   Ability to flexibly inhibit responses in a variety of circumstances (as opposed to specific ability to inhibit particular responses) assumed to emerge as part of the five-to-seven transition.

Genital stage   In Freudian theory, the final stage of psychosexual development, triggered by puberty, when the conflicts repressed at the end of the phallic stage reemerge and are resolved by transferring emotional involvement from opposite-sex parent to opposite-sex peers.

Genotype   The genetic makeup of an individual which may be expressed in many ways (phenotypes), depending on the circumstances of development. See also Phenotype.

Hemispheric lateralization   Differences in function between the right and left hemispheres of the brain.

Heritability   A numerical estimate of the proportion of variance of some attribute which is attributable to heredity, for some particular group or population in some given setting.

Horizontal décalage (Piaget)   Within a given period of intellectual growth, the lag in time as children apply the "same" intellectual structures to different content areas. For instance, concrete operational children conserve quantity before weight and weight before volume. See also Vertical décalage.

Human ethology   The application to human behavior of the research orientation based on the assumption that innate behavioral predispositions contribute to behavior development in important ways.

Identification   The process of incorporating attributes of a model into one's own personality; occurs with same- and opposite-sex models.

Incidental learning   Learning of information incidental to, or not important for, the task at hand, as when a child asked to learn a set of shapes also remembers their colors even though not instructed to do so.

Increasing specificity of discrimination   Ability of older children to discriminate, and respond to as different, stimuli which younger children respond to as the same.

Induction   Techniques of discipline in which parents attempt to control children by giving explanations or reasons why the child's behavior is good or bad. See also Power assertion; Love withdrawal.

Industry versus inferiority   Erikson's fourth stage of psychosocial development during which predominantly positive interactions with others result in a sense of industry—competent, interested in doing things—whereas predominantly negative interactions with others result in a sense of oneself as inferior.

Informal education   Learning experiences encountered in the course of day-to-day life out of school, often with tutoring from individuals not explicitly trained to do so.

Information processing   The storing and handling of information within a system. Applied to human beings, an approach to understanding and thinking as a complex of different intellectual processes engaged in by individuals having particular processing capabilities and limits.

Intelligence quotient (IQ)   A score representing the relationship between mental age and chronological age. $IQ = (MA \div CA) \times 100$. If mental age is higher than average, IQ is above 100; if mental age is lower than average, IQ is below 100. See also Mental age.

Interaction   The dependence of one factor upon the value of a second factor. The "same" virus which produces serious illness in a poorly nourished child may produce few symptoms in a well-nourished child; there is an interaction between disease severity and nutrition.

Interpersonal awareness   A general dimension of recognition of the attributes of persons and social interactions assumed to be reflected in developing ideas about friendship, role-taking, peer interactions, and other social processes.

IQ score   See Intelligence quotient.

Isolate, social   A child whose group status is characterized by low social impact as well as low social preference by other children.

Juvenile era   The first part of the school years, in Sullivan's theory, when children first begin to interact with a diversity of adults besides their parents and to spend a large proportion of their time with peers. See also Preadolescence.

Latency period   In Freudian theory, the period of psychosexual development following the phallic stage, during which psychodynamic conflicts are repressed and latent. Occurs approximately during the elementary school years.

Lateral asymmetry   (of brain function) The difference in functioning between right and left hemispheres of the brain.

Learned helplessness   Perception of oneself as unable to surmount failure, associated with "falling apart" when failure is encountered; attribution of failure to uncontrollable factors such as ability.

Libido   In Freudian theory, an innate sexual drive, assumed to be present from birth, which motivates personality.

Life span development orientation   The orientation toward psychological development which maintains that development continues throughout one's life, rather than ending at some point such as the end of adolescence.

Literacy events   Action sequences in a child's life in which the production and/or comprehension (writing, reading) of print plays some part.

Logographies   Writing systems in which picture-symbols stand for words.

Long-term memory   One's cognitive storage system; all of the meaningful information that one knows, which is retained for long periods of time. Contrast with short-term memory.

Love withdrawal   Techniques of parental discipline based on direct, non-physical expression of anger designed to arouse a child's feeling of guilt, shame, and so on; attempts to control children by expressing dislike for them, refusing to speak or listen to them, or isolating or threatening to leave them. See also Power assertion; Induction.

Media addiction   Spending time with television (or other media) to the exclusion of other activities and social interactions. Frequently an indicator of personal maladjustment.

Mental age   The age at which the average child gets a given score on a test of mental abilities, according to age norms for that test. A child who gets the same score as the average 10-year-old has a mental age of 10, regardless of chronological age. See also Intelligence quotient.

Mesomorph   One of the basic body builds; described as muscular, broad-shouldered, and thin-hipped. See also Somatotonic; Somatotype.

Metacognition   One's knowledge about one's own or others' cognitions; knowledge of persons as intelligent beings. Cf. social cognition.

Metacognitive experience   Being, or becoming, aware or conscious of some metacognition.

Metacognitive knowledge   Everything one knows about cognizing, including knowledge about persons as cognizers, tasks and their demands, and strategies for accomplishing cognitive ends.

Metamemory   Memory as knowing about knowing; one's knowledge or awareness of one's own memory and how it works.

Modeling   See Observational learning.

Moral judgment   The process through which someone decides that some action is good or bad.

Moral realism   In moral judgments, young children's tendency to think of rules as absolute, fixed, and determined by external authority. Contrast with Moral relativism.

Moral relativism   In moral judgments, the conception of rules as changeable human conventions based on reciprocal agreement among those who use them. Contrast with Moral realism.

Myelin sheath   A fatty covering of some nerve fibers which may develop some time after birth and without which the nerve fiber may not be fully functional.

Nature-nurture controversy   The centuries-old and continuing debate over the relative importance of heredity (nature) and environment (nurture) as influences on human development.

Neuroglia   Cells of supporting tissue of the brain.

Neuron   Nerve cell.

Nonconscious ideologies Beliefs and attitudes about which one has gotten such uniform messages in socialization that one is not aware that one holds them because no alternative is imaginable.

Nurturance Being concerned for and responsive to the needs of others.

Object constancy The main achievement of Piaget's sensorimotor period, where the infant realizes that objects exist independently of the infant's sensory and/or motor contact with them. See also Sensorimotor period.

Objective moral reasoning In moral judgment, judging an act as good or bad on the basis of its consequences. Contrast with Subjective moral reasoning.

Observational learning (modeling) Learning by watching others; influenced by characteristics of the model, such as power, nurturance, sex, age; direct and vicarious reinforcement; and cognitive factors.

Occupational prestige The relative social status generally attributed to some occupation.

Oedipus conflict A conflict Freud thought that boys go through during the phallic stage, characterized by close attachment to mother and jealousy and fear of father, resolved by repressing the conflict and identification with father. See also Castration anxiety; Repression; Identification; Phallic stage.

Open classrooms Classrooms based on the philosophy of giving children the freedom to learn in their own way; lesson plans, materials, classroom space, and educational objectives are kept flexible. See also Traditional classrooms.

Operant conditioning Altering the frequency of occurrence of some response by making reinforcement contingent upon that response.

Operations (Piaget) Intellectual structures which involve classes or relationships, and which are reversible. With acquisition of operations, children become capable of performing conservation, classification, serial ordering, and many other types of tasks. See also Organization; Reversibility.

Optimizing attention The ability to direct attention toward relevant attributes and to obtain desired information from the environment.

Organization (intellectual structures) A universal attribute of biological characteristics; in the case of intelligence, organization is manifested by recurrent, identifiable sequences of behavior, such as grasping, looking at, multiplication, seriation (Piaget). See also Scheme; Operations.

Partial reinforcement Maintaining or establishing an operant response with occasional reinforcement rather than by reinforcing every response.

Pathological prejudice Prejudiced attitudes which are part of an individual's personality structure. See also Authoritarian personality; Endemic prejudice.

Penis envy A motive Freud attributed to girls in the Electra conflict, which causes them to devalue femininity and to shift their attachment from mother to father. See also Electra conflict; Phallic stage.

Perceived attitude similarity The degree to which another person's attitudes are thought to be like one's own, whether or not there is actually any similarity.

Perceived similarity theory of identification The theory that children identify with individuals whom they perceive as similar to themselves.

Perceptual invariants Attributes of stimuli or relationships among stimuli which remain the same under different conditions.

Perceptual learning Changes in performance on perceptual tasks resulting from experience rather than changes in basic sensory capabilities.

Permissive parents Parents who use a minimum of discipline of any sort, believing that children should be allowed to develop in their own way without adult interference. See also Authoritarian parents; Authoritative parents.

Perseveration The tendency to keep repeating a response once it is given.

Person perception How one perceives and describes other people.

Personal space Characteristic zones of distance which people maintain from one another, depending on how well they know and like one another.

Phallic (early genital) stage Freud's third stage of psychosexual development (three to five years) when the genital area is the focus of libidinal pleasure; the stage during which the Oedipus and Electra conflicts occur. See also Genital stage; Oedipus conflict; Electra conflict.

Phenotype The observed attributes of an individual, a product of both genotype and circumstances of development. See also Genotype.

Phonological recoding In reading, translation or recoding from spelling to pronunciation.

Phonological segmentation Ability to differentiate and recognize phonemes, or sound units, in the flow of speech.

Physical attractiveness stereotype A widely held stereotype which attributes positive attributes to physically attractive persons.

Placidity-explosiveness A central orientation characterized by readiness to react in different situations and whether the reactions tend to be belligerent or calm. See also Central orientation; Emotional expressiveness-reserve.

"Plus" face A facial expression/gesture characterized by raised eyebrows, raised chin, and firmly set neck which, when displayed to another child, typically signals that the face-maker will prevail in the encounter.

Political behaviors, official Institutions and institutionalized behaviors such as political parties, governments, voting which serve to regulate and negotiate allocation of resources.

Political behaviors, unofficial Those behaviors one uses when competing or negotiating for scarce resources in one's day-to-day interactions with others.

Political socialization Socialization of children into the political world in which they live, including the development of attitudes and knowledge about their country, political processes, and government structures and officials.

Post-conventional level of moral reasoning   Kohlberg's third level of development of moral reasoning in which judgments are based on self-accepted moral principles.

Power   Holding control over rewards and punishments; a characteristic of models important in observational learning.

Power assertion   Techniques of parental discipline based on parent's physical power and control of resources; attempts to control children by such means as spankings or deprivation of privileges. See also Love withdrawal; Induction.

Power theory of identification   The theory that children identify with individuals who control rewards and punishments, whether or not the children themselves receive the rewards and punishments.

Preadolescence   The second part of the school years, in Sullivan's theory, which begins when children first begin to form close friendships marked by sensitivity to the friend as a person. See also Juvenile era.

Pre-conventional level of moral reasoning   Kohlberg's first level of development of moral reasoning in which actions are judged by their external consequences.

Pregeneralized learning   Learning of prejudicial labels and the evaluations attached to them before one has a clear understanding of what the labels mean.

Premature occupational foreclosure   Deciding against an occupation before one has sufficient information or experience to evaluate it realistically.

Preoperational period   Piaget's second major period of intellectual growth, in which the child develops the use of mental representations and symbols (such as language) but does not use them in ways indicating an understanding of the relationships among them. Characteristic of preschool children. See also Operations.

Prescriptive value orientation   Emphasis on doing good; rewarding for doing good; punishing for not doing good. Contrast with Proscriptive value orientation.

Primacy principle, in political socialization   The idea that one's political orientations are largely learned in childhood, with only minor variations in adolescence and adulthood.

Proactive structuring   Before entering the classroom, planning and preparing activities for situations which might arise in the classroom; an attribute of good classroom managers (teachers). See also Classroom management.

Process orientation toward intelligence   The tradition of studying intelligence, exemplified by Piaget, which emphasizes how children arrive at answers (whether right or wrong), flexible interviewing procedures, and universal attributes of intelligence.

Product orientation toward intelligence   The tradition of studying intelligence, which emphasizes correct answers to questions (products), IQ tests, and individual differences in intelligence.

Production deficiency Failure to spontaneously produce a response which could serve as a mediator, even when the child is able to make the response. See also Mediation deficiency; Production inefficiency.

Production inefficiency Partial but ineffective use of mediating responses, such as producing an appropriate mediating response but at a time when it cannot aid performance. See also Mediation deficiency; Production deficiency.

Proscriptive value orientation Emphasis on not doing bad; rewarding for not doing bad, punishing for doing bad. Contrast with Prescriptive value orientation.

Prosocial behaviors Socially positive behaviors such as helping, sharing, cooperating; contrast with antisocial behaviors.

Psychobiological orientation Orientation toward the study of human development and behavior which emphasizes its roots in both biology and hereditary processes, on the one hand, and in experience and socialization, on the other hand.

Psychodynamic theory (of personality) Any theory of personality which emphasizes motivational dynamics as the foundation of personality. Contrast with social learning theory.

Psychological androgyny Having about equal amounts of masculine and feminine behavior patterns; reflects the idea that masculinity and femininity are not opposite ends of a single dimension but are two independent dimensions on which any individual may be high or low.

Psychosexual stages Stages of personality development as outlined by Freud, characterized by successive changes in the locus or part of the body in which libidinal drives are focused. See also Psychosocial stages; Latency period.

Psychosocial stages Stages of personality development as outlined by Erikson, characterized by changes in predominant patterns of social interaction. See also Psychosexual stages; Industry versus inferiority.

Reciprocal role theory of identification The theory that sex roles are learned not through identification with same-sex models but from persons who interact with boys and girls in role-differentiated ways.

Reciprocity of parent-child relations Mutual influence between parent and child—what the child does is influenced by the parent, but what the parent does is also influenced by the child. To be contrasted with views that influence is unidirectional from parent to child.

Reinforcement Satisfaction or reduction of a drive. In operant conditioning, anything which changes the probability that a response will occur.

Rejected social status In studies of social status in children's groups, those children who are high on social impact but low on social preference.

Relational concept A concept defined by a relationship between objects, such as sister-brother, native-foreigner, to the left of-to the right of, rather than by properties of the objects themselves.

Reliability Applied to psychological tests, their consistency of measurement. A test that gives about the same information when children are tested twice, or when the score from one half of the test is compared to the score from the other half, is highly reliable.

Repression Excluding painful or anxiety-provoking thoughts from conscious awareness.

Retrieval In information processing, those processes through which information held in long-term store is gotten back out (retrieved) for current use.

Reversibility (Piaget) The ability to mentally perform and retrace an action or transformation, such as adding to and taking away; a property of operations. See also Operations.

s **factors of intelligence** Specific factors unique to particular intellectual tasks, such as numerical, verbal, or spatial tasks. An individual's performance depends on both *g* and *s* factors, if one assumes that there is a general factor of intelligence. See also *g* factor of intelligence.

Scheme (Piaget) Intellectual structures manifested as recurrent behavior sequences. Examples from the sensorimotor period of intellectual growth include grasping, looking at, reaching for. See also Organization.

Self-fulfilling prophecy effect Occurs when children's performance matches what someone expects of them.

Semantic integration Incorporation of new information into the context of what one already knows.

Semantic memory Memory as knowing; the entire body of meaningful information a person knows. See Long-term memory.

Semantic recoding In reading, the process of translation (or recoding) from spelling to meanings.

Sensorimotor period Piaget's first major period of intellectual growth, when the presymbolic infant's intellectual growth is evident in sensory and motor activities. See also Object constancy.

Sex-role flexibility Willingness and ability to engage in a variety of activities, perform them well, and feel good about doing them regardless of how they are sex-typed.

Sex-role identity Sense of oneself as masculine or feminine, possessing attributes prescribed by sex role standards. Compare with Sexual identity.

Sex-role stereotypes or standards General perceptions of what men and woman ought to be like, defining concepts of masculine and feminine. See also Sex-role identity.

Sex-typed behaviors Behavior considered appropriate for one sex but not the other.

Sexual identity Sense of oneself as male or female, established before three years of age.

Short-term memory Working memory, where information is first stored, but only in limited quantities and only for very short periods of time.

Sibling status Where one is located in the sibling structure of one's family of origin, as youngest child, first-born daughter, and so forth.

Sleeper effect   Patterns of parent-early child interaction correlate more highly with a child's later behavior as an adult than with the child's behavior during growing up.

Slow-to-warm-up children   Children whose temperament patterns include initial withdrawal from new situations, slow adaptability, mild intensity of reaction.

Social accommodation   Learning how others differ from oneself and how to deal with such differences. Such learning occurs especially rapidly during the school years.

Social cognition   One's knowledge and understanding of persons (including oneself), social relationships, and social institutions.

Social comparison   Evaluation of one's own social attributes or skills in relation to others around one.

Social impact   In studies of social status, the amount of influence or effect an individual has on the group.

Social learning theory   Application of learning theory principles to personality and social development; emphasis on observational learning and reinforcement, both direct and vicarious. Contrast with psychodynamic theory.

Social preference   In studies of social status, the degree to which children prefer to be with a given child or not.

Social responsibility norm   A generally accepted norm that persons should be generous or help others, by which children may judge others regardless of whether they behave according to the norm themselves.

Socialization   The process through which individuals learn the values, beliefs, and behavior patterns of their social group; the changes in an individual resulting from such social influence.

Sociogram   Diagram showing which children in a group are chosen by which other children, based on sociometric techniques.

Sociometric techniques   Techniques for studying a person's social standing among peers.

Somatotonic   The temperament originally assumed to be associated with a mesomorphic body build; described as dominant, active, self-assured, reckless, and risk-taking. See also Mesomorph.

Somatotype   Body build, such as tall and thin or short and stocky. Thought to be related to differences in temperament. See also Endomorph; Ectomorph; Mesomorph.

S-R learning theories   Theories of learning which assume that learning consists of forming associations between observable stimuli (S) and responses (R). Contrast with Cognitive psychology.

Stars, social status   In studies of social status, those children who are high in both social preference and social impact.

Status envy theory of identification   The theory that children identify with individuals whose status they envy.

Structure, intellectual   See Organization (Intellectual Structures).

Structured classroom   See Traditional classroom.

Student role   A set of behaviors required of children in classrooms whether they are girls or boys, by most teachers whether they are men or women. In the United States, the student role has more in common with sex-role standards for girls than for boys.

Subjective moral reasoning   In moral judgment, judging an act as good or bad on the basis of the actor's intentions. Contrast with Objective moral reasoning.

Superego   Internalized standards of behavior, including prohibitions (conscience) and prescriptions (ego ideal). From Freudian theory.

Syllabary   A writing system in which the symbols stand for syllables of words.

Tabula rasa   The view of the developing child associated with the British empiricist John Locke, in which the young child's mind is a "blank slate" to be written on by experience.

Teachers' role definitions   What teachers perceive as their function in the classroom and their expectations about their ability to carry out that role.

Temperament   An individual's characteristic pattern of reacting to events.

Testing play   A form of play which allows children to test their physical skills, emotional reactions, and ability to cope with different situations; a major form of play among school-aged children.

Traditional classrooms   Classrooms based on the philosophy that children learn best when materials are presented to them in an organized, structured way. Lesson plans, materials, classroom space, and educational objectives are determined by the teacher and follow a standard format for all children. See also Open classrooms.

Traditional sex-typing   Showing high acceptance of behaviors traditionally stereotyped as appropriate for one's own sex and low self-acceptance of sex-role behaviors stereotyped as appropriate for the opposite sex.

Undifferentiated sex-typing   Showing low acceptance of behaviors stereotyped as appropriate for either sex; low on both "masculine" and "feminine" behavior patterns.

Validity   Applied to psychological tests, the extent to which a test measures what it claims to measure as established by its correlation with some independent criterion of what it claims to measure.

Vertical décalage (Piaget)   Across different periods of intellectual growth, successive rediscovery of the "same" principle at each new stage of thinking. For instance, conservation of properties of objects in the concrete operational period is presaged by "conservation of objects" (object constancy) in the sensorimotor period. See also Horizontal décalage.

Vicarious reinforcement   Seeing someone else rewarded or punished for a behavior, as a result of which one may be more or less likely to perform the modeled behavior oneself.

Viscerotonic   The temperament originally assumed to be associated with an endomorphic body build; described as pleasure-loving, warm, forgiving, calm, and dependent. See also Endomorph.

Withitness   An attribute of good classroom managers (teachers), characterized by alertness to what happens throughout their classrooms, helping to prevent disciplinary incidents. See also Classroom management.

Work responses   Answers to questions which are attempts to respond in some relevant way.

REFERENCES

Aboud, F. E. A test of ethnocentrism with young children. *Canadian Journal of Behavioral Science*, 1980, *12*, 195–209.

Abram, R. S., & Cole, J. D. Maternal reactions to problem behaviors and ordinal position of child. *Journal of Personality*, 1981, *49*, 450–467.

Adams, G. R. Physical attractiveness research: Toward a developmental social psychology of beauty. *Human Development*, 1977, *20*, 217–239.

Adelson, J., & O'Neil, R. P. Growth of political ideas in adolescence: The sense of community. *Journal of Personality and Social Psychology*, 1966, *4*, 295–306.

Adjei, K. Influence of specific maternal occupation and behavior on Piagetian cognitive development. In P. R. Dasen (Ed.), *Piagetian psychology: Cross-cultural contributions*. New York: Gardner, 1977.

Adorno, T. W., Frenkel-Brunswik, E., Levinson, D. J., & Sanford, R. N. *The authoritarian personality*. New York: Harper & Row, 1950.

Ahlgren, A., & Johnson, W. Sex differences in cooperative and competitive attitudes from the 2nd through the 12th grades. *Developmental Psychology*, 1979, *15*, 45–49.

Ainsworth, M. D. S. The development of infant-mother attachment. In B. M. Caldwell & H. N. Riciutti (Eds.), *Review of child development research* (Vol. 3). Chicago: University of Chicago Press, 1973.

Allport, G. W. *The nature of prejudice*. Reading, Mass.: Addison-Wesley, 1954.

Altemeyer, R. A., Fulton, P., & Birney, K. M. Long-term memory improvement: Confirmation of a finding by Piaget. *Child Development*, 1969, *40*, 845–859.

Anastasi, A. Heredity, environment, and the question, "how?" *Psychological Review*, 1958, *65*, 197–208.

Anastasi, A. *Psychological testing*. New York: Macmillan, 1968.

Anderson, A. B., Teale, W. H., & Estrada, E. Low-income children's preschool literacy experiences: Some naturalistic observations. *The Quarterly Newsletter of the Laboratory of Comparative Human Cognition*, 1980, *2*, 59–65.

Anderson, R. B., St. Pierre, R. G., Proper, E. C., & Stebbins, L. B. Pardon us, but what was the question again? A response to the critiques of the follow through evaluation. *Harvard Educational Review*, 1978, *48*, 161–170.

287

Armsby, R. E. A reexamination of the development of moral judgments in children. *Child Development,* 1971, *42,* 1241–1248.

Armstrong, B. Illinois judge upholds IQ test use; Departs from Larry P. *APA Monitor,* November 1980, pp. 6–8.

Aronfreed, J. The nature, variety, and social patterning of moral responses to transgression. *Journal of Abnormal and Social Psychology,* 1961, *63,* 223–240.

Arvey, R. D. Some comments on culture fair tests. *Personnel Psychology,* 1972, *25,* 433–448.

Asher, S. R., Markell, A., & Hymel, S. Identifying children at risk in peer relations: A critique of the rate-of-interaction approach to assessment. *Child Development,* 1981, *52,* 1239–1245.

Atkin, C. K. *The effects of television advertising on children: First year experimental evidence.* Final Report. Office of Child Development, Department of Health, Education, and Welfare, 1975.

Atkin, C. K., & Gantz, W. *The role of television news in the political socialization of children.* Paper presented to the Political Communication Division of the International Communication Division of the International Communication Association, Chicago, 1975.

Ball, S., & Bogatz, G. A. Summative research on Sesame Street: Implications for the study of preschool children. In A. D. Pick (Ed.), *Minnesota Symposium on Child Psychology* (Vol. 6). Minneapolis: University of Minnesota Press, 1972.

Baltes, P. B., Reese, H. W., & Lipsitt, L. P. Life-span developmental psychology. In M. R. Rosenzwieg & L. W. Porter (Eds.), *Annual Review of Psychology* (Vol. 31). Palo Alto, Calif.: Annual Reviews, 1980.

Bandura, A. Influences of models' reinforcement contingencies on the acquisition of imitation responses. *Journal of Personality and Social Psychology,* 1965, *1,* 589–595.

Bandura, A. Social-learning theory of identificatory processes. In D. A. Goslin (Ed.), *Handbook of socialization theory and research.* Chicago: Rand McNally, 1969.

Bandura, A. Self-referent thought: A developmental analysis of self-efficacy. In J. H. Flavell & L. Ross (Eds.), *Social cognitive development: Frontiers and possible futures.* Cambridge: Cambridge University Press, 1981.

Bandura, A., Ross, D., & Ross, S. Imitation of film-mediated aggressive models. *Journal of Abnormal and Social Psychology,* 1963, *66,* 3–11. (a)

Bandura, A., Ross, D., & Ross, S. A comparative test of the status envy, social power, and secondary reinforcement theories of identificatory learning. *Journal of Abnormal and Social Psychology,* 1963, *67,* 527–534. (b)

Bates, J. E. The concept of difficult temperament. *Merrill-Palmer Quarterly,* 1980, *26,* 299–319.

Bates, J. E., & Pettit, G. S. Adult individual differences as moderators of child effects. *Journal of Abnormal Child Psychology,* 1981, *9,* 329–340.

Baumrind, D. Child care practices anteceding three patterns of preschool behavior. *Genetic Psychology Monographs,* 1967, *75,* 43–88.

Baumrind, D. Current patterns of parental authority. *Developmental Psychology Monographs,* 1971, *4* (1, Pt 2).

Baumrind, D. Parental disciplinary patterns and social competence in children. *Youth and Society,* 1978, *9,* 239–276.

Bayley, N. Development of mental abilities. In Paul Mussen (Ed.), *Carmichael's manual of child psychology* (3rd ed., Vol. 1). New York: John Wiley & Sons, 1970.

Bayley, N., & Schaefer, E. S. Correlations of maternal and child behaviors with the development of mental abilities: Data from the Berkeley Growth Study. *Monographs of the Society for Research in Child Development,* 1964, *29* (6, Whole No. 97).

Becker, W. C. Consequences of different kinds of parental discipline. In M. L. Hoffman & L. W. Hoffman (Eds.), *Review of child development research* (Vol. 1). New York: Russell Sage Foundation, 1964.

Bell, R. Q. A reinterpretation of the direction of effects in studies of socialization. *Psychological Review,* 1968, *75,* 81–95.

Bell, R. Q. Parent, child, and reciprocal influences. *American Psychologist,* 1979, *34,* 821–826.

Bem, D. J. *Beliefs, attitudes and human affairs.* Belmont, Calif.: Brooks/Cole, 1971.

Bem, D. J., & Allen, A. On predicting some of the

people some of the time: The search for cross-situational consistencies in behavior. *Psychological Review,* 1974, *81,* 506–520.

Bem, S. L. Sex-role adaptability: One consequence of psychological androgyny. *Journal of Personality and Social Psychology,* 1975, *31,* 634–643. (a)

Bem, S. L. Androgyny vs. the tight little lives of fluffy women and chesty men. *Psychology Today,* 1975, *9,* 58–62. (b)

Bengoa, J. M. Recent trends in the public health aspects of protein-calorie malnutrition. *WHO Chronicle,* 1970, *24,* 552–561.

Berndt, T. J. Effects of friendship on prosocial intentions and behavior. *Child Development,* 1981, *52,* 636–643. (a)

Berndt, T. J. Age changes and changes over time in prosocial intentions and behaviors between friends. *Developmental Psychology,* 1981, *17,* 408–416. (b)

Berndt, T. J. Relations between social cognition, nonsocial cognition, and social behavior: The case of friendship. In J. H. Flavell & L. Ross (Eds.), *Social cognitive development: Frontiers and possible futures.* Cambridge: Cambridge University Press, 1981. (c)

Berndt, T. J. The features and effects of friendship in early adolescence. *Child Development,* 1982, *53,* 1447–1460.

Bernstein, L. *The unanswered question.* Norton Lecture Series, Harvard University, 1973.

Berscheid, E., & Walster, E. Physical attractiveness. In L. Berkowitz (Ed.), *Advances in experimental social psychology* (Vol. 6). New York: Academic Press, 1974.

Beuf, A. *Red children in white America.* Philadelphia: University of Pennsylvania Press, 1977.

Bigelow, B. On the interdependency between stage and sequence in the development of children's friendship expectations. *The Journal of Psychology,* 1982, *110,* 121–132.

Bigelow, B. J., & La Gaipa, J. J. Children's written descriptions of friendship: A multidimensional analysis. *Developmental Psychology,* 1975, *11,* 857–758.

Bingham, J. C. Views of black and white children concerning the distribution of personality characteristics. *Journal of Personality,* 1974, *42,* 144–158.

Blanchard, R. W., & Biller, H. B. Father availability and academic performance among

third grade boys. *Developmental Psychology,* 1971, *4,* 301–305.

Bock, G., Stebbins, L. B., & Proper, E. C. *Education as experimentation: A planned variation model, Volume IV-B, effects of Follow-Through Models.* Cambridge, Mass.: Abt Associates, 1977. (Also issued by the U.S. Office of Education as National Evaluation: Detailed Effects, Vol. II-B of the Follow Through Planned Variation Experiment Series.)

Borke, H. Piaget's view of social interaction and the theoretical construct of empathy. In L. S. Siegel & C. J. Brainerd (Eds.), *Alternatives to Piaget: Critical essays on the theory.* New York: Academic Press, 1978.

Bowlby, John. *Attachment and loss* (Vol. 1). New York: Basic Books, 1969.

Bradshaw, J. L., & Nettleton, N. C. The nature of hemispheric specialization in man. *The Behavioral and Brain Sciences,* 1981, *4,* 51–91.

Brainerd, C. J. Judgments and explanations as criteria for the presence of cognitive structures. *Psychological Bulletin,* 1973, *79,* 172–179.

Brainerd, C. J. Does prior knowledge of the compensation rule increase susceptibility to conservation training? *Developmental Psychology,* 1976, *12,* 1–5.

Brainerd, C. J. Learning research and Piagetian theory. In L. S. Siegel & C. L. Brainerd (Eds.), *Alternatives to Piaget: Critical essays on the theory.* New York: Academic Press, 1978.

Brainerd, C. J., & Hooper, F. H. A methodological analysis of developmental studies of identity conservation and equivalence conservation. *Psychological Bulletin,* 1975, *82,* 725–737.

Brodsky, C. M. *A study of norms for body form—behavior relationships.* Washington, D.C.: Catholic University of America Press, 1954.

Bronson, W. C. Stable patterns of behavior: The significance of enduring orientations for personality development. In J. P. Hill (Ed.), *Minnesota Symposia in Child Psychology* (Vol. 2). Minneapolis: University of Minnesota Press, 1969.

Bronstein-Burrows, P. Patterns of parent behavior: A cross-cultural study. *Merrill-Palmer Quarterly,* 1981, *27,* 129–143.

Brophy, J. E. Interactions between learner characteristics and optimal instruction. In D.

Bar-Tal & L. Saxe (Eds.), *Social psychology of education: Theory and research.* New York: Hemisphere Publishing, 1978.

Brophy, J. E., & Evertson, C. M. *Learning from teaching: A developmental perspective.* Boston: Allyn & Bacon, 1976.

Brophy, J. E., & Good, T. L. Feminization of American elementary schools. *Phi Delta Kappan, 1973, 54,* 564–566.

Brophy, J. E., & Good, T. L. *Teacher-student relationships: Causes and consequences.* New York: Holt, Rinehart and Winston, 1974.

Brown, A. L. The development of memory: Knowing, knowing about knowing, and knowing how to know. In H. W. Reese (Ed.), *Advances in child development and behavior* (Vol. 10). New York: Academic Press, 1975.

Brown, A. L. Knowing when, where, and how to remember: A problem of metacognition. In R. L. Glaser (Ed.), *Advances in instructional psychology.* Hillsdale, N.J.: Lawrence Erlbaum Associates, 1978.

Brown, A. L. Metacognitive development and reading. In R. J. Spiro, B. C. Bruce, & W. F. Brewer (Eds.), *Theoretical issues in reading comprehension.* Hillsdale, N.J.: Lawrence Erlbaum Associates, 1980.

Brown, A. L. Learning and development: The problem of compatibility, access, and induction. *Human Development, 1982, 25,* 89–115.

Brown, A. L., & Barclay, C. R. The effects of training specific mnemonics on the metamnemonic efficiency of retarded children. *Child Development, 1976, 47,* 71–80.

Brown, A. L., & Champione, J. C. Training strategic study time apportionment in educable retarded children. *Intelligence, 1977, 1,* 94–107.

Brown, A. L., Campione, J. C., & Barclay, C. R. Training self-checking routines for estimating test readiness: Generalization from list learning to prose recall. Unpublished manuscript, University of Illinois, 1978. Cited in A. L. Brown, Metacognitive development and reading. In Rand J. Spiro et al. (Eds.), *Theoretical issues in reading comprehension.* Hillsdale, N.J.: Lawrence Erlbaum Associates, 1980.

Brown, A. L., & Lawton, S. C. The feeling-of-knowing experience in educable retarded children. *Developmental Psychology, 1977, 4,* 364–370.

Brown, A. L., & Smiley, S. S. Rating the importance of structural units of prose passages: A problem of metacognitive development. *Child Development, 1977, 48,* 1–8.

Brown, A. L., & Smiley, S. S. The development of strategies for studying texts. *Child Development, 1978, 49,* 1076–1088.

Bruce, D. J. Analysis of word sounds by young children. *British Journal of Educational Psychology, 1964, 34,* 158–169.

Bruner, J. S. *The relevance of education.* New York: W. W. Norton, 1973.

Bryan, J. H. Why children help: A review. In L. G. Wispe (Ed.), Positive forms of social behavior. *Journal of Social Issues, 1972, 28,* 87–104.

Bugental, B., Caporael, L., & Shennum, A. Experimentally produced child uncontrollability: Effects on the potency of adult communication patterns. *Child Development, 1980, 51,* 520–528.

Bukowski, W. M., & Newcomb, A. F. A naturalistic study of friendship among preadolescent children: *Patterns of development and the function of similarity.* Unpublished manuscript, 1982.

Burton, R. Generality of honesty reconsidered. *Psychological Review, 1953, 70,* 481–499.

Busby, L. J. Sex-role research on the mass media. *Journal of Communication, 1975, 25,* 107–131.

Buss, D. M., Block, J. H., & Block, J. Preschool activity level: Personality correlates and developmental implications. *Child Development, 1980, 51,* 401–408.

Camras, L. A. Facial expressions used by children in a conflict situation. *Child Development, 1977, 48,* 1431–1435.

Camras, L. A. Children's understanding of facial expressions used during conflict encounters. *Child Development, 1980, 51,* 879–885.

Carmi, G. The role of context in cognitive development. *The Quarterly Newsletter of the Laboratory of Comparative Human Development, 1981, 3,* 46–54.

Carr, T. H. Building theories of reading ability: On the relation between individual differences in cognitive skills and reading comprehension. *Cognition, 1981, 9,* 73–114.

Carr, T. C., & Evans, M. A. *Influence of learning conditions on patterns of cognitive skills in* young children. Paper presented at the Biennial Meeting of the Society for Research in Child Development, Boston, April 1981.

Cavanaugh, J. C., & Borkowski, J. G. Searching for metamemory—memory connections: A developmental study. Developmental Psychology, 1980, 16, 441–453.

Cavanaugh, J. C., & Perlmutter, M. Metamemory: A critical examination. Child Development, 1982, 53, 11–28.

Cavior, N., & Dokecki, P. R. Physical attractiveness, perceived attitude similarity, and academic achievement as contributors to interpersonal attraction among adolescents. Developmental Psychology, 1973, 9, 44–54.

Cavior, N., & Lombardi, D. A. Developmental aspects of judgment of physical attractiveness in children. Developmental Psychology, 1973, 8, 67–71.

Chandler, M. H., & Greenspan, D. Erstz egocentrism: A reply to H. Borke. Developmental Psychology, 1972, 7, 104–106.

Chandler, M. J., Paget, K., & Koch, D. A. The child's demystification of psychological defense mechanisms: A structural and developmental analysis. Developmental Psychology, 1978, 14, 197–205.

Chapman, M. Listening to reason: Children's attentiveness and parental discipline. Merrill-Palmer Quarterly, 1979, 25, 251–263.

Charbonneau, C., Robert, M., Bourassa, G., & Gladu-Bissonnette, S. Observational learning of quantity conservation and Piagetian generalization tasks. Developmental Psychology, 1976, 12, 211–217.

Charlesworth, R., & Hartup, W. W. Positive social reinforcement in the nursery school peer group. Child Development, 1967, 38, 993–1002.

Charlesworth, W. R. The ontogeny of political behavior. American Behavioral Scientist, 1982, 25, 273–293.

Chi, M. T. Short-term memory limitation in children: Capacity or processing deficits? Memory and Cognition, 1976, 4, 559–572.

Cicirelli, V. G. The relationship of sibling structure to intellectual abilities and achievement. Review of Educational Research, 1978, 48, 365–379.

Claiborn, W. L. Expectancy effects in the classroom: A failure to replicate. Journal of Educational Psychology, 1969, 60, 377–383.

Clark, K. B., & Clark, M. P. Racial identification and preference in Negro children. In T. M. Newcomb & E. L. Hartley (Eds.), Readings in social psychology. New York: Holt, 1947.

Cole, M., & Bruner, J. S. Cultural differences and inferences about psychological processes. American Psychologist, 1971, 26, 867–876.

Cole, M., & Scribner, S. Culture and thought: A psychological introduction. New York: John Wiley & Sons, 1974.

Coleman, J. S., Campbell, E. Q., Hobson, C. J., McPortland, J., Mood, A. M., Weinfeld, E. D., & York, R. L. Equality of educational opportunity. Washington, D.C.: U.S. Government Printing Office, 1966.

Collins, W. A. Effect of temporal separation between motivation, aggression, and consequence: A developmental study. Developmental Psychology, 1973, 8, 215–221.

Collins, W. A. The developing child as viewer. Journal of Communication, 1975, 25, 34–44.

Collins, W. A. Temporal integration and children's understanding of social information on television. American Journal of Orthopsychiatry, 1978, 48, 198–204.

Collins, W. A., Berndt, T. J., & Hess, V. I. Observational learning of motives and consequences for television aggression: A developmental study. Child Development, 1974, 45, 799–802.

Collins, W. A., Sobol, B. I., & Westby, S. Effects of adult commentary on children's comprehension and inferences about a televised aggressive portrayal. Child Development, 1981, 52, 158–163.

Comstock, G. The evidence so far. Journal of Communication, 1975, 25, 25–34.

Conger, J. J. Adolescence and youth: Psychological development in a changing world (2nd ed.). New York: Harper & Row, 1977.

Conger, J. J., & Miller, W. C. Personality, social class, and delinquency. New York: John Wiley & Sons, 1966.

Cooney, E. W., & Selman, R. L. Children's use of social conceptions: Towards a dynamic model of social cognition. In W. Damon (Ed.), Social cognition: New directions for child development (No. 1). San Francisco: Jossey-Bass, 1978.

Cowan, P. A., Langer, J., Heavenrich, J., & Nathanson, M. Social learning and Piaget's cognitive theory of moral development.

Journal of Personality and Social Psychology, 1969, *11*, 261–274.

Cowen, E. L., Pederson, A., Babigan, H., Izzo, L. D., & Trost, M. A. Long-term follow-up of early detected vulnerable children. *Journal of Consulting and Clinical Psychology*, 1973, *41*, 438–446.

Crandall, V. J., Dewey, R., Katkovsky, W., & Presten, A. Parents' attitudes and behaviors and grade school children's academic achievement. *Journal of Genetic Psychology*, 1964, *104*, 53–66.

Crockenberg, S., & Nicolayev, J. Stage transition in moral reasoning as related to conflict experienced in naturalistic settings. *Merrill-Palmer Quarterly*, 1979, *28*, 185–192.

Cromer, W. The difference model: A new explanation for some reading difficulties. *Journal of Educational Psychology*, 1970, *61*, 471–483.

Crook, T., Raskin, A., & Elliot, J. Parent-child relationships and adult depression. *Child Development*, 1981, *52*, 950–957.

Crosby, F., Bromley, S., & Saxe, L. Recent unobtrusive studies of black and white discrimination and prejudice: A literature review. *Psychological Bulletin*, 1980, *87*, 546–563.

Damon, W. (Ed.). *Social cognition. New directions for child development*. (No. 1). San Francisco: Jossey Bass, 1978.

Danner, F. W., & Lonky, E. A cognitive-developmental approach to the effects of rewards on intrinsic motivation. *Child Development*, 1981, *52*, 1043–1052.

Dasen, P. R. Cross-cultural Piagetian research: A summary. *Journal of Cross-Cultural Psychology*, 1972, *3*, 23–29.

Dasen, P. R. *Piagetian psychology: Cross-cultural contributions*. New York: Gardner Press, 1977.

Davidson, H. A study of the confusing letters B, D, P, Q. *Journal of Genetic Psychology*, 1935, *47*, 458–468.

Dickson, W. P. (Ed.). *Children's oral communication skills*. New York: Academic Press, 1981.

Diener, C. I., & Dweck, C. S. An analysis of learned helplessness: Continuous changes in performance strategy, and achievement cognitions following failure. *Journal of Personality and Social Psychology*, 1978, *36*, 451–462.

Diener, C. I., & Dweck, C. S. An analysis of learned helplessness: II, The processing of success. *Journal of Personality and Social Psychology*, 1980, *39*, 940–952.

Dlugokinski, E., & Firestone, I. J. Congruence among four methods of measuring other-centeredness. *Child Development*, 1973, *44*, 304–308.

Dominick, J. R., & Greenberg, B. S. Attitudes toward violence: The interaction of television exposure, family attitudes, and social class. In G. A. Comstock & E. A. Rubinstein (Eds.), *Television and social behavior. Vol. 3, Television and adolescent aggressiveness*. Washington, D.C.: U.S. Government Printing Office, 1972.

Douvan, E., & Adelson, J. *The adolescent experience*. New York: John Wiley & Sons, 1966.

Dunkin, M. J., & Biddle, B. J. *The study of teaching*. New York: Holt, Rinehart and Winston, 1974.

Dushenko, T. W., Perry, R. P., Schilling, J., & Smolarski, S. The generality of the physical attractiveness stereotype for age and sex. *Journal of Social Psychology*, 1978, *105*, 303–304.

Dweck, C. S. The role of expectations and attributions in the alleviation of learned helplessness. *Journal of Personality and Social Psychology*, 1975, *31*, 674–685.

Dweck, C. S., & Bush, E. S. Sex differences in learned helplessness: I. Differential debilitation with peer and adult evaluators. *Developmental Psychology*, 1976, *12*, 147–156.

Dweck, C. S., Davidson, W., Nelson, S., & Enna, B. Sex differences in learned helplessness: II. The contingencies of evaluative feedback in the classroom and III: An experimental analysis. *Developmental Psychology*, 1978, *14*, 268–276.

Dweck, C. S., Goetz, T. E., & Strauss, N. L. Sex differences in learned helplessness: IV. An experimental and naturalistic study of failure generalization and its mediators. *Journal of Personality and Social Psychology*, 1980, *38*, 441–452.

Dweck, C. S., & Reppucci, N. D. Learned helplessness and reinforcement responsiblity in children. *Journal of Personality and Social Psychology*, 1973, *25*, 109–116.

Edelman, M. S., & Omark, D. R. Dominance hierarchies in young children. *Social Science Information*, 1973, *12*, 103–110.

Ekman, P., & Oster, H. Facial expressions of emotions. In M. R. Rosenzweig & L. W. Porter (Eds.), *Annual review of psychology* (Vol. 30). Palo Alto, Calif.: Annual Reviews, 1979.

Elkind, D. Conceptual orientation shifts in children and adolescents. *Child Development,* 1966, *37,* 493–498.

Elkind, D. Piagetian and psychometric conceptions of intelligence. *Harvard Education Review,* 1969, *39,* 319–337.

Elkind, D. *Children and adolescents: Interpretative essays on Jean Piaget* (3rd ed.). New York: Oxford University Press, 1981.

Elkind, D., & Dabek, R. F. Personal injury and property damage in the moral judgments of children. *Child Development,* 1977, *48,* 518–522.

Ellis, S., Rogoff, B., & Cromer, C. C. Age segregation in children's social encounters. *Developmental Psychology,* 1981, *17,* 399–407.

Erikson, E. *Childhood and society.* New York: W. W. Norton, 1950.

Eron, L. Relationship of TV viewing habits and aggressive behavior in children. *Journal of Abnormal and Social Psychology,* 1963, *67,* 193–196.

Eron, L. D., Lefkowitz, M. M., Huesmann, L. R., & Walder, L. Does television violence cause aggression? *American Psychologist,* 1972, *27,* 253–263.

Exhibit A: IQ trial. Plaintiffs take the stand. *APA Monitor,* December 1977, pp. 4–5.

Exhibit B: IQ trial. State witness testifies. *APA Monitor,* January 1978, pp. 15; 18.

Farnham-Diggory, S. Cognitive synthesis in Negro and white children. *Monographs of the Society for Research in Child Development,* 1970, *35* (Whole No. 135).

Farnham-Diggory, S. The development of equivalence systems. In S. Farnham-Diggory (Ed.). *Information processing in children.* New York: Academic Press, 1972.

Feffer, M. Development analysis of interpersonal behavior. *Psychological Review,* 1970, *77,* 197–214.

Feilitzen, C. V., & Linné, O. Identifying with television characters. *Journal of Communication,* 1975, *25,* 51–54.

Feiring, C., & Lewis, M. The child as a member of the family system. *Behavioral Science,* 1978, *23,* 225–233.

Ferguson, L. R. *Personality development.* Belmont, Calif.: Brooks/Cole, 1970.

Ferguson, L. R. Personal communication, 1976.

Fitzgerald, H. E., Strommen, E. A., & McKinney, J. P. *Developmental psychology: The infant and young child* (Rev. ed.). Homewood, Ill.: Dorsey Press, 1982.

Flaherty, J. F., & Dusek, J. B. An investigation of the relationship between psychological androgyny and components of self-concept. *Journal of Personality and Social Psychology,* 1980, *38,* 984–992.

Flavell, J. H. *The developmental psychology of Jean Piaget.* Princeton, N.J.: D. Van Nostrand, 1963.

Flavell, J. H. Developmental studies of mediated memory. In H. W. Reese & L. P. Lipsitt (Eds.). *Advances in child development and behavior.* New York: Academic Press, 1970.

Flavell, J. H. *Cognitive development.* Englewood Cliffs, N.J.: Prentice-Hall, 1977.

Flavell, J. H. Metacognition and cognitive monitoring: A new area of psychological inquiry. *American Psychologist,* 1979, *34,* 906–911.

Flavell, J. H. Cognitive monitoring. In W. P. Dickson (Ed.), *Children's oral communication skills.* New York: Academic Press, 1981.

Flavell, J. H. Monitoring social cognitive enterprises: Something else that may develop in the area of social cognition. In J. H. Flavell & L. Ross (Eds.), *Social cognitive development: Frontiers and possible futures.* Cambridge: Cambridge University Press, 1981. (b)

Flavell, J. H., Botkin, P. R., Fry, C. L., Wright, J. W., & Jarvis, P. E. *The development of role-taking and communication skills in children.* New York: John Wiley & Sons, 1968.

Flavell, J. H., & Wellman, H. M. Metamemory. In R. V. Kail & J. W. Hagen (Eds.), *Memory in cognitive development.* Hillsdale, N.J.: Lawrence Erlbaum Associates, 1977.

Fleming, E. S., & Anttonen, R. G. Teacher expectancy as related to the academic and personal growth of primary-age children. *Monographs of the society for research in child development,* 1971, *36* (Serial No. 145).

Fletcher, J. M., Taylor, H. G., Morris, R., & Statz, P. Finger recognition skills and reading achievement: A developmental neuropsychological analysis. *Developmental Psychology*, 1982, *18*, 124–132.

Frenkel-Brunswik, E. A study of prejudice in children. *Human Relations*, 1948, *1*, 295–306.

Freud, A., & Dann, S. An experiment in group upbringing. In R. Eisler, A. Freud, H. Hartman, & E. Kris (Eds.), *The psychoanalytic study of the child* (Vol. 6). New York: International Universities Press, 1951.

Friedenberg, E. Z. *The vanishing adolescent.* New York: Dell Publishing, 1959.

Friedrich, L. K., & Stein, A. H. Aggressive and prosocial television programs and the natural behavior of preschool children. *Monographs of the Society for Research in Child Development*, 1973, *38* (Serial No. 151).

Fry, A. M., & Willis, F. N. Invasion of personal space as a function of the age of the invader. *The Psychological Record*, 1971, *21*, 385–389.

Furby, L. The implications of within-group heritabilities for sources of between group differences: IQ and racial differences. *Developmental Psychology*, 1973, *9*, 28–37.

Furth, H. G. Young children's understanding of society. In H. McGurk (Ed.), *Issues in childhood social development.* London: Methuen, 1978.

Gallatin, J. Political thinking in adolescence. In J. Adelson (Ed.), *Handbook of adolescent psychology.* New York: John Wiley & Sons, 1980.

Gallimore, R., & Au, K. H-P. The competence/incompetence paradox in the education of minority culture children. *The Quarterly Newsletter of the Laboratory of Comparative Human Cognition*, 1979, *1*, 32–37.

Garcia, J. The logic and limits of mental aptitude testing. *American Psychologist*, 1981, *36*, 1172–1180.

Gardner, W., & Rogoff, B. The role of instruction in memory development: Some methodological choices. *The Quarterly Newsletter of the Laboratory of Comparative Human Cognition*, 1982, *4*, 6–12.

Gazzaniga, M. S. *The bisected brain.* New York: Appleton-Century-Crofts, 1970.

Gelman, R. Conservation acquisition: A problem of learning to attend to relevant attributes. *Journal of Experimental Child Psychology*, 1969, *7*, 67–87.

Gelman, R. Logical capacity of very young children: Number invariance rules. *Child Development*, 1972, *43*, 75–90.

Gelman, R. Preschool thought. *American Psychologist*, 1979, *34*, 900–905.

Gelman, R., Bullock, M., & Meck, E. Preschoolers understanding of simple object transformations. *Child Development*, 1980, *51*, 691–699.

Gelman, R., & Gallistel, C. R. *The child's understanding of number.* Cambridge, Mass.: Harvard University Press, 1978.

Gibson, E. J. *Principles of perceptual learning and development.* New York: Appleton-Century-Crofts, 1969.

Gibson, E. J., Gibson, J. J., Pick, A. D., & Osser, H. A developmental study of the discrimination of letter-like forms. *Journal of Comparative and Physiological Psychology*, 1962, *55*, 897–906.

Gibson, E. J., & Levin, H. *The psychology of reading.* Cambridge, Mass.: MIT Press, 1975.

Ginsburg, H. *The myth of the deprived child.* Englewood Cliffs, N.J.: Prentice-Hall, 1972.

Ginsburg, H., & Opper, S. *Piaget's theory of intellectual development: An introduction.* (2nd ed.). Englewood Cliffs, N.J.: Prentice-Hall, 1979.

Ginsburg, H. J. Altruism in children: The significance of nonverbal behavior. *Journal of Communication*, 1977, *27*, 82–86.

Ginzberg, E. *Occupational choice.* New York: Columbia University Press, 1951.

Glaser, R., & Bond, L. (Eds.). Testing: Concepts, policy, practice, and research. *American Psychologist*, 1981, *36*, 997–1189.

Glick, P. C. Children of divorced parents in demographic perspective. In T. E. Levitin (Ed.) Children of divorce. *Journal of Social Issues*, 1979, *35*, 170–182.

Goetz, T. E., & Dweck, C. S. Learned helplessness in social situations. *Journal of Personality and Social Psychology*, 1980, *39*, 246–255.

Good, T. L., Biddle, B. J., & Brophy, J. E. *Teachers make a difference.* New York: Holt, Rinehart and Winston, 1975.

Goodman, M. E. *Race awareness in young children.* Reading, Mass.: Addison-Wesley, 1952.

Goodnow, J. J. Problems in research on culture and thought. In D. Elkind & J. H. Flavell

(Eds.), *Studies in cognitive development: Essays in honor of Jean Piaget.* New York: Oxford University Press, 1969.

Gordon, E. F., & Gordon, R. C. Child abuse: A review of selected aspects for the primary care physician. *Southern Medical Journal,* 1979, *72,* 985–991.

Gottman, J. J., & Parkhurst, J. T. A developmental theory of friendship and acquaintanceship processes. In W. A. Collins (Ed.), Development of cognition, affect, and social relations. *The Minnesota Symposia on Child Psychology* (Vol. 13). Hillsdale, N.J.: Lawrence Erlbaum Associates, 1980.

Gouze, K. R., & Nadelman, L. Constancy of gender identity for self and others in children between the ages of three and seven. *Child Development,* 1980, *51,* 275–278.

Greenberg, B. S., & Gordon, T. F. Social class and racial differences in children's perceptions of television violence. In G. A. Comstock, E. A. Rubinstein, & J. P. Murray (Eds.), *Television and social behavior. Vol. 5, Television's effects: Further explorations.* Washington, D.C.: U.S. Government Printing Office, 1972.

Greenfield, P. H. On culture and conservation. In J. S. Bruner, R. R. Oliver, & P. M. Greenfield. *Studies in cognitive growth.* New York: John Wiley & Sons, 1966.

Greenfield, P. M. Oral or written language: The consequences of cognitive development in Africa, the United States, and England. *Language and Speech,* 1972, *15,* 169–178.

Greenfield, P., & Lave, J. Cognitive aspects of informal education. In D. A. Wagner & H. W. Stevenson (Eds.), *Cultural perspectives on child development.* San Francisco: W. H. Freeman, 1982.

Greenstein, F. I. *Children and politics. (Rev. ed.).* New Haven, Conn.: Yale University Press, 1965.

Grusec, J. E., & Kuczynski, L. Direction of effect in socialization: A comparison of the parents' versus the child's behavior as determinants of disciplinary techniques. *Developmental Psychology,* 1980, *16,* 1–9.

Grusec, J. E., & Redler, E. Attribution, reinforcement, and altruism: A developmental analysis. *Developmental Psychology,* 1980, *16,* 525–534.

Guilford, J. P. Three facts of intellect. *American Psychologist,* 1959, *14,* 569–579.

Gutkin, D. C. The effect of systematic story changes on intentionality in children's moral judgments. *Child Development,* 1972, *43,* 187–195.

Hagen, J. W. Strategies for remembering. In S. Farnham-Diggory (Ed.), *Information processing in children.* New York: Academic Press, 1972.

Hagen, J. W., Jongeward, R. H., Jr., & Kail, R. V., Jr. Cognitive perspectives on the development of memory. In H. W. Reese (Ed.), *Advances in child development and behavior* (Vol. 10). New York: Academic Press, 1975.

Hall, J. A., & Halberstadt, A. G. Masculinity and femininity in children: Development of the children's personal attributes questionnaire. *Development Psychology,* 1980, *16,* 270–280.

Halverson, C. F., Jr., & Waldrop, M. F. The relation of mechanically recorded activity level to varieties of preschool play behavior. *Child Development,* 1973, *44,* 678–681.

Halverson, C. F., Jr., & Waldrop, M. F. Relations between preschool activity and aspects of intellectual and social behavior at age 7½. *Child Development,* 1976, *12,* 107–112.

Haney, W. Validity, vaudeville, and values: A short history of social concerns over standardized testing. *American Psychologist,* 1981, *36,* 1021–1034.

Hanson, R. A. Consistency and stability of home environmental measures related to IQ. *Child Development,* 1975, *46,* 470–480.

Harris, D., Gough, H., & Martin, W. E. Children's ethnic attitudes: II. Relationships to parental beliefs concerning child training. *Child Development,* 1950, *21,* 169–181.

Harris, L. J. Discrimination of left and right and development of the logic of relations. *Merrill-Palmer Quarterly,* 1972, *18,* 307–320.

Harris, L. J. Teaching the right brain: Historical perspectives on a contemporary fad. In C. T. Best (Ed.), *Developmental neuropsychology and education.* New York: Academic Press, 1982.

Harter, S. Pleasure derived from challenge and the effect of receiving grades on children's difficulty level choices. *Child Development,* 1978, *49,* 788–799. (a)

Harter, S. Effectance motivation reconsidered: Toward a developmental model. *Human Development,* 1978, *1,* 34–64. (b)

Harter, S. A model of intrinsic mastery motivation in children: Individual differences and developmental change. *Minnesota symposium on child psychology* (Vol. 14). Hillsdale, N.J.: Lawrence Erlbaum Associates, 1980.

Harter, S. A new self-report scale of intrinsic versus extrinsic orientation in the classroom: Motivational and informational components. *Developmental Psychology,* 1981, *17,* 300–312.

Hartley, R. Sex-role concepts among elementary school age girls. *Marriage and Family Living,* 1959, *21,* 59–64.

Hartshorne, H., & May, M. *Studies in the nature of character. Vol. 1, Studies in deceit.* New York: Macmillan, 1928.

Hartup, W. W. Peer interaction and social organization. In P. Mussen (Ed.), *Carmichael's manual of child psychology.* New York: John Wiley & Sons, 1970.

Hartup, W. W. Children and their friends. In H. McGurk (Ed.), *Issues in childhood social development.* London: Methuen, 1978.

Havighurst, R. J. *Developmental tasks and education* (3rd ed.). New York: McKay, 1972.

Helmreich, R. L., Spence, J. T., & Holahan, C. K. Psychological androgyny and sex-role flexibility: A test of two hypotheses. *Journal of Personality and Social Psychology,* 1979, *37,* 1631–1644.

Hendrickson, L. N., & Muehl, S. The effects of attention and motor response pretraining on learning to discriminate *b* and *d* in kindergarten children. *Journal of Educational Psychology,* 1962, *53,* 236–241.

Henshel, A. M. The relation between values and behavior: A developmental hypothesis. *Child Development,* 1971, *42,* 1997–2007.

Hertzig, M. E., Birch, G. G., Thomas, A., & Mendez, O. A. Class and ethnic differences in the responsiveness of preschool children to cognitive demands. *Monographs of the Society for Research in Child Development,* 1968, *33* (Whole No. 117).

Herzog, E., & Sudia, C. E. Children in fatherless families. In B. M. Caldwell & H. J. Ricciuti (Eds.), *Review of child development research.* Chicago: University of Chicago Press, 1973.

Hess, E. H. Ethology and developmental psychology. In P. Mussen (Ed.), *Carmichael's manual of child psychology* (3rd ed., Vol. 1). New York: John Wiley & Sons, 1970.

Hess, R. D., & Camara, K. A. Post-divorce family relationships as mediating factors in the consequences of divorce for children. In T. E. Levitin (Ed.), Children of divorce. *Journal of Social Issues,* 1979, *35,* 79–96.

Hess, R. D., & Torney, J. V. *The development of political attitudes in children.* Garden City, N.Y.: Anchor Books, 1967.

Hetherington, E. M. Effects of father absence on personality development in adolescent daughters. *Developmental Psychology,* 1972, *7,* 303–326.

Hetherington, E. M., Cox, M., & Cox, R. The aftermath of divorce. In J. H. Stevens, Jr., & M. Matthews (Eds.), *Mother-child, father-child relations.* Washington, D.C.: NAEYC, 1978.

Hetherington, E. M., Cox, M., & Cox, R. Play and social interaction in children following divorce. In T. E. Levitin (Ed.), Children of Divorce. *Journal of Social Issues,* 1979, *35,* 26–49.

Hetherington, E. M., & Frankie, G. Effects of parental dominance, warmth, and conflict on imitation in children. *Journal of Personality and Social Psychology,* 1967, *6,* 119–125.

Hetherington, E. M., & McIntyre, C. W. Developmental psychology. In M. R. Rosenzweig & L. W. Porter (Eds.), *Annual review of psychology* (Vol. 26). Palo Alto, Cal.: Annual Reviews, 1975.

Hill, K. T., & Sarason, S. B. The relation of test anxiety and defensiveness to test and school performance over the elementary school years: A further longitudinal study. *Monographs of the Society for Research in Child Development,* 1966, *31* (2, Whole No. 104).

Himmelweit, H. T., Oppenheim, A. N., & Vince, P. *Television and the child.* London: Oxford University Press, 1958.

Hodge, R. W., Siegel, P. M., & Rossi, P. H. Occupational prestige in the United States, 1925–1963. In D. G. Zytowski (Ed.), *Vocational behavior.* New York: Holt, Rinehart and Winston, 1968.

Hoffman, J. A., & Teyber, E. C. Some relationships between sibling age spacing and personality. *Merrill-Palmer Quarterly,* 1979, *25,* 77–80.

Hoffman, L. W. Effects of maternal employment on the child—a review of the research. *Developmental Psychology,* 1974, *10,* 204–228.

Hoffman, L. W., & Manis, J. D. Influences of children on marital interactions and parental satisfactions and dissatisfactions. In R. M. Lerner & G. B. Spanier (Eds.), *Child influences on marital and family interaction: A life-span perspective.* New York: Academic Press, 1978.

Hoffman, M. L. Parent discipline and the child's consideration for others. *Child Development,* 1963, *34,* 573–588.

Hoffman, M. L. Moral development. In P. Mussen (Ed.), *Carmichael's manual of child psychology* (3rd ed., Vol. 2). New York: John Wiley & Sons, 1970.

Hoffman, M. L., & Saltzstein, H. D. Parent discipline and the child's moral development. *Journal of Personality and Social Psychology,* 1967, *5,* 45–47.

Holden, C. Identical twins reared apart. *Science,* 1980, *207,* 1323–1328.

Honzik, M. P. Environmental correlates of mental growth: Prediction from the family setting at 21 months. *Child Development,* 1967, *38,* 337–364.

Honzik, M. P., Macfarlane, J., & Allen, L. The stability of mental test performance between 2 and 18 years. *Journal of Experimental Education,* 1948, *17,* 309–324.

Hopkins, K. D., & Bracht, G. H. Ten-year stability of verbal and nonverbal IQ scores. *American Educational Research Journal,* 1975, *12,* 469–477.

Horn, J. M., Loehlin, J. C., & Willerman, L. Intellectual resemblance among adoptive and biological relatives: The Texas Adoption Project. *Behavior Genetics,* 1979, *9,* 177–207.

Horwitz, R. A. Psychological effects of the "open classroom." *Review of Educational Research,* 1979, *49,* 71–86.

House, E. R., Glass, G. V., McLean, L. D., & Walker, D. F. No simple answers. Critiques of the Follow-Through evaluation. *Harvard Educational Review,* 1978, *48,* 128–160.

Hurley, J. R. Parental malevolence and children's intelligence. *Journal of Consulting Psychology,* 1967, *31,* 199–204.

Inhelder, B., & Piaget, J. *The growth of logical thinking from childhood to adolescence.* New York: Basic Books, 1958.

Inhelder, B., & Piaget, J. *The early growth of logic in the child.* New York: W. W. Norton, 1964.

Jeffrey, W. E., & Skager, R. W. Effect of incentive conditions on stimulus generalization in children. *Child Development,* 1962, *33,* 865–870.

Jencks, C. *Inequality: A reassessment of the effect of family and schooling in America.* New York: Basic Books, 1972.

Jensen, A. R. How much can we beset IQ and scholastic achievement? *Harvard Educational Review,* 1968, *39,* 1–123.

Johnson, C. D., & Gormly, J. Academic cheating: The contribution of sex, personality, and situational variables. *Developmental Psychology,* 1972, *6,* 320–325.

Johnson, H., and Smith, L. B. Children's inferential abilities in the context of reading to understand. *Child Development,* 1981, *52,* 1216–1223.

Johnson, M. M. Sex-role learning and the nuclear family. *Child Development,* 1963, *34,* 319–333.

Jones, W., Chernovetz, M. E., & Hansson, R. O. The enigma of androgyny: Differential implications for males and females? *Journal of Consulting and Clinical Psychology,* 1978, *46,* 298–313.

José, J. Teacher-pupil interaction as it relates to attempted changes in teacher expectancy of academic ability and achievement. *American Educational Research Journal,* 1971, *8,* 39–49.

Kagan, J. Acquisition and significance of sex typing and sex role identification. In M. L. Hoffman & L. W. Hoffman (Eds.), *Review of child development research* (Vol. 1). New York: Russell Sage Foundation, 1964.

Kagan, J. On the need for relativism. *American Psychologist,* 1967, *22,* 131–142.

Kagan, J., & Freeman, M. Relation of childhood intelligence, maternal behaviors, and social class to behavior during adolescence. *Child Development,* 1963, *34,* 899–912.

Kagan, J., & Moss, H. A. *Birth to maturity: A study in psychological development.* New York: John Wiley & Sons, 1962.

Kagan, S., & Madsen, M. C. Cooperation and competition of Mexican, Mexican-American, and Anglo-American children of two ages under four instructional sets. *Developmental Psychology*, 1971, *5*, 32–39.

Kagan, S., & Madsen, M. C. Experimental analyses of cooperation and competition of Anglo-American and Mexican children. *Developmental Psychology*, 1972, *6*, 49–52.

Kahn, R. L., & Antonucci, T. C. Convoys over the life course: Attachment, roles and social support. In *Life-span development and behavior* (Vol. 3). New York: Academic Press, 1980.

Kalish, R. A., & Knutson, F. W. Attachment versus disengagement: A life-span conceptualization. In T. Antonucci (Ed.), Attachment: A life-span concept. *Human Development*, 1976, *19*, 171–181.

Kamin, L. F. *The science and politics of I.Q.* New York: John Wiley & Sons, 1974.

Katz, L. *Developmental stages of preschool teachers*. Urbana, Ill.: ERIC Clearinghouse on Early Childhood Education, 1972.

Katz, P. A. Stimulus predifferentiation and modification of children's racial attitudes. *Child Development*, 1973, *44*, 232–237.

Katz, P. A. The development of female identity. *Sex Roles*, 1979, *5*, 155–178. (a)

Katz, P. A. *Determinants of sex-role flexibility in children*. Paper presented at the Society for Research in Child Development, San Francisco, March 1979. Cited in J. Worell, Life span sex roles. In R. M. Lerner & N. A. Busch-Rossnagel (Eds.), *Individuals as producers of their development*. New York: Academic Press, 1981. (b)

Katz, P. A., Johnson, J., & Parker, D. *Racial attitudes and perception in black and white urban school children*. Paper presented at the Annual Meetings of the American Psychological Association, September 1970.

Keeney, T. J., Cannizzo, S. R., & Flavell, J. H. Spontaneous and induced verbal rehearsal in a recall task. *Child Development*, 1967, *38*, 953–966.

Kelly, J. A., & Worrell, J. New formulations of sex roles and androgyny: A critical review. *Journal of Consulting and Clinical Psychology*, 1977, *45*, 1101–1115.

Klaus, R. A., & Gray, S. W. The early training project for disadvantaged children: A report

after five years. *Monographs of the Society for Research in Child Development*, 1968, *33* (4, Serial No. 120).

Kobasignawa, A. Utilization of retrieval cues by children in recall. *Child Development*, 1974, *45*, 127–134.

Koblinsky, S., Cruse, D. F., & Sugawara, A. I. Sex role stereotypes and children's memory for story content. *Child Development*, 1978, *49*, 452–458.

Koch, H. C. Some personality correlates of sex, sibling position, and sex of sibling among five and six year old children. *Genetic Psychology Monographs*, 1955, *52*, 3–30.

Kodera, T. L. *Cognitive classical conditioning mechanisms in infant exploratory behavior*. Unpublished doctoral dissertation, Michigan State University, 1980.

Kohlberg, L. Development of moral character and moral ideology. In M. L. Hoffman & L. W. Hoffman (Eds.), *Review of child development research* (Vol. 1). New York: Russell Sage Foundation, 1964.

Kohlberg, L. Stage and sequence: The cognitive-developmental approach to socialization. In D. A. Goslin (Ed.), *Handbook of socialization theory and research*. Chicago: Rand McNally, 1969.

Kohn, M. The child as a determinant of his peers' approach to him. *Journal of Genetic Psychology*, 1966, *109*, 91–100.

Kounin, J. S. *Discipline and group management in classrooms*. New York: Holt, Rinehart and Winston, 1970.

Kramer, J. J., & Engle, R. W. Teaching awareness of strategic behavior in combination with strategy training: Effects on children's memory performance. *Journal of Experimental Child Psychology*, 1981, *32*, 513–530.

Kun, A. Development of the magnitude-covariation and compensation schemata in ability and effort attributions of performance. *Child Development*, 1977, *48*, 862–873.

Kurdek, L. A. An integrative perspective on children's divorce adjustment. *American Psychologist*, 1981, *36*, 856–866.

Kurdek, L. A., Blisk, D., & Siesky, A. E., Jr. Correlates of children's long-term adjustment to their parents' divorce. *Developmental Psychology*, 1981, *17*, 565–579.

Kutner, B. Patterns of mental functioning associated with prejudice in children. *Psychological Monographs*, 1958, *72*, No. 7.

Laboratory of Comparative Human Cognition. What's cross-cultural about cross-cultural cognitive psychology? In M. R. Rosenzweig & L. W. Porter (Eds.), *Annual review of psychology* (Vol. 30). Palo Alto, Calif.: Annual Reviews, 1979.

Lamb, M. E. (Ed.). The role of the father in child development (2nd ed.). New York: John Wiley & Sons, 1981.

Lavine, L. O. *The development of perception of writing in pre-reading children: A cross-cultural study.* Unpublished doctoral dissertation, Cornell University, 1972. Cited in E. J. Gibson & H. Levin, *The psychology of reading.* Cambridge, Mass.: MIT Press, 1975.

Lazar, I., & Darlington, R. Lasting effects of early education: Report from the consortium for longitudinal studies. *Monographs of the Society for Research in Child Development*, 1982, *47* (Serial No. 195, Nos. 2–3).

Lee, P. C., & Wolinsky, A. L. Male teachers of young children: A preliminary empirical study. *Young Children*, 1973, *28*, 342–353.

LeFurgy, W. G., & Woloshin, G. W. Immediate and long-term effects of experimentally induced social influence in the modification of adolescent's moral judgments. *Journal of Personality and Social Psychology*, 1969, *12*, 104–110.

Leizer, J. I., & Rogers, R. W. Effects of method of discipline, timing of punishment, and timing of test on resistance to temptation. *Child Development*, 1974, *45*, 790–792.

Lepper, M. Intrinsic and extrinsic motivation in children: Detrimental effects of superfluous social controls. *Minnesota Symposium on Child Psychology* (Vol. 14). Hillsdale, N.J.: Lawrence Erlbaum Associates, 1980.

Lepper, M. R., Greene, D., & Nisbett, R. E. Undermining children's intrinsic interest with extrinsic rewards: A test of the overjustification hypothesis. *Journal of Personality and Social Psychology*, 1973, *28*, 129–137.

Lerner, R. M., Karabenick, S. A., & Meisels, M. Effects of age and sex on the development of personal space schemata towards body build. *Journal of Genetic Psychology*, 1975, *127*, 91–101.

Lerner, R. M., & Korn, S. J. The development of body-build stereotypes in males. *Child Development*, 1972, *43*, 908–920.

Lerner, R. M., & Ryff, C. D. Implementation of the life-span view of human development: The sample case of attachment. In P. Baltes (Ed.), *Life-span development and behavior* (Vol. 1). New York: Academic Press, 1978.

Lerner, R. M., & Spanier, G. B. (Eds.). *Child influences on marital and family interaction: A life-span perspective.* New York: Academic Press, 1978.

Lerner, R. M., Venning, J., & Knapp, J. R. Age and sex effects on personal space schemata toward body build in late childhood. *Developmental Psychology*, 1975, *11*, 855–856.

Lesser, G. S., Fifer, G., & Clark, D. H. Mental abilities of children from different social-class and cultural groups. *Monographs of the Society for Research in Child Development*, 1965, *30* (Whole No. 102).

Levitin, T. E. Children of divorce. In T. Levitin (Ed.), *Journal of Social Issues*, 1979, *35*, 1–25.

Levy, J., & Trevarthon, C. Metacontrol of hemispheric function in human split-brain patients. *Journal of Experimental Psychology: Human Perception and Performance*, 1976, *2*, 299–312.

Levy, J., Trevarthon, C., & Sperry, R. W. Perceptions of bilateral chimeric figures following hemispheric deconnection. *Brain*, 1972, *95*, 61–78.

Lewis, C. C. The effects of parental firm control: A reinterpretation of findings. *Psychological Bulletin*, 1981, *90*, 547–563.

Lewis, H. Culture, class, and family: Life among low-income urban Negroes. In A. Ross (Ed.), *Employment, race, and poverty.* New York: Harcourt Brace Jovanovich, 1967.

Lewis, M., & Goldberg, S. Perceptual cognitive development in infancy: A generalized expectancy model as a function of the mother-infant interaction. *Merrill-Palmer Quarterly*, 1969, *15*, 81–100.

Liben, L., & Signorella, M. L. Gender-related schemata and constructive memory in children. *Child Development*, 1980, *51*, 11–18.

Liebert, R. M., Neale, J. M., & Davidson, E. S. *The early window: Effects of television on children and youth* (2nd ed.). New York: Pergamon Press, 1982.

Livesley, W. J., & Bromley, D. *Person perception in childhood and adolescence.* London: John Wiley & Sons, 1973.

Loehlin, J. C., Horn, J. M., & Willerman, L. Personality resemblance in adoptive families. *Behavior genetics,* 1981, *11,* 309–330.

Loehlin, J. C. Psychological genetics, from the study of human behavior. In R. B. Cattell & R. M. Dreger (Eds.), *Handbook of modern personality theory.* New York: Halsted Press, 1977.

Lounsbury, K. R. *Age changes in occupational prestige: A perceptual model.* Unpublished doctoral dissertation, Michigan State University, 1973.

Lowry, C. B. *A cognitive developmental analysis of children's understanding of social relationships: Friendship, marriage, and divorce.* Unpublished doctoral dissertation, Michigan State University, 1980.

Luria, A. R. *The role of speech in the regulation of normal and abnormal behavior.* New York: Macmillan, 1961.

Lyle, J., & Hoffman, H. Children's use of television and other media. In E. A. Rubinstein, G. A. Comstock, & J. P. Murray (Eds.), *Television and social behavior. Vol. 4, Television in day-to-day life: Patterns of use.* Washington, D.C.: U.S. Government Printing Office, 1972. (a)

Lyle, J., & Hoffman, H. Explorations in patterns of television viewing by preschool age children. In E. A. Rubinstein, G. A. Comstock, & J. P. Murray (Eds.), *Television and social behavior. Vol. 4, Television in day-to-day life: Patterns of use.* Washington, D.C.: U.S. Government Printing Office, 1972. (b)

Lynn, D. B. *The father: His role in child development.* Monterey, Calif.: Brooks/Cole, 1974.

Maas, H. S. Preadolescent peer relations and adult intimacy. *Psychiatry,* 1968, *31,* 161–172.

Maccoby, E. E., & Jacklin, C. N. *The psychology of sex differences.* Stanford, Calif.: Stanford University Press, 1974.

MacKay, W. R., & Miller, C. A. Relations of socioeconomic status and sex variables to the complexity of worker functions in the occupational choices of elementary school children. *Journal of Vocational Behavior,* 1982, *20,* 31–39.

Madsen, M. C., & Shapira, A. Cooperative and competitive behavior of urban Afro-American, Ango-American, Mexican-American, and Mexican village children. *Developmental Psychology,* 1970, *3,* 16–20.

Mann, A. J., Harrell, A., & Hurt, M., Jr. *A review of Head Start Research since 1969 and an annotated bibliography.* Washington, D.C.: U.S. Government Printing Office, Department of Health, Education, and Welfare, DHEW Publication Number (OEHDS) 78-31102, 1977.

Marcus, D. E., & Overton, W. F. The development of cognitive gender constancy and sex-role preferences. *Child Development,* 1978, *49,* 434–444.

Marcus, R. F. The child as elicitor of parental sanctions for independent and dependent behavior: A simulation of parent-child interaction. *Developmental Psychology,* 1975, *11,* 443–452.

Margolin, G., & Patterson, G. R. Differential consequences provided by mothers and fathers for their sons and daughters. *Developmental Psychology,* 1975, *11,* 537–538.

Marjoribanks, K. Family and school environmental correlates of intelligence, personality, and school related affective characteristics. *Genetic Psychology Monographs,* 1979, *99,* 165–183.

Markman, E. M. Realizing that you don't understand: Elementary school children's awareness of inconsistencies. *Child Development,* 1979, *50,* 643–655.

Markman, E. M. Comprehension monitoring. In W. P. Dickson (Ed.), *Children's oral communication skills.* New York: Academic Press, 1981.

Martin, B. Parent-child relations. In F. D. Horowitz (Ed.), *Review of child development research* (Vol. 4). Chicago: University of Chicago Press, 1975.

Martin, C. L., & Halverson, C. F., Jr. A schematic processing model of sex typing and stereotyping in children. *Child Development,* 1981, *52,* 1119–1134.

Masters, J. C., & Furman, W. Popularity, individual friendship selection, and specific peer interaction among children. *Developmental Psychology*, 1981, *17*, 344–350.

Matthews, K. Caregiver-child interactions and the Type A coronary-prone behavior pattern. *Child Development*, 1977, *48*, 1752–1756.

McCandless, B. R. *Children: Behavior and development*. New York: Holt, Rinehart and Winston, 1967.

McCandless, B. R. *Adolescents: Behavior and development*. Hinsdale, Ill.: Dryden Press, 1970.

McClelland, D. C. Testing for competence rather than for "intelligence." *American Psychologist*, 1973, *28*, 1–14.

McDavid, J. W., & Harari, H. Stereotyping of names and popularity in grade-school children. *Child Development*, 1966, *37*, 453–459.

McGhee, P. E., & Frueh, T. Television viewing and the learning of sex-role stereotypes. *Sex Roles*, 1980, *6*, 179–188.

McGurk, H. *Issues in childhood social development*. London: Methuen, 1978.

McKinney, J. P. Moral development and the concept of values. In M. Windmiller, N. Lambert, & E. Turiel (Eds.), *Moral development and socialization*. Boston: Allyn & Bacon, 1980.

McKinney, J. P., Fitzgerald, H. E., & Strommen, E. A. *Developmental psychology: The adolescent and young adult* (Rev. ed.). Homewood, Ill.: Dorsey Press, 1982.

Messe, L. A., Stollack, G. E., Larson, R. W., & Michaels, G. Y. Interpersonal consequences of person perception in two social contexts. *Journal of Personality and Social Psychology*, 1979, *37*, 369–379.

Meyer, B. Development of girls' sex-role attitudes. *Child Development*, 1980, *51*, 508–514.

Midlarsky, E., Bryan, J. H., & Brickman, P. Adversive approval: interactive effects of modeling and reinforcement on altruistic behavior. *Child Development*, 1973, *44*, 321–328.

Milkovich, M., & Miller, M. with Bettinghaus, E., & Atkin, C. *The effects of television advertising on children: Exploring the relationship between television viewing and language development*. Final Report. Office of Child Development, Department of Health, Education, and Welfare, 1975.

Miller, M. M. *Factors affecting children's choices of television characters as sex role model*. Unpublished manuscript, 1975.

Miller, M. M., & Reeves, B. *Children's occupational sex role stereotypes: The linkage between television content and perception*. Paper presented at the annual meeting of the International Communication Association, Chicago, 1975.

Miller, M. M., & Reeves, B. Dramatic TV content and children's sex-role stereotypes. *Journal of Broadcasting*, 1976, *20*, 35–50.

Minuchin, P., Biber, B., Shapiro, E., & Zimiles, H. *The psychological impact of school experience*. New York: Basic Books, 1969.

Mischel, W. Metacognition and the rules of delay. In J. H. Flavell & L. Ross (Eds.), *Social cognitive development: Frontiers and possible futures*. Cambridge: Cambridge University Press, 1981.

Mondell, S., & Tyler, F. B. Parental competence and styles of problem-solving/play behavior with children. *Developmental Psychology*, 1981, *17*, 73–78.

Montemayor, R. Children's performance in a game and their attraction to it as a function of sex-typed labels. *Child Development*, 1974, *45*, 152–156.

Moss, H. A., & Kagan, J. Maternal influences on early I.Q. scores. *Psychological Reports*, 1958, *4*, 655–661.

Mussen, P. Some personality and social factors related to changes in children's attitudes toward Negroes. *Journal of Abnormal and Social Psychology*, 1960, *45*, 423–441.

Nadelman, L. Sex identity in American children: Memory, knowledge, and preference tests. *Developmental Psychology*, 1974, *10*, 413–417.

Naylor, H. Reading disability and lateral asymmetry: An information-processing analysis. *Psychological Bulletin*, 1980, *87*, 531–545.

Nelson, S. A. Factors influencing young children's use of motives and outcomes as moral criteria. *Child Development*, 1980, *51*, 823–829.

Newcomb, A. F., & Brady, J. E. Mutuality in boys' friendship relations. *Child Development*, 1982, *53*, 392–395.

Newcomb, A. F., & Bukowski, W. M. Social impact and social preference as determinants of children's peer group status. *Developmental Psychology*, in press, 1983.

Newcomb, A. F., Jeunemann, J., & Meister, J. C. *The social behavior of star, average, and isolated social standing children in their initial social encounters.* Unpublished manuscript, 1982.

Newcomb, A. F., & Meister, J. C. *Information exchange in the initial social encounters of high and low popularity children.* Unpublished manuscript, 1982.

Newell, A., & Simon, H. A. *Human problem solving.* Englewood Cliffs, N.J.: Prentice-Hall, 1972.

Nicholls, J. G. The development of the concepts of effort and ability, perception of academic attainment, and the understanding that difficult tasks require more ability. *Child Development*, 1978, *49*, 800–814.

Nye, F. I. Child adjustment in broken and in unhappy unbroken homes. *Marriage and Family Living*, 1957, *19*, 356–361.

Oetzel, R. *The relationship between sex role acceptance and cognitive abilities.* Unpublished master's thesis, Stanford University, 1961. Cited in E. Maccoby, Sex differences in intellectual functioning. In E. Maccoby (Ed.), *The development of sex differences.* Stanford, Calif.: Stanford University Press, 1966.

Olds, D. E., & Shaver, P. Masculinity, femininity, academic performance and health: Further evidence concerning the androgyny controversy. *Journal of Personality*, 1980, *48*, 323–341.

Olejnik, A. B. Adults' moral reasoning with children. *Child Development*, 1980, *51*, 1285–1288.

Olejnik, A. B., & McKinney, J. P. Parental value orientation and generosity in children. *Developmental Psychology*, 1973, *8*, 311.

Olson, D. R. Culture, technology, and intellect. In L. B. Resnick (Ed.), *The nature of intelligence.* Hillsdale, N.J.: Lawrence Erlbaum Associates, 1976.

Olson, D. R. The language of instruction: The literate bias of schooling. In R. C. Anderson, R. J. Spiro, & W. E. Montague (Eds.), *Schooling and the acquisition of knowledge.* Hillsdale, N.J.: Lawrence Erlbaum Associates, 1977.

Opie, I., & Opie, P. *The lore and language of school children.* Oxford, England: Clarendon Press, 1959.

Opie, I., & Opie, P. *Children's games in street and playground.* Oxford, England: Clarendon Press, 1969.

Orton, S. *Reading, writing, and speech problems in children.* New York: W. W. Norton, 1937.

Osipow, S. H. Some cognitive aspects of career development. In E. D. Evans (Ed.), *Adolescence: Readings in behavior and development.* Hinsdale, Ill.: Dryden Press, 1970.

Osofsky, J. D., & Oldfield, S. Parent-child interaction: Daughters' effects upon mothers' and fathers' behaviors. *Developmental Psychology*, 1972, *7*, 157–168.

Paris, S. G. Integration and inference in children's comprehension and memory. In F. Restle, R. Shiffron, J. Castellan, H. Lindman, & D. Pisoni (Eds.), *Cognitive theory* (Vol. 1). Potomac, Md.: Erlbaum and Associates, 1975.

Paris, S. G., & Carter, A. Y. Semantic and constructive aspects of sentence memory in children. *Developmental Psychology*, 1973, *9*, 109–113.

Paris, S. G., & Mahoney, G. J. Cognitive integration in children's memory for sentences and pictures. *Child Development*, 1974, *45*, 633–642.

Parke, R. D. The role of punishment in the socialization process. In R. A. Hoppe, G. A. Milton, & E. C. Simmel (Eds.), *Early experiences and the processes of socialization.* New York: Academic Press, 1970.

Parsons, J. E., Kaczala, C. M., & Meece, J. L. Socialization of achievement attitudes and beliefs: Classroom influences. *Child Development*, 1982, *53*, 322–339.

Parsons, T. Family structure and the socialization of the child. In T. Parsons & R. F. Bales (Eds.), *Family, socialization, and interaction process.* Glencoe, Ill.: Free Press, 1955.

Patterson, G. R., Littman, R. A., & Bricker, W. Assertive behavior in children: A step toward a theory of aggression. *Monographs of the Society for Research in Child Development*, 1967, *32* (Serial No. 113).

Paul, S. M. Sibling resemblance in mental ability: A review. *Behavior genetics*, 1980, *10*, 277–290.

Payne, F. D. Children's prosocial conduct in structured situations and as viewed by others: Consistency, convergence, and relationships with person variables. *Child Development*, 1980, *51*, 1252–1259.

Peery, J. Popular, amiable, isolated, rejected: A reconceptualization of sociometric status in preschool children. *Child Development*, 1979, *50*, 1231–1234.

Perfetti, C. A., & Lesgold, A. Discourse comprehension and sources of individual differences. In M. A. Just & P. Carpenter (Eds.), *Cognitive processes in comprehension*. Hillsdale, N.J.: Lawrence Erlbaum Associates, 1978.

Peterson, S. A., & Somit, A. Cognitive development and childhood political socialization. *American Behavioral Scientist*, 1982, *25*, 313–334.

Piaget, J. *Play, dreams, and imitation in childhood*. New York: W. W. Norton, 1962.

Piaget, J. *The moral judgment of the child*. Glencoe, Ill.: Free Press, 1965.

Piaget, J. *Judgment and reasoning in the child*. Totowa, N.J.: Littlefield, Adams, 1966. (a)

Piaget, J. Need and significance of cross-cultural studies in genetic psychology. *International Journal of Psychology*, 1966, *1*, 3–13. (b)

Piaget, J. *Six psychological studies*. New York: Random House, 1967.

Piaget, J. Intellectual evolution from adolescence to adulthood. *Human Development*, 1972, *15*, 1–12.

Piaget, J., & Inhelder, B. *The child's conception of space*. New York: W. W. Norton, 1967.

Piaget, J., & Inhelder, B. *Memory and intelligence*. New York: Basic Books, 1973.

Pick, H. L., Jr., & Pick, A. D. Sensory and perceptual development. In P. Mussen (Ed.), *Carmichael's manual of child psychology* (Vol. 1). New York: John Wiley & Sons, 1970.

Plomin, R., & Foch, T. T. A twin study of objectively assessed personality in childhood. *Journal of Personality and Social Psychology*, 1980, *39*, 680–688.

Porter, J. D. R. *Black child, white child: The development of racial attitudes*. Cambridge, Mass.: Harvard University Press, 1971.

Poulos, R. W., Rubinstein, E. A., & Liebert, R. M. Positive social learning. *Journal of Communication*, 1975, *25*, 90–97.

Preston, R. C. Reading achievement of German and American children. *School and Society*, 1962, *90*, 350–354.

Price-Williams, D., Gordon, W., & Ramirez, M. III. Skill and conversation: A study of pottery-making children. *Developmental Psychology*, 1969, *1*, 769.

Proshansky, H. M. The development of intergroup attitudes. In L. W. Hoffman & M. R. Hoffman (Eds.), *Review of child development research* (Vol. 2). New York: Russell Sage Foundation, 1966.

Rabban, M. Sex-role identification in two diverse social groups. *Genetic Psychology Monographs*, 1950, *42*, 81–158.

Rajecki, E. W., & Flanery, R. C. Social conflict and dominance in children: A case for a primate homology. In M. Lamb and A. Brown (Eds.), *Advances in developmental psychology* (Vol. 1). Hillsdale, N.J.: Lawrence Erlbaum Associates, 1981.

Reese, H. W. Relationships between self-acceptance and sociometric choice. *Journal of Abnormal and Social Psychology*, 1961, *62*, 472–474.

Rholes, W. S., Blackwell, J. E., Jordan, C., & Walters, C. A developmental study of learned helplessness. *Developmental Psychology*, 1980, *16*, 616–624.

Riley, P. J. The influence of gender on occupational aspirations of kindergarten children. *Journal of Vocational Behavior*, 1981, *19*, 244–250.

Roberts, J. M., & Sutton-Smith, B. Child training and game involvement. *Ethnology*, 1962, *1*, 166–185.

Rogers, C. The child's perception of other people. In H. McGurk (Ed.), *Issues in childhood social development*. London: Methuen, 1978.

Rogoff, B. Schooling and the development of cognitive skills. In H. C. Triandis & A. Heron (Eds.), *Handbook of cross-cultural psychology: Development psychology* (Vol. 4). Boston: Allyn & Bacon, 1981.

Rogoff, B., Sellers, M. J., Pirotta, S., Fox, N., & White, S. Age of assignment of roles and responsibilities to children. *Human Development*, 1975, *18*, 353–369.

Rogosch, F. A., & Newcomb, A. F. Children's understanding and use of social reputation and its effect on social organization. Paper presented at the Seventh Biennial South-

304

eastern Conference on Human Development, Baltimore, Md., 1982.

Rokeach, M. *The open and closed mind.* New York: Basic Books, 1960.

Rosenberg, B., & Sutton-Smith, B. Family structure and sex-role variations. In J. K. Cole & R. Dienstbier (Eds.), Human sexuality. *Nebraska Symposium on Motivation,* 1973. Lincoln: University of Nebraska Press, 1974.

Rosenthal, R., & Jacobson, L. *Pygmalion in the classroom.* New York: Holt, Rinehart and Winston, 1968.

Ross, D. M., & Ross, S. A. Resistance by preschool boys to sex-inappropriate behavior. *Journal of Educational Psychology,* 1972, *63,* 342–346.

Rotenberg, K. I. "A promise kept, a promise broken": Developmental bases of trust. *Child Development,* 1980, *51,* 614–617.

Rothbart, M. K., & Derryberry, D. Development of individual differences in temperament. In M. Lamb & A. Brown (Eds.), *Advances in development psychology* (Vol. 1). Hillsdale, N.J.: Lawrence Erlbaum Associates, 1981.

Rothenberg, B. Children's social sensitivity and the relationship to interpersonal competence, intrapersonal comfort, and intellectual level. *Developmental Psychology,* 1970, *2,* 335–350.

Rowe, D. C., & Plomin, R. The importance of nonshared (E_1) environmental influences in behavioral development. *Developmental Psychology,* 1981, *17,* 517–531.

Rozin, P. The evolution of intelligence and access to the cognitive unconscious. In J. S. Sprague & A. N. Epstein (Eds.), *Progress in psychobiology and physiological psychology* (Vol. 6). New York: Academic Press, 1976.

Rozin, P., & Gleitman, L. The structure and acquisition of reading II: The reading process and the alphabetic principle. In A. S. Reber & D. Scarborough (Eds.), *Toward a psychology of reading.* Hillsdale, N.J.: Lawrence Erlbaum Associates, 1977.

Ruble, D., Balaban, T., & Cooper, J. Gender constancy and the effects of sex-typed televised toy commercials. *Child Development,* 1981, *52,* 667–673.

Ruble, D., Boggiano, A. K., Feldman, N. S., & Loebl, J. H. Developmental analysis of the role of social comparison in self-evaluation. *Developmental Psychology,* 1980, *16,* 105–115.

Rule, B. B., Nesdale, A. R., & McAra, M. J. Children's reactions to information about the intentions underlying an aggressive act. *Child Development,* 1974, *45,* 794–798.

Sadker, M. Are you guilty of teaching sex bias? *Instructor,* 1972, *82,* 80–81.

Sagar, H., & Schofield, J. W. Racial and behavioral cues in black and white children's perceptions of ambiguously aggressive acts. *Journal of Personality and Social Psychology,* 1980, *39,* 590–598.

Sameroff, A. J. Early influences on development: Fact or fancy? *Merrill-Palmer Quarterly,* 1975, *21,* 267–294.

Santrock, J. W., & Warshak, R. A. Father custody and social development in boys and girls. In T. E. Levitin (Ed.), Children of divorce. *Journal of Social Issues,* 1979, *35,* 112–125.

Savin, H. B. What the child knows about speech when he starts to read. In J. F. Kavanagh & I. G. Mattingly (Eds.), *Language by ear and by eye.* Cambridge, Mass.: MIT Press, 1972.

Scarr, S. Testing for children: Assessment and the many determinants of intellectual competence. *American Psychologist,* 1981, *36,* 1159–1166.

Scarr, S., & Weinberg, R. A. Intellectual similarities within families of both adopted and biological children. *Intelligence,* 1977, *1,* 170–191.

Scarr-Salapatek, S. Genetics and the development of intelligence. In F. D. Horowitz (Ed.), *Review of child development research* (Vol. 4). Chicago: University of Chicago Press, 1975.

Schaefer, E. S. A circumplex model for maternal behavior. *Journal of Abnormal and Social Psychology,* 1959, *59,* 226–235.

Schoggen, M. An ecological study of three-year-olds at home. Nashville: George Peabody College for Teachers, November 7, 1969. Cited in J. Bruner, *The relevance of education.* New York: Norton Library, 1973.

Schooler, C. Birth-order effects: Not here, not now! *Psychological Bulletin,* 1972, *78,* 151–175.

Schwantes, F. M., Boesl, S. L., & Ritz, E. G. Children's use of context in word recognition: A psycholinguistic guessing game. *Child Development*, 1980, *51*, 730–736.

Schweinhart, L. J., & Weikart, D. P. Young children grow up: The effects of the Perry Preschool Program on youths through age 15. *Monographs of the High/Scope Educational Research Foundation,* 1980(No. 7).

Scribner, S. Recall of classical syllogisms: A cross-cultural investigation of error on logical problems. In R. J. Falmagne (Ed.), *Reasoning: Representation and process in children and adults.* New York: John Wiley & Sons, 1975.

Sears, R. R., Maccoby, E. E., & Levin, H. *Patterns of child rearing.* Evanston, Ill.: Row, Peterson, 1957.

Selman, R. L. Toward a structural-developmental analysis of interpersonal relationship concepts: Research with normal and disturbed preadolescent boys. In A. Pick (Ed.), *Minnesota Symposium on Child Psychology* (Vol. X). Minneapolis: University of Minnesota Press, 1976.

Selman, R. L. A structural-developmental model of social cognition; Implications for intervention research. *The Counseling Psychologist,* 1977, 6, 3–6.

Selman, R. L., & Byrne, D. F. A structural developmental analysis of levels of role-taking in middle childhood. *Child Development,* 1974, *45*, 803–806.

Selman, R. L., & Jaquette, D. Stability and oscillation in interpersonal awareness. A clinical-developmental analysis. In C. B. Keasey (Ed.), *Nebraska Symposium on Motivation* (Vol. 25). Lincoln: University of Nebraska Press, 1978.

Serbin, L. A., Connor, J. M., & Citron, C. C. Sex-differentiated free play behavior: Effects of teacher modeling, location, and gender. *Developmental Psychology,* 1981, *17*, 640–646.

Serbin, L. A., O'Leary, K. D., Kent, R. N., & Tonick, I. J. A comparison of teacher response to the preacademic and problem behavior of boys and girls. *Child Development,* 1973, *44*, 794–804.

Shantz, C. U. The development of social cognition. In E. M. Hetherington, J. W. Hagen, R. Kron, & A. H. Stein (Eds.), *Review of child development research* (Vol. 4). Chicago: University of Chicago Press, 1975.

Shantz, C. U., & Watson, J. S. Assessment of spatial egocentrism through expectancy violation. *Psychonomic Science,* 1970, *18*, 93–94.

Shantz, C. U., & Watson, J. S. Spatial abilities and egocentrism in the young child. *Child Development,* 1971, *42*, 171–181.

Sharabany, R., Gershoni, R., & Hofman, J. E. Girlfriend, boyfriend: Age and sex differences in intimate friendships. *Developmental Psychology,* 1981, *17*, 800–808.

Shaver, P., & Rubenstein, C. Childhood attachment experience and adult loneliness. In L. Wheeler (Ed.), *Review of personality and social psychology* (Vol. 1). Beverly Hills, Calif.: Sage Publications, 1980.

Sheldon, W. H. *The varieties of human physique.* New York: Harper & Row, 1940.

Sheldon, W. H. *The varieties of temperament.* New York: Harper & Row, 1942.

Shigetomi, C. C., Hartmann, D. P., & Gelfand, D. M. Sex differences in children's altruistic behavior and reputations for friendship. *Development Psychology,* 1981, *17*, 434–437.

Shinn, M. Father absence and children's cognitive development. *Psychological Bulletin,* 1978, *85*, 295–324.

Siegel, L. S., & Brainerd, C. J. (Eds.). *Alternatives to Piaget: Critical essays on the theory.* New York: Academic Press, 1978.

Sigel, I. E. How intelligence tests limit understanding of intelligence. *Merrill-Palmer Quarterly,* 1963, 9, 39–56.

Simon, H. A. On the development of the processor. In S. Farnham-Diggory (Ed.), *Information processing in children.* New York: Academic Press, 1972.

Singer, M. H., & Crouse, J. The relationship of context-use skills to reading: A case for an alternative experimental logic. *Child Development,* 1981, *52*, 1326–1329.

Skeels, H. M. Adult status of children with contrasting early life experiences. *Monographs of the Society for Research in Child Development,* 1966, *31* (Serial No. 105).

Slaby, R. G., & Frey, K. S. Development of gender constancy and selective attention to same-sexed models. *Child Development,* 1975, *46*, 848–856.

Smith, M. W. Alfred Binet's remarkable questions: A cross-national and cross-temporal

306

analysis of the cultural biases built into the Stanford-Binet intelligence scale and other Binet tests. *Genetic Psychology Monographs,* 1974, *89,* 307–334.

Solomon, R. L. Punishment. *American Psychologist,* 1964, *19,* 239–253.

Sontag, L. W., Baker, C. T., & Nelson, V. L. Mental growth and personality development: A longitudinal study. *Monographs of the Society for Research in Child Development,* 1958, *23* (Serial No. 68).

Spence, J. T., & Helmreich, R. *Masculinity and femininity: Their psychological dimensions, correlates, and antecedents.* Austin: University of Texas Press, 1978.

Spence, J. T., Helmreich, R., & Stapp, J. Ratings of self and peers on sex role attributes and their relation of self-esteem and conceptions of masculinity and femininity. *Journal of Personality and Social Psychology,* 1975, *32,* 29–39.

Sperry, R. W. Lateral specialization in the surgically separated hemispheres. In F. O. Schmitt & F. G. Worden, *The neurosciences third study program.* Cambridge, Mass.: MIT Press, 1974.

Staffieri, J. R. A study of social stereotype of body image in children. *Journal of Personality and Social Psychology,* 1967, *7,* 101–104.

Staffieri, J. R. Body build and behavioral expectancies in young females. *Developmental Psychology,* 1972, *6,* 125–127.

Stallings, J. Implementation and child effects of teaching practices in Follow-Through programs. *Monographs of the Society for Research in Child Development,* 1975, *40* (Serial No. 163).

Stayton, D. J., Hogan, R., & Ainsworth, M. D. S. Infant obedience and maternal behavior: The origins of socialization reconsidered. *Child Development,* 1971, *42,* 1057–1070.

Stebbins, L. B., St. Pierre, R. G., Proper, E. C., Anderson, R. B., & Cerva, T. R. *Education as experimentation: A planned variation model. Vol. IV-A, An evaluation of Follow-Through.* Cambridge, Mass.: Abt Associates, 1977. (Also issued by the U.S. Office of Education as *National Evaluation: Patterns of Effects (Vol. II-A) of the Follow-Through Planned Variation Experiment Series.*)

Steinberg, B. M., & Dunn, L. A. Conservation competence and performance in Chiapas. *Human Development,* 1976, *19,* 14–25.

Stevenson, H. W. *Children's learning.* New York: Appleton-Century-Crofts, 1972.

Stevenson, H. W. Influences of schooling on cognitive development. In D. A. Wagner & H. W. Stevenson (Eds.), *Cultural perspectives on child development.* San Francisco: W. H. Freeman, 1982.

Stodelsky, S. S., & Lesser, G. Learning patterns in the disadvantaged. *Harvard Educational Review,* 1967, *37,* 546–593.

Stotland, E. Exploratory investigations of empathy. In L. Berkowitz (Ed.), *Advances in experimental social psychology* (Vol. 4). New York: Academic Press, 1969.

Strommen, E. Friendship. In E. Donelson & J. Gullahorn (Eds.), *Women: A psychological perspective.* New York: John Wiley & Sons, 1977.

Strommen, E. A. Verbal self-regulation in a children's game: Impulsive errors on "Simon Says." *Child Development,* 1973, *44,* 849–853.

Strommen, E. A. *Front-back specificity and spatial perspective.* Unpublished manuscript, 1976.

Strommen, E. A., McKinney, J. P., & Fitzgerald, H. E. *Developmental Psychology: The school-aged child* (1st ed.). Homewood, Ill.: Dorsey Press, 1977.

Sullivan, H. S. The interpersonal theory of psychiatry. *The collected works of Henry Stack Sullivan* (Vol. 1). New York: W. W. Norton, 1953.

Suls, J., & Kalle, R. J. Children's moral judgments as a function of intention, damage, and an actor's physical harm. *Developmental Psychology,* 1979, *15,* 93–94.

Suls, J., Witenberg, S., & Gutkin, D. Evaluating reciprocal and nonreciprocal prosocial behavior: Developmental changes. *Personality and Social Psychology Bulletin,* 1981, *7,* 25–31.

Sutherland, A., & Goldschmid, M. L. Negative teacher expectation and IQ change in children with superior intellectual potential. *Child Development,* 1974, *45,* 852–856.

Sutton-Smith, B. Children at play. *Natural History,* 1971, *71,* 54–59.

Sutton-Smith, B., & Roberts, J. M. Play, toys, games, and sports. In H. C. Triandis & A. Heron (Eds.), *Handbook of cross-cultural psychology. Developmental psychology* (Vol. 4). Boston: Allyn & Bacon, 1981.

Sutton-Smith, B., & Rosenberg, B. *The sibling.* New York: Holt, Rinehart and Winston, 1970.

Tanner, J. M. *Growth at adolescence* (2nd ed.). Oxford, England: Blackwell Scientific Publications, 1962.

Tanner, J. M. Physical growth. In P. Mussen (Ed.), *Carmichael's manual of child psychology* (3rd ed.). New York: John Wiley & Sons, 1970.

Tapp, J. L., & Kohlberg, L. Developing senses of law and legal justice. In J. L. Tapp (Ed.), Socialization, the law, and society. *Journal of Social Issues,* 1971, *27,* 65–92.

Taran, J. Personal communication, 1975.

Tenney, Y. J. The child's conception of organization and recall. *Journal of Experimental Child Psychology,* 1975, *19,* 100–114.

Thomas, A., & Chess, S. *Temperament and development.* New York: Brunner/Mazel, 1977.

Thomas, A., Chess, S., & Birch, H. G. *Temperament and behavior disorders in children.* New York: New York University Press, 1968.

Thomas, A., Chess, S., Birch, H. G., Hertzig, M., & Korn, S. *Behavioral individuality in early childhood.* New York: New York University Press, 1963.

Tice, T. N. A psychoanalytic perspective. In M. Windmiller, N. Lambert, & E. Turiel (Eds.). *Moral development and socialization.* Boston: Allyn & Bacon, 1980.

Traub, R., Weiss, J., Fisher, C., & Musella, D. *Closure on openness in education.* A symposium presented at the Annual Meeting of the American Educational Research Association, New Orleans, 1973. Cited in T. L. Good, B. J. Biddle, and J. E. Brophy, *Teachers make a difference.* New York: Holt, Rinehart and Winston, 1975.

Trent, J. W., & Medsker, L. L. *Beyond high school: A psychosociological study of 10,000 high school graduates.* San Francisco: Jossey-Bass, 1968.

Turiel, E. An experimental test of the sequentiality of developmental stages in the child's moral judgments. *Journal of Personality and Social Psychology,* 1966, *3,* 611–618.

Walden, T. A. Mediation and production deficiencies in children's judgments of moral-

ity. *Journal of Experimental Child Psychology,* 1982, *33,* 165–181.

Waldrop, M. F., & Halverson, C. F., Jr. Intensive and extensive peer behavior: Longitudinal and cross-sectional analysis. *Child Development,* 1975, *46,* 19–26.

Walker, L. J. Cognitive and perspective-taking prerequisites for moral development. *Child Development,* 1980, *51,* 131–139.

Wallerstein, J. S., & Kelly, J. B. *Surviving the breakup: How children and parents cope with divorce.* New York: Basic Books, 1980.

Wasserman, G. A., & Stern, D. N. An early manifestation of differential behavior toward children of the same and opposite sex. *The Journal of Genetic Psychology,* 1978, *133,* 129–137.

Waters, H. S. Memory development in adolescence: Relationships between metamemory, strategy use, and performance. *Journal of Experimental Child Psychology,* 1982, *33,* 183–195.

Waters, H. S., & Tinsley, V. S. The development of verbal self-regulation: Relationships between language, thought, and behavior. Chapter to appear in S. J. Kuczaj (Ed.), *Language development: Language, cognition, and culture.* In press, 1981.

Watson, J. B. *Psychological care of infant and child.* New York: W. W. Norton, 1928.

Watson, J. B., & Rayner, R. Conditioned emotional reactions. *Journal of Experimental Psychology,* 1920, *3,* 1–14.

Weiss, R. S. Growing up a little faster: The experience of growing up in a single-parent household. In T. E. Levitin (Ed.), Children of divorce. *Journal of Social Issues,* 1979, *35,* 97–111.

Weisz, J. R. Learned helplessness in black and white children identified by their schools as retarded and nonretarded: Performance deterioration in response to failure. *Developmental Psychology,* 1981, *17,* 499–508.

White, R. W. Motivation reconsidered: The concept of competence. *Psychological Review,* 1959, *66,* 297–302.

White, R. W. Competence and the psychosexual stages of development. In M. R. Jones (Ed.), *Nebraska Symposium on Motivation* (Vol. 8). Lincoln: University of Nebraska Press, 1960.

White, S. W. Evidence for a hierarchical arrangement of learning processes. In L. Lip-

308

sitt & C. C. Spiker (Eds.), *Advances in Child development and behavior* (Vol. 2). New York: Academic Press, 1965.

Whiting, J. W. M. Resource mediation and learning by identification. In I. Iscoe & H. W. Stevenson (Eds.), *Personality development in children.* Austin: University of Texas Press, 1960.

Willows, D. M. Reading between the lines: A study of selective attention in good and poor readers. *Child Development,* 1974, *45,* 408–415.

Willows, D. M., & McKinnon, G. E. Selective reading: Attention to the "unattended" lines. *Canadian Journal of Psychology,* 1973, *27,* 292–304.

Windmiller, M., Lambert, N., & Turiel, S. (Eds.). *Moral development and socialization.* Boston: Allyn & Bacon, 1980.

Wolfenstein, M. *Children's humor.* Glencoe, Ill.: The Free Press, 1954.

Women on Words and Images. *Dick and Jane as victims: Sex-stereotyping in children's readers.* Princeton, N.J., 1972.

Worell, J. Life-span sex roles: Development, continuity, change. In R. M. Lerner & N. A. Bushch-Rossnagel (Eds.), *Individuals as producers of their development: A life-span perspective.* New York: Academic Press, 1981.

Yarrow, M. R., Campbell, J. D., & Yarrow, L. J. Interpersonal dynamics in racial integration. In E. E. Maccoby, T. M. Newcomb, & E. L. Hartley (Eds.), *Readings in social psychology* (3rd ed.). New York: Holt, 1958.

Youniss, J., & Volpe, J. A relational analysis of children's friendship. In W. Damon (Ed.), *Social cognition. New directions for child development: A sourcebook* (Vol. 1, No. 1). San Francisco, Jossey-Bass, 1978.

Zajonc, R. B., & Markus, G. B. Birth order and intellectual development. *Psychological Review,* 1975, *82,* 74–88.

Zellman, G. L., & Sears, D. O. Childhood origins of tolerance for dissent. In J. L. Tapp (Ed.), Socialization, the law, and society. *Journal of Social Issues,* 1971, *27,* 109–136.

Zivin, G. On becoming subtle: Age and social rank changes in the use of a facial gesture. *Child Development,* 1977, *48,* 1314–1321.

AUTHOR INDEX

SUBJECT INDEX

*This book has been set VIP, in 9 and 8 point Optima, leaded 3
and 2 points respectively. Chapter numbers are 16 point Optima
Medium and chapter titles are 20 point Optima Medium. The
overall type area is 30 by 47 ½ picas.*